IRAQ AND THE USE OF FORCE IN INTERNATIONAL LAW

Iraq and the Use of Force in International Law

MARC WELLER

Published under the Auspices of the Lauterpacht Centre for
International Law in the University of Cambridge

OXFORD
UNIVERSITY PRESS

OXFORD
UNIVERSITY PRESS

Great Clarendon Street, Oxford OX2 6DP

Oxford University Press is a department of the University of Oxford.
It furthers the University's objective of excellence in research, scholarship,
and education by publishing worldwide in

Oxford New York

Auckland Cape Town Dar es Salaam Hong Kong Karachi
Kuala Lumpur Madrid Melbourne Mexico City Nairobi
New Delhi Shanghai Taipei Toronto

With offices in

Argentina Austria Brazil Chile Czech Republic France Greece
Guatemala Hungary Italy Japan Poland Portugal Singapore
South Korea Switzerland Thailand Turkey Ukraine Vietnam

Oxford is a registered trade mark of Oxford University Press
in the UK and in certain other countries

Published in the United States
by Oxford University Press Inc., New York

British Library Cataloguing in Publication Data

Data available

Library of Congress Cataloging-in-Publication Data

Data available

Typeset by Newgen Imaging Systems (P) Ltd., Chennai, India
Printed in Great Britain
on acid-free paper by
CPI Antony Rowe,
Chippenham, Wiltshire

ISBN 978–0–19–959530–3

1 3 5 7 9 10 8 6 4 2

This book is dedicated to Nora, my one love.

Preface

This is the second in a series of monographs addressing Conflicts, Crises, and Peace Settlements in the Contemporary World. The series aims to offer international legal analyses relating to major episodes that have shaped, or are shaping, the contemporary international system. It seeks to draw out some major developments concerning the structural rules or the principal mechanisms operating within the international system that were triggered by individual episodes of crisis or conflict.

The first book in the series addressed the Kosovo conflict and the attendant issues of contested statehood, self-determination, human rights and forcible humanitarian action. This present book is mainly devoted to issues concerning the use of force, in particular the application of the United Nations collective security process, the right of individual and collective self-defence, and, again, the problem of forcible humanitarian action. It is expected that a further contribution to this series, to be commissioned at a later stage, will address the developments that followed on from the use of force in 2003, including the occupation of the territory, the treatment of detainees in theatre and elsewhere, Iraq's transition to self-government, and the associated problems of state-building in a highly complex and hostile environment.

In accordance with the aims of the series, this book seeks to offer legal analysis and comment that is of sufficient depth to be of interest to the international law community. However, an attempt has been made to write in a way that renders the work accessible to a wider audience interested in international relations and contemporary history. As with the first volume in the series, this remains something of an experiment, and it is hoped that an appropriate balance among these aims can be found as further volumes emerge.

Marc Weller
Lauterpacht Centre for International Law
University of Cambridge

Acknowledgements

This book was written under some pressure of time. I am most grateful for the extraordinary speed with which Oxford University Press embraced the project. As before, Merel Alstein and John Louth of the Press were superb and supportive commissioning editors. Benjamin Roberts guided the production process swiftly and with the flexibility required to meet the ambitious time-schedule. Many thanks to Glynis Dyson and Ashley Bailey for their excellent copy-editing and proofreading, and to Katie Nobbs who supported the editorial process as always in a supremely calm and competent manner. Ms Lottie Garrett and Mr Simon Lafferty very kindly helped with typing at a critical stage.

I am indebted to the four anonymous readers arranged by the Press, who offered very helpful suggestions at an early stage. More detailed comments were received at a later point, also from others, including Dr Philip Towle of the Department of Politics and International Studies in the University of Cambridge. The chapters on the role of UK legal advice in particular have benefited from additional comments from particularly knowledgeable individuals, although I was not always in a position to take their suggestions fully on board. In addition, Professor Claus Kress of the University of Cologne and Chris Griggs alerted me to some issues previously neglected in the presentation. The responsibility for any remaining failings in this work remains, of course, mine alone.

I have occasionally drawn on my previous work generated alongside the twists and turns of the Iraqi episode, beginning with the materials published in the *Cambridge International Documents Series* in 1990. This long-standing involvement with the Iraq issue made it possible to generate this work expeditiously. However, the greatest impetus for generating the book was derived from the materials freshly made available by the UK Chilcot enquiry into the Iraq war. These materials are in many respects extraordinary. It does the UK government credit to have offered them for public release, knowing full well that considerable scholarly and public criticism would ensue. Of course, there are other documents that have not yet been released and that may not be released in the foreseeable future. Nevertheless, it was felt that the available materials have stabilized sufficiently to warrant fresh scholarly examination at this point.

In acknowledging those who have supported the writing of this book, it is impossible to ignore the indefatigable Nona, Oma and the tag-team of Tetas. Without their timely intervention, and the unending patience and forbearance of Nora, it would not have been possible to finish the script. Little Nina and baby Lorenz deserve special praise for crying as little as they possibly could to help facilitate this project. I give them all my respect and love.

Table of Contents

Table of Cases

INTERNATIONAL COURT OF JUSTICE

ICJ ADVISORY OPINIONS

List of Abbreviations

AJIL	*American Journal of International Law*
BYIL	*British Yearbook of International Law*
DSM	Downing Street Memos
ECOWAS	Economic Community of West African States
FAO	Food and Agricultural Organization
FCO	Foreign and Commonwealth Office
IAEA	International Atomic Energy Agency
ICJ	International Court of Justice
ICRC	International Committee of the Red Cross
IDI	Institut de Droit International
IK	M Weller (ed), *Iraq and Kuwait: The Hostilities and their Aftermath* (1993)
ILC	International Law Commission
KBD	E Lauterpacht et al. (eds), *The Kuwait Crisis: Basic Documents* (1991)
KDP	Kurdish Democratic Party
NILR	Netherlands International Law Review
SYBIL	Singapore Year Book of International Law
UN	United Nations
UNESCO	UN Education, Scientific and Cultural Organization
UNICEF	United Nations International Children's Fund
UNIKOM	United Nations Iraq-Kuwait Observation Mission
UNMOVIC	UN Monitoring, Verification and Inspection Commission
UNSCOM	UN Special Commission
WHO	World Health Organization
WMD	weapons of mass destruction

1

Introduction

The prohibition of the use of force by states is the greatest achievement of twentieth century civilization. The traumatic experience of mechanized warfare in the trenches of Verdun and elsewhere in World War I removed the gloss from the militaristic tradition of the pre-war age. Faced with public pressure against the prospect of another war, states solemnly declared in the name of their respective peoples that they condemned recourse to war for the resolution of international controversies. More specifically, they 'renounced war as a means of national policy in their relations with one another'.[1] Instead, the parties agreed that solutions to all disputes or controversies that might arise between them, of whatever nature or whatever origin, would be sought through peaceful means alone.[2]

After the next cataclysmic conflict of World War II, that commitment was recast in the form of the UN Charter, and supported by an enforcement mechanism which, it was hoped, would save succeeding generations from the scourge of war.[3] In a profound shift from previous cabinet politics, which employed war as an extension of policy by another means, Article 2(4) of the Charter required that states refrain in their international relations not only from the use of force, but from the very threat of the use of force.

The renunciation of war as a means of advancing national policy was more than just a cynical gesture of the statesmen of the time. It represented a fundamental shift in human history. Up to that point, war had been accepted as a predominantly legitimate and often glorious way of defending or advancing national interests and of enforcing international obligations. However, since 1945 discussions about the use of force in international relations have had to be conducted against the background of the claim that launching an aggressive war may constitute a 'crime against peace'. Already in 1954, a Draft Code of Offences against

---

[1] See the somewhat touching account by JT Shotwell, *War as an Instrument of National Policy* (1929).

[2] Treaty Providing for the Renunciation of War as an Instrument of National Policy. Signed at Paris on 27 August 1928, entered into force 24 July 1929, and still listed by the United States as a treaty in force, available at <http://www.state.gov/documents/organization/38569.pdf>.

[3] UN Charter, Preamble: 'to save succeeding generations from the scourge of war, which twice in our lifetime has brought untold sorrow to mankind'.

the Peace and Security of Mankind had been developed by the United Nations International Law Commission, covering:[4]

Any act of aggression, including the employment by the authorities of a State of armed force against another State for any purpose other than national or collective self-defence or in pursuance of a decision or recommendation of a competent organ of the United Nations.

Even during the difficult Cold War years, the presumption against war was maintained.[5] Despite the many challenges to the prohibition of the use of force, international lawyers from the East and West principally agreed on the content of the relevant rules.[6] Breaches of the prohibition were inevitably justified by the relevant states in terms of an exception to the rule (self-defence), rather than through denial of its binding force.[7] While keen to portray their own conduct as lawful, states also sought to preserve the prohibition as a key structural rule of the international system from which they, too, would benefit.

Although the UN system could not function during the Cold War period in terms of enforcing peace, the Security Council and the General Assembly nevertheless provided an arena in which the lawful and unlawful use of force could be relatively easily distinguished through the interpretations of third states. For instance, while the Security Council was unable to condemn the Soviet invasion of Afghanistan, the submissions of third states to the Council, and the condemnation of the action in the General Assembly, easily overcame Moscow's self-serving justification.[8] Hence, despite occasional rival claims to the lawful use of force, the content of the rule has, for the most part, remained clearly understood among governments. Force can only be justified either on the basis of an express mandate from the Security Council, or by way of individual or collective self-defence in response to an actual or imminent armed attack.

The end of the Cold War presented an opportunity to activate the enforcement mechanisms attached to the prohibition of the use of force. During the 1980s, Iraq was involved in a highly destructive war against Iran. The two sides

---

[4] 1954 Draft Code of Offences against the Peace and Security of Mankind, Art 2(1), available at <http://untreaty.un.org/ilc/texts/instruments/english/draft%20articles/7_3_1954.pdf>. The crime of aggression has now been incorporated into the Rome Statute of the International Criminal Court, Art 5(1)(d), although this will only be activated some time after the definition of the crime has been agreed. See <http://untreaty.un.org/cod/icc/statute/romefra.htm>. See below, p. 261.

[5] See, generally, C Gray, (2008) *International Law and the Use of Force*; M Wood, 'The Law on the Use of Force: Current Challenges' (2007) 11 SYBIL 1; T Franck, (2002) *Recourse to Force*; or the classic, I Brownlie, (1963) *The Use of Force by States in International Law*.

[6] For instance, this was demonstrated by a collection of essays on the individual aspects of the prohibition of the use of force from a Soviet bloc and a Western perspective published at the conclusion of the Cold War, in WE Butler, (1989) *The Non-use of Force in International Law*.

[7] *Case Concerning Military and Paramilitary Activities in and against Nicaragua* (1986) ICJ Rep 14, paras 207, 208.

[8] For example General Assembly Resolutions ES-6/2 of 14 January 1980, 35/37 of 20 November 1980, and 36/34 of 18 November 1981.

were unable to terminate hostilities, despite efforts by the UN Secretary-General. However, the end of the Cold War 'unfroze' the Security Council. While the Council had found it difficult to become involved in major crises involving the interests of its permanent members, due to the possible application of the veto by one of the five permanent members of the Security Council, this now changed. The threat of concerted action in the Council was credited as having pushed Iran and Iraq into accepting a termination of hostilities.

This was followed by decisive action in the Council with respect to the invasion of Kuwait in 1990. While Kuwait and the coalition states cooperating with it reserved the right to respond in self-defence, they also obtained a Council mandate.[9] Resolution 678 (1990) granted legal authority to forcibly reverse this breach of the peace. It remains contested whether the operation was ultimately carried out under the auspices of self-defence or collective security. But in its day the Resolution heralded, finally, the possibility of a functioning collective security system.[10] Indeed, the vision of a New World Order briefly became plausible. As the then President of the United States, George HW Bush, explained to Congress and the world in September 1990:[11]

Today that new world is struggling to be born, a world quite different from the one we've known. A world where the rule of law supplants the rule of the jungle.

But it seemed far from clear that the rule of the jungle would be overcome. While Kuwait had been an example of decisive action in the face of classic, state-to-state aggression, different challenges were emerging. With the end of the Cold War, the UN system of collective security sought to adapt to these new challenges. There were some notable early successes. The UN had played a key role in ending some of the protracted conflicts fought on the periphery of the Cold War (Namibia, South Africa, Angola, Mozambique, Cambodia, Central America). But the transition from a bipolar world did not yield a piece dividend, nor did it signify the end of history. Conflicts continued to occur, although now mainly *within* states rather than between them.

The Cold War realignment in Europe led to the outbreak of ethnoterritorial disputes in eastern and central Europe. Georgia, Moldova, Azerbaijan, and the former Yugoslavia were soon engulfed by violence, ethnic cleansing and, in at least one instance, genocide. Outside Europe, challenges to the territorial definition of states remained comparatively rare. But in Africa, anarchy (Somalia),

---

[9] That reservation is contained in the Preamble to Resolution 661 (1990) imposing the initial set of enforcement measures in relation to Iraq/Kuwait.

[10] C Greenwood, 'New World Order or Old: The Invasion of Kuwait and the Rule of Law' (1992) 55(2) MLR 153; C Warbrick, 'The Invasion of Kuwait by Iraq (Part I)' (1991) 40 ICLQ 482 and C Warbrick, 'The Invasion of Kuwait by Iraq (Part II)' (1991) ICLQ 965; M Weller, 'The United Nations and the *Jus ad Bellum*' in P Rowe, (1993) *The Gulf War 1990–91 in International and English Law* 29.

[11] Reproduced in S Chesterman *et al.*, (2008) *Law and Practice of the United Nations* 33f.

protracted internal conflict (Sudan, Democratic Republic of Congo), and geno-cide (Rwanda) erupted with similar vigour.

These developments led to a significant debate about one of the key princi-ples underpinning the prohibition of the use of force—sovereignty. Sovereignty describes the supreme authority of the state to determine its internal and external relations, subject only to the dictates of international law. The prohibition of the use of force, and the attendant prohibition of armed intervention, protects states from armed interference in the exercise of their sovereign powers, and ensures that they can retain the physical space of sovereign decision-making—their ter-ritorial integrity. However, the dramatic internal conflicts of the 1990s led to an understanding that sovereignty does not really reside in the state as such—the state is merely an abstraction, a legal construct, a concept. Instead, the actual sov-ereign is the people. Where the organs of the state or effective authorities within it are actively involved in destroying that sovereign, they cannot at the same time rely on the doctrine of sovereignty to protect them from external interest.

This realization fed into the debate about a right to forcible humanitarian action spawned by television images of intense human suffering. Up to the end of the Cold War, that doctrine was widely derided. It was seen as a potentially dangerous cover for unending intervention operations by self-interested states. However, when faced with stark images of human suffering, the terms of the debate changed. As the UN Secretary-General put it in his seminal Agenda for Peace: 'The time of absolute and exclusive sovereignty, however, has passed; its theory was never matched by reality'.[12] Instead, the UN began to engage in ever-more ambitious and complex humanitarian rescue operations, including attempts to reconstitute disintegrating or 'failing' states.

The challenge to the traditional view of sovereignty also extended to the ques-tion of democratic governance. Previously, it was accepted that any effective authority was entitled to govern, merely because it did. Now, the idea that the will of the people formed the basis of the authority to govern was reconsecrated. There were demands to enact this requirement, through the use of force if neces-sary. The UN authorized the forcible restoration of democratic governance in Haiti, for instance—a practice replicated in a surprising number of instances on the African continent, where such action was taken by regional states, mainly without a UN mandate.

There were other new challenges, one of which concerned the proliferation of weapons of mass destruction. Previously, the International Atomic Energy Agency (IAEA) had been able to prevent their spread under the terms of the 1969 Nuclear Non-Proliferation Treaty. But with technological advances in places like India, Pakistan, Libya, North Korea, and, indeed, Iraq, the international non-proliferation regime was severely challenged by a number of threshold states throughout the 1990s.

---

[12] Agenda for Peace, A/47/277, 17 June 1992, para 17.

Another area of concern related to so-called 'rogue states'. These were countries that did not play by the international rules of the game. They were pariah states that had nothing to gain from compliance with international legal regimes. Hence, they could violate them without fear of penalty.

A third dimension concerned international terrorism. Even before the 9/11 attacks, it was evident that powerful non-state groups were forming transnational networks. These groups had no specific demands that could be addressed or coherent structure that could be reasoned with. The United States, in particular, became the subject of terror attacks, with the assault on the *USS Cole* in Yemen, and the bombing of US embassies in Kenya and Tanzania.

While each of these three challenges was regarded as dangerous in itself, there was considerable concern that they might combine and create an unprecedented threat to Western security. Rogue states might acquire nuclear weapons or biological and chemical agents. They might use these against Western targets or, worse still, pass them on to terrorist movements, with devastating consequences.

The 9/11 attacks on New York and Washington brought that message home in a powerful way. Even without the use of weapons of mass destruction (in this case, civilian airliners) massive damage was inflicted on the United States. Attacks in London, Madrid, Egypt, and Bali demonstrated that the threat was not restricted to US territory. And an incident on the Tokyo underground appeared to presage the use of weapons of mass destruction on a massive scale.

The UN convened a high-level panel to study new threats. It concluded that they were best engaged through international cooperation and action under the UN umbrella.[13] International legal rules, the panel opined, were sufficient to accommodate international action that might be necessary to prevent or defeat new security challenges.

However, by the time the panel reported, the United States had already adopted a different tack. International cooperation through the UN, in accordance with international legal rules, was not a top priority of the newly incoming US administration of George W Bush. Instead, it saw the unipolar moment as an opportunity to act in support of values supported by the United States and which it held to be universal.

Furthermore, it had been demonstrated previously that force could be used effectively and at limited cost towards such ends. Even in the final years of the Cold War, under President Ronald Reagan, the United States began to assert itself more forcefully through military means on the international stage. This took three forms. First, it engaged in a more active policy of resisting Soviet strategic advances around the globe. For instance, under what became known as the Reagan Doctrine, the United States mounted covert operations in support of armed rebel movements operating in Nicaragua, Angola, and Mozambique. US military support for the mujahideen armed opposition to the Soviet-installed

---

[13] UN General Assembly 59th Session, A/59/564, 2 December 2004.

regime in Afghanistan became so strong and sustained that it was funded from publicly acknowledged sources in the US budget. Second, the United States engaged in the direct use of force to pursue its strategic aims in its own neighbourhood, as exemplified by the invasions of Granada and Panama. And, third, it became increasingly willing to use air strikes for more limited aims, including bombings in response to terrorist acts in Libya, Afghanistan, Sudan, and Iraq.

The US-led coalition operation to liberate Kuwait had demonstrated the devastating superiority of the US military when operating under the Powell Doctrine of employing overwhelming force for a singular aim. More limited operations since then had shown that force could also be used on a smaller scale, with 'surgical precision', in pursuit of limited political objectives. These operations had triggered little international condemnation. The United States therefore possessed a unique tool equally suited for major or minor warfare.

Initially, while the United States did not itself feel under threat, this potential was employed proactively, mainly in pursuit of a humanitarian agenda. An initial use of limited force had in fact been undertaken immediately after the liberation of Kuwait. US and allied forces intervened in Iraq in support of threatened minority populations that were being persecuted by the Saddam Hussein's Goverment. The operation was not strictly authorized by the UN, but could be said to be consistent with UN resolutions. Shortly before leaving office, US President Bush (Senior), under a formal UN mandate, dispatched US Marines to prevent the starvation of thousands of Somalis. Subsequently, US armed forces facilitated the ousting of the Cedras regime from Haiti, again under a formal UN mandate. In 1995, after European-led efforts failed to end the massacre in Bosnia, NATO, again under US leadership, launched a short but decisive bombing campaign against Bosnian-Serb targets, ending the three-and-a-half-year bloody conflict in a matter of five days. This was followed by the massive NATO aerial campaign against Yugoslavia during the Kosovo crisis of 1999. That operation, again, did not rest on a formal mandate from the UN, although it could be argued to have been consistent with demands made by the Security Council.

Upon conclusion of the Kuwait conflict, the Security Council imposed comprehensive ceasefire terms on Iraq. This included the requirement to surrender for destruction its weapons of mass destruction (nuclear, biological, chemical) and longer-range delivery vehicles, and to accept long-term monitoring as a safeguard against the reacquisition of that capability. This process was meant to be administered by a UN Special Commission (UNSCOM). However, Iraq complied very hesitantly, often obstructing the work of the arms inspectors.

To address this difficulty, the Security Council adopted a practice of informal authorization of limited forcible action undertaken by the United States and the United Kingdom. The Council acted on the understanding that the authorization originally granted to states cooperating with the Government of Kuwait, in cases of material breach of the UN cease-fire, was revived. However, towards the latter part of the decade, when US and UK armed forces appeared to be acting outside the control of the Council, that informal approach fell into disrepute. This tension came to a head when both states launched a 70-hour aerial campaign against Iraq late in 1998, under the name Operation Desert Fox. Several Council members objected that there was no mandate for enforcement of UN demands relating to Iraq.

Even under the liberal Clinton administration of the 1990s, therefore, the utility of the use of force appeared to have been proven. At times, action was undertaken under a formal UN mandate, or at least in pursuit of an informal consensus expressed in the Council. On other occasions, it was deemed sufficient to point to UN identification of certain aims. These could then be pursued through force. It must be noted, however, that this view was only applied in cases of overwhelming humanitarian emergency. Such situations were legally covered, it was thought, by the emerging doctrine of humanitarian intervention. According to that doctrine, it was legally permissible for states to act to prevent or terminate situations of overwhelming humanitarian suffering if no other means was available.

There is, however, another basis for the use of force in the absence of a UN mandate. This is the doctrine of self-defence. The 9/11 outrage was immediately recognized by the UN and others as an armed attack triggering the right of self-defence. The United States and her allies answered decisively, arguing that the use of force was the only possible means of terminating further attacks emanating from Al Qaida bases in Afghanistan. The Taliban Government was toppled during the operation, although this was mainly attributed to the actions of local armed opposition forces acting in concert with the United States and its allies.

By this time, the Government had used force, occasionally on a large scale, to repel armed aggression (Kuwait), to advance humanitarian motives (Iraq, Somalia, Bosnia, Kosovo), in defence of democracy (Haiti), to promote the disarmament of Iraq, and to defend itself against terrorist threats (Sudan, Afghanistan). In each of these cases, a reasonable legal argument could be made, based either on a UN mandate, on the emerging right to counter humanitarian emergencies, or on self-defence. However, in the wake of 9/11, the United States considered whether force might also be available in broader circumstances. Iraq became the focus of these considerations.

To the US administration, and also the UK Government, Iraq appeared to combine all the elements of evil that had previously been engaged through the use of force. Iraq had invaded two of its neighbours, Iran and Kuwait. It had attacked its own population causing massive humanitarian emergencies. It had used weapons of mass destruction (chemical weapons) both internally and against Iran. It had acquired a biological weapons capacity and, as was revealed at the end of the Kuwait conflict, had been well on the way to developing nuclear weapons, and right under the nose of the IAEA inspection regime. Thereafter, it had defied mandatory UN resolutions providing for its disarmament. It was difficult to deny that Iraq under Saddam Hussein posed a threat to its neighbours. Moreover, should he decide to pass on weapons of mass destruction to terrorists, it might also pose an incalculable risk to the United States and the West.

The problem was that self-defence did not permit action to forestall risks from taking shape. Traditionally, it was recognized that a state may defend itself against imminent attack. However, the US doctrine of preventative war, to destroy threats that were still gathering, could not be reconciled with that doctrine. Nevertheless, public pronouncements by the US administration, and in particular the neoconservative elements within it, began to apply this approach to Iraq.

Of course, the international system is not defenceless when specific threats emerge. It is true that self-defence is strictly limited in terms of the trigger event—only an actual or imminent armed attack of some severity will do.[14] Moreover, the aim, scope, and scale of self-defence must be proportionate to the armed attack, and strictly necessary to defeat it. But collective security, by contrast, can be far broader.[15] The Security Council can act in a preventative way to forestall a breach of the peace or an act of aggression. It can authorize the use of force for purposes other than self-defence.[16] This can include, uncontroversially, a mandate to enforce disarmament obligations.[17] But such broad authority is constrained by the procedural requirement of obtaining a decision from the 15 members of the Council, including the five permanent members, who have been delegated the task of deciding on matters of peace and war by the UN membership.[18] Hence, under the UN system, war remains prohibited as a means of national policy (other than self-defence), but it can be a means of international policy provided it is backed by a collective security mandate.[19]

The difficulty was twofold. First, the Bush administration had little faith in the functioning of the collective security mechanism. It held the strong view that the United States was entitled to ensure its own protection, through the use of force if necessary. Second, the UN apparatus is not an autonomous mechanism. It consists of, and is reflective of, the views of a wide range of states, which did not subscribe to the analysis of the United States and the United Kingdom relating to the urgency of the Iraqi threat. While there was a strong willingness of most states to help ensure, through increased pressure, that Iraq would comply with its existing disarmament obligations, few were willing to go further. This unease was not lessened by talk in the United States about regime change. It seemed apparent that the collective security mechanism would be invoked for aims that went significantly beyond compliance with UN arms inspections.

---

[14] For example Gray (above n 3) 128–156.

[15] For example M Bedjaoi, (1994) *The Security Council and the Rule of Law.*

[16] See generally D Saraooshi, (2000) *The UN and the Development of Collective Security.*

[17] The Council has also used its Chapter VII powers generally in relation to weapons of mass destruction and their proliferation, eg in Resolution 1540 (2004).   [18] UN Charter, Art 27.

[19] The best discussion of this issue can be found in D Bowett, 'Collective Security and Collective Self-defence' in M Rama-Montaldo (ed), (1994) *El derecho international en un mundo en transformacion* 425.

Considerable tension over the Iraq issue therefore emerged. Under the threat of armed action, Iraq re-engaged with the arms inspection effort. This time, the Security Council raised the bar of Iraqi compliance. Inspections were to be more intrusive than before, and Iraqi prevarication would no longer be tolerated. The United States and the United Kingdom claimed that Resolution 1441 (2002) permitted them to act unilaterally after the Council had merely 'considered' Iraqi compliance. Others, however, were of the view that action could only be taken once expressly authorized by the Council, following submission of a report by UN inspectors detailing further material breaches by Iraq of its arms control obligations. While Iraq was initially hesitant to comply with the new inspections regime, by March 2003 it was cooperating much more actively. Regardless, at that point, the United States and the United Kingdom launched a large-scale military invasion of Iraq, leading to the removal of the Saddam Hussein Government and occupation of the country.

This development generated sharp international controversy and claims that the UN system had not only been circumvented, but fatally wounded. On the other hand, the Iraq episode highlighted the strong commitment of Western public opinion to the principle of legality in international affairs. While it was acknowledged that lawfulness should not, in itself, determine whether a war should be launched, it was equally clear that such a venture could not take place without a legal basis. Legality was thus a necessary, but not a sufficient condition. On the eve of the invasion, in London alone, over one million people marched against the war, in large part because they believed it to be unlawful.

This reflected widespread apprehension about the possible use of force, which was especially strong among European states. Arguing that only Europe had experienced the consequences of devastating war on its territory, several European leaders opposed the gradual emergence of a sense that force might, after all, again be used as an extension of national politics. But Europe was divided. Several of the 'new' states that attributed their liberation from Soviet domination to US support were strongly supportive of the US position, and looked to the United States to safeguard their newfound independence (including Poland, Georgia, and the Baltic Republics). Even within 'Old Europe' a significant rift emerged, pitting, for instance, the United Kingdom, Spain, and Italy against Germany and France over the issue of the use of force against Iraq.

The decision to go to war was not only questioned in public opinion. The UN Secretary-General claimed that it was illegal. In the Netherlands, a public inquiry ruled that the war had indeed been undertaken with insufficient legal foundation. And in the United Kingdom, a protracted debate ensued about the legal view adopted by the Attorney General. Under British constitutional convention, his advice was crucial to the launch of an invasion.

Through leaks to the press, it emerged that the Blair Government had committed itself at an early stage to support the US agenda of regime change in Iraq. It had then set out to help channel US activism into 'going the UN route'. However, published documents raised doubts as to the authenticity of its commitment to the arms inspection effort, given the wider aim of regime change.

The matter became more controversial still when it emerged that Foreign Office Legal Advisers had consistently taken the view, before and after the adoption of Resolution 1441 (2002), that the use of force would not be lawful unless authorized by a further Security Council decision. In 2010, the Chilcot Inquiry published hitherto confidential internal documents that shed light on the legal advice given in this instance. It emerged that the Attorney General, who had ultimately given the green light for the invasion, appeared to have changed his mind at a very late stage and for reasons that were not immediately obvious.

The Iraq episode has not been concluded. As was widely predicted, public order in Iraq collapsed. Sectarian violence and terrorism directed against the local population and international forces and officials present in Iraq have continued, as has the debate about both the moral and political wisdom of invading, and the lawfulness of the operation. A number of important questions remain unanswered. The first concerns the relevance of international law to the use of force, especially at a time when governments feel under threat by new security challenges. Can the existing legal rules sufficiently accommodate such threats, or was the case for preventative self-defence perhaps a necessary and acceptable one? How can we reconcile condemnation of the Iraq operation with the fact that Saddam Hussein was, in the words of the UK Prime Minister, a 'monster', abusing and torturing his own population? Was regime change not, after all, an appropriate answer? And finally, can we really rely on the alternative of collective action through the Security Council, when the Council often does not function effectively? At the end of the day, do we not need to reserve the option of unilateralism? Finally, how should we take account of the law in our domestic decision-making on peace and war? Where a clear decision is required as to whether a proposed war is lawful or not, can we rely on international law? After all it is, in the minds of some, an uncertain field, subject to interpretation by individuals who might come under considerable political pressure to deliver the 'politically necessary' result.

This book cannot claim to resolve all these questions. Instead, it presents and analyses developments in the Iraqi episode from an international legal perspective. This episode reflects virtually all the questions concerning the use of force that have arisen over the past two decades, from collective security action in the face of aggression, to forcible humanitarian action, claims of the preventative use of force, and auto-interpretation and implementation of purported UN mandates. The book only addresses these aspects of the *jus ad bellum*, the claim to be entitled to go to war. It does not consider the *jus in bello*, the laws of war that apply within armed conflicts. Other important aspects are also excluded, such as a detailed consideration of the sanctions mechanism, the human rights and humanitarian situation before, during, and after the war against Iraq, and the questions of occupation and state-building that arose in the wake of the removal of Saddam Hussein.

It should also be noted that this case is not free of irony. When President Bush Senior rang in the New World Order in 1991, he did so with reference to Resolution 678 (1990), which authorized international action to liberate Kuwait. In 2003, the purported 'revival' of that very same Resolution by his son, in justification of the second war against Iraq, seemed to some, at least at first, to herald the collapse of that dream.

2

Iraq and Kuwait

Iraq invaded Kuwait at the very moment the international community was seeking to reorganize itself at the conclusion of the Cold War.[1] The transition from the Cold War system was a profound one. The dissolution of the Warsaw Pact and of the Soviet Union removed with one stroke the bipolar system of global security, or insecurity, that had existed for close to half a century. Nuclear deterrence, previously the guarantee against a war between the two contending superpowers, became less relevant. In fact, both sides formally announced a decision to de-target one another. As the possibility of strategic nuclear exchange receded, the question of the involvement of great powers in other forms of overt and covert warfare became more pertinent. An initial peace dividend was already being paid out in relation to the proxy wars that had been nourished by the Cold War confrontation and that were now running out of fuel. Peace agreements in Central America, Cambodia, Namibia, Angola, and Mozambique became possible, supported by complex peace support operations mounted by the United Nations. Even in South Africa, the changed global strategic situation facilitated the transition from apartheid to majority governance. In fact, the conclusion of another conflict involving Iraq—the Iran–Iraq war—was a central achievement of the Security Council during this period of reawakening.[2]

The invasion of Kuwait by Iraq appeared to be fundamentally out of step with these optimistic developments. The forcible absorption of one state by its more powerful neighbour, based on territorial claims and other grounds, seemed to hark back to another age. During the League of Nations era, the failure to reverse aggression and territorial aggrandizement (Japan in Manchuria, Italy in

[1] This chapter draws on the author's collection of materials in E Lauterpacht *et al.* (eds), (1991) *The Kuwait Crisis: Basic Documents* (hereinafter 'KBD'), and on M Weller (ed), (1993) *Iraq and Kuwait: The Hostilities and their Aftermath* (hereinafter 'IK'). It updates earlier assessments of the Gulf crisis that appeared in 'The Kuwait Crisis: A Survey of some Legal Issues' (1991) 3 *African Journal of International and Comparative Law* 1; and 'The United Nations and the Jus ad Bellum' in P Rowe (ed), (1993) *The Gulf War 1990–1 in International and English Law* 29.

[2] Ironically, of course, the invasion of Kuwait prompted Iraq to agree to a settlement of most issues left unresolved by the ceasefire of 1988. For the agreement between Iraq and Iran, including the full withdrawal of troops and the recognition of the common border, as established in 1975, see S/21528, 14 August 1990, S/21556, 8 August 1990, and the Secretary-General's Report, S/21803, 21 September 1990, all reprinted in KBD, 69. See also M Weller, 'The Use of Force and Collective Security' in IF Decker and HHG Post (eds), (1991) *The Gulf War of 1980–1988* 71.

Abyssinia, and Germany in Czechoslovakia) had eventually resulted in the overthrow of the system of collective security by the Axis Powers. Iraq's aggression against Iran, a decade before its invasion of Kuwait, had triggered little international response at a time when the UN Security Council—the world's answer to the Hitlerite and Japanese aggression of the 1930s—was unable to act due to deadlock among the superpowers. Clearly, Iraq expected to establish facts on the ground that would consolidate over time. Even if there were any kind of decisive international opposition to its move, Iraq could still negotiate a partial withdrawal from a position of strength and retain far more than it had had before, both in terms of territorial possessions and of strategic power over the militarily weak states of the Gulf.

The key states of the global community were, therefore, faced with two challenges. On the one hand, they had to ensure that the armed aggression would be reversed in a way that left no benefit for the aggressor. Otherwise, the prohibition of the use of force would have been weakened at the very point of the reconstruction of a global order. Even during the Cold War years, the prohibition of the use of force had obtained the rank of a peremptory norm of international law.[3] Peremptory norms are regarded by the organized international community as a whole as non-derogable.[4] They apply to all states under all circumstances, and states cannot suspend or abrogate their application. Moreover, serious violations of a peremptory rule trigger important consequences in the international system. States must not recognize the results of the infraction.[5] They must not assist the offending state in maintaining the situation brought about by the violation. And they should cooperate in order to ensure a reversal of the situation brought about in breach of the key principle of global order concerned.[6]

Kuwait was, in fact, a key test case for the doctrine of serious violation of peremptory norms. The international response to the clear and unambiguous armed invasion of Kuwait would determine whether the UN International Law Commission, which had pioneered this concept (initially designated as 'crimes of

---

[3] See, for instance, the detailed investigation conducted in 1988, at the conclusion of the Cold War period, by L Hannikainen, (1988) *Peremptory Norms (Jus Cogens) in International Law* Ch 8, addressing the prohibition of the use of force. More recently, see A Orakhelashvili, (2006) *Peremptory Norms in International Law* 50: 'The prohibition of the use of force by states undoubtedly forms part of *jus cogens*'.   [4] Vienna Convention on the Law of Treaties, Art 53.

[5] Before the ILC re-designated such offences as 'serious violations of peremptory norms', it referred to crimes of states. The legal consequences are the same, the new designation notwithstanding. See A de Hoogh, (1996) *Obligations Erga Omnes and International Crimes*.

[6] See the International Law Commission's Articles on State Responsibility, Art 41, which reads: '1. States shall cooperate to bring to an end through lawful means any serious breach within the meaning of Article 40 [on serious breaches of peremptory norms]. 2. No State shall recognize as lawful a situation created by a serious breach within the meaning of Article 40, or render aid or assistance in maintaining that situation'. See also the ILC commentary on Art 41, reproduced in J Crawford, (2002) *The International Law Commission's Articles on State Responsibility* 249, and, for instance, the ruling of the International Court of Justice in relation to this point in the Advisory Opinion on the *Legal consequences of the Construction of a Wall in the Occupied Palestinian Territory* (2004) ICJ 136.

state'), had advanced beyond actual practice of states, or whether the responses of states would conform to the rule in reality.

If the first important structural aspect of the episode related to the credibility of the prohibition of the use of force, and its legal nature of a high status rule within the emerging international constitutional system, the second issue was one of process. The question was whether the armed action by Iraq would simply be reversed through the application of collective self-defence, or whether it would also lead to a revival and reconstitution of the UN's collective security mechanism. This chapter will try to answer this question through a review of developments following upon the invasion of Kuwait. However, it will first be necessary to set out the political and legal background to these developments.

I. Background to the Conflict

Baghdad launched a large-scale invasion of Iran in September 1980, accompanied by air strikes ranging deep into Iranian territory. The Iraqi authorities claimed to be entitled to use force. The border with Iran, they asserted, had been wrongly fixed in the middle of the strategic Shatt al-Arab waterway. The 1975 Algiers agreement establishing the boundary line was null and void. Hence, Iraq was merely enforcing its legal right to its own territory. Moreover, Iran was also guilty of subversive actions against Iraq, and there had been limited border incursions by regular Iranian armed forces. In fact, Iran was attempting to export its Islamic Revolution by fostering an uprising among the large Shia population in the south of Iraq. There had been terrorist outrages in that context, such as the assassination attempt directed against the Iraqi Foreign Minister, Tariq Aziz. Hence, there was a right to self-defence in order to prevent further actions of that kind.

A desperate war ensued, estimated to have cost the lives of at least half a million combatants and civilians, and probably many more. The conflict involved massive aerial and missile attacks against civilian targets (the war of the cities), the use of chemical weapons, initially by Iraq and later also by Iran, and the deployment of Iranian child soldiers in large numbers. While Iran had managed to displace Iraqi forces from its territory within two years, the conflict continued until a cease-fire was reached on 20 August 1988.

The eventual achievement of the cease-fire in 1988 was seen as something of a triumph for international diplomacy conducted through the United Nations. In line with its 'toothless' practice during the Cold War years, the Security Council had merely been able to consider 'the situation between Iran and Iraq'. In Resolution 479 (1980), it had called upon both parties equally to refrain from further force and settle their disputes peacefully. There had been no identification of Iraq as the aggressor and no characterization of its action as an unlawful armed invasion. Instead, the parties were invited to resort to conciliation or mediation in order to resolve the territorial dispute.

The tide turned in 1982. By then, Iran had managed to push Iraqi forces out of its territory. The Council called for an immediate cease-fire.[7] However, only Iraq, now on the losing side, accepted unconditionally. The Council called upon Iran to do likewise, but the conflict continued.[8] Iraq, previously the aggressor, could now claim to be the victim of an unjustified use of force by virtue of Iran's excessive self-defence.[9] Self-defence is a provisional right, which applies only until the consequences of an armed attack have been reversed or the Council takes the measures necessary to restore international peace and security.[10] The attack had ceased and the right to self-defence lapsed at that point. Moreover, while the initial cease-fire call by the Council in itself may not have been the measure necessary to suspend self-defence under Article 51 of the UN Charter, it turned into such a measure once it had been accepted by Iraq. At that point, the Council had established the conditions that rendered further fighting unnecessary for the purpose of terminating an armed attack.[11]

Iran indicated that it would only accept a cease-fire in exchange for Iraq's unconditional surrender, reparations in the order of US$ 150,000 million, the overthrow of the regime of Saddam Hussein, and the institution of a commission of enquiry into the origin of the conflict. Given the intransigence of Iran, and its inability to terminate hostilities, the Council was constrained to reiterate its cease-fire call, and to focus on condemning the practices of the parties during the conflict. This included the heavy losses in civilian lives and extensive damage caused to cities, property, and the economic infrastructure. It also hinted at instituting the commission of enquiry into the origins of the war sought by Iraq in support of the mediation mission of the UN Secretary-General.[12]

It was not until 1986, however, that the Council became more actively involved. By that time, there were the first signs of the Cold War thaw. Cooperation in the Council between the United States and the USSR started to become possible. Moreover, the horrendous consequences of the Iran–Iraq war for its civilian—and, indeed, combatant—victims, raised grave international concern. This included reports of the use of chemical weapons. The Council deplored these practices in Resolution 582 (1986). In a concession to Iran, it also 'deplored the initial actions which gave rise to the conflict between the Islamic Republic of Iraq' while it also criticised Tehran by deploring 'the continuation of the conflict'.[13] The Council sought expert advice and concluded that Iraq had

---

[7] Resolution 514 (1982).   [8] Resolution 522 (1982).
[9] SH Amin, 'The Iran-Iraq Conflict: Legal Implications' (1982) 31 ICLQ 167, 186.
[10] UN Charter, Art 51; KH Kaikobad, 'Jus ad Bellum: Legal Implications of the Iran-Iraq War' in IF Decker and HHG Post, (1992) *The Gulf War of 1980 to 1988*; but see Y Dinstein, (1998) *War, Aggression and Self-defence* 219, claiming that one may continue 'hammering at them up to the time of their total defeat'. On the suspension of the right by the Council, see the discussion below in Chapter 5, 132–144.   [11] This argument is made by Weller (above n 2) 71, 89.
[12] Resolution 540 (1983).   [13] Resolution 582 (1986) para 1.

indeed used chemical weapons against Iranian forces, strongly condemning this practice in a Council Presidential Statement.[14] The same statement again condemned the continuation of the war. By October 1986, the Council reiterated its cease-fire call to the parties, hinting that it might take further measures to back that call.[15]

In the meantime, both states intensified their campaign against shipping in the Gulf. Iraq had sought to interrupt oil tanker traffic and other shipping to Iran for some time. Iran had responded by targeting shipping bound for Iraq, but also for its supporters, Saudi Arabia and Kuwait. In the end, external states, including the United States, began to escort tankers through an increasing naval presence. However, while most states, including the United States and USSR, shared an interest in maintaining the flow of oil from the Gulf, this was distinctly not a collective security exercise. Instead, some states claimed to be acting in self-defence of their own flag vessels when mounting the patrols. In pursuit of this argument, a number of Kuwaiti tankers were re-registered to the United Kingdom, which was operating the Amilla patrol, and even the USSR. The United States also extended its protection to other friendly states.[16]

An escalation in the conflict occurred at the end of 1986. The Security Council referred, initially in a Presidential Statement, to the fact that the prolongation of the conflict, which continued to exact an appalling toll of human life, would 'endanger peace and security in the region'. This language still did not cross the threshold to UN Charter, Chapter VII action, but did give an indication to the parties that the Council was moving towards possible action, beyond Chapter VI meditation efforts. On 20 July, the Council adopted Resolution 598 (1987), which determined to end all military actions between Iran and Iraq. It also determined 'that there exists a breach of the peace as regards the conflict between Iran and Iraq'. This finding under Article 39 of the UN Charter located the Resolution within Chapter VII on enforcement action. Moreover, the Council specifically invoked Articles 39 and 40, covering provisional measures adopted by the Council. Now adopting mandatory language ('demands', instead of 'calling upon' or 'urging' the parties), the Council insisted on a discontinuation of all military action and the withdrawal of forces to the internationally recognized boundary. The cease-fire would be stabilized through UN monitoring. Moreover, Iran and Iraq were called upon to achieve a 'comprehensive, just and honourable settlement, acceptable to both sides' through further mediation by the UN Secretary-General.[17] The Council threatened to take 'further steps to ensure compliance with this resolution'.[18]

---

[14] S/17932, 21 March 1986.
[15] Resolution 588 (1986), para 3, indicating that the Council would meet again to consider the outcome of the mediation efforts of the Secretary-General.
[16] See C Gray, 'The British Position with Regard to the Gulf Conflict (Iran-Iraq): Part II' (1991) 40 ICLQ 464.   [17] Resolution 598 (1987), para 4.
[18] Ibid, para 6.

However, negotiations were slow. In the meantime, there was evidence that both sides were now using chemical weapons.[19] Both the United States and the USSR increased diplomatic pressure on Iran and Iraq at this point to come to a settlement, and preparations were made to impose sanctions upon them. This pressure finally took effect. By August 1988, the elements of a peace deal were in place. According to a choreography negotiated by the UN Secretary-General, and memorialized by the Council President, a cease-fire took effect at 03.00hours GMT on 20 August 1988, to be followed by additional negotiations by the parties.[20]

The war had economically exhausted both sides. Iraq had contracted significant debts from its Arab neighbours, including Kuwait. Heavy Iraqi pressure notwithstanding, Kuwait was unwilling simply to forgive this debt. There were also differences over oil pricing and production rates. Iraq claimed that Kuwait was engaging in economic warfare against Iraq in keeping production up and prices low. Moreover, Iraq claimed that Kuwait was 'stealing' its oil by drilling sideways under the border in the area of the Rumeila oil field, and by extracting oil from underground reservoirs that lay, principally, on the Iraqi side. The stage was set for the next round of hostilities, although the international response would be vastly different to the international inaction that had accompanied the Iran-Iraq conflict. This misplaced Iraqi expectation that its action would not be opposed, may have been due in part to a misunderstanding of the US position in the matter. In a discussion with US Ambassador April Glaspie held six days before the invasion, she had indicated that the United States would have 'no opinion on the Arab-Arab conflicts, like your border disagreement with Kuwait'.[21] This statement has at times been taken as something of an (unintended) US green light for the armed action. In truth, however, the overall context of the discussion indicates the opposite intention. The US emissary attempted to convey US concern about the massive deployment of Iraqi armed forces taking shape on the Iraq-Kuwait border. However, the altogether too-subtle tone of that intercession was evidently lost on the Iraqi leadership. While high-ranking officials at the State Department were considering how to issue a sterner warning over the following days, events took a more dramatic turn.[22]

II. The Invasion of Kuwait and the Immediate Response

In addition to its economic demands, Iraq maintained two claims in relation to Kuwait as such. First, it asserted that the boundary line had been inaccurately drawn and that a larger part of the Rumeila oil field straddling the boundary,

---

[19] Resolution 612 (1988).   [20] S/20095 (1988), 8 August 1998.
[21] A full transcript of the discussion is reproduced in P Auerswald, (2009) 1 *Iraq, 1990–2006* 58, 63.   [22] See RN Haass, (2009) *War of Necessity, War of Choice* 56.

territory at the port of Um Quasr, and the strategic islands of Warba and Bubiyan should all appertain to Iraq.

In addition to this territorial claim, Iraq also asserted a far broader one, based on the doctrine of decolonization, in particular the rule of *uti possidetis*, which requires that a newly independent state inherits the boundaries of the former colonial territory. Iraq had been fashioned out of three former provinces of the Ottoman Empire—the *vilayets* of Mosul, Baghdad, and Basra. One of these, the gubernatoriate of Basra, it was asserted, had in fact included Kuwait. While the Sheikh of Kuwait exercised independent powers, he nevertheless acknowledged his dependence on Basra by occasionally rendering tribute to the governor of Basra and, in 1897, accepted the title of *Qaim Maqam* from him.[23] In view of Turkish pressure to consolidate the integration with Basra, the Sheikh turned to Britain for protection. This was eventually granted in 1899, when the Sheikh signed an agreement binding him not to alienate any territory without British consent.[24] At the time, there was much discussion (and international rivalry) about the construction of a strategic railway line from the Gulf to Baghdad. London encouraged Kuwait to consolidate its claim to suitable territory for its terminus, in particular in the area of the contested island of Warba. However, that project did not materialize as had originally been envisaged. The British Government then concluded an agreement with the Ottoman Imperial government which would have confirmed that 'the territory of Kuwait...constitutes and autonomous *kaza* of the Ottoman Empire'.[25] The Sheikh would, 'as heretofore', fly the Ottoman flag, although with the word 'Kuwait' inscribed on it. However, in view of the outbreak of the Great War, the agreement remained unratified. Instead, the British again encouraged the Sheikh to reassert his independence from the Ottoman Empire, now the enemy in war.[26]

After the war, Britain exercised mandatory powers in relation to Iraq.[27] These powers were extinguished when Iraq gained full independence and was made a member of the League on Nations on 3 October 1932.[28] Iraq had been required to assure the League before independence that it did not have territorial claims against its neighbours. However, almost immediately upon independence, Iraq made such claims in relation to Kuwait.

The United Kingdom and Kuwait had terminated the agreement of 1899 relating to British protected status in an exchange of notes of 1961. But Iraqi threats against Kuwait led to the stationing of British troops there, and subsequently to the deployment of an Arab League security force.[29] After a change in government in Baghdad, Iraq and Kuwait concluded an Agreed Minute of 4 October 1963, in which Iraq expressly recognized 'the independence and complete sovereignty

[23] RV Pillai and M Kuwar, 'The Political and Legal Status of Kuwait' (1962) 11 ICLQ 108, 109.
[24] Agreement of 23 January 1899, in KBD, 9f.
[25] Agreement of 29 July 1913, in KBD, 33f.   [26] Ibid, 37.
[27] Decision of the Council of the League of Nations, 27 September 1927, in KBD, 42.
[28] Ibid, 45.   [29] Ibid, 51ff.

of the State of Kuwait' within the boundaries specified at the time of Iraqi inde-pendence.[30] After another change in government, however, Iraq asserted its claim to Kuwait once more. However, the Agreed Minute was a formal treaty, duly reg-istered with the United Nations.[31] While Iraq argued that it lacked ratification from its Parliament, it was internationally treated as a definite renunciation of any claim to Kuwait as a whole or parts of its territory that Iraq may have had.

At about midnight local time, on the night of 1 August 1990, a massive Iraqi force crossed the border into Kuwait. Almost immediately, delegates to the Security Council in New York were alerted. They met for an informal session at UN headquarters at around 3.00am and quickly hammered out the essential elements of a draft resolution. The Council convened formally at 5.08am, and the debate was opened with a passionate speech from the ambassador of Kuwait. He described the desperate situation in his country, stating that although the Government was still in control, the Emir and most of his family had sought ref-uge in Saudi Arabia. He added that:[32]

It is now incumbent on the Council to shoulder all its responsibilities and to maintain international peace and security. The Council is responsible for the protection of Kuwait and its security, sovereignty and the territorial integrity, which have been violated. In order to shoulder all its responsibilities and to carry out its tasks, the Council is urgently requested to demand that Iraq withdraw immediately and unconditionally all its forces to the positions in which they were located on 1 August 1990.

Iraq, on the other hand, rejected the intervention of the Council in the affair. The ambassador advanced the following view:[33]

First, the events taking place in Kuwait are internal matters which have no relation to Iraq.

Secondly, the Free Provisional Government of Kuwait requested my Government to assist it to establish security and order so that the Kuwaitis would not have to suffer. My Government decided to provide such assistance solely on that basis.

Thirdly, the Iraqi Government energetically states that Iraq is pursuing no goal or objective in Kuwait and desires cordial and good-neighbourly relations with Kuwait.

Fourthly, it is the Kuwaitis themselves who in the final analysis will determine their future. The Iraqi forces will withdraw as soon as order has been restored. This was the request made by the Free Provisional Government of Kuwait. We hope that it will take no more than a few days, or at the most a few weeks.

Fifthly, there are reports that the previous Kuwaiti Government has been overthrown and that there is now a new Government. Hence, the person in the seat of Kuwait here represents no one, and his statement lacks credence.

Sixthly, my Government rejects the flagrant intervention by the United States of America in these events. This intervention is further evidence of the co-ordination

---

[30] Ibid, 56f.   [31] 485 UNTS 321.
[32] Provisional Verbatim Record of the UN Security Council, S/PV.2932, 2 August 1990, 3ff.
[33] Ibid, 11ff.

and collusion between the United States government and the previous Government of Kuwait.

My country's Government hopes that order will be swiftly restored in Kuwait and that the Kuwaitis themselves will decide upon their future, free from any outside intervention.

It is interesting to note that Iraq did not attempt to justify the invasion with reference to a claim to the territory of Kuwait, the alleged 'theft' of oil from the Rumaila oilfield through so-called 'slant drilling' underneath the border line, or that Kuwait had flooded the international market with cheap crude, thereby depressing prices and damaging Iraq's economic interests. These points had been made in the political arena, but it seemed that even Iraq understood that that they would not provide the basis for a legal argument in the Security Council.[34] Instead, Iraq justified its actions on the grounds of an alleged invitation to intervene by a provisional revolutionary government. This argument was swiftly rejected by the Council, as it had been by a large majority of the UN membership in the cases of Hungary, Czechoslovakia, and Afghanistan.[35] After all, Iraq itself had brought that purported government into Kuwait in the wake of the invasion. And, in terms of fact, there was no evidence of a significant revolutionary movement within Kuwait itself.[36] As the US delegate to the Council pointed out:[37]

While the Iraqi invasion was carefully planned and professionally executed, the Iraqis at one salient point made a serious mistake. Instead of staging their *coup d'état* and installing this so-called free provisional government before the invasion, they got it the wrong way around: they invaded Kuwait and then staged the *coup d'état* in a blatant and deceitful effort to justify their action—like the effort they have just made here.

The condemnation of the Iraqi action in the Council was unanimous, although Yemen failed to participate in the vote on Resolution 660 (1990), having been unable to receive instructions from its capital. That Resolution determined that the Iraqi invasion of Kuwait was a breach of international peace and security. Initially, the draft text had indicated that an act of aggression had taken place, but that wording was changed at the urging of the Soviet delegation. In substance there was no difference, as both formulations constituted a finding under Article 39 of the UN Charter, which must precede enforcement measures under Articles 41 and 42.

Still, as opposed to the diplomatic and imprecise language usually employed when urging 'the parties' or some other unspecified entity to cease hostilities, the

---

[34] Compare the Iraqi memorandum, reprinted in KBD, 73.

[35] See the illuminating survey of practice in L Doswald-Beck, 'The Legal Validity of Military Intervention by Invitation of the Government' (1985) 56 *British Yearbook of International Law* 189.

[36] Iraq failed for days to produce the so-called 'Revolutionary government' and, when it did, it appeared to consist of Iraqi army officers and affiliated personnel.

[37] Provisional Verbatim Record of the UN Security Council (above n 32), 12ff.

Resolution clearly named Iraq as being responsible for the invasion. In that way, it reflected a very distinct change from the attitude exhibited a decade earlier, after Iraq's invasion of Iran.

The Council condemned the invasion, and, by way of a provisional measure adopted explicitly under Article 40 of the UN Charter, it demanded 'that Iraq withdraw immediately and unconditionally all its forces to the positions in which they were located on August 1, 1990'. By adopting this wording, the Council avoided having to make an instant pronouncement on the validity of territorial claims in the context of the withdrawal.[38] Thus, even if Iraq had a valid claim to certain territories, such as Warba and the Bubiyan Islands, it was required to withdraw fully and re-establish the status quo. The Resolution did, however, indicate that certain issues could be made subject to immediate negotiations.

The Iraqi Government precluded negotiations when it announced the annexation of Kuwait less than a week after the invasion. Again, this measure was rejected by the Council with unanimity in Resolution 662 (1990), which demanded that it must be rescinded.[39] In that Resolution, the Council also affirmed the legitimacy of the Government of the state of Kuwait, by then in exile in Saudi Arabia.[40] In calling upon all states, international organizations, and specialized agencies not to recognize the annexation, and to refrain from any action or dealing that might be interpreted as indirect recognition of the annexation, the Resolution in effect mirrored the consequences arising from the unlawful acquisition of territory in general international law.

Iraq challenged this action of the Council when it required the closure of diplomatic and consular missions in Kuwait. Under the 1961 Vienna Convention, the termination or suspension of diplomatic relations is a sovereign act of the states which establish such relations.[41] Acceptance of the order to close the missions would have amounted to acknowledgement of the authority of the state of Iraq to act on behalf of Kuwait. Although a protest would have been sufficient, a number of states kept their embassies in Kuwait open to underscore the refusal of the international community to accept the validity of the annexation. The Council supported this attitude, demanding, in Resolution 664 (1990), that Iraq rescind its orders for the closure of diplomatic and consular missions in Kuwait and the withdrawal of diplomatic immunity of their personnel, and refrain from any such actions in the future.

---

[38] Under Art 40, such pronouncements would in fact be impermissible.

[39] Provisional Verbatim Record of the UN Security Council, S/PV.2934. See also the pronouncements of the Arab League, the European Commission, the Gulf Cooperation Council, the Non-Aligned Movement, the Nordic Countries, and the Organization of American States on this matter, reprinted in KBD, Ch 8.

[40] Resolution 661 (1990) had already referred to the aim of restoring the legitimate Government of Kuwait. On the Government in exile, see UN Doc S/21666, reprinted in KBD, 185.

[41] Arts 43 and 45 of the Vienna Convention, 500 UNTS 95. See also the 1963 Vienna Convention on Consular Relations, 596 UNTS 261.

When Iraq attempted to enforce its decision concerning the closure of embassies and consulates, the response in the Security Council was once again unanimous.[42] In Resolution 667 (1990) it expressed outrage at the violations by Iraq of diplomatic premises in Kuwait, and at the abduction of personnel enjoying diplomatic immunity and of foreign nationals who were present on these premises, and issued a veiled threat that non-compliance might trigger further enforcement measures, in addition to economic sanctions.[43] In this way, the Council did act very much in accordance with the expectation established in the doctrine of *jus cogens*, and its protection through the concept of serious violations of peremptory norms triggering collective responses noted at the outset of this chapter.

III. Economic Sanctions

Iraq had initially announced its desire to withdraw quickly from Kuwait. Before adopting enforcement measures, the Security Council gave the Government of Iraq four days to furnish evidence of the seriousness of its declarations. Much hope was placed on inter-Arab mediation efforts in this respect, but these were not successful. Hence, in Resolution 661 (1990) the Council imposed economic sanctions.[44] Following upon earlier, limited sanctions relating to Southern Rhodesia and South Africa, these were very comprehensive. They covered the importation from, or exportation to, Iraq and occupied Kuwait, of all commodities and products, shipment of such items, the rendering of services and funds, etc. Only supplies intended strictly for medical purposes were exempt. Moreover, in relation to foodstuffs, exemptions could be granted in humanitarian circumstances.

The Secretary-General was requested to report within 30 days of the adoption of Resolution 661 (1990) on progress in its implementation. To examine these reports, and to seek further information from states concerning the actions taken, the Sanctions Committee was established with membership identical to that of the Security Council.[45]

The request directed at the Secretary-General to report within 30 days on implementation was misunderstood by some members of the organization. Jordan, for example, initially appeared to interpret this stipulation as allowing for a 30-day period within which to decide upon the adoption of sanctions. However, Resolution 661 (1990) was binding from the moment of its inception and demanded immediate implementation. Similarly, the right of Member States

---

[42] Provisional Verbatim Record of the UN Security Council, S/PV.2940, 16 September 1990.

[43] In fact, this episode served to reunite the Council, which was in danger of division over the issue of exceptions to the economic sanctions under Resolution 661 (1990).

[44] See, in considerable detail, D Bethlehem, (1991) *The Kuwait Crisis: Sanctions and their Economic Consequences*.

[45] The Sanctions Committee had its first meeting on 9 August 1990, when it elected the delegate of Finland as its chairperson. See KBD, 197.

to consult the Council with respect to special economic hardship in accordance with Article 50 of the UN Charter did not imply that, pending a grant of relief, sanctions would not have to be implemented. This was made clear at the very first substantive session of the Sanctions Committee.[46]

Generally, however, compliance with Resolution 661 (1990) was surprisingly solid.[47] National measures implementing sanctions were adopted in some 140 jurisdictions.[48] Allegations concerning violations of the embargo were comparatively rare, and seldom substantiated.[49]

On one issue, however, consensus within the Security Council and the Sanctions Committee was threatened. A large number of foreign workers were stranded in occupied Iraq and Kuwait. Many were not permitted or were unable to leave, and lacked supplies of food and medicine. Whereas the Sanctions Committee was able to grant certain exemptions, for example with respect to the use of aircraft, including Iraqi aircraft, to return mainly Western nationals, it had more difficulty in accepting that relief shipments for the remaining foreigners should be permitted. This issue was complicated by Iraq's demands that it would only permit entry of food shipments if they were also made available to Iraqi civilians. This demand was contextually linked with the view, put forward in the Council by Yemen and Cuba, that food supplies were generally exempt from the application of Resolution 661 (1990). Reference was made to the provision in that Resolution for exceptions in case of 'humanitarian circumstances'.[50]

However, the Council determined that it had to make a specific finding of humanitarian circumstances within Iraq before being able to permit food supplies. The Sanctions Committee requested the Secretary-General to ascertain whether such circumstances prevailed in Iraq. Perhaps unwilling to participate in this highly emotional debate, the Secretary-General reported back that he did not have the means to furnish such a finding. He was then requested to report with particular reference to children under 15 years of age, expectant mothers, and the sick and elderly.[51] In the event, the Sanctions Committee authorized the dispatch of one Indian ship carrying humanitarian supplies, provided that the supplier country could guarantee, through the involvement of agencies like the respective national Red Cross societies, that this food would only be used for its intended purpose.[52]

---

[46] A/AC.25/SR.2, 4.   [47] For example S/21715, reprinted in KBD, 200.

[48] See Bethlehem (above n 44); CC Joyner, 'Sanctions, Compliance and International Law: Reflections on the United Nations' Experience Against Iraq' (1991) 31(1) *Virginia Journal of International Law* 1.

[49] Some unspecified allegations were made by the United States and certain other powers immediately before and after the Council adopted Resolution 665 (1990) concerning the naval blockade, A/AC.25/SR.3, 5. However, these apparently related mostly to Iraqi attempts to breach the embargo, rather than violations by other states.

[50] Medical supplies were totally exempt from the application of Resolution 661 (1990).

[51] Resolution 666 (1990).

[52] Statement by the Chairman of the Committee established by Resolution 661 (1990) concerning the Situation between Iraq and Kuwait, 14 September 1990, reprinted in KBD, 234.

Only after the adoption of the provisional cease-fire in Resolution 686 (1991), terminating the eventual hostilities, the Council endorsed a fact-finding mission by Under-Secretary-General Martti Ahtisaari, whose report indicated that great suffering was occurring among the Iraqi population.[53] On 23 March 1991 the Sanctions Committee determined that relevant humanitarian circumstances prevailed within Iraq.

IV. Naval and Aerial 'Interdiction'

The United States and Great Britain, which had deployed significant naval forces in the region, decided to institute a naval 'interdiction' campaign a week after the adoption of Resolution 661 (1990). This measure engendered some controversy. It was taken under the following request of the Emir of Kuwait, made from exile in Saudi Arabia:[54]

Kuwait is grateful to all those Governments that have taken a principled stand in support of Kuwait's position against aggression and occupation by Iraq. It is considered essential that these efforts be strengthened so that the provisions of the relevant Security Council resolutions be fully and effectively implemented.

In the exercise of its inherent right of individual and collective self-defence and pursuant to Article 51 of the Charter of the United Nations, Kuwait should like to notify you that it has requested some nations to take such military or other steps as are necessary to ensure the effective and prompt implementation of Security Council Resolution 661 (1990).

This request was made to the United States, Great Britain, and a number of other states, and it was immediately accepted by the United States and Great Britain. Both states stressed that the operation was undertaken in the exercise of the right to self-defence. Britain, in addition, added that:

...the Kuwaiti request is put firmly in the context of the economic sanctions, as was given in the drafting of it which I read out: '... other steps as are necessary to ensure that economic measures designed to restore our rights are efficiently implemented'.[55]

This formulation, cited from the text of the request actually made by the Kuwaiti Government to the British authorities, differs slightly from the wording of the request as relayed to the Security Council in the above communication. It does not refer to steps necessary to ensure the implementation of Resolution 661 (1990), but is couched in more general language. It appears that the wording had in fact been agreed in advance by the British and Kuwaiti legal advisers, to avoid giving the impression of a unilateral act, taken at the request of Kuwait, to enforce sanctions that had been adopted by a collective body, that is, the United Nations.

---

[53] UN Press summary, 3 March 1991, 5.

[54] Letter to the Security Council, S/21498, 13 August 1990.

[55] Transcript of a press conference given by the British Foreign and Commonwealth Minister of State, William Waldegrave, 13 August 1990, reprinted in KBD, 245.

However, the politicians were less subtle than the British lawyers. US President George HW Bush, his Secretary of State James Baker, UK Prime Minister Margaret Thatcher, and her Foreign Secretary Douglas Hurd, all spoke of a request to enforce UN sanctions, in addition to the right of self-defence, when they announced the 'interdiction'. And the United States, in its official communication to the Council, affirmed that the operation was indeed designed to ensure that sanctions would be effective and that Resolution 661 (1990) would not be violated.[56]

This assertion led to an unnecessary and acrimonious debate in the Council. In a closed emergency session, a wide range of delegations, including those very friendly to the United States and Britain, such as Canada, made it clear that it was for the Council alone to authorize the enforcement of its sanctions by military force. Although Resolution 661 (1990) did not formally invoke the provision, economic sanctions were adopted under the authority of Article 41 of the UN Charter, which relates specifically to measures 'not involving the use of armed force'.[57] The initiation of a blockade, even if semantically converted into an interdiction, was a belligerent act falling clearly and explicitly within the ambit of Article 42. As such, it would have required further authorization by the Council. In this case, however, the members of the Council had not even been consulted about the measure.

This fact had been confirmed in previous practice. In 1966, the United Kingdom specifically requested Council authorization when it came under pressure from the majority of newly independent states at the UN to use naval force in support of sanctions covering Southern Rhodesia after its unilateral declaration of independence.[58] It had done so in the clear belief that the action would not be lawful in the absence of such an authorization (in fact it had refused previous requests to that end). The Council in consequence had called upon:[59]

...the Government of the United Kingdom of Great Britain and Northern Ireland to prevent, by the use of force if necessary, the arrival at Beira of vessels reasonably believed to be carrying oil destined for Southern Rhodesia, and empowers the United Kingdom to arrest and detain the tanker known as Joanna V upon her departure from Beira in the event her oil cargo is discharged there.

In that case, of course, there was no underlying right to self-defence that could have been invoked in the alternative. Here, it was not really disputed in the Council that the US and British action was lawful in the exercise of the right to collective self-defence, upon the request from Kuwait.

---

[56] Letter to the Security Council, S/21537, 16 August 1990.

[57] This explicit wording of Art 41 does not leave room for the idea that authority to enforce economic sanctions militarily is somehow implied in the concept of economic sanctions. Of course, if Resolution 661 (1990) had requested states to cooperate in implementation through military force, then it would have been a measure adopted under Art 42. But no such request had been made.

[58] The sanctions were in fact not formally adopted under Chapter VII, covered oil and petroleum products, and were adopted in Resolution 216 (1966).   [59] Resolution 221 (1966).

It might have been argued, of course, that self-defence was no longer available. After all, the Council had adopted sanctions Resolution 661 (1990). Conceivably, this could have been considered sufficient to suspend the operation of the right to self-defence. According to Article 51 of the UN Charter, that right applied only provisionally, until the Council had taken the measures necessary to maintain international peace and security. But, as opposed to other texts that had been negotiated jointly, sanctions Resolution 661 (1990) had been very carefully drafted by the United States alone. It contained a preambular reference affirming 'the inherent right of individual or collective self-defence in response to the armed attack by Iraq against Kuwait, in accordance with Article 51 of the Charter'. In addition, it stated that the application of economic sanctions should not 'prohibit assistance to the legitimate Government of Kuwait'. Hence, the Resolution itself made clear that self-defence would continue to apply.

Nevertheless, few delegations interpreted these provisions as encouraging unilateral action outside the framework agreed by the Council. In particular, the reference to Article 51 was seen as a customary reiteration of a well-known provision of the Charter, which was not relevant, at least while the Council was able to discharge its primary responsibility for the maintenance of international peace and security. While most delegations felt that Resolution 665 (1990) had been precisely the 'measure necessary' to suspend the right of self-defence pending Council action, in adopting the US draft of the text, they had in fact agreed that self-defence survived as an option.

In effect, neither Britain nor the United States used lethal force unilaterally before a UN mandate was granted. Britain asserted that it was merely monitoring compliance with Resolution 661 (1990) by interdicting shipping. The United States did actually fire shots across the bow of an Iraqi vessel a week before Resolution 665 (1990) was adopted but, when this had no effect, the vessel was not boarded, disabled, or sunk.[60]

The affair generated mistrust among Council members, who were wary of losing control over the UN operation in the Gulf at the very moment when the Council was, for the first time, able to operate as originally foreseen. The danger of threatening unanimous support in the Council for the tough measures instituted against Iraq led the United States to go back to the Council and ask for a mandate, although it was asserted that, legally, this would not be necessary.

This time, members of the Council were more mistrustful, and it took 10 days of intense negotiations to adopt Resolution 665 (1990). A reference to the blockade as an act on behalf of Kuwait had to be deleted, as it would have hinted at application of the right to self-defence. Instead, in more vague terms, it referred to states 'cooperating with the government of Kuwait'. An initial draft had foreseen

---

[60] R McLaughlin, 'United Nations Mandated Naval Interdiction Operations in the Territorial Sea' (2002) 51 ICLQ 249. See also C Greenwood, 'New World Order or Old? The Invasion of Kuwait and the Rule of Law' (1992) 55 MLR 153, 161.

authority to use 'minimum force as may be necessary to prevent maritime trade in breach of the embargo' including 'all necessary action in accordance with the Charter (ie under Article 51) including use of such air, sea and land forces as may be necessary to ensure complete compliance'.[61] This wording seemed to mix language from Article 42 of the Charter providing for the use of force in the pursuit of collective security with self-defence.

In the end, the Resolution as adopted was only indirectly linked to Chapter VII, through a preambular reference back to Resolution 661 (1990) and its Chapter VII character. Article 42 of the UN Charter was also deliberately not referred to, although the measure was adopted under its authority. That article empowers the Council to:

... take such action by the air, sea, or land forces as may be necessary to maintain or restore international peace and security. Such action may include demonstrations, blockade, and other operations by air, sea, or land forces of Members of the United Nations.

Article 42 was specifically not invoked to preclude an expansive interpretation of the authority granted. It was thus made clear that no action other than a naval interdiction, that is, no action of land or air forces, which were also mentioned in the article, had been authorized at this point. Moreover, instead of the use of 'minimum force' as originally proposed by the US at the insistence of the Chinese, the states deploying maritime forces in the area were called upon to use such measures 'commensurate to the specific circumstances as may be necessary' to halt all inward and outward maritime shipping in order to inspect and verify their cargoes and destinations and to ensure strict implementation of the provisions related to such shipping laid down in Resolution 661 (1990). It was, however, generally accepted that this included the possible use of force, with only China taking a different view. In fact, China made a unilateral statement upon adoption of the Resolution, asserting that the use of force had been positively ruled out. However, this view was not in line with the negotiating history of the Resolution, was rejected by the majority of the Council members, and was more of an attempt by China to allow passage of the Resolution without publicly abandoning its objection to the use of force against less-developed nations. The measure was expressly placed under 'the authority of the Security Council'. Indeed, the states concerned were requested to coordinate their action through the Military Staff Committee. Furthermore, the Council expressly committed itself to the monitoring of the implementation of the measure.

The legal nature of the Resolution raised some doubts.[62] First, it was asserted that it was legally defective, given the failure expressly to refer to Article 42. However,

---

[61] As reported in H Freudenschuss, 'Between Unilateralism and Collective Security: Authorizations of the Use of Force by the UN Security Council' (1994) 5 *European Journal of International Law* 492, 495.

[62] See, in detail, D Sarooshi, (1999) *The United Nations and the Development of Collective Security* 200ff; LE Fielding, 'Maritime Interceptions: Centrepiece of Economic Sanctions in the

there is no requirement in the UN Charter to do so. It was also alleged that the mandate adopted was in fact too broad, rendering it inappropriate for collective security, which can be extended only to quite specific grants of authority when the Security Council delegates quite specific powers to individual states. But the mandate is in fact well circumscribed, particularly when compared to subsequent practice of the Council. Finally, there was an objection that the Council failed to supervise the operation, as collective security would demand. However, in this instance, there was an unprecedented measure of supervision, or at least involvement, foreseen by virtue of the reference to coordination of the operation through the Military Staff Committee. In reality, though, the Committee met only once in relation to the naval interdiction and took no role in the substantive coordination of the action. But this fact concerns the way the text was implemented, not its design or the emphasis it placed on the collective security dimension.

The United States and Great Britain made unilateral statements at the time of the adoption of the Resolution, highlighting their position on the issue of self-defence. US Ambassador Thomas Pickering said that the Resolution clearly 'does not diminish the legal authority of Kuwait and other States to exercise their inherent right', in apparent reference to self-defence. The British delegate also referred to self-defence, but then emphasized the need for further measures to be agreed by the Security Council, if necessary. However, a number of other delegations insisted that no further unilateral measures should be taken. Kuwait itself appeared to accept that Resolution 665 (1990) constituted a measure necessary in the sense of Article 51. If, in consequence, Kuwait's right to individual self-defence had been suspended pending Council action, then the United States and Great Britain could not of course invoke a derived right of collective self-defence on its behalf.

However, it cannot be seriously doubted that the reference to the right to self-defence in Resolution 661 (1990) carried over to subsequent action. There is, of course, academic debate on this point. One, extreme position suggests that no measure adopted by the Council can be capable of suspending self-defence, unless the victim state of the armed attack itself accepts this.[63] This view is based on the claim of self-defence as an inherent right, aiming to secure the survival of the state under any circumstance. Only the state concerned is in a position to determine what is necessary for its survival. However, this position would deny to the Council the very right it is specifically accorded in Article 51 of the UN Charter. It is also inconsistent with the notion that Article 51 is a provisional right, ancillary to the collective security provisions. After all, the article is actually placed in Chapter VII of the UN Charter governing collective security.

New World Order' (1993) 53 *Louisiana Law Review* 1191, 1227ff; rightly opposing R Lavalle, 'The Law of the United Nations and the Use of Force, Under the Relevant Security Council Resolutions of 1990 and 1991, to Resolve the Persian Gulf Crisis' (1992) 23 *Netherlands Year Book of International Law* 3, 24.

[63] EV Rostow, 'Until What? Enforcement Action or Collective Self-defence?' (1991) 85 AJIL 506, 512.

Another view requires an express decision by the Council, ordering a state to desist from the continued exercise of the right.[64] However, there is no support for that proposition in either the Charter and its *travaux preparatoires*, or in Council practice. At the other extreme, there is the view that any action by the Council, or least any action adopted under Chapter VII, suspends the right to self-defence.[65] After all, why would the Council have adopted the measure if it did not regard it as the measure necessary to maintain international peace and security at that time? But this would be 'an implausible—indeed absurd—interpretation', potentially depriving a state of the right to defend itself due to any pronouncement of the Council, however ineffectual.[66] As Greenwood points out, this attitude also makes it highly unattractive for a state under attack to turn to the Council at all if it risks trading its right to self-defence for an ineffective pronouncement from the Council.[67] The correct, and dominant, view remains that self-defence is only suspended when the action taken by the Council, if implemented, would reverse the armed attack, and when such action is backed by enforcement measures capable of achieving this result. Whether or not this is the case is, as Bowett noted, a matter of objective assessment if the Council itself has offered no guidance.[68]

In this instance, self-defence—an inherent right—clearly remained available to Kuwait, if the measures adopted by the Council failed to achieve their stated aim of reversing the occupation of Kuwait. However, there was a strong expectation on the part of the Council that states cooperating with the Government of Kuwait would do so in the context of collective security, and under the authority that had been granted.

In spite of the dispute surrounding its creation, Resolution 665 (1990) was important for the subsequent practice of the Council. Following on from Resolution 221 (1966), concerning the Southern Rhodesia embargo, the Council confirmed very clearly that sanctions in themselves do not carry with them implied authorization of their enforcement. For that purpose, a specific mandate from the Council is required. Moreover, it re-established a mode of action for the Council delegation that would be applied with some frequency thereafter.[69] One might also note that the Resolution was left in place even after the liberation of Kuwait, in parallel with the continued operation of sanctions Resolution 661 (1990). At that point, self-defence was no longer available. A formal cease-fire had terminated the authority to use force according to Resolution 678 (1990).

[64] D Greig, 'Self-defence and the Security Council: What does Article 51 Require?' (1990) 40 ICLQ 366, 389, 401.

[65] R Mullerson, 'Self-defence in the Contemporary World' in LF Damrosch and DJ Scheffer, (1991) *Law and Force in the New International Order* 3, 10: 'From the moment the Council adopted these measures (661 and 665) and imposed them on Iraq, the inherent right of self-defence was replaced by collective measures'.

[66] O Schachter, 'United Nations Law in the Gulf Conflict' (1991) 85 AJIL 452, 458.

[67] Greenwood (above n 60) 164.

[68] DW Bowett, (1958) *Self-defence in International Law* 195ff; Y Dinstein, (1998) *War, Aggression and Self-defence* 196f.

[69] For example Haiti, the former Yugoslavia: see McLaughlin (above n 60).

However, the authority granted in Resolution 665 (1990) persisted, and was, from that point onwards, the only legal basis for sanctions enforcement action.

The collective security dimension was strengthened further in the wake of Iraqi interference with some of the remaining foreign embassies in Kuwait. In Resolution 670 (1990) the Council confirmed that Resolution 661 (1990) applied to all means of transport, including aircraft, in effect pronouncing an aerial blockade. However, states were not empowered to use force to achieve compliance with the aerial embargo. Operative paragraph 7 referred to applicable general international law and to the Chicago Convention on International Civil Aviation of 7 December 1944.[70] That Convention had been amended in 1984 to include a specific provision prohibiting the use of weapons against civil aircraft in flight.[71]

With the adoption of Resolution 670 (1990), the Council had exhausted the catalogue of measures short of active hostilities against Iraq. In light of reports concerning atrocities committed by the Iraqi occupation forces in Kuwait,[72] the Council turned to drafting Resolution 678 (1990).

V. Authorization of the Use of Force Against Iraq

At the very moment when the permanent members of the UN Security Council appeared to be inching towards a new resolution which would empower states to end the illegal occupation of Kuwait by military means, Iraq called on the General Assembly to hear its case and adopt a resolution discouraging the use of force.[73] In the Assembly all members have an equal voice, and it is, therefore, dominated by the large number of neutral and non-aligned states. These have traditionally displayed a hostile attitude towards the application of military force against a developing nation, especially when a great power like the United States is involved. Iraq was hoping to employ the solidarity of fellow developing nations to preclude military action by the international coalition which was assembling in the Gulf.

In terms of law, only the Security Council can issue orders, directives, and demands. The Assembly, by contrast, can only make recommendations, which lack binding force. To avoid a conflict of authority, the Assembly is barred from pronouncing on resolutions relating to matters of peace and international security which are under consideration by the Council. In practice, however, the Assembly has never been averse to discussing cases that were under deliberation in the Council. Arguably, the Assembly can even adopt recommendatory

---

[70] 15 UNTS 295.
[71] Protocol Relating to the Amendment to the Convention on International Civil Aviation, 18 May 1984, 23 *International Legal Materials* 705.
[72] See S/PV.2959, S/PV.2960, S/PV.2962, and KBD, Ch 6.
[73] A/45/236/Cor.1, set out in KBD, 193.

resolutions on issues which the Council has been precluded from addressing due to a veto.

However, Iraq seriously miscalculated the attitude of the neutral and non-aligned members. First, their views had already been heard in the Council, where they were represented by states ranging from Malaysia and Columbia to Yemen and Cuba. The neutral and non-aligned nations had generally supported the tough sanctions adopted against Baghdad. Furthermore, in the opening debate of the Assembly in September 1990, Iraq had been condemned just as strongly and consistently as it had been in the Council.

Thus, the General Committee of the Assembly, which manages its business, refused to admit a special agenda item on the danger of a military confrontation in the Gulf, as proposed by Iraq.[74] Instead, the members of the Committee delivered a strong denunciation of Baghdad's attitude. The general discussion in the Assembly on the Kuwait crisis must also have been discouraging for the Iraqi Government. In stark contrast to the usual diplomatic language employed to describe acts of aggression (for example, 'the situation in Afghanistan'), the respective agenda item was concerned with 'Iraqi aggression and the continued occupation of Kuwait in flagrant violation of the Charter of the United Nations', and condemnation was once again nearly unanimous. Iraq's attempt to split the international community failed spectacularly.

Instead, the Security Council offered the Government of Iraq a tough choice in Resolution 678 (1990). Unless it was willing to implement Resolution 660 (1990) and all subsequent relevant resolutions, and furnished concrete evidence of that desire, the Council authorized Member States cooperating with the Government of Kuwait to use all necessary means to uphold and implement Resolution 660 (1990) and all subsequent relevant resolutions, and to restore international peace and security in the area. It left Iraq a final pause of goodwill, up to 15 January 1991, to comply before force was used.

There was no doubt in the Council that the term 'all necessary means' was meant to cover the use of military force.[75]

A. Was Resolution 678 (1990) validly adopted?

The legal validity of Resolution 678 (1990) was attacked, in particular by the delegations of Iraq, Yemen, and Cuba, in the debate preceding its adoption.[76] However, in accordance with long-standing international jurisprudence, a resolution of a properly constituted organ of the UN which is passed in accordance with the UN's rules of procedure, and which is declared by its President to have

---

[74] The agenda item as adopted concerned 'Iraqi Aggression and the continued occupation of Kuwait in flagrant violation of the Charter of the United Nations', A/45/250, 10.

[75] It was precisely for this reason that Cuba and Yemen voted against the Resolution, and China abstained. See Provision Verbatim Record of the UN Security Council, S/PV.2963, 29 November 1990.   [76] Ibid, 19, 31, 52 respectively.

been so passed, must be presumed to have been validly adopted.[77] Resolution 678 (1990) was adopted by 12 votes to 2, with China abstaining. The argument that the mandate granted in the Resolution is defective because it had not attracted the 'affirmative' vote of China required by the UN Charter is misplaced. As the International Court of Justice (ICJ) has confirmed:[78]

... the proceedings of the Security Council extending over a long period supply abundant evidence that presidential rulings and the positions taken by members of the Council, in particular its permanent members, have consistently and uniformly interpreted the practice of voluntary abstention by a permanent member as not constituting a bar to the adoption of resolutions.

Resolution 678 (1990) was adopted with specific reference to Chapter VII of the UN Charter. Again, the failure to formally invoke Article 42 as a source of authority was not decisive. There is no formal requirement for such an invocation and there is no practice of the Council that might add to the provisions of the Charter in that respect. Indeed, Article 42 had never been invoked expressly. Neither Resolution 83 (1950), which concerned assistance to repel the armed attack against the Republic of Korea during the Korean War, nor Resolution 221 (1966), which authorized the United Kingdom to use force, if necessary, to prevent the arrival of oil destined for Southern Rhodesia at the harbour of Beira, contained such a reference. In fact, the wording of Resolution 678 (1990) mirrored the wording of Article 42, thus hinting at the source of its authority. In case of doubt, the principle of interpretation prevails, which holds that 'when the Organization takes action which warrants the assertion that it was appropriate for the fulfilment of one of the stated purposes of the United Nations, the presumption is that such action is not *ultra vires* the Organization'.[79]

The formal requirement of Article 39 concerning a finding of a threat to the peace, breach of the peace, or act of aggression was fulfilled in this case. Such a finding, which had to be made in order to permit recommendations or decisions by the Council under Article 42, had already been made in Resolution 660 (1990), only hours after the invasion. Legally, at least, the Council was also entitled to authorize the use of military force, despite the fact that sanctions had arguably not been given long enough to take effect. Article 42 does not require the actual exhaustion of peaceful remedies, as it were. There is no objective test in this respect. Instead, according to Article 42, it is for the Council to 'consider' that the measures provided for in Article 41 are inadequate.[80] This is essentially a political function. The finding was inherent in the terms of Resolution 678 (1990).

---

[77] *Legal Consequences for States of the Continued Presence of South Africa in Namibia (South West Africa) Notwithstanding Security Council Resolution 276* (1970) 1971 ICJ 16, 22.   [78] Ibid.

[79] *Certain Expenses of the United Nations (Article 17, paragraph 2, of the Charter)* (1962) ICJ Reports 167f.

[80] O Schachter, 'United Nations Law in the Gulf Conflict' (1991) 85 AJIL 452, 462; BH Weston, 'Security Council Resolution 678 (1990) and Persian Gulf Decision-making: Precarious Legitimacy' (1991) 85 AJIL 516, 528.

The failure to utilize the mechanisms provided for in Article 43 of the UN Charter did not impinge on the validity of the measure.[81] That provision provides for Member States to make available to the Council on its call and in accordance with a special agreement, armed forces and other assistance necessary for the purpose of maintaining peace and security. Article 43 obliges members to respond to a call from the Council, but the Council is not required to make use of the facilities offered by its members. The function of Article 43 is to provide the non-permanent members and non-members of the Council with some form of guarantee that their forces and facilities will only be used in accordance with an agreement with the Council, that is, they have an influence over their contribution, and, if a special agreement has been negotiated, that they know in advance what form that contribution might take. No such agreements have ever been concluded. This has not inhibited the Council from authorizing force in what is by now a very large number of instances of delegated Chapter VII mandates.

According to Article 46 of the UN Charter, plans for the application of armed force are to be made by the Security Council with the assistance of the Military Staff Committee. However, the fact that the Council is meant to pre-plan for possible uses of force does not mean that it cannot authorize force when such plans have not been made, either through the Military Staff Committee, or through other means.

Nor does the UN Charter require under Article 47 that the Council itself must direct the armed forces operating on its behalf. The Military Staff Committee exists to 'advise and assist' the Council in the execution of its function, including the employment and command of forces placed at its disposal. It is true that the Charter foresees that the Committee 'shall' also be responsible for the strategic direction of armed forces. But this concerns, only and expressly, those forces 'placed at the disposal of the Council'. That is to say, the article would find application in instances where the UN is mounting its own operation under its own command, as was the case, for instance, in the UNISOM II operation for Somalia. This would not apply to delegated tasks falling instead under Article 48 of the Charter, permitting military action decided by the Council to be undertaken by Member States. Moreover, Article 47 refers to the use of the Military Staff Committee 'under the Security Council'. If it is a servant of the Council, it can be assumed that the Council has authority to dispense with the services of the Committee if they are not deemed necessary. Finally, prior practice at the time (Southern Rhodesia), and a very large number of subsequent instances since, have demonstrated the unchallenged ability of the Council to authorize military operations without involvement of the largely defunct Committee.[82]

---

[81] See ND White, (1993) *Keeping the Peace* 103; Sarooshi (above n 62) 144.

[82] If there were any doubts remaining over the formal validity of Resolution 678 (1990), Art 106 of the UN Charter concerning transitional security arrangements might perhaps have been invoked.

B. Delegation of authority and collective security

If the adoption of Resolution 678 (1990) could not be challenged, there remained important questions relating to its legal nature and effect. The first concerned the question of whether the authorization was in fact compatible with the concept of collective security, or whether it was merely an affirmation of the right to self-defence enjoyed by the coalition states in any event. If it was collective security, then a second question arises concerning the basis of authority in the UN Charter under which the decision was taken.

Collective security and collective self-defence differ in a number of important aspects. The most important distinction relates to the trigger point. Self-defence is only and exclusively available in case of an actual or imminent armed attack. It cannot be activated by any other factor. Collective security can address a variety of circumstances that are much broader than an armed attack. According to Article 39 of the UN Charter, the Security Council can respond with enforcement measures, including the authorization to use force, to a mere 'threat to the peace'. This reflects the fact that the UN was designed as a means to maintain peace, through 'effective preventative measures' if necessary. Second, such broad authority is, however, balanced by the fact that collective security can only be exercised on the basis of a mandate expressly granted by the Council. This requires compliance with the collective decision-making procedures, including the possibility of a veto. Self-defence, on the other hand, is available immediately, without the need to go through any procedural steps. It is triggered by the armed attack itself and applies as soon as the attack is imminent or underway. However, the initial auto-interpretation by the victim state as to the existence of an armed attack is subject to subsequent review, and possible challenge, by the Security Council.

Third, the victim state can itself select any other state it wishes to invite to contribute to its defence. Only states so invited can rely on the right of collective self-defence. Under collective security, the Council will determine whether the UN itself will act (although with forces assigned to it by Member States), whether it will authorize regional organizations or arrangements to act for it, or whether it will delegate authority to individual states or coalitions.

A further important difference lies in the fact that self-defence action is strictly limited by what is necessary and proportionate to the armed attack. The right ceases to apply once the attack has been repelled. Collective security, on the other hand, can extend the mandate to use force to achieve other aims that go beyond the expulsion of an aggressor. It is up to the Council to determine when the mandate concludes. This can be achieved either through a decision terminating the authorization, through sun-set clauses indicating the circumstances when authority will lapse already in the authorizing resolution, through the establishment of a formal cease-fire, or through implied conduct of the Council.

A final difference concerns the supervision of the action. In self-defence, the defending state must report its action to the Council immediately. This enables the Council to review the claim to the use of force and possibly reject it. Alternatively, the Council can endorse the use of force, adopt its own collective security action in relation to it, or remain indifferent. Beyond such reporting, the Council does not become involved in the conduct of the operation. In the case of collective security, there is a stronger reporting requirement, and possibly an expectation that the Council will contribute to the strategic direction of the use of force. Moreover, the Council would ordinarily be expected to be in a position to terminate the mandate it has granted at any time, as part of its overall strategic control over any collective security operation.

Self-defence	Collective security
Triggered by armed attack	Triggered by threat to peace
Applies immediately	Subject to involving process requirements
Initial auto-interpretation, subject to Council review	Collective determination of facts and consequences
Self-selecting coalition	Collective appointment of privileged actors
Force limited to that which is necessary to reverse armed attack	Extension of force available determined by Council
Reporting to the Council	Strategic direction by Council or coordination (in theory)
Law of armed conflict applies	In forcible humanitarian operations, UN mandated personnel may enjoy additional protection
Issues of neutrality may arise if it is not clear which party is actually entitled to invoke self-defence	Can there be neutrality in relation to collective security?
Right to use force ceases when armed attack has been reversed	Authority to use force ends as stipulated in the mandate, or if suspended by Council
Peace settlement subject to negotiations	Authority to use force extends to imposition of international or even internal settlement terms, and their enforcement through military means

In view of the veto, collective security practice generally, and use of force especially, in the Council was extraordinarily limited up to the instance of Kuwait. In addition to the enforcement of sanctions concerning Southern Rhodesia, already noted above, the Council determined the existence of an armed attack by North Korea on the South.[76] That appeared to confirm that the conditions in Article 51 of the UN Charter were met and action could be taken in self-defence.[83] However, the Council also determined that this attack constituted a breach of the peace, moving the resolution to the territory of

[83] Clearly, this episode has been studied very widely. A more recent assessment can be found in W Stueck, 'The United Nations, the Security Council, and the Korean War' in V Lowe et al. (eds), (2008) *The United Nations Security Council and War* 265.

Chapter VII action in accordance with Article 39 of the Charter. In substance, the Council:[84]

Recommends that the Members of the United Nations furnish such assistance to the Republic of Korea as may be necessary to repel the armed attack and to restore international peace and security in the area...

It is also to be noted that the Resolution did not use the term 'authorizes' when addressing the use of force. Instead, it 'recommends'. This would ordinarily not be sufficient if a mandate in excess of what is permissible under self-defence is intended. On the other hand, the text contains elements related both to self-defence and collective security.

Repelling the armed attack appears to relate to self-defence. Restoring peace and security in the area, on the other hand, is widely taken as a reference to the collective security function of the Council. In a further resolution, the Council recommended that the operation be conducted under a unified command and requested that it be led by the United States. This recommendation and request might be taken to strengthen the collective security thesis, as it would be unusual for the Council to involve itself in the administration of a self-defence campaign. Moreover, the Council authorized the force to fly the UN flag.[85] While there was no provision for strategic guidance or control being exercised by the Council, there was a more intensive reporting requirement than would ordinarily expected in the case of self-defence.

In view of this, it is unsurprising that commentators are divided when considering the nature of the action. While some hold it to be collective security, others see in the Resolutions merely an authoritative affirmation of the right to self-defence that was available in any event, or perhaps a hybrid of the two.[86] In reality, the circumstances of the adoption of the Resolutions were such that it would be inappropriate to go either way. The Resolutions deliberately combine elements of both propositions.

The double nature of these Resolutions was related to the circumstances of their adoption—the Soviet Union boycotted the proceedings of the Council at the time.[87] Hence, there was a temptation to use the opportunity and load the Resolution with as many elements of authorization as was deemed useful. On the other hand, the Soviet Union was expected to return to the Council at any

---

[84] Resolution 83 (1950).   [85] Resolution 84 (1950).

[86] A Chayes, 'The Use of Force in the Persian Gulf' in LF Damrosch and DJ Scheffer, (1991) *Law and Force in the New International Order* 3, 10.

[87] As the UN Record indicates, the USSR (S/1517, S/1579) stated that the Security Council resolution of 27 June had no legal force since it had been adopted by only six votes, the seventh being that of the Kuomintang representative, who had no legal right to represent China. Moreover, although the United Nations Charter required the concurring votes of all five permanent members of the Council for any decision on an important matter, the above resolution had been passed in the absence of two permanent members of the Council the USSR and China. That position was supported by Czechoslovakia (S/1523) and Poland (S/1545).

time. It was, therefore, essential to argue that the action was in fact self-defence, and, therefore, not subject to immediate Council control. Hence, the Resolutions exhibited features reflecting both concepts on nearly every issue: the trigger point (armed attack and breach of the peace), the extent of authority (reversing the armed attack and maintaining international peace and security), the appointment of authorized actors (states furnishing assistance to South Korea but acting under a unified command under the control of the United States, appointed by the Council), and the enhanced reporting. Even the award of the right to fly the UN flag was carefully balanced by the fact that it would be flown along with the flags of force-contributing states.

This finding of the *sui generis* nature of the Resolutions may also be of assistance when considering the nature of Resolution 678 (1990),[88] which recalls in its Preamble the Council's responsibility to maintain and preserve international peace and security. This points in the direction of collective security. The Council is also determined to secure full compliance with its decisions. This includes securing compliance with all Council resolutions previously adopted on Iraq/ Kuwait and the restoration of peace and security in the area. This is clearly a collective security mandate, and it is a mandate 'authorized' by the Council, going beyond the mere 'recommendation' in the Korean case. Moreover, the Council subjected the authority to use force to a final opportunity, as a pause for goodwill, for Iraq to comply with its withdrawal requirement. Self-defence was available immediately, not merely after the exhaustion of that period, on 15 January 1990. If all this, taken together, confirms the view that Resolution 678 (1990) was a collective security measure, then it can also be seen as one that was, on an objective analysis, likely to achieve the termination of the armed attack. Hence, on this reading, it would displace a claim to self-defence.[89]

On the other hand, the Council assigned the authority to act to states cooperating with the Government of Kuwait. In line with collective self-defence, it is the defending state itself that picks the members of its defensive coalition.[90] Resolution 678 (1990) was addressed to Member States cooperating with the Government of Kuwait. Israel, for example, was not covered by the Resolution.[91] It was left to Kuwait to determine which states would participate in the operation; those that did not cooperate with the Kuwaiti Government did not enjoy the special legal status conferred upon them by the Resolution.

---

[88] Greenwood (above n 60) 169 refers to a deliberate degree of ambiguity in these instances; the UK position also appears to have been somewhat ambiguous, having moved from an assertion of self-defence to reference to action 'under the authority of' the Council resolution: C Warbrick, 'The Invasion of Kuwait by Iraq' (1991) 40 ICLQ 482, 487.

[89] KH Kaikobad, 'The Gulf Wars 1980–88 and 1990–91' (1992) 63 BYIL 299, 350.

[90] Schachter (above n 66) 459. On the self-defence view, see EV Rostow, 'Until What? Enforcement Action or Collective Self-defence?' (1991) 85 AJIL 506, 509.

[91] Of course, when Israel suffered missile attacks by Iraq during the conflict, it would have been entitled to act under its own right of self-defence, but it came under heavy pressure not to respond. Iraq's ploy of involving Israel in the conflict sought to generate complications in regard to the Arab members of the coalition.

The legal effect of the authorization was to exempt the Member States cooperating with the Government of Kuwait from compliance with obligations that would have been violated if the acts envisaged were undertaken in the absence of such authorization. In other words, the states involved could rely on an authorization to act which precluded the wrongfulness of that action, assuming it remained within the authority granted. The Resolution also clarified that the action undertaken was not inconsistent with the purpose and principles of the United Nations in the sense of Article 2(4) of the UN Charter concerning the prohibition of the threat or use of force.

In effect, a legal imbalance had been established between the forces cooperating with the Government of Kuwait, on the one side, and Iraq, on the other. States which participated in the coalition effort or furnished assistance were not liable to lawful counter-attack, as Iraq could not invoke the right of self-defence against the action of the coalition forces. This issue was particularly relevant when Iraq threatened to retaliate against Turkey after Ankara granted permission for the use of its airfields to coalition air forces. The question arose whether such an attack against Turkey would trigger the application of the NATO Treaty.[92] In view of the special situation created by Resolution 678 (1990) the answer would have been affirmative.

The principal element of the mandate was focused on implementing Resolution 660 (1990). That Resolution was focused only on securing the withdrawal of Iraqi forces to the positions they held on 1 August 1990, that is, a reversal of the armed attack. There was no reference to strategic guidance and direction from the Council. However, there was an enhanced requirement to keep the Council 'regularly' informed on the progress of the action.

Once again, therefore, the text exhibits a dual nature, although it points more in the direction of collective security than the Korean resolutions. Again, the reason for this unique approach is to be found in the political circumstances that obtained at the time. Kuwait was the first instance of the application of the New World Order foreseen by US President Bush. There was a good possibility that a consensus on resisting Iraqi aggression could be nurtured through the steps necessary to liberate Kuwait. On the other hand, Kuwait and her key ally, the United States, were not willing to place their faith in the functioning of the collective security machinery. The consensus that made the adoption of Resolution 678 (1990) possible might have crumbled at any moment.

It is therefore best to see the Resolution as an invitation to proceed according to the collective security paradigm. However, it preserved the freedom of action of the states involved to proceed unilaterally, if need be, outside of the control of the Council. Whether or not this was an instance of collective security would, therefore, depend on the way action was taken by the coalition under the terms of the Resolution.

---

[92] North Atlantic Treaty, 34 UNTS 243, Art 5.

As was noted above, with respect to the authority under which the Resolution was adopted, the text itself did not point to a single source of authority under the Charter. Again, this would have precluded the flexibility that was intended. An express reference to Article 42 would have ruled out the deployment of an alternative argument if that had become necessary in view of the coalition at a later stage. In principle, of course, the natural presupposition would be that the Resolution was hinged on Article 42, even if this was not made express. It is the only provision in Chapter VII (other than self-defence) contemplating the use of force. Others have pointed to Article 40 covering provisional measures. However, the article allows the Council only to call upon the parties to undertake certain provisional steps before it 'decides'. This would be inconsistent at least with a collective security authorization, although it would permit clarification of the applicability of the right to self-defence.

Another argument is to see Article 39 as the source of Council action in this case. In principle, however, Article 39 has a procedural function, clearing the way for Council action through a finding of a threat to peace, breach of the peace, or act of aggression.[93] It confirms the power of making recommendations according to Chapter VI of the Charter. Arguably, it also furnishes the Council with an additional basis of authority, to adopt recommendations under Chapter VII, although independently of any other provision in that chapter (that is, Articles 40, 41, and 42). However, decisions, rather than recommendations, are expressly related to measures to be taken 'in accordance with Article 41 and 42'. Hence, the actual source of authority for decisions authorizing force can only be found in those articles, and not in Article 39 itself. This would leave room for a Korea-style recommendation to Member States to assist in the defence of a state in response to an armed attack, where there exists an underlying right to self-defence. But it would not permit authority to use force under collective security powers in excess of self-defence.

Finally, Article 48 has been proposed as the basis for action in this instance. It provides that Member States shall take the action required to carry out the decisions of the Council as determined by the Council. Article 48 is not intended to establish a source of authority for the Council. Instead, it amplifies the obligations of Member States to comply with Council decisions already contained in Articles 24 and 25 of the Charter, and clarifies that the Council is free to assign enforcement tasks to some or all UN members, depending on circumstances.[94] In that sense, Article 48 can be invoked in relation to the action of states under Council authority, but the authority to use delegated force would still, ultimately, be drawn from Article 42, the actual basis of the delegation performed according to Article 48.

[93] BH Weston, 'Security Council Resolution 678 and Persian Gulf Decision-making: Precarious Legitimacy' (1991) 85 AIL 516, 522.

[94] See, eg Schachter (above n 80) 463; LM Goodrich, E Hambro, and LP Simons, (1969) *Charter of the United Nations* 334; J-P Cot and A Pellet, (2nd edn, 1991) *La Charte des Nations Unies* 749.

Overall, therefore, the better view is that the source of authority in this instance depends on whether the Council was acting as an agency of collective security, or whether it merely confirmed the right to self-defence. In the former case, its action was based in Article 42, read in conjunction with Article 48. In the latter, its action was based on Articles 39 and/or 40. But this issue was deliberately left open. Which of the two would apply was left to future developments, in particular the way action would be conducted under the resolution. This may be an unusual result, and in many ways an unsatisfactory one. One might say that the basis of the authority must have been clear at the point when it was granted. Otherwise it could be said that states using force produce the legal authority for the use of force while using force. But the realities of international life are not always such that they fit neatly into the classificatory boxes provided for in the UN Charter, and in the minds of even dedicated and brilliant legal commentators. Moreover, the states in question would not actually generate the authorization in question through their own forcible conduct. Self-defence was available in any event, independently of a possible exercise of collective security powers. There also existed a mandate for collective security, but whether it would be actualized depended on the way the states exercising the mandate would conduct the operation.

VI. The Outbreak and Conduct of Hostilities and the Extent of the Authorization to Use Force under Resolution 678 (1990)

On 9 January 1991, Tariq Aziz, the Iraqi Foreign Minister, and US Secretary of State James Baker, met in Geneva for some six-and-a-half hours. Despite the length of these talks, they were not successful. Apparently, the Iraqi envoy was presented with a letter from President Bush, demanding Iraq's immediate and unconditional withdrawal from Kuwait, in line with Resolution 660 (1990). This proved unacceptable to Iraq, whose government also rebuffed mediation efforts by the UN Secretary-General and the Soviet Union.

At 7.00pm EST (3.00am Baghdad time) on 16–17 January 1991, a massive aerial attack was launched against Iraq and Iraqi forces in Kuwait. Coalition forces gained full air superiority and proceeded systematically to destroy both the military and, controversially, also elements of the civilian infrastructure of Iraq (which could only remotely be connected to the war efforts).

The international community's response to the outbreak of hostilities was varied.[95] The Government of Kuwait initially announced that a military operation had been launched under its right to self-defence. Saudi Arabia referred to the armed implementation of Arab and Islamic resolutions, in addition to resolutions of the Security Council. The Western members of the coalition, in particular

---

[95] The responses to the outbreak of hostilities are reproduced in Weller (above n 1) section III.5.

the United States, the United Kingdom, France, Canada, Italy, and, indirectly, Turkey, affirmed that they were participating in an exercise of collective security.

A number of neutral and non-aligned states regretted the outbreak of hostilities, but few complained of a breach of international law. Yemen saw the operation as a flagrant challenge to the will of the international community, as peaceful procedures had not been exhausted. Cuba asserted that the use of force was illegal, and not covered by Chapter VII of the UN Charter. Iraq complained of an act of aggression.

The members of the coalition were subject to legal limitations in executing the conflict. International law frowns upon war and violence, and exceptions to the prohibition of the use of force by states are very narrowly defined. Military operations in the Gulf were subject to three legal limitations. First, the authority to use force was not only granted by Resolution 678 (1990), but also limited by its terms. Second, principles of general international law, including the principle of proportionality, were applicable to the conflict. Third, operations had to be conducted within the constraints imposed by humanitarian law (or the laws of war, also known as *jus in bello*).[96]

In the case of the Kuwait conflict, the most specific restraints on the application of force were provided by the enabling Resolution 678 (1990) itself. The words 'necessary means' indicated that no blanket authorization for the use of force had been granted. In line with the principles of general international law, which furnished the second type of restraint, the doctrine of proportionality required that the mildest possible means be employed to achieve a lawful objective and that no 'unreasonable or excessive' action be undertaken.[97] The principle of proportionality was affirmed by the ICJ in the *Nicaragua v United States* case, but its precise content has been subject to much dispute.[98] However, it is certain that proportionality in international law did not require weighing the goal of liberating Kuwait against the possible human costs necessary to achieve it, with a view to deciding whether or not the operation as such was legally defensible. The Security Council, to which states have delegated the highest authority in matters of peace and security, had already determined that military measures, with all their consequences, were legitimate in this case. It was only the amount of force utilized to achieve that goal that could be subject to legal dispute.

The degree of military force necessary to fulfil the mandate granted by the UN depended to a large extent on the Iraqi authorities. The more vigorously the Iraqi forces resisted, the more determined the international coalition had to be in its attempts to subdue them in and around Kuwait. Military planners were

---

[96] See C Greenwood, 'Customary International Law and the First Geneva Protocol of 1977 in the Gulf Conflict' in P Rowe (ed), (1993) *The Gulf Conflict in International and English Law* 63; FJ Hampson, 'Means and Methods of Warfare in the Conflict in the Gulf' in Rowe (ibid) 89ff.

[97] See 'The Caroline (Exchange of diplomatic notes between Great Britain and the United States, 1842)' (1906) 2 *Digest of International Law* 409; and RY Jennings, 'The Caroline and MacLeod Cases' (1932) 32 AJIL 82.   [98] (1986) ICJ Rep 122.

not legally obliged to risk the lives of their own soldiers by restricting their free-dom of action unduly. There was a certain margin of safety operating in favour of the forces arrayed against Iraq. Of course, enemy combatants could not be subjected to 'unnecessary' suffering, for example through the use of exploding bullets. Civilians, and cultural and religious objects, were to be spared altogether in accordance with humanitarian law, which provided the third legal restraint on military operations.

A number of practical consequences flowed from these considerations. Clearly, air attacks against Iraq's military infrastructure were permissible. Command and control centres, airfields, and missile bases within Iraq were used in support of the occupation forces in Kuwait. They had to be put out of action if the actual removal of Iraqi forces from Kuwait was to be achieved with limited casualties among the coalition. With one tragic exception, it appears that the aerial attacks were generally limited to military or infrastructure installations, although civil-ian casualties did occur.

The attacks against Iraqi forces held in reserve behind the border with Kuwait, both by air and during the land campaign, were also covered by legal authority. However, while the land offensive of the coalition progressed it was argued that even more ambitious military measures could be undertaken, including those nec-essary to extract reparations from Iraq, topple its government, and try its members for crimes against peace and for war crimes. This argument was made with refer-ence to the goals which had been established in Resolution 678 (1990). Particular emphasis was placed on the wording in operative paragraph 2, relating to the estab-lishment of 'peace and security in the area'. However, as noted above, this wording was a reflection of the terms of Article 42. It was a procedural device, pointing indi-rectly to the source of authority for the operation and was not, in the view of the majority of delegation to the Security Council, intended substantially to broaden the mandate. When Resolution 678 (1990) was adopted, the Yemeni delegate to the Council pointed to the danger of a wider interpretation, but the fact that all the other states expressing a restrictive view voted in favour of the Resolution, indi-cated that they assumed that the restrictive view had been accepted.[99]

UN forces had been used previously on occasion to safeguard or re-establish the constitutional systems of states in distress. The most notable example of this was the massive UN intervention in the Congo in 1960. At the time, however, there was only one precedent for a mandate to *remove* an established government by military means.[100] In October 1950, the General Assembly adopted a resolu-tion which contained implicit authorization for the forcible unification of Korea

---

[99] Provisional Verbatim Record of the UN Security Council, S/PV.2963, 29 November 1990, 31. The United States and Britain did not refer to a wide interpretation of the relevant provision prior to the adoption of the resolution.

[100] Since the Kosovo operation, this situation has changed. Most notably, the UN Security Council authorized the forcible restoration of the government of President Aristide of Haiti, who had been deposed through a counter-constitutional coup.

and specifically referred to the establishment of a 'unified, independent and democratic Government of Korea'.[101] In the end, North Korea was not defeated and this goal could not be realized. In any event, the case did not establish a viable precedent in terms of law. The resolution on Korea was adopted by the UN General Assembly, an organ with limited authority in matters of peace and security. The Security Council, which has primary responsibility in that field, was unable to accept such a mandate, due to the Soviet veto. However, the very fact that it was felt necessary to obtain approval at least from the General Assembly is instructive. In that case, a previous resolution of the Security Council, authorizing the use of force to repel the invasion of the Republic of Korea, did include the same formulation concerning the restoration of international peace and security in the area involved in Resolution 678 (1990).[102] Nevertheless, an explicit authorization for effecting a change in the governmental structure of Korea was legally necessary.[103]

The imprecise reference in Resolution 678 (1990) to the restoration of peace and security did not amount to a substantive grant of authority, and an extensive interpretation of that phrase was therefore barred.[104] This was the position taken by all parties at the time and confirmed, subsequently, by the statement of senior US and UK figures.[105]

However, Resolution 678 (1990) not only authorized the use of force to implement Resolution 660 (1990), relating to the withdrawal of Iraqi forces from Kuwait, but also referred to 'all subsequent relevant Resolutions'. Would this reference have permitted the use of force to implement goals which were mentioned in other resolutions on Kuwait? The destruction of Kuwaiti oilfields and the apparent mistreatment of prisoners of war and civilians brought the issues of reparations and war crimes trials to mind.

On closer inspection, it emerged that the relevant previous Resolutions 670 and 674 (1990) only invited states to collate information concerning possible claims for reparations, and the Iraqi authorities were merely reminded of their responsibility in the commission of grave breaches of humanitarian law. A reminder concerning responsibility and the invitation to record claims for compensation were not intended, nor were capable, of being enforced militarily. This was made clear

---

[101] Resolution 376 (1975).

[102] Resolution 83 (1950). Korea had, of course, been subject to the attention of the UN before the invasion, and the UN had previously found that a unified government should be established. Nevertheless, a specific authorization to use force to effect such a change was required.

[103] Greenwood (above n 60) 170 states that in the case of Korea, the General Assembly was only requested to legitimize an operation that had already been decided. Even if that was the case, it is still relevant that a resolution from the General Assembly was deemed desirable to cover the proposed operation north of the 38th parallel.

[104] Sarooshi (above n 62) 179 goes so far as to indicate that 'the purported delegation by the Council of this broad power to member states is unlawful'.

[105] See the statements by US President Bush and Brent Scowcroft, Colin Powell, and John Major in Ch 4 of this work, p 109.

by the Malaysian delegate to the Security Council, whose views tended to reflect those held by most neutral and non-aligned countries. He stated upon adoption of Resolution 678 (1990): 'The resolution does not provide a blank cheque for excessive and indiscriminate use of force. The Council has certainly not authorized actions outside the context of its Resolutions 660 (1990), 662 (1990) and 664 (1990)'.[106] These Resolutions related to the withdrawal requirement and the nullification of the purported annexation of Kuwait. There was no mention of an intervention in the political structure of Iraq, nor of military enforcement of claims for reparations and criminal justice.

Of course, the international community could easily have widened the mandate of the coalition fighting in the Gulf by adopting further enabling resolutions at the UN. This is precisely what happened, but only after active hostilities had ended, when the Council adopted cease-fire Resolution 686 (1991).

VII. Extent of the Use of Force and the Temporary Cease-fire

On 29 January 1991, 12 days after the commencement of the aerial campaign, the United States and the USSR, in a joint statement, offered Iraq a cease-fire in exchange for full and unconditional withdrawal: 'a cessation of hostilities would be possible if Iraq would make an unequivocal commitment to withdraw from Kuwait'.[107] However, it was added that such a commitment would have to be backed by immediate, concrete steps leading to full compliance with the Security Council resolutions.

Three days after this declaration had been issued, Soviet envoy Yevgeny Primakov went to Baghdad to pursue further negotiations.

Despite urgent calls for a meeting of the Security Council from the very onset of hostilities, the Council only convened on 14 February—four weeks after the commencement of the aerial campaign. On 15 February, the Iraqi Revolutionary Command Council began hinting that a withdrawal might be possible. However, in a formal statement, it conditioned such an action on a whole series of requirements, including the withdrawal from the region of the United States and her allies, the withdrawal of Israel from Palestine, guaranteed acceptance of Iraq's territorial claims, and the withdrawal of all Security Council measures against Iraq.[108] Two days later, Tariq Aziz went to Moscow, and a peace plan emerged, which was communicated to the Council. Iraqi forces would withdraw from Kuwait City within four days, and within 21 days from all of Kuwait. The withdrawal would be supervised by UN peace-keeping troops. There would be a

---

[106] Provisional Verbatim Record of the UN Security Council, S/PV.2963, 19 November 1990, 74.

[107] Joint Statement, 29 January 1991, reproduced in Auerswald (above n 21) 382.

[108] Iraqi Statement, 15 February 1991, reproduced in Auerswald (above n 21) 407.

release of all prisoners of war and the Council would rescind its resolutions after two-thirds of the withdrawal had been completed. This latter point was difficult for the Council to accept since it would have meant an automatic lifting of economic sanctions even before a full withdrawal, and the annulment of all of the Council's pronouncements concerning the Kuwait crisis.

These conditions were answered by an ultimatum issued by US President Bush. The United States granted the Iraqi authorities one day to declare that they would withdraw fully and unconditionally, and to provide evidence of the seriousness of their intentions. In effect, the coalition gave the Government of Iraq a final opportunity to refute the presumption that a massive land campaign would be 'necessary' in order to implement UN resolutions.

Tariq Aziz, the Iraqi Foreign Minister, who flew to Moscow to refine the withdrawal proposal, apparently dropped the condition concerning the automatic termination of economic sanctions upon the completion of two-thirds of the withdrawal. At this point it seemed as if a land campaign could indeed be averted. In fact, the UN Secretariat began to assemble an observer force which could have been dispatched to the Gulf at short notice to supervise the withdrawal. The differences in the positions of Iraq and the coalition concerning the time frame for withdrawal and for the exchange of prisoners of war could have been bridged by the Security Council when it met just before the expiry of the ultimatum.

Legally, it appeared very difficult to justify the launching of a potentially destructive land war at that juncture. There were conflicting signals emanating from the Iraqi Government. The Revolutionary Command Council in Baghdad was still formulating proposals designed to rule out the return of the legitimate government of Kuwait, even after a withdrawal. Iraq's envoys in Moscow and at UN headquarters were ambiguous about the annulment of the purported annexation of Kuwait and the renunciation of territorial claims—two points that were indisputably part of the UN 'war-aims', which had to be fulfilled prior to an acceptance of a cease-fire. But a clear word from the Iraqi delegate to the UN, uttered five minutes before the expiry of the ultimatum, might have been sufficient to resolve the issue. However, instead of unambiguous acceptance of all UN requirements, the Iraqi Government insisted on one condition. Apparently interested in averting the threat of war crimes trials and reparations, it argued again that 'after the end of the withdrawal of Iraqi forces from Kuwait, the causes for the corresponding resolutions of the Security Council would cease to exist, so those resolutions of the Security Council would cease to be in effect'.

This proposition was flawed. Arguably, the economic sanctions would have come to an end once a full withdrawal was in effect and once the legitimate government had been restored to Kuwait. This was actually implied in a preambular paragraph of sanctions Resolution 661 (1990). But it would have required a formal finding on the part of the Security Council that these conditions had been fulfilled. The Council could have decided that sanctions should be kept in place pending settlement of the questions of war crimes trials and reparations. In fact, the Council later affirmed that economic sanctions would continue to apply even after the permanent cease-fire took effect. In addition, Iraq apparently expected some sort of guarantee that the two issues of war crimes and reparations, which had been covered in Resolutions 670 (1990) and 674 (1990), would not be raised in the future.

Kuwait, and possibly select third states, would have retained their right to conduct proceedings against alleged war criminals and demand reparations independent of the Security Council, even if Baghdad's request for a rescinding of the Resolutions had been granted. These claims were not primarily derived from the authority of the Council, but were also based on general international law. Although the settlement of the issues of war crimes trials and reparations would not have needed to be a necessary precondition for accepting a cease-fire and withdrawal, the Council was unwilling to give up its authority to enforce these claims at a later stage.

Nevertheless, on the eve of the land offensive, Moscow produced a formal six-point peace plan, providing for a full withdrawal within 21 days. However, again 'immediately after the withdrawal from Kuwait has been completed', the reason for all other UN Security Council resolutions would lose their meaning and would be lifted'.[109]

When reports of mass killings of civilians in Kuwait and of the wholesale destruction of the economic infrastructure of the country (in particular the incineration of oil installations) reached the UN, hopes of avoiding a land offensive were lost in any event.[110] On 23–24 February 1991, a massive land operation of coalition forces commenced. The rapid success of the coalition soon led to calls for intervention by the Security Council to demand an immediate cease-fire. On 26 February, the Soviet delegate relayed to the Council a message from Saddam Hussein to President Mikhail Gorbachev. That message read: 'The Iraqi leadership has decided in accordance with Resolution 660 (1990) immediately to withdraw all its troops from Kuwait. The order to that effect has already been issued'. However, initially no cease-fire was achieved, although a number of delegations strongly argued in favour of one. Instead, the Council sought authoritative assurances from the Iraqi Government that it was willing to accept all resolutions concerning Kuwait. On 27 February, Iraq complained to the Council that its forces were being attacked during their withdrawal.[111] Later that day, Iraq declared unconditionally and officially that it 'agrees to comply fully the Security Council Resolution 660 (1990) and all the other Security Council Resolutions'.[112] In the meantime, the tragic episode of the 'Turkey shoot' against retreating Iraqi forces

---

[109] Six-point Soviet Plan, 22 Febraury 1991, reproduced in Auerswald (above n 21) 411.
[110] Haass (above n 22) 126. Critical on this point, J Quigley, 'The United States and the United Nations in the Persian Gulf War: New Order or Disorder' (1992) 25 *Cornell International Law Journal* 1, 12.   [111] Iraq Letter to the Security Council, S/22274, 27 February 1991.
[112] Iraq Letter to the Security Council, S/22275, 27 February 1991.

(see below) continued to play out until President Bush announced a cease-fire, which took effect at midnight on 27 February.

The question arose as to whether the coalition had been entitled to continue operations after Iraqi forces had effectively been surrounded, defeated, and were in the process of actual withdrawal under fire. Clearly, at that point, the Iraqi forces were no longer resisting but evidently in retreat. However, the US President had issued National Security Directive 54 of 15 January 1991, stating the US war aims. That directive specifically authorized force to 'destroy the Republican Guards as an effective fighting force' in the longer term.[113]

Under the terms of Resolution 678 (1990), the application of military force should have ceased when it was no longer 'necessary' to achieve the goals established by the UN. The requirement of necessity and proportionality also prevailed if the action had been undertaken in pursuit of self-defence. Had the Government of Iraq accepted the obligation of a full and unconditional withdrawal prior to the initiation of the land campaign, an immediate cease-fire would have been required. With the initiation of the land battle, however, the situation apparently changed. Some members of the Council seemingly recognized that it would not be possible to freeze the position of the coalition troops until they had achieved and secured their objectives. In addition, in demanding Iraq's acceptance of all UN resolutions before contemplating a cease-fire, Council members appeared to have at least implicitly accepted the wider interpretation of the mandate contained in Resolution 678 (1990), which allowed for the implementation of secondary goals of the UN, such as the apprehension of war criminals and the possible extraction of reparations from Iraq by military means. On the other hand, these views were not fully shared by all members of the Council. Clearly, the representative of the coalition forces and their allies were not responsive to the cease-fire proposals put forward by the neutral and non-aligned states.

In any case, the failure of the Security Council to call for a cease-fire did not imply a mandate for the excessive use of force against Iraqi troops, which were still protected by the second branch of international law applicable to the conflict—the laws of war. According to the regulations annexed to the Fourth Hague Convention of 1907, the right of belligerents to adopt means of injuring the enemy is not unlimited. More specifically, it is especially forbidden 'to kill or wound an enemy who, having laid down his arms, or having no longer means of defence, has surrendered at discretion and to declare that no quarter will be given'.[114] Iraqi soldiers had to be given a reasonable opportunity to lay down their arms—an obligation enforced with rigour in numerous war crimes trials at the conclusion of the Second World War. In practice, in other instances, the coalition forces on the ground did at least formally comply with that requirement. The surrender of several units was achieved without casualties. Nevertheless, there was no

---

[113] Reproduced in Auerswald (above n 21) 356, 357. See Haass (above n 22) 115.
[114] Art 23.

mass surrender. Instead, Iraqi units attempting to withdraw were engaged in the process, in particular from the air, in circumstances that made surrender difficult, if not impossible. The 'Turkey shoot' in particular, is difficult to defend and filled many of the soldiers participating in it with deep unease.[115] On that occasion, large numbers of Iraqi soldiers, some of them in civilian cars stolen in Baghdad, others in military vehicles over-laden with looted items, others still in a regular military convoy, were engaged from the air while on the only major highway leading out of Kuwait northwards into Iraq. They were backed up on the highway, often immobile, and picked off by coalition aircraft one by one when in evident retreat. A grizzly assemblage of hundreds of dead bodies and burnt-out vehicles remained.

In addition to this episode at the conclusion of hostilities, other issues arose during the conflict. This included, for instance, the devastating use of fuel-air explosives and the 'innovatory tactic' of bulldozing trenches and bunkers, burying alive the Iraqi soldiers therein and making it unnecessary to overpower them by more conventional means.[116] Moreover, it appeared that the US-led coalition had apparently embarked upon the implementation of other, wider goals in continuing operations. In addition to removing Iraq's forces from Kuwait, the long-term military potential of Iraq was to be reduced to make future aggression impossible, or at least less likely. The destruction of Iraq's nuclear research facilities marked the sharp end of this policy. It could not legitimately be argued that these facilities were in any way connected with the ongoing armed conflict. Moreover, strikes were directed at other targets that were of an unambiguously economic character, such as power stations. The coalition later argued that it only addressed infrastructure targets of relevance to the war effort. Electricity installations were targeted but only those 'powering military systems'.[117] It appears that these installations did not contribute to Baghdad's immediate war effort, however, but were destroyed anyway, perhaps to contain Iraq in the long run.

The wholesale destruction of Iraq's civilian economic infrastructure in pursuit of this policy would have been in excess of the requirement of 'necessity' in the terms of Resolution 678 (1990) and in general international law, and also in terms of the *jus in bello*. The UN's post-action assessment of the damage to the civilian infrastructure clearly raised questions in this respect. An initial WHO/UNICEF mission found, for instance:[118]

The mission found in Baghdad that normal life had come almost to a halt. The city's citizens now spend much of their time in family support preoccupations, searching for food, trying to find water, and improvising cooking and heating amidst an acute shortage of all kind of fuel. Baghdad has no public electricity, no telephone, no gasoline for civilian vehicles, and less than 5 per cent of its normal water supplies. Toilets go unflushed, and unpumped raw sewage is backing up and overflowing in residential areas.

---

[115] Quigley (above n 110) 15.   [116] Hampson (above n 96) 105.
[117] Cited in Greenwood (above n 96) 72.
[118] WHO/UNICEF Special Mission Report to Iraq, S/22328, 4 March 1991.

A second mission, led by Under Secretary-General Martti Ahtisaari and comprising representatives from various relevant UN agencies, found:

> ...nothing that we had seen or read had quite prepared us for the particular form of devastation which has now befallen the country. The recent conflict has wrought near-apocalyptic results upon the economic infrastructure of what had been, until January 1991, a rather highly urbanized and mechanized society. ...Iraq has, for some time to come, been relegated to a pre-industrial age...

Following the cease-fire declared unilaterally by the United States, the Council met on 2 March 1991 to discuss the situation and consider a draft resolution. The draft affirmed that all previous Council resolutions on Kuwait would continue to have effect and demanded their implementation by Iraq. In particular, Iraq was required to rescind its actions purporting to annex Kuwait, accept liability for reparations and return all seized Kuwaiti property, release all detained Kuwaiti and third-state nationals, including prisoners of war, and cease air operations. In an extraordinary paragraph, the Council recognized that 'during the period required for Iraq to comply' with these demands, 'the provisions of paragraph 2 of Resolution 678 (1990) remain valid'. This provision was bitterly attacked in the Council by the delegates of Yemen and Cuba, who rightly saw in it an extension of the mandate concerning the use of force contained in Resolution 678 (1990).[119] In effect, the Council was adopting a view on the permissibility of the use of force which was even broader than the widest possible interpretation of that Resolution. Some members emphasized that a resumption of hostilities should be avoided, but in adopting the US draft as Resolution 686 (1991), the members of the coalition were given great latitude of action by the Council. However, it is to be noted that this continuing authority was still subject to the requirements of necessity and proportionality, which would have barred the resumption of force for most or all purposes other than self-defence of the occupation forces.

VIII. The Formal Cease-fire

In Resolution 687 (1990), the Security Council established the terms of peace for Iraq. The Government in Baghdad formally accepted that Resolution, including its obligation to consent to the demarcation of the boundary with Kuwait, to accept limitations on its armaments, including the inspection of possible nuclear, bacteriological, and chemical warfare installations, to provide for the payment of compensation, and to return persons and property taken from Kuwait.

The cease-fire terms, comprehensive though they appeared, were lacking in at least two respects. They did not impose restrictions upon Iraq with respect to the

---

[119] See C Gray, 'After the Cease-fire: Iraq, the Security Council and the Use of Force' (1994) 65 BYIL 136, 139ff.

treatment of individuals present in its territory, in particular the Kurds and Shiites. Also conspicuously absent from the Resolution were the issues of war crimes and crimes against peace. Most prisoners of war were rapidly repatriated, without an investigation into individual responsibility for grave breaches of the Geneva law. The political and military leadership of Iraq was also not seriously threatened with war crimes proceedings or even prosecutions for launching an aggressive war. Considering that it may well have been the issue of individual responsibility which kept the Iraqi Government from accepting an entirely unconditional withdrawal before the land offensive started, this is perhaps surprising.

One further issue connected with the cease-fire talks was of particular interest in light of the reason for the conflict in the first place. The Iraqi delegation, when addressing the Council before the adoption of Resolution 687 (1991), voiced the following opinion:[120]

The Security Council has never before imposed disputed international boundaries on States Members of the United Nations. Recognized international boundaries represent a basic pillar of the territorial integrity of States. Therefore, the views of all States concerned should be taken into consideration. Iraq views this question and the manner in which it has been addressed in this draft resolution as an infringement upon its sovereignty and territorial integrity. The text contravenes operative paragraph 3 of Resolution 660 (1990), which calls upon Iraq and Kuwait to begin negotiations for the resolution of their differences, and among those differences is that of boundaries. Iraq reserves its right to demand its legitimate territorial rights in accordance with international law.

In Resolution 687 (1991), the Security Council, acting under Chapter VII of the UN Charter:

2. Demands that Iraq and Kuwait respect the inviolability of the international boundary and the allocation of islands set out in the 'Agreed Minutes Between the State of Kuwait and the Republic of Iraq Regarding the Restoration of Friendly Relations, Recognition and Related Matters', signed by them in the exercise of their sovereignty at Baghdad on 4 October 1963 and registered with the United Nations and published by the United Nations in document 7063, United Nations Treaty Series, 1964;

3. Calls on the Secretary General to lend his assistance to make arrangements with Iraq and Kuwait to demarcate the boundary between Iraq and Kuwait, drawing on appropriate material including the map transmitted by Security Council document S/22412 and to report back to the Security Council within one month.

The Iraqi Government accepted the provisions of that Resolution, but in identical letters[121] addressed to the Secretary-General and to the President of the Security Council, dated 6 April 1991, it made some:

...preliminary comments on the juridical and legal aspects of this resolution, so as to encourage men of conscience in the countries members of the international community

---

[120] Provisional Verbatim Record of the UN Security Council, S/PV.2981, 3 April 1991, 32.
[121] Iraq's Written Agreement to Comply with Resolution 687 (1991), S/22456, 18 April 1991.

and world public opinion to make an effort to understand the truth as it is and the need to ensure the triumph of justice...

With reference to Resolution 687 (1991), the letter continued:

In fact, the resolution constitutes an unprecedented assault on the sovereignty, and the rights that stem therefrom, embodied in the Charter and in international law and practice. For example, where the question of boundaries is concerned, the Security Council has determined in advance the boundary between Iraq and Kuwait. And yet, it is well known, from the juridical and practical standpoint, that in international relations boundary issues must be the subject of an agreement between States, since this is the only basis capable of guaranteeing the stability of frontiers.

Moreover, the resolution fails to take into account Iraq's view, which is well known to the Council, that the provisions relating to the boundary between Iraq and Kuwait contained in the 'Agreed Minutes Between the State of Kuwait and the Republic of Iraq Regarding the Restoration of Friendly Relations, Recognition and Related Matters' dated 4 October 1963, have not yet been subjected to the constitutional procedures required for ratification of the Agreed Minutes by the legislative branch and the President of Iraq, thus leaving the question of the boundary pending and unresolved. The Council has nevertheless imposed on Iraq the line of its boundary with Kuwait. By acting in this strange manner, the Council itself has also violated one of the provisions of Resolution 660 (1990), which served as the basis for its subsequent resolutions. In its paragraph 3, Resolution 660 (1990) calls upon Iraq and Kuwait to resolve their differences through negotiations, and the question of the boundary is well known to be one of the main differences. Iraq officially informed the Council that it accepted Resolution 660 (1990) and was prepared to apply it, but the Council has gone beyond this legal position, contradicting its previous resolution, and adopted an iniquitous resolution which imposes on Iraq, an independent and sovereign State and a Member of the United Nations, new conditions and a boundary line which deprive it of its right to establish its territorial rights in accordance with the principles of international law. Thus, the Council is also depriving Iraq of its right to exercise its free choice and to affirm that it accepts that boundary without reservation.

In a letter to the Secretary-General dated 23 April 1991, the Iraqi Minister for Foreign Affairs raised similar points, arguing that the demarcation of the Kuwait-Iraq boundary could not be 'imposed' by the Security Council.[122] Nevertheless, the Iraqi Government expressed a willingness to participate in the work of the Demarcation Commission established in pursuance of paragraph 3 of Resolution 687 (1991). 'We do this because the circumstances forcing our acceptance persist', the Iraqi Minister for Foreign Affairs added.

In making these assertions and claims, the Iraqi Government appeared to be laying the groundwork for another challenge to the international boundary with Kuwait, which require brief comment.

The power of international organizations to make binding decisions rests upon a grant of authority from their membership. The UN, an organization enjoying objective legal personality, is accorded such authority in general terms, *inter alia*,

---

[122] Letter, S/22558, 2 May 1991, Annex II.

in Article 25 of the UN Charter, which states that the members of the United Nations agree to accept and carry out the decisions of the Security Council. In order to ensure prompt and effective action by the United Nations, its members have conferred on the Council primary responsibility for the maintenance of international peace and security and, in Article 24 of the Charter, they have agreed that in carrying out its duties under this responsibility the Council acts on their behalf. In adopting Resolution 687 (1991), the Council acted explicitly under Chapter VII of the Charter.

Resolution 687 (1991) was adopted in accordance with the requirements established in the Charter for the application of Chapter VII. It followed upon a finding of the Council, made under Article 39 of the Charter, that a breach of the peace and security as regards the Iraqi invasion of Kuwait had occurred. It far exceeded the number of votes required for its adoption. The Resolution was even expressly accepted by the Iraqi Government.

In legal terms, of course, acceptance of paragraph 2 of Resolution 687 (1991) was not necessary. While some of the provisions of the Resolution (mostly involving procedural issues, such as the setting-up of certain commissions, etc) required cooperation from the Iraqi Government, the Security Council *demanded* that Iraq and Kuwait respect the inviolability of the international boundary and the allocation of islands set out in the 1963 Agreed Minutes. Thus, paragraph 2 of Resolution 687 (1991) is not phrased in recommendatory language. It is absolute and immediate in its binding effect and application, establishing an independent legal obligation for both states in accordance with Article 25 of the UN Charter.[123]

It must be noted, however, that this obligation is, in fact, a reflection of the pre-existing legal situation. The boundary between Iraq and Kuwait was reaffirmed in the legally binding 1963 Agreed Minutes, to which Resolution 687 (1991) explicitly refers. Thus, there is no room for the argument, put forward by the Iraqi Government, that the Council had 'imposed' the solution of an ongoing boundary dispute. Rather, the Council recognized the legal situation that had resulted from the consent of Iraq and the state of Kuwait when establishing and reaffirming their common boundary on numerous occasions over the past decades. As the representative of India explained when addressing the Council at its 2,981st meeting:[124]

In this particular case we find that the boundary between Iraq and Kuwait was agreed upon by the highest authorities or the respective countries as two fully independent and sovereign States. Furthermore, they both took the precaution to register their agreement with the United Nations. Thus, the Council is not engaging itself in establishing any new boundary between Iraq and Kuwait. What it is doing is to recognize [sic.] that such a boundary, agreed to by the two countries in the exercise of their full sovereignty, exists and to call [sic.] upon them to respect its inviolability.

---

[123] See also Gray (above n 119) 147ff.
[124] Provisional Verbatim Record of the UN Security Council, S/PV.2981, 3 April 1991, 78.

Seen in this light, paragraph 2 of Resolution 687 (1991) is not in itself an original source of the legally established boundary line. Rather, it serves to internationalize the obligation to respect the boundary as freely established between Iraq and the state of Kuwait. In future, a failure to recognize the international boundary between Iraq and Kuwait on the part of the authorities of Iraq, or its violation by those authorities, would amount to a violation of Resolution 687 (1991) and thus of Article 25 of the UN Charter. This effect of paragraph 2 of Resolution 687 (1991) is emphasized in paragraph 4 of that Resolution, which formally guarantees the boundary line.

The international guarantee of the boundary is not inconsistent with the terms adopted by the Security Council in Resolution 660 (1990). In operative paragraph 2 of that Resolution the Council *demanded* the immediate and unconditional withdrawal of Iraqi forces from all Kuwaiti territory. By contrast, the wording adopted in paragraph 3 relating to negotiations of differences between Iraq and Kuwait was not necessarily mandatory. This distinction in language is amplified in Resolution 661 (1990), in which the Council adopted certain enforcement measures after having determined that Iraq had failed 'to comply with paragraph 2 of Resolution 660 (1990)'. There is no mention of a failure to implement paragraph 3, despite the fact that Iraq had in effect made negotiations impossible, indicating that the call for negotiations did not amount to a mandatory measure.

In any case, it is to be noted that negotiations did take place, including negotiations conducted under the aegis of the League of Arab States, as indicated under paragraph 3 of the Resolution. It was the Iraqi Government that frustrated that process by purporting to annex the state of Kuwait. Furthermore, the suggestion of negotiations cannot in itself be taken to cast doubt upon the validity of the boundary between Iraq and Kuwait. It is the essence of negotiations that the states involved are not compelled to relinquish their rights if they do not wish to do so. Furthermore, it is not established that negotiations were meant to cover territorial issues. Rather, Kuwait might argue that negotiations were to focus only and exclusively on the modalities of an Iraqi withdrawal from the territory of the state of Kuwait. To hold otherwise would amount to an admission that Iraq was to be granted concessions as the result of the unprovoked aggression it had launched against Kuwait. This could not have been the intention of the Council.

In terms of substance, Resolution 687 (1991) provides for the demarcation of the international boundary between Iraq and the state of Kuwait under the aegis of the UN. This procedure relates simply to the geographical description and physical demarcation of a long-established boundary line. The Demarcation Commission, established pursuant to Resolution 687 (1991), is, therefore, accorded only a limited, technical function. There is no room for delimitation, or even a quasi-judicial role of the Commission, as it is explicitly bound to demarcate the boundary line agreed between Iraq and the state of Kuwait in the 1963 Agreed Minutes.

Although no further consent on the part of Iraq was necessary to establish the definite nature of that boundary line, the Iraqi Government gave its consent to the procedure for demarcation envisaged in operative paragraph 3 of

Resolution 687 (1991). The Secretary-General, in his letter to the Minister of Foreign Affairs of Iraq, dated 1 May 1991, recalled that Resolution 687 (1991) had been adopted under Chapter VII, and found that the acceptance of its terms by both governments involved had provided the 'necessary element of consent' in that respect.[125] In accordance with the obligation thus undertaken, the Iraqi Government participated in the work of the Demarcation Commission. Having accepted the mandate of the Demarcation Commission, the Iraqi Government was henceforth precluded from challenging its authority.[126] In the event, the Commission adopted a ruling that deviated from the expected line. In particular, the boundary appeared to have been moved northwards in the region of Um Quasr, including critical harbour installations on the Kuwaiti side.[127]

IX. Conclusion

The response of the international community to the invasion of Kuwait was unprecedented. The aggression was condemned immediately, and tough economic sanctions were imposed and administered effectively through the Council's own mechanism, the Sanctions Committee, as enforcement measures. To that extent, action was consistent with the concept of collective security. With respect to military enforcement, the membership of the UN was willing to engage in an experiment. As there were no forces at the disposal of the UN, the military enforcement of its resolutions was delegated to the coalition of states cooperating with the Kuwaiti Government. The Council did not foresee that it would direct military operations itself. Instead, where the naval enforcement of sanctions was concerned, the Council foresaw coordination of a broad international effort through the Military Staff Committee. However, that option was not taken up by coalition powers. Instead, a looser form of delegated authority was constructed in the shape of Resolution 678 (1990). The Resolution authorized states cooperating with the Kuwaiti Government to use force. The question remains as to the characterization of the Resolution and the ensuing operation.

Apart from those flatly denying the legality of the military campaign, three possible views have already been noted. First, the operation may have been an act of collective self-defence. Second, it may have amounted to a mixture of self-defence and collective security, the UN Security Council having clarified,

---

[125] Letter, S/22558, 2 May 1991, Annex III.

[126] Since this chapter was concluded, the Boundary Commission has adopted a line of demarcation which does not exactly match the previously assumed boundary line. That decision has been endorsed by the Security Council.

[127] On the boundary and delimitation, see M Mendelson and SC Hulton, 'The Iraq-Kuwait Boundary' (1993) 64 *British Yearbook of International Law* 135; M Mendelson and SC Hulton, 'Les décisions de la Commission des Nations Unies sur la démarcation de la frontière entre l'Iraq et le Koweit' (1993) *Annuaire français de droit international* 178; J Klabbers, 'No More Shifting Lines: The Report of the Iraq-Kuwait Boundary Demarcation Commission' (1994) 43 ICLQ 904.

through the authorization contained in Resolution 678 (1990), that Kuwait was entitled to rely on the right of collective self-defence, and having authoritatively defined the content of that right, that is, the outer limit of the permissive use of force. Third, the operation could be considered as one undertaken in pursuit of collective security, although none of the means established in the UN Charter for the management of such operations were utilized. The action would have been mandated under the authority of Article 42 (without formally invoking it) and its conduct would have been delegated to states cooperating with Kuwait under Article 48.

The UN Secretariat took a somewhat ambiguous position on this issue. Secretary-General Javier Perez de Cuellar asserted that 'this is not a UN war'. His Chief Legal Adviser later clarified that, although the operation had not been undertaken under Article 42, it was covered by Chapter VII of the Charter.[128] The Secretary-General, in his report on the work of the organization, later wrote:[129]

Another important aspect is that enforcement action was not carried out exactly in the form foreseen by Articles 42 *et sequentia* of Chapter VII. Instead, the Council authorized the use of force on a national and coalition basis.

To help address the question of how the action was actually conducted, Dan Sarooshi has drawn three tests from his exhaustive examination of the delegation of Security Council powers under Article 42. First, the action has to have a clearly defined (and therefore limited) forcible mandate. Second, the action must be conducted under the control of the Council. And, third, the Council must, at all times, be in a position to terminate the mandate.[130]

First, there is the limitation of the mandate. Resolution 678 (1990) has been sharply criticized in this respect. It has been asserted that its terms were unduly open and potentially subject to a very expansive interpretation.[131] The reference to international peace and security, in particular, can be invoked in that context. Two points arise. First, the original understanding of Resolution 678 (1990) was clear and undisputed. Until some time after the conclusion of the operation, there was no serious argument from any state suggesting that the Resolution permitted anything other than the liberation of Kuwait. This included the United States and the United Kingdom. Both formally confirmed their understanding of the limited authority that had been granted. To this day, the leading political figures involved in the matter at the time adhere to that view.[132] The reference to peace and security, based in the Korean precedent, did not add substantive authority

---

[128] American Society of International Law, *Proceedings of the 85th Annual Meeting* (1991) 431. For further discussion, see Ch 4 .

[129] J Perez de Ceullar, (1991) *Report of the Secretary-General on the Work of the Organization* 8. For the consequences for naval action between authorization of the use of force under Article 51 or Article 42, see Ch 7.   [130] Sarooshi (above n 62) 32ff, 155.

[131] BH Weston, 'Security Council Resolution 678 and Persian Gulf Decision-Making: Precarious Legitimacy' (1991) 85 AJIL 516, 518.   [132] See Ch 4, 109.

going beyond that aim, although it clarified that force could be used beyond the boundaries of occupied Kuwait if necessary to achieve it. Once the liberation of Kuwait had been achieved, and a formal cease-fire was in place, that authority ceased. However, it has to be admitted that in the period of the provisional cease-fire according to Resolution 686 (1991) and the adoption of the definite cease-fire, an unspecific and unclear situation obtained. The Council appeared to have confirmed that Resolution 678 (1990) continued to operate and that force remained available during that interim period for a wide variety of purposes. This can perhaps only be explained by the confusion of the situation that prevailed upon termination of hostilities, and by the justified eagerness on the part of the Security Council to reassert its authority in the matter.

The argument that the authority granted in 1990 can be revived many years later, and deployed in favour of operations with an entirely different aim, was only generated some time afterwards, and is not really attributable to the terms of Resolution 678 (1990) itself.[133] That argument is not based on a genuine interpretation of the Resolution. The fact that it was permitted to gain traction in the early implementation practice of the Council relating to the cease-fire, which will be considered in Chapter 4, can be attributed to laxity in legal advice in the UN Secretariat at the time. This interpretation was as erroneous in law as it turned out to be dangerous in practice. It overrode the clearly established limits of the use of force in Resolution 678 (1990) and the definite establishment of a formal cease-fire through Resolution 687 (1991).

The conduct of operations raises more difficult questions. The Council merely required reporting on action undertaken in the exercise of its mandate. Even that reporting was hesitant. Once military operations had commenced, the Council was not involved in any form of supervision or even control. Clearly, the coalition powers, led by the United States, were unwilling to tolerate strategic direction of the war by committee. The action was undertaken entirely within national chains of command and any suggestion that the Council had an operational role would have been rejected out of hand.

Of course, it could be argued that the requirement of Council supervision or control is fulfilled, as long as the Council has the ability at any time to terminate the mandate, or require states to change the modalities of the use of force. One commentator, therefore, concludes that the delegation of authority to the coalition was 'legally acceptable'. However, this would mean conflating the second criterion of collective action with the third. The exercise of control or supervision implies a more continuous review of action, if not its actual strategic direction. Moreover, in this instance, the Council found it very difficult to reassert control and authority as events progressed—unsurprisingly, given the controlling role of key coalition states of the Council at the time.

---

[133] See J Lobel and M Ratner, 'Bypassing the Security Council: Ambiguous Authorizations to Use Force, Cease-fires and the Iraqi Inspection Regime' (1999) 93 AJIL 124.

It is difficult to imagine, for instance, that the Council itself, had it exercised strategic direction, would have been able to endorse the way the conflict was conducted. According to the Powell Doctrine, overwhelming force was employed. The coalition comprised 29 states and 750,000 personnel. The campaign consisted, in the first place, of a devastating air campaign lasting for some four weeks. The campaign went beyond the targeting of strictly military and related assets and impacted heavily on the civilian economic infrastructure of the country. It was not focused on Kuwait, but instead on Iraq, including in particular its capital, Baghdad. The methods and means employed during the land operation would also not have been very widely acceptable, at least in their more extreme forms.

The issue of the possible termination of the mandate also raises questions. The Council was, in fact, barred from pronouncing itself on the continuing necessity of using force in the early stages of the campaign. As events progressed, and as Iraq appeared to accept a withdrawal, voices in favour of a suspension of hostilities grew louder. In view of Iraq's hedged commitments to a withdrawal, it was, in fact, necessary to continue operations. But the Council was not placed at the heart of the debate about this issue. Clearly, the assumption was that once the operation was underway, only the coalition powers, in particular the United States, could determine its conduct and possible termination. The failure of the Council to assert itself in the final phases (the 'Turkey shoot') is noteworthy in this respect. Of course, this was not really attributable to the Council as an abstract institution, or an actor in its own right. Instead, it was an arena in which the coalition powers exercised a dominant influence at the time.

The coalition gained much from the double-headed nature of Resolution 678 (1990). The political legitimacy of the operation was greatly enhanced by the claim to the collective security elements of the mandate. A very broadly based alliance could be constructed against Iraq, both militarily and politically, including important elements of the Arab world. However, the underlying reserve of self-defence persisted and dominated throughout, as was evident in the conduct of the operation entirely independently of the Council. The benefits obtained were not traded for an acceptance of the attendant collective security process requirements one would ordinarily accept. Hence, in the way the operation was actually conducted the claim to collective security was denied.

On the part of the wider Council membership, there were nevertheless grounds to place the operation in the context of collective security.[134] Rather than dwelling on the deficiencies of the action, or pointing to the potential dangers of the delegation of mandates that were then implemented without supervision, it was felt more constructive to look to the future. It was more convenient to join in with the victors and celebrate the fact that, for the first time in UN history, naked aggression and annexation had been overturned. In claiming that this was a victory for collective

---

[134] See ND White, 'From Korea to Kuwait: The Legal Basis of United Nations Military Action' (1998) 20 *International History Review* 597.

security, the hope may have been to try and build on this precedent and improve performance of the collective security mechanism over time. This would have included building confidence on the part of the US and Western states that forcible intervention, where necessary, could be delivered within a UN framework.

The UN did pick up on many of the elements that had been pioneered during the Kuwait conflict. Comprehensive sanctions administered by sanctions committees were deployed and refined over the decades to come. This included military sanctions enforcement under express authorization of the Council. Forcible mandates proliferated in relation to issues other than the reversal of aggression, in particular where delivery of humanitarian aid and the stabilization of divided and threatened states were concerned. In fact, the humanitarian dimension of the Iraq-Kuwait conflict was the next major issue to confront the Council at the very point when hostilities were being terminated.

3

Forcible Humanitarian Action

Can armed force be used to protect human beings from the excesses of their own governments? This question has dogged humanity for centuries. Moral philosophers and legal scholars throughout the ages have claimed that there exists a right, or perhaps even a duty, to intervene in cases of tyrannical government and evident abuses of power by a sovereign in relation to his subjects.[1] However, with the consolidation of the modern state system, these voices have been increasingly side-lined. In the absolutist age, the sovereign was held to be bound by God, or by a compact with his subjects, to refrain from excessive abuses of his otherwise absolute powers. In extreme cases, some argued, threatened populations had a right to resist. External powers might be entitled to support such resistance. Ironically, the doctrine of popular sovereignty that replaced absolutism undermined that view.

The enlightenment social contract that was assumed to exist would ordinarily have limited the exercise of sovereign powers. The sovereign would no longer be empowered to act manifestly in disregard of those, on whose corporate will, his right to rule depended. Liberal theory also postulated the existence of certain basic rights upon which the state could never encroach. However, the enlightenment was a brief moment, instantly overshadowed by the advent of the concept of the nation state. The nation, and with it the state, was assumed to be more than a voluntary association of citizens for their common good. It was a metaphysical entity through which nations expressed their history and destiny. Nothing was allowed to interfere with that sacred process.

The nation state was enveloped in the doctrine of national sovereignty, which proclaimed that only the state itself could determine its internal powers and external obligations. While even the super-sovereign states accepted that they could limit their freedom of action by contracting into international legal obligations, they also insisted on an increasingly rigid doctrine of non-interference and non-intervention in the internal affairs of the state.[2]

Interventions did take place during the nineteenth century, when the doctrine of super-sovereignty was established. A few were carried out with humanitarian

---

[1] For example, S Murphy, (1996) *Humanitarian Intervention: The United Nations in an Evolving World* 35ff; R Vincent, (1974) *Non-Intervention and International Order* 19ff.
[2] See EC Stowell, (1921) *Intervention in International Law* passim; Vincent (above n 1) 20–141.

motives. The rescue of Maronite Christians of Mount Lebanon in 1860–1861 is often cited as the principal example. Some 11,000 Christians were killed by Druze inhabitants, and 100,000 displaced. The Ottoman authorities belatedly calmed the situation. A French intervention force was also dispatched. However, this occurred under an agreement with Turkey providing for the dispatch of up to 12,000 troops. When a French force eventually arrived, the humanitarian emergency had abated.[3] The late deployment of the French troops, and the fact that their presence was based on agreement with Turkey, undermine the value of this episode as a precedent in favour of genuine humanitarian intervention. It has been asserted that there is not in fact a single genuine case of humanitarian intervention in nineteenth-century history; others cite the cases of Greece (1827–1830), Crete (1866–1868), the Balkans (1875–1878) and Macedonia (1903–1908).[4]

The debate about the true motives and facts surrounding these historical instances now seems quaint. They occurred when the modern prohibition on the use of force contained in the UN Charter did not yet exist. There was at the time no commitment to renounce war as a means of national policy. Moreover, instances invariably took place on the periphery of the European Concert system. The rules of the game ordinarily in operation among the central players were not necessarily applied externally, or in relation to the crumbling Ottoman Empire. If anything, the discussion on these cases demonstrates the desperation of those seeking to establish a foundation for a modern right of forcible humanitarian action after the advent of the UN Charter and up to the Iraq episode of 1991. There were few modern precedents that could be invoked after 1945, and international standards and doctrine strongly opposed argument in favour of such forcible action.

I. Standards, Practice, and Doctrine up to 1991

The prohibition of the use of force contained in Article 2(4) of the UN Charter is comprehensive. Traditionally, the only exceptions permitting force were the 'inherent' right of self-defence, and action by the Security Council mandated under Chapters VII and VIII of the Charter. 'Thus, there is no room for the concept of humanitarian intervention to continue to exist, in addition to the UN Charter, as a rule of customary international law' even if there existed evidence for the prior existence of such a rule, an authoritative commentary on the UN Charter concludes.[5]

---

[3] I Pogany, 'Humanitarian Intervention in International Law: The French intervention in Syria Re-Examined' (1986) 35 ICLQ 182.

[4] See, at length, GJ Bass, (2008) *Freedom's Battle: The Origins of Humanitarian Intervention*; TB Knudsen, 'The History of Humanitarian Intervention: The Rule or Exception?', paper presented at the 50th ISA Annual Convention, New York, 15–18 February 2009, available at <http://www.allacademic.com/meta/p_mla_apa_research_citation/3/7/0/8/0/p370801_index.html>.

[5] B Simma (ed), (2nd edn, 2002) *The Charter of the United Nations: A Commentary* 130.

Beyond the prohibition of the use of force, the UN Charter does not contain a specific prohibition of intervention for states. Article 2(7) only expressly prohibits intervention by the UN organs in matters essentially within their domestic jurisdiction, with the exception of enforcement action under Chapter VII. However, the prohibition of intervention as applied to states has been repeatedly confirmed in authoritative standard-setting instruments of the UN General Assembly, which are regarded as authentic interpretations of Charter principles. In particular, the UN Friendly Relations Declaration, adopted by consensus at the UN's twenty-fifth anniversary, provides:[6]

No state or Group of states has the right to intervene, directly or indirectly, for any reason whatever, in the internal or external affairs of any state. Consequently, armed intervention and all other forms of interference or attempted threats against the personality of the State or against its political, economic and cultural elements, are in violation of international law.

The denial of 'any reason whatever' in justification of intervention would exclude armed action in favour of humanitarian motives. Moreover, 'any military occupation, however temporary', of foreign territory, or the 'use of armed forces of one State which are within the territory of another State with the agreement of the receiving State, in contravention of the conditions provided for in the agreement or any extension of their presence in such territory beyond the termination of the agreement' are considered acts of aggression.[7] In its Declaration on the Enhancement of the Effectiveness of the Principle of Refraining from the Threat or Use of Force in International Relations, the UN General Assembly added, once again, that:[8] 'No consideration of whatever nature may be invoked to warrant resorting to the threat or use of force in violation of the Charter'.

The prohibition on intervention is not only based in Article 2(4) of the Charter when force is involved. It also exists in parallel in customary international law. Already in 1949, the International Court of Justice (ICJ) had held that:[9]

... the alleged right of intervention as the manifestation of a policy of force, such as has, in the past, given rise to most serious abuses and such as cannot, whatever be the present defects in international organization, find a place in international law. Intervention is perhaps still less admissible in the particular form it would take here; for, from the nature of things, it would be reserved for the most powerful States, and might easily lead to perverting the administration of international justice itself.

---

[6] Resolution 2625 (XXV) (1970); see also the Declaration on the Inadmissibility of Intervention in the Domestic Affairs of States and the Protection of their Independence and Sovereignty, Resolution 2131 (XX) (1965).

[7] Definition of Aggression, Resolution 3314 (XXIX) (1974), Art 3.

[8] UN General Assembly Resolution 42/22 (1987).

[9] *United Kingdom v Albania (Corfu Channel case)* (1949) ICJ Rep 4, 35.

The ICJ subsequently defined intervention in the *Nicaragua v United States* case as follows:[10]

A prohibited intervention must accordingly be one bearing on matters in which each State is permitted, by the principle of State sovereignty, to decide freely. One of these is the choice of a political, economic, social and cultural system, and the formulation of foreign policy. Intervention is wrongful when it uses methods of coercion in regard to such choices, which must remain free ones. The element of coercion, which defines, and indeed forms the very essence of prohibited intervention is particularly obvious in the case of an intervention which uses force, either in the direct form of military action, or in the indirect form of support for subversive or terrorist armed activities within another State.

It may be useful to distinguish at this point a number of related concepts. Interference in the internal affairs of another state is considered an unfriendly act, although not necessarily an unlawful one. For instance, if one state criticized the human rights performance of another in a diplomatic note, this was tradition-ally considered interference. It is now clear, however, that such pronouncements alone are not precluded by virtue of international law. Intervention occurs, on the other hand, where one state undertakes public acts targeted within the domestic jurisdiction of another without the latter's consent. For instance, if one state were to deploy a humanitarian rescue mission on the territory of another without its consent, that would traditionally amount to an act of intervention. The interven-ing state would replace one aspect of public administration in another state with its own. Classically, some authors consider this a 'dictatorial' intervention as the target state would be left no option but to bow to the will of the intervenor.

Where an intervention aims to supplant an existing government through clan-destine action, for instance through support for a rebel movement, the term fre-quently used is that of 'subversive' intervention. Intervention in defence of an existing democratic order is termed 'pro-democratic action' and tends to take place either where an incumbent, democratically mandated government is dis-placed by a counter-constitutional coup, or where an existing government refuses to transfer power to those who have been democratically mandated by a clear election result. In the 1980s, the United States added the concept of counter-intervention, arguing that it would be entitled to assist a rebel movement if the Soviet Union or its allies supported the existence of a contested government in another state (Afghanistan, Angola, Mozambique, Nicaragua).

By contrast, humanitarian intervention does not ordinarily aim to change the governmental structure of the state concerned. It is specifically targeted towards assisting the imperilled population of another state, but limited to that aim. Rescue of one's own nationals abroad is not normally considered part of this context. This, instead, is covered by an extension of the right to self-defence.

---

[10]   (1986) ICJ Rep 14, 106.

Genuine humanitarian intervention is often presented as a remedy to widespread and systematic human right violations. This would include cases where the government itself is causing the violations, for instance through a policy of repression, extermination, or forced displacement (ethnic cleansing), and overwhelming emergencies that may not be the result of governmental abuse, but occur as a result of natural disaster, crop failure, breakdown of authority, and resulting in insecurity and famine. In addition, humanitarian intervention covers situations where there is no longer a central government in place (Somalia), the government is unwilling to admit to and address a major humanitarian emergency (Sudan in the 1980s), or it has lost control over the territory where the emergency occurs and is, therefore, unable to act. Hence, forcible humanitarian action is undertaken as a temporary measure with the aim of addressing or preventing a large-scale humanitarian emergency that threatens the lives of a significant segment of a population.

Intervention involving the use of force is not only prohibited by virtue of the non-intervention doctrine, but is also a breach of Article 2(4) of the UN Charter.[11] Such cases are generally characterized as forcible, or armed intervention. On the other hand, where consent of the target state has been given, no issue of intervention arises.

In summary, forcible humanitarian action can be defined as:

The individual or collective threat or use of force strictly necessary and proportionate to addressing an actual or imminent humanitarian emergency threatening the survival of a significant segment of a population undertaken in the absence of host state consent.

In the *Nicaragua* case, the ICJ confirmed that the provision of 'strictly humanitarian aid to persons or forces in another country, whatever their political affiliations or objectives, cannot be regarded as unlawful intervention, or as in any other way contrary to international law'.[12] At the same time, it ruled out the use of force as a means of ensuring or monitoring human rights or pursuing humanitarian objectives.[13] However, even the rendering of mere humanitarian aid without the consent of the target state has remained highly contested. The issue arose during the 1980s when major humanitarian emergencies continued to threaten the lives of large population groups, in particular in Ethiopia and Sudan. These situations occurred at a time of intensive internal armed conflict. Restriction of food supplies was seen by the governments of both states as a strategic means of defeating the rebel movements that had taken control of significant parts of the state territory. United Nations attempts to achieve humanitarian access were often impeded.[14]

The issue of humanitarian access and state consent had already been raised by the International Committee of the Red Cross (ICRC) in preparations for the negotiations that led to the adoption of the two additional protocols to the 1949

---

[11] Ibid, 109.

[12] Ibid, 114f; See N Rodley, 'Human Rights and Humanitarian Intervention: The Case Law of the World Court' (1989) 38 ICLQ 321, 327.   [13] Ibid.

[14] This led to the establishment of the famed 'Operation Lifeline Sudan'.

Geneva Convention. Protocol II addresses internal armed conflicts, including the humanitarian dimension. The original ICRC concept foresaw an obligation on the part of states to accept humanitarian aid rendered in circumstances of extreme humanitarian emergency. However, during the diplomatic drafting conference, 'many states showed themselves to be more concerned with preserving their national sovereignty than with undertaking to facilitate relief action in all circumstances'.[15] Protocol II therefore provides that:[16]

If the civilian population is suffering undue hardship owing to a lack of the supplies essential for its survival, such as foodstuffs and medical supplies, relief actions for the civilian population which are of an exclusively humanitarian and impartial nature and which are conducted without any adverse distinction shall be undertaken subject to the consent of the High Contracting Party concerned.

Hence, the wording of the provision as eventually adopted, appears to privilege the requirement of state consent even for strictly humanitarian relief rendered by humanitarian agencies over the survival of a population.[17]

The prestigious Institut de Droit International (IDI) addressed this issue afresh in 1989. At its session in Santiago de Compostela, it considered proposals for forcible humanitarian action in times of extreme humanitarian distress. However, after intensive discussion, its concluding document, 'Protection of Human Rights and the Principle of Non-Intervention in the Internal Affairs of States', ruled out the threat or use of force for humanitarian purposes:[18]

An offer by a State, a group of States, an international organization or an impartial humanitarian body such as the International Committee of the Red Cross, of food or medical supplies to another State in whose territory the life or health of the population is seriously threatened cannot be considered an unlawful intervention in the internal affairs of that State. However, such offers of assistance shall not, particularly by virtue of the means used to implement them, take a form suggestive of a threat of armed intervention or any other measure of intimidation; assistance shall be granted and distributed without discrimination.

The Institut also argued that states in whose territories these emergency situations exist should not arbitrarily reject such offers of humanitarian assistance. However, instead of contemplating forcible action by states where such offers were rebuffed, the Institut noted the option of collective measures permitted under the UN Charter in case of large-scale systematic human rights violations, pointing to the possibility of Security Council action.[19]

---

[15] ICRC, (1987) 'Commentary on the Additional Protocols of 8 June 1977 to the Geneva Conventions of 12 August 1949' 1476.   [16] Protocol II, Art 18.
[17] The ICRC Commentary adds that consent is not left to the discretion of parties. Instead, where the survival of the population is threatened, 'relief action must take place': ICRC (above n 15) 1479. The Commentary does not offer justification for that finding, however laudable it may be. Nonetheless, this view subsequently attracted broader support (see below).
[18] Article 5, available at <http://www.idi-iil.org/idiE/resolutionsE/1989_comp_03_en.PDF>. On subsequent resolutions, see below.   [19] Article 2.

The campaign for securing a right to humanitarian access continued in the UN General Assembly. Instead of confirming an obligation of states to accept humanitarian relief in times of grave emergency, the resulting text stipulated the opposite, invoking the sovereignty and territorial integrity of states. It confirmed that 'humanitarian assistance should be provided with the consent of the affected country and in principle on the basis of an appeal by the affected country'.[20] However, the words 'should' and 'in principle' pointed to the increasing acceptance that states should not be able arbitrarily to refuse genuine offers of strictly humanitarian relief when the survival of their populations is at stake. As will be noted below, this view was strengthened in subsequent practice. But there was no support of any kind for the proposition that forcible humanitarian action might be permissible, even where a government—conceivably unlawfully—refuses humanitarian access where the survival of a significant segment of the population is concerned.

These restrictive international standards reflected post-1945 practice. While there was no shortage of cases of overwhelming humanitarian need, there were only a handful of instances of forcible responses, and these were not justified by way of humanitarian intervention.

The first concerned East Pakistan.[21] Following contested elections in the territory, which is geographically separated from the rest of Pakistan by hundreds of miles, unrest broke out, leading to a declaration of independence. During the fighting that ensued, over one million refugees poured into neighbouring India. India intervened with force, initially formally invoking humanitarian motives before the UN Security Council. However, when the final record of the Council debate was generated, that reference was struck from the record by the Indian representative. Instead, the mission was justified as a response to what was labelled 'refugee aggression'—caused by the outpouring of East Pakistanis—and to border incursions mounted by Pakistani forces against India. The consequent collapse of Pakistani rule in the territory, which led to its independence as Bangladesh, was entirely coincidental.

In a similar vein, Vietnam failed to invoke the doctrine of humanitarian intervention as a reason for its invasion of Cambodia in 1978. There, the Khmer Rouge were administering an absurd regime of terror, targeting broad segments of the population in a campaign that became known as 'the killing fields'. An estimated one to two million people died. Vietnam overthrew the Khmer Rouge and installed its own replacement government—claiming this as an accidental consequence of a limited military operation triggered by Cambodian border incursions and aggression occasioned by internal opposition forces.[22]

---

[20] Resolution 46/182, XX (19 December 1991).

[21] See T Franck and N Rodley, 'After Bangladesh: The Law of Humanitarian Intervention by Military Force' (1973) 67 AJIL 275.

[22] G Clintworth, *Vietnam's Intervention in Cambodia in International Law* (1989) 59ff.

Another example was the invasion of Uganda by Tanzania in 1979. At the time, the Idi Amin Government was committing grave atrocities against segments of the Ugandan population, resulting in around 300,000 deaths. Tanzania, however, chose to legally justify its action, which led to the overthrow of the Amin regime, as a limited self-defence measure, triggered by Ugandan border incursions and attempts to annex part of its neighbouring territory. The termination of the terror administered by Idi Amin was claimed to be coincidental and the result of efforts of domestic opposition to the dictator.[23] Tanzania's Leader, Julius Nyerere, otherwise not averse to contributing new precedents to international law, 'felt that they had to find a legal pretext for an action which on the face of it contravened Article 2(7)'.[24]

In the same year, France deposed Jean-Bedel Bokassa, who had declared himself Emperor of the Central African Republic and administered and despoiled it through a regime of extreme brutality. As France does not possess a common border with that territory, the usual justification of limited self-defence action in response to border incursion could not be applied. Instead, France relied on the invitation of the Government it had itself installed through the intervention.[25]

A number of other forcible actions were undertaken during this period that resulted in changes in government. However, these were not generally in response to overwhelming humanitarian emergencies, and were not contextualized as such by the intervening states, and thus do not need to be considered in detail in this context. These included US action in the Dominican Republic (1965), Grenada (1983), and Panama (1989/90), and Soviet interventions in Hungary (1956), Czechoslovakia (1968), and Afghanistan (1979). These actions were justified by a mixture of arguments drawing in part on purported invitations by the governments concerned, authority allegedly granted by regional organizations, and the defence of nationals and military personnel: 'Hence, there has thus far been no unambiguous case of state reliance on the right of humanitarian intervention'.[26] The intervention operations that could be considered in this context were in any event overwhelmingly rejected as unlawful.

The state practice noted here thus rejects, rather than supports, the existence of a doctrine of humanitarian intervention in international law. In the few instances where the doctrine could have been applied, even the states that would have benefited from invoking it failed to do so. This failure has been attributed to their belief that no such justification existed in international law. Moreover,

---

[23] SK Chaterjee, 'Some Legal Problems of Support Role in International Law: Uganda and Tanzania' (1981) 30 ICLQ 755; F Hassan, ''Realpolitik' in International Law: After the Tanzanian Uganda Conflict' (1981) 17 *Willamette Law Journal* 859; UO Umozurike, 'Tanzanian Intervention in Uganda' (1982) 20 *Archiv des Voelkerrechts* 301.

[24] P Calvocoressi, 'A Problem and Its Dimension' in N Rodely (ed), (1992) *To Loose the Bands of Wickedness* 1, 9.

[25] When that initial argument appeared somewhat dubious, France later pointed to the humanitarian situation in the country.

[26] AC Arend and RJ Beck, (1993) *International Law and the Use of Force* 137.

states were also unwilling to contribute to a practice that might have been seen as evidence of the emergence of such a doctrine. There was a sense that such a precedent could ultimately be invoked against them, or could lead to increased instability in the international system by undermining the prohibition of the use of force.

This was very much evident in the legal scholarship of the time of the Iraqi intervention operation. Some argued in favour of the doctrine, either on the basis of its roots in liberal human rights, its purported nineteenth-century history, or on the basis of broader, conceptual considerations about the nature of the state.[27] But the majority of legal scholars felt obliged to stick by the state practice they were meant to analyse when establishing the status of legal rights or obligations. They concluded that there was no justification for forcible humanitarian action in international law.[28] The position in law at the end of the Cold War period was perhaps best summarized in a UK Foreign and Commonwealth Office (FCO) document:[29]

...the overwhelming majority of contemporary legal opinion comes down against the existence of a right of humanitarian intervention, for three main reasons: first, the UN Charter, and the corpus of modern international law do not seem specifically to incorporate such a right; second, state practice in the past two-centuries, and especially since 1945, at best provides only a handful of genuine cases of humanitarian intervention, and, on most assessments, none at all; and finally, on prudential grounds, that the scope for abusing such a right argues strongly against its creation.

The document famously concluded that 'in fact, the best case that can be made in support of humanitarian intervention is that it cannot be said to be unambiguously illegal'.[30] While the document did not state the formal legal position of the FCO, it nevertheless highlighted the shift that subsequently occurred in relation to this finding. The United Kingdom led the way in restoring the argument of forcible humanitarian action to some international respectability, and did so mainly in the context of the developments that took place in Iraq after the liberation of Kuwait.

---

[27] F Teson, (3rd edn, 2005) *Humanitarian Intervention* (now also taking account of post-Cold War practice); R Lillich, 'Humanitarian Intervention: A Reply to Ian Brownlie and a Plea for Constructive Alternatives' in JN Moore (ed), (1974) *Law and Civil War in the Modern World* 229; WD Verwey, 'Humanitarian Intervention' in A Cassese (ed), (1986) *The Current Legal Regulation of the Use of Force* 57.

[28] The list is long, but see, eg Arend and Beck (above n 26) 113ff; M Akehurst, 'Humanitarian Intervention' in H Bull (ed), (1984) *Intervention in World Politics*; I Brownlie, 'Humanitarian Intervention' in Moore (above n 27) 217; TJ Farer, 'An Enquiry into the Legitimacy of Humanitarian Intervention' in LF Fisler Damrosch and DJ Scheffer, (1991) *Law and Force in the New International Order* 159; V Kartashkin, 'Human Rights and Humanitarian Intervention' in Fisler Damrosch and Scheffer (ibid) 203; P Malanczuck, (1993) *Humanitarian Intervention and the Legitimacy of the Use of Force*; P Hilpold, 'Humanitarian Intervention: Is there a Need for a Legal Reappraisal?' (2001) 12 *European Journal of International Law* 437; N Ronziti, (1985) *Rescuing Nationals Abroad and Intervention of Grounds of Humanity*.

[29] UK Foreign Policy Document No 148 (1986) 57 BYIL 614, 619.   [30] Ibid.

II. Resolution 688 (1991) and Initial Forcible Humanitarian Action in Iraq

On 2 April 1991, Turkey alerted the UN Security Council to the fact that some 220,000 civilians were massing along its border with Iraq. They were being attacked by artillery and helicopters and deliberately driven out of their country. In fact, the Kurds in northern Iraq and Shia populations in the south had been encouraged by the United States and other countries to mount a uprising with a view to displacing Saddam Hussein.[31] US President Bush had declared on 15 February 1991:[32]

... there is another way for the bloodshed to stop, and that is for the Iraqi military and the Iraqi people to take matters into their own hands to force Saddam Hussein the dictator to step aside and to comply with the United Nations resolutions and then rejoin the family of peace-loving nations.

However, this left them exposed to a very brutal response by Iraqi armed forces returning from the Kuwait campaign or which had been held in reserve to respond to such an uprising. 'These actions violate all norms of behaviour towards civilian populations and constitute an excessive use of force and a threat to the region's peace and security', Turkey indicated.[33] Iran also reported that the method by which the Iraqi military had dealt with the uprising had already led to an exodus of 110,000 civilians, which was likely to rise to half a million.[34] In fact, in the end there were around 1.5 million displaced civilians. In view of this situation, France requested an urgent meeting of the Council to discuss the abuses committed against the Iraqi population, in particular in Kurdish-inhabited areas: 'By virtue of the repercussions in the region, this situation constitutes a threat to international peace and security'.[35]

The invocation by both delegations of the concept of international peace and security was meant to bring what would otherwise have been considered an issue internal to Iraq into the ambit of potential action by the UN Security Council. Under Article 2(7) of the UN Charter, UN organs are not authorized to intervene in matters that fall essentially within the domestic jurisdiction of states. However, the principle does not preclude enforcement measures undertaken by the Council under Chapter VII of the Charter. According to Article 39, enforcement measures require a determination by the Council that an issue threatens international peace and security, or that there has been a breach of the peace or an act of aggression. In previous practice, the definition of what might constitute a threat to international

---

[31] L Freedman and D Boren, ' 'Safe Havens' for the Kurds in Post-war Iraq' in N Rodley, (1992) *To Loose the Bands of Wickedness* 43, 45.   [32] Ibid, quoted at 47.
[33] Letter to the Security Council, S/22435, 3 April 1991.
[34] Letter to the Security Council, S/22447, 4 April 1991.
[35] Ibid.

peace and security was expanded. The Council had taken enforcement action in relation to southern Rhodesia and South Africa.[36] The first concerned unilateral, opposed secession with the aim of perpetuating white minority governance in the territory prior to decolonization. The second addressed the maintenance of the apartheid system. Both could be considered essentially internal matters. Nevertheless, it had become accepted that so-called 'internal colonialism' administered by racist regimes was a matter of international concern and could amount to a threat to international peace and security. However, this was a special category of case emanating from the context of decolonization.

Hence, consideration by the Security Council of a matter that fell within the domestic jurisdiction of a state outside of this specific context remained, at that time, a delicate one. The French request for a meeting, therefore, sought to demonstrate the international dimension of an otherwise internal matter. Civilians were being persecuted inside Iraq, but their spill-over into neighbouring territories constituted a threat to international peace and security, which opened the door for Council action.

France followed up its initiative by placing a draft resolution before the Council. Delegations expressed their adherence to the principle of non-intervention, but also recognized the gravity of the humanitarian situation. Romania, for instance, noted that 'the armed repression of the Iraqi population can be a legitimate concern of the international community. However, Council action should not be taken as a precedent'.[37] Ecuador confirmed that the 'human pressure' exerted by one million civilians on the borders of Iraq's neighbours constituted a threat to peace. Russia, Austria, Belgium, and Italy also drew attention to the external dimensions of the crisis.[38] Zaire noted that the issue was exclusively humanitarian, and that the draft text had been amended to refer to the principle of non-intervention. Similarly, the Ivory Coast emphasized the resolution's reference to Article 2(7) of the Charter. India indicated that this had addressed some concerns, but that the Council should only have addressed the external dimensions of the crisis, leaving internal matters to more appropriate UN bodies.[39] China made an oblique statement, emphasizing Article 2(7) of the Charter, but accepting that the situation was one of great complexity.[40]

The United Kingdom, on the other hand, directly objected to the assertion that Article 2(7) could be a bar to action in this case.[41] Germany declared that the persistent and brutal persecution of a minority population required immediate steps on the part of the Council.[42] Anticipating future Council practice, Denmark declared that the 'magnitude of the human suffering', along with

---

[36] In addition to limited economic sanctions in both cases, in Resolution 221 (1966) the Council had even authorized military measures for naval sanctions enforcement.

[37] Provisional Verbatim Record of the UN Security Council, S/PV.2982, 5 April 1991, 22ff.

[38] Ibid, 56ff.   [39] Ibid, 62.   [40] Ibid, 54.   [41] Ibid, 63.

[42] Ibid, 134; also Luxembourg, 73.

the transborder problems made it 'natural' for the international community to address the matter through the Council.[43] France, the sponsor of the draft resolution, indicated that:[44]

Violations of human rights, such as those now being observed, become a matter of international interest when they take on such proportions that they assume the dimension of a crime against humanity.

Resolution 688 (1991) was adopted by 10 votes to 3 (Cuba, Yemen, Zimbabwe), with China and India abstaining. The Resolution recalled Article 2(7), but noted the Council's responsibilities under the Charter for the maintenance of international peace and security. This pointed the way towards possible invocation of Chapter VII. In a further preambular paragraph (not linked to the threat to peace), the Council also noted that it was deeply *disturbed* by the magnitude of the human suffering involved. Moreover, the Preamble expressed its grave concern at:

the repression of the Iraqi civilian population in many parts of Iraq, including most recently in Kurdish populated areas which led to a massive flow of refugees towards and across international frontiers and to cross border incursions, which threaten international peace and security in the region...

The Council came close to clearing the way for action by finding a threat to peace and security under Article 39, not through the suffering of the Iraqi population, but through the cross-border consequences of the movement of persons. It has been asserted that the subsequent reference to the 'consequences' of the Iraqi repression makes it clear that no Article 39 finding was in fact provided.[45] This, however, is not quite accurate. While the repression in itself did not amount to a threat to international peace and security, the Resolution nevertheless confirmed that the resulting flow of refugees, or at least the border incursions, did formally constitute such a threat. In principle, Chapter VII action would have been possible, and this was in fact originally intended. However, it emerged in Council consultations that China would not permit passage of a resolution formally adopted under Chapter VII in this instance. Hence, there was no mention of 'acting under Chapter VII', or the alternative invocation of a specific article from Chapter VII, which has since come invariably to denote the Chapter VII character of a Council resolution.

Nevertheless, under previous practice, the Council decision was not devoid of legal meaning.[46] Applying the rationale of the *Namibia* opinion of the ICJ, it was still possible that the Council was making binding demands upon Iraq, even if these were not accompanied by enforcement action or expressly based on

---

[43] Ibid, 135; also Sweden, 136.   [44] Ibid, 53.

[45] R Zacklin, (2010) *The United Nations Secretariat and the Use of Force in a Unipolar World* 14.

[46] N Rodley, 'Collective Intervention to Protect Human Rights' in Rodley (above n 31) 14, 31.

Chapter VII. Article 25 of the UN Charter requires states to 'accept and carry out' the decisions of the Security Council. The Court found:[47]

It has been contended that Article 25 of the Charter applies only to enforcement measures adopted under Chapter VII of the Charter. It is not possible to find in the Charter any support for this view. Article 25 is not confined to decisions in regard to enforcement action but applies to 'the decisions of the Council' adopted in accordance with the Charter.

In the substantive parts of the text of Resolution 688 (1991), the Council:

1. *Condemns* the repression of the Iraqi civilian population in many parts of Iraq, including most recently in Kurdish populated areas, the consequences of which threaten international peace and security in the region;

2. *Demands* that Iraq, as a contribution to removing the threat to international peace and security in the region, immediately end this repression and expresses the hope in the same context that an open dialogue will take place to ensure that the human and political rights of all Iraqi citizens are respected;

3. *Insists* that Iraq allow immediate access by international humanitarian organizations to all those in need of assistance in all parts of Iraq and to make available all necessary facilities for their operations;

4. *Requests* the Secretary-General to pursue his humanitarian efforts in Iraq and to report forthwith, if appropriate on the basis of a further mission to the region, on the plight of the Iraqi civilian population, and in particular the Kurdish population, suffering from the repression in all its forms inflicted by the Iraqi authorities;

The Council also appealed to Member States and humanitarian organizations to contribute to the humanitarian relief effort on behalf of the refugees and the displaced.

Minutes after the adoption of the text, the United States announced in the Council that its air force would begin air-dropping humanitarian supplies into Iraq, expecting Iraq to permit this effort without interference.[48] The following day, the United States demanded that Iraq cease military operations in the north, and announced that Iraqi fixed-wing or rotary aircraft would henceforth no longer be permitted to operate north of the 36th parallel. Under the original cease-fire agreed by the United States, only Iraqi fixed-wing military aircraft were prohibited from operating in Iraqi airspace.[49] Resolution 686 (1991) establishing the temporary UN cease-fire conditions had confirmed this.[50] However, this had

---

[47] ICJ *'Legal Consequences for States of the Continued Presence of South Africa in Namibia (South West Africa) Notwithstanding Security Council Resolution 276 (1970)'* 1971 ICJ 14, 52; see also R Higgins, (1963) *The Development of International Law through the Political Organs of the United Nations* 263; and R Higgins, 'The Advisory Opinion on Namibia: Which UN Resolutions are Binding under Article 25 of the Charter?' (1992) 21 ICLQ 270.

[48] Ibid, 57.

[49] General Norman Schwarzkopf, who concluded the initial ceasefire for the coalition, later claimed that he had been 'suckered' into exempting Iraqi helicopters. Iraq had argued that these were needed for the purpose of internal transport in the wake of the withdrawal from Kuwait.

[50] Paragraph 3(c).

not included the rotary-wing aircraft that were now being deployed against the Kurdish population. Moreover, a formal cease-fire entered into force on 11 April 1991, terminating the right to use force against Iraq which had been granted in Resolution 678 (1991).[51]

On 8 April 1991 the UK Prime Minister, John Major, announced that he was introducing an action plan building on Resolution 688 (1991) to the European Council. This consisted of humanitarian air-drops delivered by the UK air force which were already on the way. Second, he proposed the establishment of a 'safe haven in Northern Iraq under United Nations control where refugees, particularly Kurds...could be safe from attack and able to receive relief supplies'.[52]

Iraq immediately protested against the US/UK airdrops, to which France would also later contribute, which, Iraq claimed, 'infringe the sovereignty of Iraq in a shameful violation of the principles of international law and constitutes direct interference in the internal affairs of Iraq'.[53] Nevertheless, the US President, after further consultations with the British, persisted and, in addition, announced the establishment of safe havens in northern Iraq on 16 April. He indicated that a greatly expanded and more ambitious relief effort would now be undertaken:[54]

If we cannot get adequate food, medicine, clothing, and shelter to the Kurds living in the mountains along the Turkish-Iraq border, we must encourage the Kurds to move to areas in northern Iraq where the geography facilitates rather than frustrates such a large-scale relief effort.

Consistent with United Nations Security Council Resolution 688 (1991) and working closely with the United Nations and other international relief organizations and our European partners, I have directed the US military to begin immediately to establish several encampments in northern Iraq where relief supplies for these refugees will be made available in large quantities and distributed in an orderly way.

I can well appreciate that Kurds may have good reason to fear for their safety if they return to Iraq. And let me reassure them that adequate security will be provided at these temporary sites by US, British and French air and ground forces, again consistent with United Nations Security Council Resolution 688 (1991). ...

The UK Foreign Secretary confirmed that 'We are not talking of a territorial enclave, a separate Kurdistan or a permanent UN presence. We support the territorial integrity of Iraq'.[55]

He added subsequently that the operation sought to offer humanitarian aid, 'as authorized by Security Council Resolution 688 (1991)'.[56] However, the line

---

[51] Letter of the President of the Security Council to Iraq confirming the establishment of the formal cease-fire, S/22485, 11 April 1991.

[52] Statement by the Prime Minister, 8 April 1991, reproduced in M Weller (ed), (1993) *Iraq and Kuwait: The Hostilities and their Aftermath* (hereinafter, 'IK'), 714.   [53] S/22459, 8 April 1991.

[54] US President, News Conference, 16 April 1991, in IK, 717.

[55] House of Commons Statement, 15 April 1991, in IK, 716f.

[56] House of Commons Statement, 17 April 1991, in IK, 720.

taken by the United Kingdom remained that the action was consistent with the Resolution, rather than authorized by it. It was clear that Resolution 688 (1991) did not in itself furnish authority for action. First, it had not been adopted under Chapter VII of the UN Charter. Second, while it required Iraqi cooperation with humanitarian relief agencies, this would not ordinarily be considered to include US air-borne divisions.[57] Even if it had been a Chapter VII resolution, it did not authorize the deployment of foreign military forces on Iraqi soil without Iraqi consent. In the same vein, there was no authorization of the aerial exclusion zone. The external establishment of such a zone, backed by the threat of the use of force for its enforcement, also constituted a violation of Article 2(4) of the Charter, unless authorized by a Council mandate, by self-defence or, arguably, the doctrine of forcible humanitarian action.

The United States, United Kingdom, and France deployed rapidly on the ground, arranging for secure food distribution centres and shelters for very large numbers of displaced populations in northern Iraq. A significant number of other states joined in the operation. After difficult negotiations with the UN headquarters, a Memorandum of Understanding was reached to support the handing-over of the operation to the UN.[58] It was agreed that up to 500 lightly armed UN security guards would be deployed in the distribution centres. This was not a peace-keeping operation on Iraqi soil and did not suggest measures to defend the safe areas against Iraqi incursion. The guards were not mandated to intervene in issues lying outside of the protection of UN resources.[59] Instead, Iraqi security forces were kept out of the north due to a combination of the presence of Kurdish resistance fighters, and the inability of the Iraqi military to operate against them in the absence of air cover, which was precluded by the no-fly zone. Moreover, coalition forces retained a rapid reaction force in neighbouring Turkey to deter Iraqi encroachment into northern Iraq, which proceeded to administer itself autonomously from that point onwards.[60]

A new Memorandum of Understanding was concluded with Iraq in November 1991, permitting a UN humanitarian presence 'wherever such presence may be needed' in Iraq.[61] The presence of up to 500 UN guards carrying only side arms (pistols) was confirmed, along with their right to communicate freely between their areas of deployment.

Coalition members pointed out that their action had been strictly limited to implementing the aims established by the Council in Resolution 688 (1991). This concerned the termination of repression against vulnerable groups, in particular

---

[57] It was argued, however, that, given the intended handover of the operation to the UN, it could be seen to fall under the exhortation of Resolution 688 (1991) to cooperate with the UN when stemming the humanitarian crisis; see Rodley (above n 46) 31.

[58] S/22663, 18 April 1991, 30 ILM 860.

[59] See Office of the Executive Delegate of the Secretary General, 12 June, in IK, 627, 631.

[60] Freedman and Boren (above n 31) 43.

[61] UN-Iraq Memorandum of Understanding, 24 November 1991, in IK, 647.

in the north, and the free delivery of humanitarian aid until the operation could be taken over by the UN.

III. Action Relating to Southern Iraq

While the humanitarian situation improved somewhat, from October 1991 Iraq proceeded to restrict the inflow of relief supplies to the north and south. Moreover, the UN Special Rapporteur on the Situation of Human Rights in Iraq found that the violations committed by the Iraqi authorities were so grave and massive that an exceptional response was required. In view of this exceptional case, he proposed the deployment of human rights observers with full access to all parts of Iraq.[62] This proposal became more urgent during the summer of 1992. In an unprecedented step, the UN Special Rapporteur, Mr Max van der Stoel, who operated under a mandate from the UN Commission on Human Rights, addressed a communication directly to the UN Security Council.

The Special Rapporteur had gained knowledge of an Iraqi plan to 'wipe out' the Shiite population of the southern marsh area of Iraq. This would take the form of full-scale military attacks against villages. There had already been forced relocation, restrictions on foodstuffs, and artillery attacks against civilian concentrations. Moreover, a programme to drain the marshes had been proposed. Since the Council had been seized of the matter through Resolution 688 (1991), and in view of the link between the human rights situation and peace and security in the area, the Special Rapporteur now appealed to the Council for action. In particular, he proposed the deployment of unarmed human rights monitors.[63]

The response in the Council was very hesitant. A debate ensued about whether or not the Special Rapporteur was permitted to address the Council. It was argued that the human rights function should remain restricted to other bodies operating under the authority of the General Assembly.[64] In the end, the Special Rapporteur was permitted to speak, and indicated that attacks against civilians continued both in the north, in relation to Kurdish areas, and in the south. This included the use of fixed-wing aircraft. Moreover, Iraq continued to maintain a food blockade in relation to the north and south of Iraq.[65] In the ensuing discussion, Council members strongly condemned the Iraqi action. Russia, for instance, indicated that 'the world community will not stand for any further delay' in implementing Resolution 688 (1991) and that Iraq would face 'serious consequences' if it persisted in its confrontation with the Security Council.[66] However,

---

[62] E/CN.4/199231, 18 February 1992, in IK, 671, 695; the UN Commission on Human Rights encouraged the Special Rapporteur to develop this plan for an 'exceptional' response.

[63] S/24386, 30 July 1992.

[64] S/3105, 11 August 1992. Such reservations were expressed by India, China, and Ecuador.

[65] See IK, 703.   [66] Ibid, 708.

no action was taken in the Council at that point, or subsequently. Instead, the coalition took action once more.

The UK Prime Minister announced on 18 August 1992 that the coalition would[67] 'monitor the situation from the air and whilst we are doing that to ensure the security both of the Shias and of their aircraft we will instruct the Iraqis not to fly in that area'.

The UK Foreign Minister noted that not every action taken 'has to be underwritten by a specific provision in a UN resolution provided we comply with international law. International law recognizes extreme humanitarian need'.[68] He also drew attention to the fact that this overwhelming need had been attested by the appropriate UN agencies. An FCO spokesman added that this action was justified 'in response to a situation where there was demonstrably overwhelming humanitarian need. This action was in support of UN SCR 688'.[69]

The operation commenced on 27 August 1992. US President Bush affirmed that the purpose of the mission was to monitor the situation through surveillance flights. To facilitate this, a no-fly zone was implemented south of the 32nd parallel. This statement was flanked by a formal declaration by the coalition powers. The declaration noted that, especially in view of the use of air power against the southern Shiites, 'the survival of very large sections of the population' was now at risk, and required aerial monitoring. It added, 'to be clear':

No threat to coalition operations over southern Iraq will be tolerated. The Iraqi government should know that coalition aircraft will use appropriate force in response to any indication of hostile intent as defined in previous démarches. Inter alia, illumination and/or tracking of aircraft with fire control radars and any other action deemed threatening to coalition aircraft, such as intrusion of Iraqi aircraft into the no-fly zone, would be an indication of hostile intent.[70]

Once again, it was asserted that the coalition operation was strictly limited to the aims established by the Council, as supplemented by the report of a best-placed, objective international agency, the Special Rapporteur. As it would have been impossible to place unarmed human rights monitors in the area in the absence of Iraqi consent, aerial monitoring represented the mildest form of intervention capable of achieving the aim stipulated by the Rapporteur. In order to monitor in safety, coalition planes had to be protected by the no-fly zone. If challenged while so doing, force would be used in self-defence.

Initial patrolling of the zones was relatively routine. However, on 27 December 1992 a US jet, after having issued a radio warning, shot down an Iraqi fighter that had intruded into the no-fly zone in the north.[71] On 6 January 1993 Iraq was reported to be strengthening its anti-air defences in the southern zone. The

[67] Interview Transcript, 18 August 1992, in IK, 723.
[68] Secretary of State, interview, 19 August 1992, ibid.   [69] 20 August 1992, in IK, 724.
[70] Statement Issued by member of the Coalition, 26 August 1992, in IK, 725.
[71] In IK, 733.

coalition set a 48-hour ultimatum for the removal of those weapons.[72] Initially, it appeared that Iraq was complying.[73] However, Iraq also interfered with UN flights transporting personnel into the territory and mounted incursions into the Demilitarized Zone on the border with Kuwait.[74] The coalition responded by attacking anti-air installations in southern Iraq and their associated command and control facilities. The United Kingdom asserted:[75]

The action was taken in self-defence to ensure the safety of coalition aircraft patrolling the no-fly zone and following the démarche made by the coalition of 6 January 1993. In that démarche we demanded that Iraq take steps within 48 hours to ensure that its aircraft and surface-to-air missiles did not pose a threat to coalition aircraft operating south of the 32nd Parallel. Those aircraft are there to monitor Iraqi compliance with UN Security Council Resolution 688 (1991) which demanded that Iraq end the repression against her civilian population. The Iraqis initially appeared to comply with the terms of the démarche but subsequently violated it by putting in place missile batteries which threatened allied aircraft. The coalition have tonight acted to restore conditions which do not pose a threat to our aircraft.

The UK Secretary of Defence confirmed that the action had been taken 'in self-defence under international law and is both a necessary and a proportionate response to the serious threat posed to the safety of coalition aircraft'.[76] In this instance, the concept of serious threat appeared to have moved from actual targeting by Iraqi anti-air installations (locking on), to the mere presence of such installations that might target coalition aircraft. Moreover, in order to be able to invoke the right to self-defence of military aircraft flying in Iraqi airspace without Iraqi consent, a legal basis was required. In the absence of formal authorization through Resolution 688 (1991), this could only be based on a right to forcible humanitarian action.

The United States, however, appeared to place the action into the context of two presidential statements from the UN Security Council, having found that Iraq was in material breach of its obligations under the cease-fire regime: 'We stand ready to take additional forceful action with our coalition partners if Iraq continues to flout the will of the international community and if it continues to disregard its international obligations'.[77]

The French position also sought to hinge the operation on the terms of the cease-fire, rather than a right to self-defence. Noting the Iraqi incursions into the Demilitarized Zone, the inhibition of UN flights, and the presidential statements from the Security Council holding Iraq in material breach of the cease-fire, the French Government stated that the action was founded 'on the resolutions authorizing the use of force, in particular Resolution 678 (1991)'.[78] However, the

---

[72] Interview with the UK Defence Secretary, 8 January 1993, in IK, 735.
[73] White House Statement, 9 January 1993, in IK, 736.   [74] See IK, 736f.
[75] Statement from No 10 Downing Street, in IK, 738.   [76] Ibid.
[77] US Press Statement, 13 January 1993, in IK, 739.
[78] French Ministry of Foreign Affairs, Press Statement, 14 January 1991.

spokesperson also referred to the coalition ultimatum and the warning directed against Iraq, connected with the southern no-fly zone. The UN Secretary-General, who was visiting Paris on the same day, stated in a similar vein:[79]

The raid yesterday, and the forces that carried out the raid, have received a mandate from the Security Council, according to Resolution 678 (1990) and the cause of the raid was the violation by Iraq of Resolution 687 (1991) concerning the cease-fire.

This view included the requirements established in Resolution 688 (1991) among the terms of Resolution 687 (1991) establishing the cease-fire terms for Iraq. However, a UN spokesman later clarified that the no-fly zone was not in fact specifically authorized by a UN resolution, but he understood that the Member States involved considered that there was authorization within the overall framework of the relevant resolutions, specifically Resolution 688 (1991).[80]

The issue of Iraqi repression had been addressed separately by the Council because it would not have been possible to obtain the necessary votes if the internal situation within Iraq had been made subject to the Chapter VII requirements of the cease-fire resolution. China had threatened to veto. Hence, both issues were kept deliberately separate by the Council, and Resolution 688 (1991) was not formally adopted under Chapter VII, nor did it contain authorization for the use of force. While the UN Secretary-General reported on compliance with Resolution 688 (1991) as part of his regular reports on Iraq's conduct, although under a separate heading, there was no agreement in the Council to the effect that the requirements of Resolution 688 (1991) were now part of Resolution 687 (1991).[81]

France, in fact, withdrew its initial statement in an 'Official Declaration' issued by its Foreign Ministry. It distinguished between the issue of securing Iraqi compliance with the arms embargo and Resolution 687 (1991), on the one hand, and the issue of affording protection to the threatened populations in the north and south of Iraq, on the other:

France has participated on two occasions, within the framework of global agreement, in aerial raids over the past week against military targets south of the 32nd parallel. Those targets constitute a threat to the freedom of overflight of coalition aircraft in the exclusion zone.[82]

Russia also issued a rather oblique statement. It pointed to the pronouncement of the Council President, but also to the coalition démarche, as clear cut signals to 'stop disregarding decisions taken by the United Nations'. Russia noted that the 'action of the coalition forces in Iraq was taken in the context of the international community's efforts to ensure the observance of a decision jointly adopted under

---

[79] UN Press Release, 14 January 1993.   [80] Ibid, 742.
[81] For example S/23699, 11 March 1992.
[82] Official Declaration issued by the Ministry for Foreign Affairs of France, 21 January 1993, in IK, 752.

UN aegis to alleviate the consequences of Iraqi aggression'.[83] At that point, there did exist an informal consensus on forcible action in the Council, although it was a limited one concerning the humanitarian dimension.

Four days after the initial operation, US aircraft shot down a further Iraqi MIG-29 fighter in the northern no-fly zone, declaring that the action had been taken in self-defence.[84] That same day, the United States launched a missile strike against an alleged nuclear facility near Baghdad. This had been 'designed to achieve the goals of United Nations Security Council Resolutions 687, 707, and 715, namely to ensure that Iraq never again acquires weapons of mass destruction'.[85] Russia responded more cautiously, indicating that action against Iraq had to be adequate and should follow 'only agreed decisions'. It now appeared necessary to review what would be required in the Council.[86] France also expressed reservations, claiming that this latest action exceeded what had been agreed among the coalition and others.[87] In fact, this action undermined the cautious consensus that had underpinned the other parts of the operation in the Council.

There then followed further armed action against Iraqi anti-air installations in both northern and southern no-fly-zones. These were triggered by the firing of anti-air missiles at US aircraft, or the targeting of US aircraft by anti-air radar.[88]

The aerial exclusion zones re-entered international headlines in 1996. At that time, factional fighting had broken out between the Kurdish Democratic Party (KDP) and the Patriotic Union of Kurdistan vying for power in the north. The KDP had entered into an agreement with the Hussein Government to ensure its victory. Baghdad deployed its armed forces in pursuit of an invitation by the KDP, assisting it in the retaking of the key cities of Irbil and Sulaymaniya. The United States responded with a cruise missile attack against Iraq—although, oddly, it targeted the south, rather than the north.[89] Moreover, the southern no-fly zone was extended northwards, to the 33rd parallel, coming close to the capital Baghdad. France did not support the extension, but continued to contribute to the monitoring of the zone in its previous dimension. However, France withdrew entirely from the enforcement of the northern zone at the end of 1996, arguing that the humanitarian need had subsided. It terminated its remaining support for the southern zone in the wake of Operation Desert Fox—a 70-hour US/UK bombing campaign against Iraq. While that attack was mainly connected with Iraq's failure to contribute to the UN arms inspection effort, it also had implications for the credibility of the maintenance of the humanitarian zone.

---

[83] Statement by the Russian Foreign Ministry, 14 January 1993, in IK, 744f.
[84] US Press Release, 17 January 1993, in IK, 745.   [85] Ibid.
[86] Statement by the Russian Foreign Ministry, 18 January 1993, in IK, 749.
[87] Press Briefing by the French Foreign Minister, 20 January 1993, in IK, 751.
[88] US Press Release, 19 January 1993, in IK, 749.
[89] DM Malone, (2006) *The International Struggle over Iraq* 100.

Armed confrontations in relation to the no-fly zones continued, with increasingly broader rules of engagement following the motto of Operation Desert Fox to diminish and degrade Iraq's military potential. In 2001, it appeared that the situation might escalate, as the United States and United Kingdom struck targets outside the no-fly zone. However, it was argued that this was an isolated incident, and in fact concerned a command and control facility linked directly to the air-defence infrastructure in the south. Hence, it was necessary to visit that target if efforts to repress the southern air defence were to be successful.[90] In reality, however, operations started to take on a broader scale.

The raid triggered an enquiry by Iraq to the UN Secretary-General, who refused to offer a view on the lawfulness, or otherwise, of the no-fly zones. He reported that certain UN members were claiming authority in this respect under the resolutions of the Council, but that it was for the Council alone to determine whether 'its resolutions are of such a nature and effect as to provide a lawful basis for the "no-fly-zones" and for the actions that have been taken for their enforcement'.[91]

At least one of the members of the Council involved in the operations had doubts about the lawfulness of the mission. The continued maintenance of the no-fly zones in Iraq was in fact subjected to periodic review by the UK Attorney General. Noting that force is in principle prohibited in circumstances other than self-defence or Chapter VII authorization by the UN Security Council, he recalled that, in addition, the Law Officers had previously accepted that a 'respectable legal argument' could be made in relation to overwhelming humanitarian necessity as a further justification of the use of force. But the arguments put to him by the relevant branches of the government in favour of maintaining the no-fly zones had not focused on an ongoing humanitarian emergency. Instead, they had pointed to the fact that such an emergency would arise if the no-fly zones were removed. Hence, in his view, it was becoming 'more questionable whether a respectable legal argument can be maintained that force is justified on grounds of overwhelming humanitarian necessity' in Iraq. He concluded that 'it is still *possible* to argue that the maintenance of the No Fly Zones is justified', adding that this judgment was a 'very fine one'.[92]

The Attorney General reiterated that this legal basis could not justify military action for other, ulterior motives, such as action to punish Saddam Hussein, or to enforce other UK or US objectives in the area. Moreover, it would be 'vitally important to keep constantly in view the precarious nature of the legal basis for the UK and US action in the No Fly Zones'.[93]

By this time, the maintenance of the no-fly zones appeared to be based on two rationales. The southern zone, subsequent testimony revealed, was mainly

---

[90] Chilcot Testimony, 26 November 2009, 141.   [91] S/2001/160, 21 February 2001.
[92] David Brummell to Tom McKane, 12 February 2001, para 13 (emphasis in original).
[93] Ibid, para 15.

retained as its existence was necessary in order to support the existence of the northern zone. In relation to the northern zone, it was argued that 'there was a severe risk that Saddam Hussein would recommence his attacks and the repression', should the zone be discontinued.[94] In a way, therefore, the justification moved towards one of anticipatory humanitarian action, arguing that an overwhelming humanitarian emergency would arise in the future, unless action was taken (or maintained in place) in the present.

However, armed actions in and around the no-fly zones continued to increase. From 2002 onwards, in the run-up to the 2003 war, the United States adopted a strategy of so-called 'spikes'. This used strikes in and around the no-fly zones to leave the Iraqi regime in a state of uncertainty about the timing of a more major aerial campaign as a precursor to the invasion that was now widely expected.[95] A few days before the launch of the invasion, action against the no-fly zones was again increased, to ensure the suppression of Iraqi air defences in preparation for the major bombing campaign that was to follow.[96] The United Kingdom reportedly opted out of this action, named 'Operation Southern Focus', believing that that the authority to patrol the zones did not extend to the preparation of an invasion.[97]

IV. The UK Claim Relating to Forcible Humanitarian Action

The United Kingdom appeared to be the only state endorsing humanitarian action in relation to Iraq outright and in legal terms, although even this was subsequently qualified. The principled UK view was also highlighted in a major policy speech of Prime Minister Tony Blair. He proclaimed 'The Doctrine of the International Community' in his famous Chicago speech, in which he set out five criteria for UK intervention in internal conflicts.[98] In view of the unique UK view, it is appropriate to consider the position of the principal 'norm entrepreneur' in this instance, before addressing the wider reception of the UK argument.

---

[94] Sir Michael Wood, Chilcot Testimony, 26 November 2009, 132.
[95] B Woodward, (2004) *Plan of Attack: The Road to War* 83, 100, 102, 236.
[96] M Gordon and B Trainor, (2007) *Cobra II* 79f.　　[97] Ibid, 80.
[98] 24 April 1999. The tests were: 'First, are we sure of our case? War is an imperfect instrument for righting humanitarian distress; but armed force is sometimes the only means of dealing with dictators. Second, have we exhausted all diplomatic options? We should always give peace every chance, as we have in the case of Kosovo. Third, on the basis of a practical assessment of the situation, are there military operations we can sensibly and prudently undertake? Fourth, are we prepared for the long term? In the past we talked too much of exit strategies. But having made a commitment, we cannot simply walk away once the fight is over; better to stay with moderate numbers of troops than return for repeat performances with large numbers. And finally, do we have national interests involved? The mass expulsion of ethnic Albanians from Kosovo demanded the notice of the rest of the world. But it does make a difference that this is taking place in such a combustible part of Europe'. See <http://www.number10.gov.uk/Page1297; http://keeptonyblair forpm.wordpress.com/blair-speech-transcripts-from-1997–2007/#chicago>.

In 1992, the British FCO submitted a memorandum to Parliament, indicating that:[99]

We believe that international intervention without the invitation of the government of the country concerned can be justified in cases of extreme humanitarian need. This is why we were prepared to commit British forces to Operation Haven, mounted by the Coalition in response to the refugee crisis involving the Iraqi Kurds.

The memorandum also emphasized that the deployment of these forces was 'entirely consistent' with the objectives of Resolution 688 (1991). Hence, it was undertaken in pursuit of the aims established in the Resolution, although not legally based on it.

In subsequent testimony, Tony Aust, of the FCO Legal Advisers, confirmed that Resolution 688 (1991) did not mandate Operation Provide Comfort in northern Iraq. Instead:[100]

... the practice of states does show over a long period that it is generally accepted that in extreme circumstances a state can intervene in another state for humanitarian reasons. I think before doing so though a state would have to ask itself several questions. First of all, whether there was a compelling and an urgent situation of extreme humanitarian distress which demanded immediate relief. It would have to ask itself whether there was any other practical alternative to intervening in order to relieve the stress, and also whether the action could be limited in time and scope.

In making this statement, he noted that international law develops to meet new situations and 'that is what we are seeing now in the case of Iraq'. His statement claiming a new right in customary law was subsequently refined. When the United Kingdom felt constrained to justify the threat of the use of force against Yugoslavia, made by NATO in September 1998 in view of the increasingly dramatic situation in Kosovo, Baroness Symons indicated to Parliament:[101]

There is no general doctrine of humanitarian necessity in international law. Cases have nevertheless arisen (as in northern Iraq in 1991) when, in the light of all the circumstances, a limited use of force was justifiable in support of purposes laid down by the Security Council but without the Council's express authorization when that was the only means to avert an immediate and overwhelming humanitarian catastrophe. Such cases would in the nature of things be exceptional and would depend on an objective assessment of the factual circumstances at the time and on the terms of relevant decisions of the Security Council bearing on the situation in question.

This statement expressly backtracked from the earlier claim to a formal right to humanitarian intervention. Instead, action was very firmly placed in the context

---

[99] Reproduced in (1992) 63 BYIL 825.
[100] Reproduced in DJ Harris, (6th edn, 2004) *Cases and Materials in International Law* 950.
[101] Baroness Symons, UK Parliamentary Debates, House of Lords, 16 November 1998, WA 140.

of Security Council pronouncements, and the exceptional nature of any action without a formal mandate was emphasized.

It is not easy to grasp the essence of the UK position. The reference to state practice over a long period would appear to indicate an argument based on customary international law. As it is difficult to establish a new rule in this case, reference is made to its purported historical pedigree. Nevertheless, somewhat inconsistently with the position he has taken elsewhere, Sir Michael Wood QC, the former FCO Legal Adviser, testified to the Chilcot Inquiry that the right of forcible humanitarian action:[102]

> Is regarded by the British Government as being derived from customary international law, and the essence of it, I think, is that if something like the Holocaust were happening today, if the Security Council were blocked, and you couldn't get an authorization from it, then it simply cannot be the law that states cannot take action to intervene in that kind of situation, an emergency of that scale.

However, subsequent statements conflict with the initial explanation, locating the right within custom, or considering it at least, to be 'derived from customary international law'. Indeed, Baroness Symons' statement directly opposes the assertion of a general right to humanitarian intervention. Instead, reference is made to an overwhelming humanitarian catastrophe as a truly exceptional circumstance that can justify intervention. But 'overwhelming humanitarian circumstances' is not in itself a justification for the use of force, unless it is argued that this is merely the standard triggering the application of what, after all, is a right to humanitarian intervention or, better, an exception to the prohibition of the use of force. If there is no such exceptional right, then there would be three alternative options.

First, overwhelming humanitarian circumstances may constitute distress or necessity. According to the law of state responsibility, distress concerns situations where an otherwise unlawful action is the only way of preserving the very lives of those placed in the care of the state taking the action.[103] Of course, the intervention would in reality be undertaken in relation to populations under the immediate care of another state in reality. Hence, one would need to broaden the definition of the concept, assuming perhaps that all states have responsibility of care in relation to humanity. The other concept drawn from state responsibility is necessity. Necessity is described as the only way to safeguard an essential interest against grave and imminent peril.[104] However, the violation concerned must not seriously impair the interests of the state whose rights are being violated, or of the international community as a whole. It could be argued that an armed intervention would, by definition, seriously impair the rights of the target state and of the international community as a whole.

The International Law Commission (ILC) Articles on State Responsibility clarify that they are not intended to enlarge or expand upon the law on the use

---

[102] Sir Michael Wood, Chilcot Testimony, 26 November 2009, 119f.
[103] ILC Articles on State Responsibility, Art 24.   [104] Ibid, Art 25.

of force. They are without prejudice to the UN Charter and their provisions are to be interpreted in accordance with the Charter.[105] While thus not modifying the law on the use of force, they are nevertheless reflective of it. This is evidenced by the treatment of another aspect of the use of force in addition to necessity and distress—self-defence.[106] All three belong to the category of circumstances precluding wrongfulness. That is to say, an action (say, the use of force) is prima facie a violation of international law. However, due to the circumstances triggering the action, it is nevertheless not internationally wrongful. The UK approach to forcible humanitarian action would be consistent with this approach.

An alternative view would be that of 'unlawful but legitimate' action. This proposition argues that humanitarian intervention remains prohibited by the use of force. However, when such an action is undertaken in response to genuine humanitarian circumstances and pursued only in the interests of the affected population (as opposed to the self-interest of the intervening state), and the action is strictly necessary and proportionate, then it will not be internationally condemned. While the organized international community would be unwilling to accept a precedent in favour of a rule of intervention, it might also fail to insist on the application of the prohibition of the use of force in such a case, and the consequences ordinarily triggered by the violation do not flow.

As will be noted below, this was the position adopted by a significant number of scholars and expert commissions in the wake of the Kosovo intervention of 1999. However, the approach is difficult to reconcile with an assumption that governmental action, in order to be legitimate, must at a minimum also be lawful. This point was made by a former senior Foreign Office lawyer who was involved in all aspects of the evolving Iraq episode over the years.[107] If international law is to be law, rather than a collection of rules of convenience, the claim that it applies under all circumstances is an important one. The law itself needs to provide sufficient flexibility to accommodate the exigencies of international life. It does so by providing recognized exceptions to the prohibition of the use of force, and the possibility that the Security Council may offer additional authorization. However, if, ultimately, extra-legal considerations prevail, the nature of the legal order is called into question.

A third possible interpretation of the UK position is not substantive, but procedural. Humanitarian intervention as a claimed right of states does not exist. However, the Security Council as the principal organ of collective security can authorize forcible humanitarian action under the powers transferred to it by all states party to the UN Charter. Where, in exceptional circumstances, the Council is unable to give such authorization, states, coalitions of states, or regional organizations may nevertheless act. However, there are a number of requirements that have to be met. The Council itself must have determined that there exists

---

[105] Ibid Art 59.   [106] Ibid, Art 21.
[107] Elisabeth Wilmshurst, Chilcot Testimony, 26 January 2010 12f.

an overwhelming humanitarian emergency that is sufficiently severe to threaten international peace and security. It must also have indicated the minimum necessary action to avert or end the humanitarian catastrophe. Finally, while the granting of a formal mandate may have proved impossible, there must nevertheless have been widespread support for the action.

This view would be in line with UK action over Iraq, Sierra Leone, and Kosovo.[108] In all these instances, the humanitarian emergency was reliably and objectively attested. The Council had found that the situations in question constituted a threat to international peace and security. The action taken was deliberately, and indeed expressly, focused on what the Council had determined to be the minimum necessary for addressing the situation. In Iraq, coalition action focused on terminating repression by effectively excluding Iraqi armed forces from the north through the no-fly zone. The other aim established in Resolution 688 (1991) concerned humanitarian assistance. Its delivery was facilitated initially through air-drops, and subsequently through a military presence on the ground in the safe haven areas. In Sierra Leone the Council, in Resolution 1162 (1998) and subsequent texts, had called for action to ensure peaceful and stable conditions in the country. The United Kingdom limited its actions to maintaining a safe environment within which other international actors, and the Sierra Leone Government, could operate. In Kosovo the Council, in Resolution 1199 (1998), had demanded the cessation of repression, the withdrawal of Yugoslav military and paramilitary forces, and the rapid implementation of an interim autonomy arrangement. NATO's aims in the ensuing military campaign were tailored to match these requirements exactly.

As proven by the subsequent discussion in the UK Government about the invasion of Iraq, this approach implied a risk. Action 'à la Kosovo' seemed to be possible in a wider sense—that is to say, the idea that the demands of the Council might also be enforced in other contexts was advanced by politicians. This would have included demands for Iraqi cooperation with the arms inspection process made over a whole series of Chapter VII resolutions of the Council, from Resolution 687 (1991) to Resolution 1441 (2002). However, the Foreign Office Legal Advisers strongly opposed this view.[109] They drew a clear distinction between the case of Kosovo and that of the disarmament of Iraq. As indicated by the Legal Adviser at that time, Sir Michael Wood QC, in relation to the UK position, 'the fact that the Council has laid down the common purpose is necessary, but not sufficient, condition for States to act unilaterally' in pursuit of humanitarian motives.[110]

Sir Franklin Berman, a former Legal Adviser whose tenure spanned both the Iraq and Kosovo episodes, explained the UK view at the time, which was

---

[108] See below, 91–94.   [109] See Ch 6, 206.

[110] M Wood, 'The Principle of Non-Intervention in Contemporary International Law', Chatham House Discussion Group Presentation, 28 February 2007, available at <http://www.chathamhouse.org.uk/files/6567_il280207.pdf>.

admittedly a complex one. The argument went in three stages. First, the Security Council would authoritatively express the 'common purposes' of the organized international community:[111]

It must be plain that no State could conceivably claim to be acting in the Council's stead unless it was acting in pursuit of purposes the Council itself had already laid down. The fact that the Council had already laid down clear purposes and goals was crucial to the legal argument put forward by my own country as the basis for creating the 'Safe Havens' in Northern Iraq in 1991, and then elaborated in somewhat less convincing circumstances by the North Atlantic Alliance for Kosovo in 1999.

However, the articulation of aims by the Council would not be sufficient in itself: 'Chaos would ensue from the establishment of a doctrine that Member States were empowered to take upon themselves the enforcement of Council decisions'.[112] Instead, a collective identification of aims by the Council:[113]

... was not being advanced as a positive empowering factor in its own right, but in a purely negative sense; in other words, it was there to make plain that the States in question were precisely not claiming for themselves the right to lay down the purposes of the international community in whose name they were acting, but were operating in aid of common purposes laid down by the only duly authorised organ, the Security Council. ...
... there is no legal basis under which any State (which for present purposes would include any group of States) can appoint itself the Security Council's enforcement arm. The Charter could not be clearer: the Security Council is given the sole prerogative to act, and part of its prerogative is to 'determine' whether the action required to carry out its decisions for the maintenance of international peace and security is to be taken by some Member States (Article 48 of the Charter).

This view would, therefore, preclude unilateral action in pursuit of UN aims. Nevertheless, humanitarian action is said to be possible in the absence of Council authorization, through application of the 'Dutch thesis'. When justifying the Kosovo intervention in the Council, the Netherlands argued:[114]

... if, however, due to one or two permanent members' rigid interpretation of the concept of domestic jurisdiction, such a resolution is not attainable, we cannot sit back and simply let the humanitarian catastrophe occur. In such a situation we will act on the legal basis we have available, and what we have available in this case is more than adequate.

This sounds a little like the argument of the 'unreasonable veto' put by the UK Prime Minister in relation to the Iraqi disarmament issue.[115] Action would be possible if a small, but controlling minority of one or two others were to take an unreasonably rigid position on non-intervention. In fact, however, this is not quite accurate. In contrast to Tony Blair's concept of an unreasonable veto, in the Dutch instance there would be underlying justification for the use for force to which recourse could be had in the event of a failure by the Council to

---

[111] F Berman, 'The UN Charter and the Use of Force' (2006) 10 SYBIL 9, 15.
[112] Ibid, 16.   [113] Ibid.   [114] Below, p. 97.   [115] See Ch 6, 215–216.

authorize action. The Netherlands did not reveal what the legal basis would be in this instance, although it confirmed its adequacy. One presumes that it can only be a doctrine of overwhelming humanitarian emergency, either as a circumstance precluding wrongfulness, or as justification for the use of force in terms of humanitarian intervention.

Sir Franklin Berman added some additional meat to the third stage of the UK position:[116]

Does this rule out any possibility for the lawful use of individual or collective force by States where the Security Council has failed to act? If so, how do we account for the cases of Northern Iraq in 1991 and Kosovo in 1999? I do not myself believe that it does—provided that the conditions and limitations are properly weighed. Article 2(4) of the Charter, for example, the prohibition on the threat or use of force, is so clearly predicated, by its very wording, on the concepts of consistency or inconsistency with the purposes and principles of the United Nations, and infringements of sovereignty and territorial integrity, that I see little virtue in a refusal, as a matter of principle, even to examine whether particular uses of force may, or may not, be compatible with those predicates. And the 'Safe Havens' operation in Northern Iraq was unambiguously and credibly based (the Kosovo intervention less convincingly so) on temporary emergency relief of extreme humanitarian need, which certainly bears comparison with those two Charter predicates.

The solution offered by Sir Franklin appears to be a weighing of values to which the UN Charter and Article 2(4) itself refer. The balancing of human values in the Charter with notions of sovereignty and territorial integrity would take account of the temporary nature of the operation, the fact that it is exclusively humanitarian aid that is being rendered, rather than pursuit of self-interest by the intervening state, and the extreme humanitarian need being addressed.[117] Despite the elegance of its phrasing it is not entirely clear, however, where this process differs from outright acceptance of the doctrine of humanitarian intervention. The doctrine performs exactly that balancing function. The difference seems to lie in the previous, authoritative articulation of overriding international community interest in the matter through the Council (threat to the peace), coupled with an objective finding of overwhelming need. But, as already noted, this is essentially a procedural requirement, rather than a substantive one. The Council confirms the facts and sets the aims, but does not authorize their forcible implementation.

In view of the express statement by Baroness Symons that the United Kingdom does not believe in a right of humanitarian invention, recently restated by

---

[116] Berman (above n 111) 17.

[117] See also J Currie, 'NATO's Humanitarian Intervention in Kosovo: Making or Breaking International Law' (1998) *Canadian Yearbook of International Law* 303; and, for a somewhat more cautious view, A James, 'The Concept of Sovereignty Revisited' in A Schnabel and R Thakur, (2000) *Kosovo and the Challenge of Humanitarian Intervention* 334.

Sir Michael Wood QC, what then is the overall position? Perhaps one might summarize the points that are clear:

- There is no formal doctrine of humanitarian intervention, but, in circumstances of extreme humanitarian distress, human values and the doctrine of non-intervention need to be balanced against the specific factors of the situation. Such balancing is inherent even in Article 2(4).
- However, action can only be taken if the UN Security Council has determined that the matter is of overwhelming international interest (threat to the peace), and if it has laid out the minimum action required for averting or terminating the emergency.
- The action must be strictly necessary (no other means), proportionate to the emergency, and restricted to the pursuit of the aims established by the Council.

This view was reflected in part by guidelines on humanitarian intervention operations issued in 2000 by the then UK Foreign Secretary, Robin Cook. The guidelines suggest six (in reality, five) criteria for action, which are presumably to be read cumulatively:[118]

- The principle that armed force should only be used as a last resort.
- The recognition that immediate responsibility rests with the state concerned, recognizing, however, that 'sometimes a state would like to act but cannot' while other states refuse to halt the violence or cause it themselves.
- The existence of an overwhelming humanitarian catastrophe, which the host government has shown it is unwilling or unable to prevent or is actively promoting. There must be 'convincing evidence of extreme humanitarian distress on a large scale', requiring urgent relief.
- It must be objectively clear that there is no practicable alternative to the use of force to save life.
- Any force used should be proportionate to achieving the humanitarian purpose and carried out in accordance with international law. It must be likely to achieve its objective, and the scale or potential of actual human suffering must justify the dangers inherent in military action.
- Force should be used collectively. No individual state should reserve to itself the right to act on behalf of the international community. This may include coalition action or action through regional organizations, but 'our own preference would be that, wherever possible, the authority of the Security Council should be secured'.

This announcement was followed up by a UK initiative in the Security Council, which sought to introduce such criteria for Council action in the face of grave humanitarian emergencies. However, the initiative was not taken up. In any

---

[118] Reprinted in (2000) 71 BYIL 646.

event, the criteria are broader than the view summarized above. While action through the Security Council is the clear preference, it seems to be less dependent on actual pronouncements by the Council. Hence, action is possible, even in the absence of such pronouncements, if the humanitarian emergency is credibly attested in another way, and provided action is taken in a multilateral context.

The UK Secretary of State for Foreign and Commonwealth Affairs expanded on the subject once again in 2003. He indicated:[119]

Action should be taken only to prevent genocide or major loss of civilian life that could destabilize other states and threaten international peace and security. In those circumstances, force should be used only as a last resort and when a Government have demonstrated their unwillingness or inability to end large-scale civilian suffering within their jurisdiction.

There also has to be a pragmatic element. The same of actual or potential human suffering must justify the risks and dangers of military action, and there must be clear and relevant objectives and the military means to ensure a high probability of success. The use of force in such circumstances should be collective and limited in scope to actions necessary and proportionate to achieving the humanitarian objective. It must also respect humanitarian law and the Geneva Convention.

However, it appeared that the UK Government was not willing to commit itself definitely to this firm set of criteria, only part of which appear to be legal. It was added that this is 'only one possible way of expressing the conditions under which intervention should take place'. Moreover, the reference to a threat of destabilization of external states and the resulting threat to international peace and security appears to be a reference to criteria for Security Council action. However, the Foreign Secretary had also indicated in this statement that another Rwanda should be prevented at all cost, presumably referring to the possibility of unilateral action in the face of UN inaction.

V. The Reception of the Iraq Precedent into Wider Practice

International coalition action in relation to Iraq was not widely criticized. Indeed, there was an element of informal consensus in the Security Council underpinning the action.[120] Overall, four positions may be distinguished in that respect. Cuba and Yemen continued to oppose the action. A number of states had doubts, but did not prevent the operations (in particular, China). The larger group of states, which initially included Russia, favoured action but was unwilling to commit to it. Finally, the coalition states defended the action, but generally without purporting to support the establishment of a right of forcible humanitarian action of wider applicability. As noted above, the United Kingdom initially appeared to

---

[119] HC Deb, Vol 314, cols 206–207, 11 November 2003, (2003) 74 BYIL 817.
[120] See also Ch 4.

formally embrace such a right on the basis of state practice, allegedly accepted as law over a prolonged period (the 'Aust statement'), but later adopted a far more hesitant attitude that linked the action more firmly to the pronouncements of the Security Council.

In subsequent practice, there was very considerable proliferation of Council action in relation to internal emergencies. This included the issuing of forcible mandates to UN-led forces, to regional organizations or arrangements, and even to coalitions of states.[121] These mandates were either finely focused, for instance on ensuring conditions for the safe delivery of humanitarian assistance, or were framed in wider, more general terms.[122] While many of the relevant resolutions continued to refer to the external ramifications of humanitarian circumstances (refugee movements, regional instability caused by the spill-over of internal conflict), this pretence was at times abandoned. The situation in Somalia in 1992, for example, was considered so shocking that the Council recognized:

... that the magnitude of the human tragedy caused by the conflict in Somalia, further exacerbated by the obstacles being created to the distribution of humanitarian assistance, constitutes a threat to international peace and security...

Hence, it was clear by that point that humanitarian suffering in itself could constitute the threat to international peace and security necessary to displace the obligation of non-intervention in Article 2(7) of the UN Charter and permit Council action.[123] While each of these instances were said to be based on unique circumstances (in deference to China and some other delegations) it was not possible to prevent the consolidation of Council practice in this regard.[124] Clearly, by the mid-1990s it was no longer possible to argue that the Council itself lacked in principle the power to mandate the use of force—even in relation to situations that were entirely internal—if the humanitarian emergency was sufficiently grave.[125] In another instance, the Council also mandated forcible action in response to a counter-constitutional coup.[126] While it was pointed out that Resolution 688 (1991) was not itself a Chapter VII text, it is fair to say that this subsequent practice was rooted in that early precedent.[127]

The Council also adopted the concept of safe havens pioneered in northern Iraq. In Resolution 836 (1993) it committed the UN force UNPROFOR and NATO air power to the protection of 'safe areas' in Bosnia and Herzegovina from

[121] See, in detail, S Chesterman, (2001) *Just War or Just Peace* 112–219.

[122] See the particularly useful review in C Gray, (3rd edn, 2008) *International Law and the Use of Force* 294–428.   [123] Resolution 794 (1992), Preamble.

[124] For example Resolution 794 (1992), Preamble: '*Recognizing* the unique character of the present situation in Somalia and mindful of its deteriorating, complex and extraordinary nature, requiring an immediate and exceptional response'.

[125] Initial instances of action are Somalia, Bosnia, Haiti, Rwanda, Zaire-Rwanda, Albania, Sierra Leone, Central African Republic, Eastern Timor, Democratic Republic of Congo, etc.

[126] Resolution 940 (1994) on Haiti. See also Sierra Leone, below, 226–232.

[127] See D Sarooshi, (1991) *The United Nations and the Development of Collective Security*.

bombardment, armed incursion, or the deprivation of humanitarian aid supplies.[128] However, this collapsed disastrously when the 'safe area' of Srebrenica was overrun by Bosnian-Serb forces without any opposition from the UN troops stationed there, or from NATO air power.[129] Some 7,000 men and boys were then systematically massacred. This experience, coupled with the collapse of the increasingly ambitious US mission to re-establish constitutional governance in Somalia, led to a temporary halt in the 'new interventionism' of the Council.[130] This, in turn, contributed to the failure of the UN to take measures to stem the 1994 genocide in Rwanda, which led to between 800,000 and one million deaths in the space of just a few months. After considerable soul-searching in the wake of these disasters, the Council re-engaged in intervention operations, and Chapter VII mandates have since abounded in relation to complex internal emergencies and conflicts.[131]

If this practice makes it impossible to question the authority of the Council to carry out, or mandate, forcible humanitarian action, the issue of a possible right of states to act in the absence of such a mandate is more controversial. Council practice cannot in itself furnish evidence of acceptance of a practice as law in this regard. The intention of the Council, and of the states voting in it, was clearly directed towards action under UN authority. The practice, however voluminous, cannot, therefore, be taken into account when considering whether general international law now recognizes a right of unilateral (or coalition) intervention for humanitarian purposes. A further problem lies in the legal character of the prohibition on the use of force as a '*jus cogens*' rule. A particularly high threshold of consistent, virtually uniform, and widely representative practice would be required, along with the specific intent of states to modify the prohibition by admitting a new exception to it.[132] When compared with this requirement, practice subsequent to the Iraq interventions of 1991–1992 appears somewhat thin.[133]

---

[128] Also Resolutions 815 (1993) and 824 (1993).

[129] See M Weller, 'Peace-keeping and Peace-Enforcement in Bosnia and Herzegovina' (1996) 56 *Zeitschrift fuer Auslaendisches Offenliches Recht und Voelkerrecht* (*Heidelberg Journal of International Law*) 1.

[130] J Mayall (ed), (1996) *The New Interventionism, 1991–1994*; see also M Berdal and S Economides, (2007) *United Nations Interventionism, 1991–2004*; LM Howard, (2008) *UN Peacekeeping in Civil Wars*.

[131] See, in particular, Brahimi Report on United Nations Peace Operations, S/2000/809.

[132] A *jus cogens*, or 'peremptory norm' of general international law, is one 'accepted and recognized by the international community as a whole as a norm from which no derogation is permitted and which can be modified only by a subsequent norm of general international law having the same character': Vienna Convention of the Law of Treaties, Art 53. On the difficult issue of modifications of *jus cogens* rules, see, eg J Sztucki, (1974) *Jus Cogens and the Vienna Convention on the Law of Treaties* 109–114; L Hannikainen, (1988) *Peremptory Norms in International Law* 265–269; A Orakhelshvili, (2006) *Peremptory Norms in International Law* 104–133.

[133] A Cassese, 'A Follow-Up: Forcible Humanitarian Countermeasures and *Opinio Necessitatis* (1999) 10(4) *European Journal of International Law* 791; RC Santopadre, 'Deterioration of Limits on the Use of Force and Its Perils: A Rejection of the Kosovo Precedent' (2003) 18 *Saint John's Journal of Legal Commentary* 369.

The first case concerns Liberia, which in fact commenced before the Iraqi episodes. In August 1990 the Economic Community of West African States (ECOWAS), led by Nigeria, intervened in the ongoing civil conflict in Liberia. It did so 'first and foremost to stop the senseless killing of innocent civilian nationals and foreigners, and to help the Liberian People to restore their democratic institutions'.[134]

The action was not originally mandated by the Council, but retroactively endorsed by it.[135] At a later stage, the UN launched a combined UN-regional mission in relation to that state.

The case of Sierra Leone is also invoked as an example of forcible humanitarian action. In that instance ECOWAS was operating under a narrow UN mandate concerning sanctions enforcement.[136] However, in 1998 it forcibly removed the regime of Major Jonny Paul Koroma, who had seized power the previous year. Despite the absence of a mandate for this action, and a subsequent mandate defending the reinstituted government against a further rebel onslaught, ECOWAS's action was again commended by the Council.[137]

In fact, Koroma soon returned to office, along with other so-called 'warlords' under an internationally brokered power-sharing arrangement that was supposed to help end the protracted civil conflict. However, instability and chaos prevailed. In 2000, UK armed forces played a key role in restoring a modicum of order. While UK military personnel were initially introduced to secure the evacuation of foreign nationals, they also patrolled in Freetown and its immediate environs in coordination with the UN mission in the country. A more significant confrontation was triggered by the capture of 11 UK service personnel. In Operation Barras, UK forces penetrated deeper into the hinterland and, in a demonstration of force, defeated the so-called 'West-Side Boys', a splinter faction of the Armed Forces Revolutionary Council that had contributed significantly to insecurity and terror in the country.[138]

While the initial coalition operation in northern and southern Iraq commanded the informal support of the Security Council, and ECOWAS obtained retroactive support for its interventions in Liberia and Sierra Leone, the situation was different in relation to Kosovo. In that instance, the Security Council condemned the repression by Serb authorities in Kosovo, and demanded the withdrawal or cantonment of security forces. It also demanded the accelerated conclusion of a peace agreement between the Yugoslav Government and the Kosovo opposition

---

[134] Letter by the Nigerian delegation to the UN Security Council, summarizing the decision of the Standing Mediation Committee, UN Doc. S/21485, 10 August 1990.

[135] The Council, in its first resolution on the crisis in 1993, expressly commended ECOWAS 'for its efforts to restore peace, security and stability in Liberia': Resolution 788 (1992), para 1.

[136] Resolution 1132 (1997). See L Berger, 'State Practice Evidence of the Humanitarian Intervention Doctrine: The ECOWAS Intervention in Sierra Leone' (2001) 11 *Indiana International and Comparative Law Review* 605.

[137] Resolution 1156 (1998), para 1, which 'welcomed the return to Sierra Leone of its democratically elected President'; and Resolution 1162 (1998), commending ECOWAS. Also Resolution 1231 (1999) relating to the next round of fighting. See also Gray (above n 122) 411ff.

[138] See W Fowler, (2004) *Operation Barras*.

forces. When aggressive counter-insurgency tactics resulted in the displacement of around 300,000 ethnic Albanians in September 1998, NATO threatened to use force. After a provisional peace deal broke down in January 1999, and a peace settlement attempt failed in February/March, NATO launched a massive aerial campaign. The campaign resulted in the displacement of Yugoslav armed forces from the territory, which declared independence in 2008 after a prolonged period of international administration under UN authority.[139]

Not unlike the situation in Iraq in 1991, the initial threat of the use of force by NATO was backed by an informal consensus in the Security Council. The same applied to the Rambouillet peace conference of February 1999, which was also conducted under the shadow of the threat of force by NATO against Yugoslavia should it refuse a negotiated settlement. However, that consensus collapsed along with the peace process. When force was used by NATO, this led to a very sharp confrontation in the Council. Russia noted that the doctrine of humanitarian intervention is 'in no way based on the Charter or other generally recognized rules of international law'.[140] Belarus complained of an unqualified act of aggression, 'no rationale, no reasoning presented by NATO can justify the unlawful use of military force and be deemed acceptable'.[141] China opposed 'interference in the internal affairs of other States, under whatever pretext or in whatever form'.[142] China added that 'it is only the Security Council that can determine whether a given situation threatens international peace and security and can take appropriate action'. India opposed the doctrine of humanitarian intervention:

Among the barrage of justifications we have heard, we have been told that the attacks are meant to prevent violations of human rights. Even if that were to be so, it does not justify unprovoked military aggression. Two wrongs do not make a right.

On the side of the proponents of the use of force in this instance, the United Kingdom offered a formal legal justification:

The action being taken is legal. It is justified as an exceptional measure to prevent an overwhelming humanitarian catastrophe. Under present circumstances in Kosovo, there is convincing evidence that such a catastrophe is imminent. . . . Every means short of force have been tried to avert this situation. In these circumstances, and as an exceptional measure, military intervention is legally justifiable. The force now proposed is directed exclusively at averting a humanitarian catastrophe, and is the minimum judged necessary for that purpose.[143]

However, most other states were less clear in their statements. France, Canada, and Germany referred to humanitarian considerations more generally or drew attention to the relevant Security Council resolutions.[144] Opinion differed among states not directly involved in the issue. Gambia, Malaysia, and Argentina

---

[139] Resolution 1244 (1999).
[140] Provisional Verbatim Record of the UN Security Council, S/PV.3988, 24 March 1999, 4.
[141] Ibid, 15.   [142] Ibid, 12.   [143] Ibid, 12.   [144] Ibid, 5, 9.

appeared to accept that it had become 'necessary' to act outside of the Council.[145] Other states that at least noted the grave humanitarian circumstances were Slovenia, Bahrain, Albania, and Bosnia & Herzegovina. Gabon, on the other hand, indicated its opposition to the use of force as a matter of principle, having preferred further efforts at peaceful resolution.[146] However, an attempt by Belarus, India, and the Russian Federation to obtain condemnation of the action failed decisively. The draft determining that NATO action amounted to a flagrant violation of the UN Charter was not adopted, having received only three votes in favour (China, Namibia, and the Russian Federation) and 12 votes against.[147] The fact that 12 states actively voted against is significant, perhaps confirming the thesis that genuine humanitarian action may at least be immune for international censure

An action brought before the ICJ by Yugoslavia, which sought cessation of the use of force by way of interim measures, was equally unsuccessful.[148] Yugoslavia argued that Article 2(4) of the UN Charter did not leave room for the doctrine of humanitarian intervention. Subsequent practice had not changed this position and no change in customary law had been proven, or even asserted, by NATO states.[149] Most respondents did not engage the argument in substance, as the case did not progress beyond the initial jurisdictional debate. However, Belgium claimed that the existing Security Council resolutions 'provide an unchallengeable basis of the armed intervention. They are clear, and they are based on Chapter VII of the Charter'.[150] Moreover, Belgium also referred to the concept of humanitarian intervention, noting that 'NATO intervened to protect fundamental values enshrined in jus cogens and to prevent an impending catastrophe, recognized as such by the Security Council'. Moreover, NATO had not questioned the political independence and the territorial integrity of Yugoslavia. Accordingly, this 'is an armed humanitarian intervention, compatible with Article 2, paragraph 4, of the Charter, which covers only intervention against the territorial integrity or political independence of a State'. Belgium also invoked the doctrine of necessity defined in what was then Article 33 of the UN International Law Commission Draft Articles on State Responsibility. In this instance, a breach of legal obligation would be justified by the need to safeguard, in the face of grave and imminent peril, values that are higher than those protected by the rule that has been breached.

The debate on humanitarian intervention in Kosovo was carried forward through a number of high-level governmental enquiries. The UK House of Commons Foreign Affairs Committee determined 'at the very least, the doctrine of humanitarian intervention has a tenuous basis in current international

---

[145] Ibid, 10ff.　　　[146] Ibid, 10.　　　[147] S/1999/328, 26 March 1999; ibid, 55.

[148] Yugoslavia initiated proceeding through a letter dated 26 April 1999, adding a request for provisional measures on 28 April: ibid, 321f.

[149] ICJ, Uncorrected transcript, CR/99/14 (translation), 10 May 1999.

[150] ICJ, Uncorrected transcript, CR/99/15 (translation), 10 May 1999.

customary law, and...this renders NATO action legally questionable'.[151] However, the Committee also argued that the intervention was morally justified. Similarly, a Netherlands committee of legal experts, commissioned by the Netherlands Ministry for Foreign Affairs, concluded that 'current international law provides no legal basis for such intervention, and... no such legal basis is yet emerging'.[152] Nevertheless, the committee also noted 'that it is no longer possible to ignore the increasingly perceived need to intervene in situations where fundamental human rights are being or are likely to be violated on a large scale, even if the Security Council is taking no action'. A report of the Danish Institute of International Affairs offered a similar view. It clearly stated that 'under current international law there is no right for states to undertake humanitarian intervention in another state without prior authorization from the UN Security Council'.[153] Yet, this report, too, noted growing support amongst governments and legal experts in favour of a right to intervene. Moreover, the report found that criticism of unauthorized interventions was muted. While this might:[154]

...evidence a greater acceptance that humanitarian intervention without Security Council authorization may be necessary and justified in extreme cases...these events do not amount to the conclusion that a legal right of humanitarian intervention without Security Council authorization has been established under international law. It is premature to assess whether such a right may be emerging under international law.

The high-level Independent International Commission on Kosovo, chaired by Richard Goldstone of South Africa and Carl Tham of Sweden, provided considerable evidence confirming the existence of a humanitarian necessity at the time of the intervention. It highlighted the 'need to close the gap between legality and legitimacy', apparently taking the view that the operation was not strictly legal, but should nevertheless not be condemned.[155]

In scholarship, the overwhelming view concurred with these assessments. While few found the operation to be lawful, most argued that it was nevertheless somehow legitimate.[156]

---

[151] HC Session 1999–200, Foreign Affairs Committee, Fourth Report, Kosovo, Volume 1, at li.

[152] Advisory Committee on Issues of Public International Law, Advisory Council on International Affairs, Joint Advisory Report, *Humanitarian Intervention*, Report No 13, 13 April 2000.

[153] Danish Institute of International Affairs, *Humanitarian Intervention* (1999) 123.

[154] Ibid.

[155] Independent International Commission on Kosovo, *Kosovo Report* (2000) 10.

[156] For example S Blockmans, 'Moving into UN Chartered Waters: An Emerging Right to Unilateral Humanitarian Intervention' (1999) 12 *Leiden Journal of International Law* 759; A Cassese, 'Ex Iniuria Ius Oritur: Are We Moving Towards International Legitimation of Forcible Humanitarian Countermeasures in the World Community?' (1999) 10(1) *European Journal of International Law* 23; H Daniel, 'The Kosovo Intervention: Legal Analysis and a More Persuasive Paradigm' (2002) 13 *European Journal of International Law* 597; N Kirsch, 'Review Essay: Legality, Morality, and the Dilemma of Humanitarian Intervention after Kosovo' (2002) 13(1) *European Journal of International Law* 323; JS Morton, 'The Legality of NATO's Intervention in Yugoslavia in 1999: Implications for the Progressive Development of International Law' (2002) 9 *ILSA Journal*

VI. Emerging International Standards?

For the upcoming General Assembly session of the autumn of 1999, UN Secretary-General Kofi Annan proposed a debate, with a view to reaching a consensus on how concerns for human rights and for state sovereignty could be balanced.[157] At the outset of the session, the Secretary-General described the:[158]

…dilemma of what has been called 'humanitarian intervention': on the one side, the question of the legitimacy of an action taken by a regional organization without a United Nations mandate; on the other, the universally recognized imperative of effectively halting gross and systematic violations of human rights with grave humanitarian consequences.

The Secretary-General noted that while the world cannot stand aside when gross and systematic violations of human rights are taking place, intervention must be based on legitimate and universal principles. He then admitted that:[159]

This developing norm in favour of intervention to protect civilians from wholesale slaughter will no doubt continue to pose profound challenges to the international community. Any such evolution in our understanding of state sovereignty and individual sovereignty will, in some quarters, be met with distrust, scepticism and even hostility. But it is an evolution that we should welcome.

In the debate that followed in the Plenary of the General Assembly, a significant divergence of views was discernible. Some states continued to attack the very

---

of International and Comparative Law 75; A Pellet, 'Brief Remarks on the Unilateral Use of Force' (2000) 11(2) *European Journal of International Law* 385; B Simma, 'NATO, the UN and the Use of Force: Legal Aspects' (1999) 10(1) *European Journal of International Law* 1; J Currie, 'NATO's Humanitarian Intervention in Kosovo: Making or Breaking International Law?' (1998) 36 *Canadian Yearbook of International Law* 303; T Gazzini, 'NATO Coercive Military Activities in the Yugoslav Crisis (1992–1999)' (2001) 12 *European Journal of International Law* 391; C Greenwood, 'Humanitarian Intervention: The Case of Kosovo' (1999) 10 *Finnish Yearbook of International Law* 141; DH Joyner, 'The Kosovo Intervention: Legal Analysis and a More Persuasive Paradigm' (2002) 13 *European Journal of International Law* 597; D Kritsiotis, 'The Kosovo Crisis and NATO's Application of Armed Force against the Federal Republic of Yugoslavia' (2000) 49 ICLQ 330; HB McCullough, 'Intervention in Kosovo: Legal? Effective?' (2001) 7 *ILSA Journal of International and Comparative Law* 299; J Merriam, 'Kosovo and the Law of Humanitarian Intervention' (2001) 33 *Case Western Reserve Journal of International Law* 111; JA Miller, 'NATO's Use of Force in the Balkans' (2001) 45(1–2) *New York Law School Law Review* 91; W Moorman, 'Humanitarian Intervention and International Law in the Case of Kosovo' (2002) 36 *New England Law Review* 775; GK Walker, 'Principles for Collective Humanitarian Intervention to Succor Other Countries' Imperiled Indigenous Nationals' (2992) 18 *American University International Law Review* 35; NJ Wheeler, 'Humanitarian Intervention after Kosovo' (2001) 77(1) *International Affairs* 113; D Wippman, 'Kosovo and the Limits of International Law' (2001) 25 *Fordham International Law Journal* 129; R Zacklin, 'Beyond Kosovo: the United Nations and Humanitarian Intervention' (2001) 41 *Virginia Journal of International Law* 923.

[157] Kofi Annan, 'Two Concepts of Sovereignty', *The Economist*, 18 September 1999, 49.
[158] Verbatim Record of the Fourth Plenary Session, A/54/PV.4, 2.   [159] Ibid, 3.

notion of intervention on humanitarian grounds.[160] China directly attacked the Secretary-General's thesis of a changing balance between sovereignty and human rights, arguing that human rights are:[161]

...in essence, the internal affair of a given country...when the sovereignty of a country is put in jeopardy, its human rights can hardly be protected effectively....Sovereign equality, mutual respect for State sovereignty and non-interference in the internal affairs of others are the basic principles governing international relations today. In spite of the major changes in the post-cold war international situation, these principles are by no means out of date. Any deviation from or violation of these principles would destroy the universally recognized norms governing international relations and would lead to the rule of hegemonism; if the notion of 'might is right' should prevail, a new gun-boat policy would wreak havoc, the sovereignty and independence by virtue of which some small and weak countries protect themselves would be jeopardized and international peace and stability would be seriously endangered.

Others had sympathy for the need to counter grave humanitarian emergencies, but also argued that the Security Council must remain the 'sole organ competent to decide on the action to be taken in cases where the principle of non-intervention needs to be interpreted with due regard to the existence of violations of international humanitarian law'.[162] France, one of the participants of the Kosovo operation, emphasized that there can be circumstances when an urgent humanitarian situation dictates that immediate action must be taken. However, in the view of the French delegate, such an approach:

...must remain exceptional. We must take care, as in the case of Kosovo, to reintegrate this action into the context of the Charter. Our fundamental rule is that it is for the Security Council to resolve crisis situations.

Germany, while declaring the Secretary-General's argument on sovereignty as 'brilliant', also effectively denied unilateral humanitarian intervention. It emphasized the very special circumstances of the situation in Kosovo, adding that the action:

...must not set a precedent for weakening the United Nations Security Council's monopoly on authorizing the use of legal international force. Nor must it become a licence to use external force under the pretext of humanitarian assistance. This would open the door to the arbitrary use of power and anarchy and throw the world back to the nineteenth century.

Similarly, Jamaica argued that the principles of international law affecting the sovereignty of states and the use of force should not be brushed aside, giving rise

---

[160] For example Mexico, Verbatim Record of the Eleventh Plenary Session, A/54/PV.11, 32; Russia, Verbatim Record of the Sixth Plenary Session, A/54/PV.6, 12; Iraq, Verbatim Record of the Twelfth Plenary Session, A/54/PV.12, 28; Vietnam, Verbatim Record of the Sixteenth Plenary Session, A/54/PV.16, 17; Libya, Verbatim Record of the Nineteenth Plenary Session, A/54/PV.19, 16.   [161] Verbatim Record of the Eighth Plenary Session, A/54/PV.8, 16.
[162] Guatemala, ibid.

to a right to unilateral action.[163] However, there was also understanding for the need to act where the Security Council was unable to do so.[164] New Zealand indicated that 'collective action to try to put a stop to a humanitarian disaster involving genocide and the most serious crimes against humanity should never be held hostage to the veto'.[165] Sweden appeared strongly to endorse the primacy of the Security Council and the need to obtain a mandate for forcible action, otherwise 'we run the risk of anarchy in international relations'.[166] Nevertheless, Sweden also agreed that:

When human life is threatened on a massive scale, it is not possible to remain passive. Humanitarian intervention has to be assessed on a case-by-case basis, in view of the value at stake and whether all other means have been exhausted. The effects on international law and international security at large have to be considered as well.

Saudi Arabia stated that:

... resort to military force without a United Nations mandate to resolve such problems might not be the ideal way to settle international crises, but it becomes an unavoidable necessity whenever the Security Council, due to disunity and disagreements between its permanent members fails to fulfil its role in maintaining the world peace and security.

Italy supported the concept of developing rules that would govern the new relationship between sovereignty and human rights.[167]

The Netherlands engaged with the thesis of the Secretary-General in the most direct way:[168]

Since 1945, the world has witnessed a gradual shift in that balance, making respect for human rights more and more mandatory and respect for sovereignty less and less stringent. An elaborate body of international human rights law has come to counterbalance the dictates of paragraphs 4 and 7 of Article 2. Today, human rights have come to outrank sovereignty. Increasingly, the prevailing interpretation of the Charter is that it aims to protect individual human beings, not to protect those who abuse them. Today, we regard it as a generally accepted rule of international law that no sovereign state has the right to terrorize its own citizens. Indeed, if the Charter were to be written today, there would be an Article 2(8) saying that nothing contained in the present Charter shall authorize Member States to terrorize their own people.

---

[163] Verbatim Record of the Seventeenth Plenary Session, A/54/PV.17, 3.

[164] For example Georgia, Verbatim Record of the Fourth Plenary Session, A/54/PV.4, 24; Denmark, Verbatim Record of the Ninth Plenary Session, A/54/PV.9, 37.

[165] Verbatim Record of the Seventeenth Plenary Session, A/54/PV.17, 11, although this might also be taken to indicate only opposition to the veto, while not necessarily endorsing unilateral action should a veto occur.

[166] Verbatim Record of the Seventh Plenary Session, A/54/PV.7, 32.

[167] Verbatim Record of the Eighth Plenary Session, A54/PV.8, 20f; see also the interesting discourse offered by Singapore, Verbatim Record of the Twelfth Plenary Session, A/54/PV.12, 24. Slovenia indicated that a search for criteria for intervention needs to be mounted, Verbatim Record of the Thirteenth Plenary Session, A/54/PV.13, 15.

[168] Verbatim Record of the Thirteenth Plenary Session, A/54/PV.13, 23.

Hungary also endorsed the view that the:

... traditional concept of the principle of national sovereignty is undergoing a progressive evolution ... national sovereignty is becoming less acceptable as a justification for Governments in cases of serious violations within their countries of universally recognized international legal standards.

Poland followed suit, expressly accepting humanitarian intervention as a means of last resort, given that 'the walls of sovereignty cannot be used to conceal and legitimize the abuse of human rights and fundamental freedoms. Sovereignty cannot mean impunity for genocide and human rights abuses'.[169] Uganda formally declared:[170]

It is vital for all of us to recognize the sanctity of the right to life. We are glad to note that the evolution of international law on human rights no longer condones country's internal affairs [sic]. The principle of non-interference in the internal affairs of States has been so fundamentally eroded that the international community should now openly adopt a definitive convention which will permit instant intervention in cases of massive threats to the right to life.

The UN Secretary-General himself commented on this debate in his subsequent Annual Report to the General Assembly. Referring to the cases of Rwanda and Bosnia and Herzegovina (Srebrenica), he indicated that 'if the reason to my address last year to the General Assembly is any guide, I fear that we may still prove unable to give a credible answer to the question of what happens next time we are faced with a comparable crime against humanity'.[171]

An answer was offered by another international high-level commission to address the problem of humanitarian intervention in the wake of Kosovo, supported and sponsored by Canada. The Commission on Intervention and State Sovereignty identified a 'responsibility to protect'. In its view:[172]

- State sovereignty implies responsibility, and the primary responsibility of protection of its people lies with the state itself.
- Where a population is suffering serious harm as a result of internal war, insurgency, repression, or state failure, and the state in question is unwilling or unable to halt or avert it, the principle of non-intervention yields to the international responsibility to protect.

The Committee emphasized, however, the expectation that in principle this responsibility should be exercised through the UN Security Council. It considered the issue of unilateral humanitarian intervention, arguing that it would be

---

[169] Verbatim Record of the Seventeenth Plenary Session, A/54/PV.17, 6.
[170] Verbatim Record of the Fifty-fourth Plenary Session, A/54/PV.54, 34.
[171] *Report of the Secretary General on the Work of the Organization*, A.55/1, 5.
[172] International Commission on Intervention and State Sovereignty, *The Responsibility to Protect: Report of the International Commission on Intervention and State Sovereignty* (2001) ii.

impossible to reach a consensus on the matter. From this finding, it drew the conclusion that pressure on the Council had increased to ensure, through its own action, that individual states or ad hoc coalitions did not feel constrained to act in the most extreme circumstances.[173]

The 'responsibility to protect' doctrine was taken up by the UN Secretary-General—who created the post of Special Adviser on the subject—and by the UN General Assembly. Most recently, in the 2005 World Summit outcome document, universal adherence to this doctrine was confirmed. In line with the doctrine, the General Assembly placed primary responsibility to protect populations from atrocities on their own governments. However, it confirmed that:[174]

…we are prepared to take collective action, in a timely and decisive manner, through the Security Council, in accordance with the Charter, including Chapter VII, on a case by case basis and in cooperation with regional organization as appropriate, should peaceful means be inadequate and national authorities are manifestly failing to protect their populations from genocide, war crimes, ethnic cleansing and crimes against humanity.

In opposition to the original report on the responsibility to protect[175] and (perhaps) the aims of the then UN Secretary-General, Kofi Annan, there is no clarification here relating to a possible unilateral right of action. Emphasis is placed entirely on collective action through the Security Council.

The Institut de Droit International (IDI) was also unable to form a clear view on the issue when it revisited the issue of forcible humanitarian action. In its 1999 Berlin session, it confirmed that the UN organs can take action:

In case of systematic and massive violations of humanitarian law or fundamental human rights, States, acting individually or collectively, are entitled to take diplomatic, economic and other measures towards any party to the armed conflict which has violated its obligations, provided such measures are permitted under international law.

There was no clarification of what exactly was permitted. In 2003, at Bruges, the IDI confirmed that individual states do not have the right arbitrarily and unjustifiably to reject a bona fide offer exclusively intended to offer humanitarian assistance. In case of such a rejection, however, it would be up to the Security Council to adopt 'necessary measures'.[176] Most recently, at its Santiago session, members of the IDI were unable to agree on the legal issues concerning forcible humanitarian action. Expressly reserving the issue of the lawfulness or otherwise of such action, the IDI stipulated instead that, if military action is undertaken, the sole objective of such action would be to put an end to genocide, large-scale crimes against humanity, or large-scale war crimes.[177]

---

[173] Ibid, 54f.
[174] 2005 World Summit Outcome, A/60/L.1, 15 September 2005.
[175] Above n 173.
[176] Available at <http://www.idi-iil.org/idiE/resolutionsE/2003_bru_03_en.PDF>.
[177] Available at <http://www.idi-iil.org/idiE/resolutionsE/2007_san_03_en.pdf>.

VII. Conclusion

What, then, was the overall impact on international law of forcible humanitarian action relating to Iraq? It may be argued that this was an atypical instance of the use of force, directed against a pariah state at the very point when it had suffered a major defeat—and a defeat that was administered in the context of collective security. Hence, the world at large appeared to have lined up against Iraq, and there was no diplomatic backing or strong appetite to defend its legal position. One might also note the comparative scarcity of academic comment when compared to the Kosovo episode.[178] Nevertheless, Iraq did have a significant impact. While it is generally noted that Resolution 688 (1991) did not give Chapter VII authorization for the use of force, it is widely overlooked that the forcible action that ensued was, nevertheless, based on an informal consensus in the Council. Moreover, the determination by the Council that Iraqi repression of its own population was unacceptable, and the demand that it must cease, was an important step forward in Council practice. This also marked the beginning of a trend, now consolidated, which confirmed the authority of the Security Council to take Chapter VII action in instances of this kind, even if it did not do so expressly in Resolution 688 (1991).

In terms of the development of international doctrine, Iraq, and, to a lesser extent, Liberia and initial action concerning Sierra Leone, were the only precedents that could be used in support of the argument that a new justification for the use of force was available in international custom by the time of the Kosovo operation.[179] The UK's pronouncements in this respect served to crystallize the purported new rule, notwithstanding subsequent clarification by the FCO that this had not in fact been intended. In this instance, the position of a single state— and apparently one widely misunderstood—did have a very significant effect. True, it did not assure victory for those arguing in favour of humanitarian intervention. But previously, proponents of the doctrine had been relatively isolated, and at times regarded as idealists arguing on the basis of concepts, rather than state practice accepted as law. The UK's willingness to argue formally that action in Iraq was justified as a matter of right overturned this presumption. Forcible humanitarian action was now at least a respectable position to take.[180]

---

[178] Compare the references above, n 156.

[179] For example, C Greenwood 'Pre-emptive Use of Force' (2003) 4 San Diego International Law Journal 7.

[180] Indeed, the debate is now far more diverse and vibrant than before: see, eg FK Abiew, (1999) *The Evolution of the Doctrine and Practice of Humanitarian Intervention*; S Chesterman, (2003) *Just War or Just Peace? Humanitarian Intervention and International Law*; EA Heinze, 'Humanitarian Intervention: Morality and International Law on Intolerable Violations of Human Rights' (2004) 8(4) *International Journal of Human Rights* 471; M Brenfors, 'The Legality of Unilateral Humanitarian Intervention: A Defence' (2000) 69 *Nordic Journal of International Law* 413; IM Marcus, 'Humanitarian Intervention without Borders: Belligerent Occupation or Colonization?' (2002) 25 *Houston Journal of International Law* 99; C Poltak, 'Humanitarian Intervention: A Contemporary

The NATO armed action against Yugoslavia in 1999 disrupted what might otherwise have been considered a gradual consolidation of practice (if not *opinio juris*) around the Iraqi precedent. The sharp division among states undermined the argument of an emerging consensus in favour of intervention. However, this division was not as pronounced as was initially assumed. In the subsequent, broader debate about intervention launched by the UN Secretary-General in the autumn of 1999, there was some opposition to the intervention thesis, but also support from a surprising range of states. This positive momentum was exploited through the 'responsibility to protect' initiative. In the end, that initiative was tamed by focusing it exclusively on the expectation that the Security Council would take action in the face of genocide, ethnic cleansing and crimes against humanity. Unilateral action was not addressed. Nevertheless, the acceptance of 'responsibility to protect' as a principle was important, as it confirmed an emerging understanding of the changing notion of sovereignty in this respect. This has not led to a guarantee of action by the Council in the face of severe humanitarian emergencies (Myanmar/Sudan), but it has given credence to the argument that forcible humanitarian action may not, in fact, require a new legal rule justifying it. Instead, it may be based on more conceptual considerations concerning the state and its relation with its constituents that are inherent within the international system. One such view accepts that there is no tension between sovereignty and human rights. Indeed, this view denies that forcible humanitarian action involves the prohibition of the use of force at all, as action is being taken on behalf of the true sovereign—the people.[181]

According to this view, international law recognizes that a government or effective authorities can lose the power to represent the state fully under certain circumstances. This phenomenon is becoming increasingly evident in international practice in a number of areas, such as responses to counter-constitutional coups, the recognition of internationally privileged self-determination movements, and the disenfranchisement of effective authorities claiming to represent populations under their control in circumstances of civil conflict. One additional area of application of this doctrine is forcible humanitarian action. Where a government forcibly exterminates a constitutionally relevant segment of its population, or denies to it that which is necessary for its survival, or seeks forcibly to

Interpretation of the Charter of the United Nations' (2002) 60(2) *University of Toronto Faculty of Law Review* 1; A Roberts, 'The So-Called "Right" of Humanitarian Intervention' (2000) 3 *Yearbook of International Humanitarian Law* 3; JE Rytter, 'Humanitarian Intervention without the Security Council, from San Francisco to Kosovo—and Beyond' (2001) 70 *Nordic Journal of International Law* 121; J Welsh (ed), (2004) *Humanitarian Intervention and International Relations*; N Wheeler, (2000) *Saving Strangers*; P Alston and E Macdonald, (2008) *Human Rights, Intervention, and the Use of Force*; JL Holzgrefe and RO Keohane, (2003) *Humanitarian Intervention*.

[181] This view was first advanced by M Weller, 'Sovereignty and Suffering: The Legal Framework' in J Harris (ed), (1995) *The Politics of Humanitarian Intervention* 35; see also M Weller, 'Access to Victims: Reconceiving the Right to Intervene' in WP Heere, (1999) *International Law and The Hague's 750th Anniversary* 353.

displace it, it cannot claim to represent that population. The assumption that effective control over territory and population equals the exclusive power of the state to speak on the international plane is altered in such circumstances. Instead of exclusively allocating this power to the government or effective authority, international action can be taken directly on behalf of a population faced with such an emergency. It is preferable for the UN Security Council, or another objective, best-placed agency to determine that a state of fundamental dissociation exists, and to identify authoritatively the nature and extent of the action that must be taken on behalf of the population in question. However, individual states, coalitions, or regional organizations or arrangements can act directly where such guidance is not available and an immediate response is required.

The application of this theory is particularly well illustrated by both the Iraq and the Kosovo episodes. In Iraq, action was taken in relation to two large population segments exposed to attack from their own government. This action was taken directly on behalf of the populations concerned, to ensure their minimum interests of survival and safety. These aims had been authoritatively identified by the Council in relation to the north, and by the UN Special Rapporteur on Human Rights in Iraq—a best-placed, international agency—in relation to the south. In Yugoslavia, action in accordance with the minimum requirements of a large, constitutionally relevant segment of the population was carried out by NATO, which carefully tailored its action to meet the essential requirements identified by the UN Security Council, demanding that Belgrade cease repression in Kosovo, withdraw forces, and accept a political settlement. At the conclusion of the conflict, the UN Security Council took over. It accepted that Belgrade could not, under the circumstances it had generated, fully represent and govern in relation to Kosovo. Instead, it established an international operation to act temporarily on behalf of the local sovereign—the population—to the exclusion of the formerly effective Belgrade authorities.

While the Iraq episode marked the beginning of arguments in favour of forcible humanitarian action in the post-Cold War environment, it also served to confirm some of the fears of those who held that the doctrine had to be opposed at all costs, given the risk of its abuse. It is regrettable that enforcement of the no-fly zones was gradually conflated with other aims pursued by the only two states that remained in the international coalition—the United States and United Kingdom. Of particular note was a widening of claims to self-defence while patrolling the zones. Ordinarily, the right extended only to defence against enemy aircraft or air-to-ground installations at the point of attacking coalition planes. This was made manifest by radar lock-on. Subsequently, the detection (painting) of over-flying planes was considered sufficient indication of imminent attack. This was later expanded to the mere fact that enemy radar was active. Subsequently, the very existence of anti-air installations within the no-fly zones rendered them liable to attack. Finally, this was extended from the no-fly zones (themselves significantly expanded without any visible justification in 1996) to the wider Iraqi anti-air and command and control infrastructure, also outside the zones.[182]

In addition to the degradation of the understanding of the conditions of self-defence, this process also undermined the humanitarian action argument. It became increasingly difficult to detect the overwhelming humanitarian emergency that was purportedly being addressed by the operation. The UK Attorney General was informed that there was no such emergency at the time, but one might occur if the zones were withdrawn. The evident abuse of the humanitarian argument from 1996 onwards, when a gradually increasing campaign to diminish and degrade the Iraqi military was conducted, served to undermine the position of those supporting the doctrine on principle. The fact that the no-fly zones were used to prepare the ground for the eventual invasion of Iraq in 2003 added to that result.

---

[182] On this progression, see C Gray, 'From Unity to Polarization: International Law and the Use of Force Against Iraq' (2002) 13 *European Journal of International Law* 1, 16. See, for instance, UK practice in 2002, claiming strict self-defence, but also confirming that action was taken against the 'integrated air defence system': (2002) 73 BYIL 863.

4

The UNSCOM Inspection Regime, Material Breaches, and Desert Fox

The implementation of the disarmament obligations imposed upon Iraq occupied the United Nations and key governments throughout the 1990s,[1] during which period the threat or use of force was present. Initially, this process was administered informally, through cooperation of the UN Secretary-General and the UN Special Commission (UNSCOM) arms inspectors, the UN Security Council, and the three key members of the international coalition that had removed Iraq from Kuwait: the United States, the United Kingdom, and France. However, the consensus supporting that action started to crack once the divergent interests of UN Member States, and Iraq's persistent refusal to cooperate, began to take their toll. The policy of force thus became more controversial as time progressed.

I. The Cease-fire and the Disarmament Obligations

The Security Council adopted the cease-fire terms for Iraq in Resolution 687 (1991). The cease-fire entered into force upon Iraq's acceptance of those terms on 11 April 1991.[2] Resolution 687 (1991) was adopted under Chapter VII of the UN Charter, 'bearing in mind its objective of restoring international peace and security in the area as set out in recent Council resolutions'.[3] Clearly, the obligations contained in the Resolution, and in subsequent Chapter VII resolutions

---

[1] ML Cornell, 'A Decade of Failure: The Legality and Efficacy of United Nations Actions in the Elimination of Iraqi Weapons of Mass Destruction' (2001) 16 *Connecticut Journal of International Law* 325; LF Damrosch, 'The Permanent Five as Enforcers of Controls on Weapons of Mass Destruction: Building on the Iraq "Precedent"' (2002) 13(1) *European Journal of International Law* 305; CJ Oudraat, 'UNSCOM: Between Iraq and a Hard Place' (2002) 13(1) *European Journal of International Law* 139; D Fleck, 'Developments of the Law of Arms Control as a Result of the Iraq-Kuwait Conflict' (2002) 13(1) *European Journal of International Law* 105; SD Murphy, 'Efforts to Address Iraqi Compliance with UN Weapons Inspections' (2002) 96 AJIL 956; TM Franck, 'Inspections and Their Enforcement: A Modest Proposal' (2002) 96(4) AJIL 899.

[2] Letter from the President of the Security Council to the Permanent Representative of Iraq to the United Nations, S/22485, 11 April 1991: 'The members of the Security Council have, accordingly, asked me to note that the conditions established in paragraph 33 of resolution 687 (1991) have been meet and that the formal ceasefire referred to in paragraph 33 of that resolution is therefore effective'.   [3] Resolution 687 (1991), penultimate preambular paragraph.

on this issue,[4] were in themselves binding upon Iraq, by virtue of Articles 24 and 25 of the UN Charter. The power of the Security Council to impose arms control terms upon a state, in apparent derogation from that state's perception of sovereignty, cannot be questioned in this instance. The Resolution arose from a genuine breach of international peace and security, duly certified in accordance with Article 39 of the Charter.[5] It was adopted in accordance with the procedural requirements of the Charter, by 12 votes to 1, with two abstentions.[6] In fact, while protesting against its terms in great detail, Iraq formally accepted the Resolution.[7] This decision was ratified by the Iraqi National Assembly.[8]

However, in its letter of acceptance, Iraq indicated that it had 'no choice but to accept this resolution'.[9] It added numerous caveats and reservations, claiming to have been forced into acceptance. Nevertheless, Iraq could not rely on protests made at the time of acceptance, and, indeed, subsequently, to try and undermine the legal validity of its consent. Baghdad itself relied upon the legal regime instituted as a result of having accepted the Resolution and cooperated in relation to most of its elements. Neither could Iraq argue that the Resolution was imposed in violation of *jus cogens* rules relating to the threat or use of force. After all, the text emanated from a Chapter VII decision taken by the Council in the exercise of its primary responsibility for the maintenance of international peace and security. It was the outcome of Iraq's own unlawful armed action against Kuwait. Hence, the legal force of the arms control obligations incumbent upon Iraq was not only based on Chapter VII powers of the Security Council but also on state consent.[10] Moreover, the obligations relating to disarmament and arms control were reinforced in supplementary exchanges of letters and status agreements with UNSCOM and its successor, the UN Monitoring, Verification and Inspection Commission (UNMOVIC) and the International Atomic Energy Agency (IAEA).[11]

The terms of the cease-fire foresaw three phases in the disarming of Iraq in relation to weapons of mass destruction (WMD), related items, and delivery vehicles (missiles) of a range above 150km.[12] First, Iraq was required to make a full

---

[4] See especially UN Security Council Resolutions 699 (1991), 707 (1991), and 715 (1991).

[5] Resolution 660 (1990), penultimate preambular paragraph.

[6] Record of the 2981st meeting of the UN Security Council, S/PV.2981, 3 April 1991, 82.

[7] Identical Letters from the Permanent Representative of Iraq to the United Nations Addressed Respectively to the Secretary-General and the President of the Security Council, 4 April 1991, S/22456, 8 April 1991, reprinted in M Weller, (1993) *Iraq and Kuwait: The Hostilities and their Aftermath* 397, final paragraph.

[8] Letter from the Permanent Representative of Iraq to the United Nations Addressed to the President of the Security Council, S/22480, 11 April 1991, in Weller (above n 7) 400.

[9] Above n 7.

[10] Compare, for instance, the arms control obligations imposed upon West Germany through the Western European Union arms control regime after World War II.

[11] Beginning with exchanges of letters between Iraq and the UN Secretary-General of 6 and 17 May 1991, available at <http://www.un.org/Depts/unmovic/new/documents/letters.pdf>.

[12] These are set out in section C of Resolution 687 (1991).

declaration of proscribed items within 15 days of the adoption of the Resolution. Within 45 days, a plan was to be devised which would provide for the destruction of those items within a period of another 45 days. Within 120 days, a long-term monitoring plan was to have been approved, which would ensure that Iraq was not able to acquire proscribed weapons in the future. However, in reality this plan went unimplemented. Iraq complied hesitantly with the requirements of the UN and IAEA weapons inspectors. No full declaration of prohibited items was made. Instead, partial declarations were offered, roughly coinciding with the advancing level of knowledge achieved through the work of inspections teams on the ground, aerial monitoring, and national technical means. A cat-and-mouse game developed over access to sensitive facilities, the capturing of documentary evidence, and the search for proscribed weaponry.[13] UNSCOM and IAEA teams were repeatedly denied access to Iraqi installations. There were even attempts to retrieve documents seized by arms inspectors, and other obstructions were put in their way.[14] Iraq also threatened, at an early stage, the safety of Special Commission aerial surveillance flights over Iraq.[15] The Security Council responded to these developments by dispatching High Level Missions to Iraq and reinforcing Iraq's obligations in further resolutions and presidential statements.[16]

II. Development of the Theory of Material Breach and Initial Uses of Force

This failure of Iraq to comply unconditionally with the Resolution led to the question of possible remedies, including the use of force. It appeared impossible to renew the consensus within the Security Council and obtain a fresh mandate for coalition forces. Russia and China were no longer inclined to allow the passage of such express authorization. However, in Resolution 707 (1991), the Council had already determined that Iraq's serious violations constituted a 'material breach of the relevant provisions of resolution 687 (1991) which established a cease fire and provided the conditions essential to the restoration of peace and security in the region'.[17] In February 1991, the Council noted a 'further material breach' in a presidential statement, also warning Iraq 'of the serious consequences of con-tinued material breaches of resolution 687 (1991)'.[18] In July 1992, the Council

---

[13] On the early phase of implementation, see Weller (above n 7) Ch 12.
[14] These early developments are detailed in ibid, 499–536.
[15] Note by the President of the Security Council dated 10 April 1992, S/23803, 10 April 1992, reprinted in Weller (above n 7) 533.
[16] In particular UN Security Council Resolutions 707 (1991) and 715 (1991). Reference to some particularly relevant presidential statements will be made below.
[17] Resolution 707 (1991) para 1.
[18] Statement by the President of the Security Council, S/23663, 28 February 1992.

reminded Iraq, in a further presidential statement, that the disarmament provisions had been agreed to by Iraq as 'a condition precedent to the establishment of a formal cease-fire'.[19]

These statements reflected the legal position developing within the UN Secretariat in August 1992.[20] It was argued that the cease-fire, established according to Resolution 687 (1991), may have been a formal one, but it was not necessarily definitive. It could be suspended if Iraq failed to comply with essential obligations contained in the Resolution. In that case, the authority to use force established in Resolution 678 (1990) would revive. However, it was also made clear that the Security Council controlled this process.

Before addressing the application of this proposition, it needs to be assessed in principle. The revival argument, however convenient it may have appeared at the time, was seriously deficient in a number of important aspects.

A. Flaws in the revival argument

The revival argument was daring, or perhaps indeed reckless, in that it disregarded important facts concerning the Security Council resolutions on which it was based, was rooted in major confusions relating to general international law as it applied to them, and allowed room for abuse in terms of its implementation process.

1. *The relevant resolutions*

In order to revive authority to use force, that authority must exist in the first place. Hence, the first question was whether the legal authority granted in Resolution 678 (1990) could conceivably cover the enforcement of arms control obligations established in Resolution 687 (1991).

Resolution 678 (1990) authorized the use of all necessary means to uphold and implement Security Council Resolution 660 (1990) and all subsequent relevant resolutions and to restore international peace and security in the area. Resolution 660 (1990) required the Iraqi withdrawal from Kuwait. There was no argument to the effect that the reference to 'all subsequent relevant resolutions' granted additional authority in relation to other resolutions adopted before Resolution 678 (1990), for instance relating to the return of stolen or looted property. However, it was subsequently asserted that the reference to the restoration of international peace and security furnished additional authority for the use of force, beyond the liberation of Kuwait.

---

[19] Statement by the President of the Security Council, S/24240, 6 July 1992.
[20] That advice has not been made public. This section draws heavily on the account of former Assistant Secretary-General for Legal Affairs, Ralph Zacklin, in (2008) 'The United Nations Secretariat and the Use of Force in a Unipolar World', Hersch Lauterpacht Memorial Lectures, and R Zacklin, (2010) *The United Nations Secretariat and the Use of Force in a Unipolar World* 18ff.

In reality, the reference in the Resolution concerned the collective security dimension of the authorization, placing it within the framework of UN Charter, Chapter VII action.[21] The reference was included in the Resolution in deference to the Korean precedent, which had used a similar formula:[22]

Recommends that the Members of the United Nations furnish such assistance to the Republic of Korea as may be necessary to repel the armed attack and to restore international peace and security in the area.

As noted in Chapter 2, the Korean precedent shares certain features with the Kuwait episode. In both cases, action by the Security Council was underpinned by the right of self-defence. Collective security action, as it were, reinforced collective self-defence. The reference to international peace and security in the area points to the fact that the Council was exercising its powers in response to threats to the peace, breaches of the peace, or acts of aggression. According to Article 39 of the UN Charter, it is for the Council to decide what measures shall be taken 'to maintain or restore international peace and security'. As Edwin D Williamson, the then US State Department Legal Adviser, explained:[23]

The last phrase in Resolution 678 was borrowed from Resolution 83, which was passed shortly after the North Koreans invaded South Korea in June of 1950. In that case, it was the basis for the United Nations' authority to push North Korea back beyond the original border rather than having to stop at the 38th parallel. Similarly, *the goal of Resolution 678 was to get Iraq to pull back to its August 1 position*. But once the battle had started, we did not think that Resolution 678 required the coalition to stop at the Kuwait-Iraq border.

However, as Williamson clarified, not having to stop at the border had a tactical meaning. Restoring peace and security in the area did permit military operations to reach into Iraq proper if necessary to liberate Kuwait, but only towards that end, during the ongoing self-defence operation. It was not meant to establish open-ended authority to use force for further aims, as yet unspecified and extending into the indefinite future.[24] This was also the UK view:[25]

At an early stage, the British government had indicated that it did not regard Resolution 678 (1990) as restricting the field of operations to Kuwait itself, but any extension would be on the basis that it was necessary to achieve the liberation of Kuwait, not to achieve any purpose beyond the Resolution, in particular not to overthrow Saddam Hussein.

---

[21] See the UK representative on the adoption of Resolution 687 (1991), S/PV.2981, 3 April 1991, 111ff.   [22] Resolution 83 (1950).
[23] The Bush (41st) Administration, in MP Scharf and PR Williams, (2010) *Shaping Foreign Policy in Times of Crisis: The Role of International Law and the State Department Legal Adviser* 87f (emphasis added).
[24] Ibid, 89: 'I was worried very much about our ability to go in to Iraq to take further action, because…Resolution 678 only allowed us to use force to restore peace and security in the area'.
[25] C Warbrick, 'Current Developments: Public International Law' (1991) 40 ICLQ 965, 966ff.

The Netherlands inquiry into the war with Iraq later confirmed that it would be difficult to accept within the system of collective peace and security as laid down in the UN Charter, that member states 'acquire a mandate to use force that is unlimited in time and geographical area'.[26] This view was also confirmed at the point of the adoption of the Resolution: 'The Council has certainly not authorized action outside the context of its resolutions 660 (1990), 662 (1990) and 664 (1990)'.[27] (Resolutions 662 and 664 concerned the purported annexation of Kuwait.) Moreover, the limits of the mandate, and its failure to offer authority 'to go to Baghdad' in pursuit of wider aims, has been consistently confirmed by the key protagonists ever since. Former President George HW Bush and his National Security Adviser Brent Scowcroft indicated expressly that 'going in and occupying Iraq, thus unilaterally exceeding the UN mandate, would have destroyed the precedent of international response to aggression we hoped to establish'.[28]

Colin Powell added that the United States was unwilling to 'move the goalposts' as it was heading an international coalition 'carrying out a clearly defined UN Mission. That mission was accomplished'.[29] From the UK side, the then Prime Minister John Major added:[30]

When the conflict began, it did so under international law. UN Security Council Resolutions set out the war aims, and on that basis the House of Commons and other political assemblies supported the liberation of Kuwait. ... The Resolutions did not support the destruction of the Iraqi regime, for the very good reason that no Arab nation would have joined the coalition against Iraq if they had. There was no Resolution empowering the allies to go into Baghdad and drag Saddam out by the heels.

It is, therefore, disingenuous to argue that the original mandate granted in Resolution 678 (1990) extended beyond the liberation of Kuwait. If that is true, it is also not possible that a revival of that mandate at a subsequent stage could justify action in pursuit of additional aims.

Other issues arise. Resolution 678 (1990) assigned the authority to use force to 'member states cooperating with the government of Kuwait'. As the Resolution was somewhat ambiguous in terms of whether it authorized collective security or recognized collective defence, the reference to Kuwait, the state exercising the primary right of self-defence in this instance, was natural. However, the cease-fire terms imposed by Resolution 687 (1991) were clearly an exercise of the collective security powers of the Security Council. It would have been absurd to argue that Kuwait would retain the right to select states for the purpose of

---

[26] Report of the Dutch Committee of Inquiry on the War in Iraq (2010) 57 NILR 79, 100. This was reflected in the official advice tendered by the Netherlands Legal Advisor, ibid, 105, which, as reported by the inquiry, stated that 'authority to use force' was 'limited to ending the illegal occupation of Kuwait by Iraq'. [27] Malaysia, S/PV.2963, 29 November 1990, 74.

[28] GHW Bush and B Scowcroft, 'Why We Didn't Remove Saddam?', *Time Magazine*, 2 March 1998, reproduced in J Ehrenberg, (2010) *The Iraq Papers* 27.

[29] C Powell, (1995) *My American Journey* 526.

[30] J Major, (1999) *The Autobiography* 240.

implementing the Council's demand in this respect. Moreover, in none of the subsequent instances of the use of force, including the eventual invasion of Iraq, did the United States or United Kingdom argue to have done so at the invitation of Kuwait.[31] Moreover, Kuwait formally indicated that it had not requested the operations.

An additional problem was that even if the authority contained in Resolution 678 (1990) could be revived, the mandate granted therein, whatever its interpretation, could not anticipate enforcement of a resolution which did not exist at the time of adoption of Resolution 678 (1990).[32] It is true that subsequent resolutions, including Resolution 1441 (2002), consistently refer to previous resolutions, including Resolution 678 (1990). However, none of these resolutions, other than Resolution 686 (1991), attach authority to use force to the demands made against Iraq subsequent to the adoption of Resolution 678 (1990).

2. The cease-fire and the material breach argument

Resolution 686 (1991), rather than transporting the authority granted in Resolution 678 (1990) into the indefinite future, was in fact express in limiting it. That Resolution concerned the provisional cease-fire.

In Resolution 686 (1991) the Security Council noted the 'suspension of offensive combat operations' by the forces of Kuwait and states cooperating with it. The Council demanded that Iraq take certain immediate actions, for instance, to rescind the purported annexation of Kuwait, to release prisoners, to provide information on mines, etc. It expressly recognized that during the period required for Iraq to comply with these demands, the provisions of paragraph 2 of Resolution 678 (1990) remained valid.[33] It is important to note this express confirmation, as it is absent from subsequent Council texts following the formal cease-fire.

Resolution 687 (1991) provided for the formal cease-fire. That this was intended not merely as a temporary suspension of military operations is clear from Resolution 686 (1991), which confirmed that implementation of its terms would be followed by 'a definite end to the hostilities'.[34] Indeed, the Council committed itself to securing the 'rapid establishment of a definite end to the hostilities' and the withdrawal of foreign forces and decided to remain 'actively seized' of the matter.[35] The complex provisions of Resolution 687 (1991) have

---

[31] For example V Lowe, 'The Iraq Crisis: What Now?' (2003) 52 ICLQ 859, 866.

[32] On this point see the interesting discussion between Michael Matheson of the Office of the Legal Adviser, US Department of State, and Paul Szaz in *Proceedings of the 92nd Annual Meeting of the American Society of International Law* (1998) 137 et seq; C Schaller, 'Massenvernichtungswaffen und Präventivkrieg—Möglichkeiten der Rechtfertigung einer militärischen Intervention im Irak aus völkerrechtlicher Sicht' (2002) 62 *Zeitschrift für öffentliches ausländisches Recht und Völkerrecht* 641, 646; and S Murphy, 'Assessing the Legality of Invading Iraq' (2003–4) 92 *Georgia Law Journal* 173, 181.   [33] Resolution 686 (1991), para 4.

[34] Ibid, preamble, which also records the intention of the coalition forces to bring their presence in Iraq to an end.   [35] Ibid, para 8,

led one observer to consider it in substance 'a peace treaty'.[36] While the Council affirmed its previous 13 resolutions, in this context, it did so with the specific exception of the terms that had been expressly changed in the Resolution. This included explicitly the establishment of 'a formal cease-fire'. Hence, the Council did in fact terminate the previous authorization to use force expressly. This point is generally overlooked by the US/UK Governments searching for authority to use force subsequently.

Resolution 687 (1991) also specifically affirmed the commitment of all Member States to the sovereignty, territorial integrity, and political independence of Iraq. This is a direct reference to Article 2(4) of the UN Charter, prohibiting the use of force against the 'territorial integrity or political independence' of states. Hence, the prohibition of the use of force was to operate again in relation to Iraq upon establishment of the formal cease-fire.

The definite nature of the cease-fire was confirmed by several delegations addressing the Council upon adoption of Resolution 687 (1991). For instance, India repudiated any suggestion that the cease-fire might be conditional:[37]

My delegation has always advocated that the institution of a formal cease-fire must not be made contingent upon implementation of open-ended conditions indefinite in terms of time-bound implementation. In fact, we have consistently attached great importance to and called for the promulgation of a definitive, formal cease-fire...We therefore welcome that this formal cease-fire will become effective upon official notification by Iraq to the Secretary General and to the Security Council of its acceptance of the provision of the draft resolution. That is a noteworthy improvement on resolution 686 (1991).

The United States referred to the Resolution as laying the groundwork for a permanent cease-fire that would become effective upon certification of Iraq's acceptance.[38] France referred to 'a proper' cease-fire.[39] Russia indicated that the 'crux of the resolution just adopted is to turn the temporary cessation of hostilities into a permanent cease-fire'.[40]

The Resolution confirmed that 'a formal cease fire is effective' upon notification by Iraq to the UN Secretary-General and to the Security Council of its acceptance of those terms.[41] Iraq formally accepted the Resolution on 11 April 1991 and a formal cease-fire entered into force.[42] The authority of states cooperating with the Government of Kuwait to use force, therefore, terminated at that point.

---

[36] C Gray, 'After the Cease-Fire: Iraq, the Security Council and the Use of Force' (1994) 65 BYIL 135, 144.   [37] S/PV.2981, 3 April 1991, 72ff.

[38] Ibid, 82.   [39] Ibid, 92.   [40] Ibid, 98.   [41] Resolution 687 (1991), para 33.

[42] Letter from the President of the Security Council to the Permanent Representative of Iraq to the United Nations, S/22485, 11 April 1991: 'The members of the Security Council have, accordingly, asked me to note that the conditions established in paragraph 33 of resolution 687 (1991) have been meet and that the formal cease-fire referred to in paragraph 33 of that resolution is therefore effective'.

3. Material breach

The revival argument sought to overturn this result by finding that the cease-fire was contingent on Iraq's performance of the obligations contained in Resolution 687 (1991). In order to achieve this, it relied upon a concept from the law of treaties. Article 60 of the Vienna Convention on the Law of Treaties provides that a material breach by one party to a treaty permits the other to suspend or terminate that treaty under certain circumstances. This applies in particular to material breaches, ie violations of a provision essential for the accomplishment of the object and purpose of the treaty.[43] The accomplishment of the disarmament obligations in Resolution 687 (1991) would amount to such an essential objective.

However, the doctrine of material breach is a reflection of the reciprocal interests that will tend to be accommodated in a treaty. In cases of bilateral treaties, it would be unreasonable to expect only one side to perform agreed obligations if the other side does not.[44] This is also applied to multilateral treaties, where a party is 'specifically affected by the breach'.[45] In this instance, however, there was no legal relationship between individual Member States of the Security Council and Iraq.[46] The relationship existed only between Iraq and the Council itself. Hence, no state, including members of the Council, could claim a breach of obligations to which they were a party. Nor could they claim to be specifically affected by such a breach.[47]

Nevertheless, the US Department of State Legal Adviser appeared to take a rather simplistic view, conflating the US-negotiated initial cease-fire with Resolution 687 (1991):[48]

The situation that now exists is that there is a cease-fire among parties involved in an armed conflict, on the one side Iraq and on the other, the coalition forces, primarily led by the United States but including other forces. If there are violations of the cease-fire resulting in a material breach, the usual recourse of the side is to use necessary and proportionate force to deal with those breaches.

Ruth Wedgwood also argues that it was the United States itself that initially concluded the agreement to cease operations with Iraq, before Resolutions 686

---

[43] Vienna Convention on the Law of Treaties, 1155 UNTS 661, Art 60(3)(b).

[44] See, generally, S Rosenne, (1985) *Breach of Treaty*.

[45] Vienna Convention, Art 60(2)(b).

[46] This is analogous to the judgment by the International Court of Justice in the *South West Africa* cases, where two former members of the League of Nations Council sought to bring an action against South Africa on account of the fact that they had been a member of that body when it established the mandate for South West Africa. The Court declined to hold that the two states could claim a legal interest in the matter sufficient to bring an action. South West Africa cases (*Ethiopia v South Africa*; *Liberia v South Africa*), Second Phase, judgment, 18 July 1966.

[47] AM Weisburd, 'The War in Iraq and the Dilemma of Controlling the International Use of Force' (2004) 39 *Texas International Law Journal* 521, 535.

[48] M Matheson, 'Legal Authority for Use of Force Against Iraq' (1998) 92 *American Society of International Law Proceedings* 136, 141.

(1991) and 687 were adopted.[49] However, that agreement did not contain the disarmament obligations at issue. Hence, Iraq's violations of these obligations could not overturn that initial cease-fire agreement. Moreover, the revival argument related to the authority granted in Resolution 678 (1990) and the termination of the authority to use force in Resolution 687 (1991). A possible violation by Iraq of obligations undertaken in relation to the United States, or the coalition powers, did not affect that legal relationship.

More decisive is the point that the law of treaties and concepts drawn from it could not offer a justification for the use of force. The Vienna Convention itself recalls the obligation contained in Article 2(3) that all disputes must be settled by peaceful means, and the attendant prohibition of the use of force.[50] With the adoption of the formal cease-fire, the prohibition of the use of force once again applied to Iraq. The prohibition of the use of force is a *jus cogens* rule from which no derogation is permitted. Only the recognized exceptions of self-defence, arguably forcible humanitarian action, and a Chapter VII mandate can authorize the use of force. The invocation of the very concept of material breach is, therefore, fundamentally misplaced in this context.

Nevertheless, it has been argued that a cease-fire is a special case. If a cease-fire is considered to be in essence merely an armistice or truce (that is, just a temporary suspension of hostilities), then special rules apply. Where one side violates an armistice, the other is entitled to resume hostilities. This thesis is supported with reference to the Fourth Hague Convention Respecting the Laws and Customs of War on Land. Article 40 of its Annex provides that 'Any serious violation of the armistice by one of the parties gives the other party the right of denouncing it, and even, in cases of urgency, or recommencing hostilities immediately'.[51] However, this provision was adopted before the modern prohibition of the use of force came into being. Current practice under the authority of the UN Security Council instead emphasizes the stability of armistices or cease-fires. For instance, the Council held that an armistice, concluded with a view to a return to permanent peace in the region, stabilized over a period of two-and-a-half years and 'is of a permanent character'.[52] It strongly rejected the claim that force could be used in response to violations of its terms.

The *lex specialis* governing forcible responses to the obligation contained in a cease-fire is in fact the right to self-defence. Violations of cease-fire terms other than the reinstituted prohibition of the use of force cannot trigger a resumption of hostilities. This was made clear by the UN Secretary-General in 1956 in answer to what he termed the 'confusion' of the parties in this respect.[53] As the Council itself had indicated, there is no case for forcible retaliation in such

---

[49] R Wedgwood, 'The Enforcement of Security Council Resolution 687: The Threat of Force against Iraq's Weapons of Mass Destruction' (1998) 92 AJIL 724, 726.

[50] Vienna Convention, Preamble.

[51] Reproduced in A Roberts and R Guelff, (3rd edn, 2000) *Documents on the Laws of War* 67.

[52] Resolution 95 (1951).   [53] SC 11th yr, Suppl April–June, 49, S/3659, paras 6f.

circumstances. To emphasize this point, the Secretary-General proceeded to give the cease-fire element a legal status as an independent obligation 'compliance with which was conditioned only by reciprocity in respect of the implementation of the same obligation [ie, not to use force] of the other parties to the agreement'. The Secretary-General also confirmed that self-defence applied in those circumstances within the strict confines of the definition of that right in the UN Charter.[54] That is to say, it can only be an answer to 'an armed attack' and the measures taken have to be necessary proportionate. Accordingly, there would be no case for a general resumption of hostilities.

Hence, short of the full-scale resumption of hostilities by one side, which triggers the application of the right to self-defence on the part of the victim state, a cease-fire violation by one side does not entitle the other to suspend or terminate it and resume hostilities. For instance, when fighting broke out after the conclusion of the Israel-Syria Armistice agreement of 20 July 1949, the Council determined that this had occurred in violation of Article 2(4) of the UN Charter. Evidently, that provision was brought back into operation through the armistice.[55] Moreover, when considering instances of the use of force in that context, the Council found that these had violated the armistice, but still insisted that the parties comply with it. There was no suggestion that such a violation would suspend or terminate the armistice. In a close parallel to the present case, the Council also noted that it had itself imposed a cease-fire upon the parties.[56] This, too, was not invalidated by the failure of one or other party to comply—to the contrary, the Council insisted on continued compliance, expressly in the context of the operation of Article 2(4) in relations between the parties.[57] This practice has been consistently applied over the decades.[58]

In the present instance, no side claimed that Resolution 687 (1991) ceased to operate. Even when states were using force in response to supposed material breaches purportedly suspending the cease-fire resolution, there was still strong insistence on continued compliance with the terms of the cease-fire by Iraq. Once again, this outcome highlights the inappropriate nature of the doctrine of material breach (which would suspend or even terminate the obligation for both sides) in relation to cease fires, and in particular those imposed under Chapter VII authority.

4. Process

Finally, the doctrine of material breach as it applies to treaties rules out the unilateral suspension or termination of the treaty in question. Instead, an involving process applies.[59] Moreover, the Vienna Convention on the Law of Treaties entirely precludes the unilateral application of the material breach argument

---

[54] Ibid, paras 44f.   [55] Resolution 92 (1951).   [56] Resolution 54 (1948).
[57] Resolution 93 (1951).
[58] For example Resolution 258 (1968); see AE David, (1975) *The Strategy of Treaty Termination* 267.   [59] Vienna Convention on the Law of Treaties, Art 65.

where the treaty itself provides for a mechanism to address it.[60] In this instance, Article 34 of Resolution 687 (1991) expressly provided for the Council to 'take such further steps as may be required for the implementation of this resolution and to secure peace and security in the area'. This provision asserted, on the one hand, that it was for the Council itself to ensure implementation of its resolutions and their potential enforcement. However, the unusual reference to peace and security in the area also clarified that any claimed mandate under Resolution 678 (1990) in that respect had firmly reverted back to the Council.[61]

What has been said above applies principally in relations between states. The question remains whether the Security Council itself may be entitled to adopt this doctrine in its own practice, as the principal 'owner' of the cease-fire and its terms. However, most of the objections to the application of the material breach doctrines would also apply in that context. The original authority did not go beyond the liberation of Kuwait. While the Council could easily have adopted fresh authority for other purposes, it did not do so. Given the power of the Council to adopt a mandate at any time, it is not necessary to import the law of treaties doctrine of material breach into its practice. It would be for the Council, in the application of its own powers, to determine how to respond to any breach of cease-fire terms without reference to the material breach standard. Moreover, as was noted above, material breach implies the suspension or termination of the very obligation the Council would be intent on enforcing.

B. Application of the material breach argument

The material breach argument was initially supported, if not generated, by the UN Secretariat's own Legal Counsel. This had political, rather than legal reasons. At the time, there was stalemate in the Council. On the one hand, there was agreement that Iraq's obstruction in relation to the disarmament objectives was unacceptable. On the other hand, there was also the realization that Member States in the Council would not be prepared to offer a fresh, express mandate for the enforcement of Resolution 687 (1991). At that point, the idea of applying the material breach theory had appeal. However, it was not designed as a source of authority for unilateral action. Instead, it was meant to furnish a way for the Council to authorize force informally:[62]

Since the original authorization had emanated from the Security Council acting under the powers vested in it by the Charter, in the Legal Counsel's view the precondition for any renewed use of force was that the Security Council must agree that such a violation had taken place. This did not necessarily require a new resolution, it could, for example, take

---

[60] Ibid, Art 60(4).

[61] Some commentators have pointed in this context to the exercise of this power in response to Iraq's concentration of forces on the Kuwaiti border of 1994. See Resolution 649 (1994).

[62] R Zacklin, (2010) *The United States Secretariat and the Use of Force in a Unipolar World* 19.

the form of a Presidential Statement [of the Council]. The important point was that there needed to be an institutional finding of the Security Council acting as a collective organ.

The Legal Counsel also argued that a finding of a breach by the Council was not enough. Instead, the Security Council had to communicate that states were entitled to use all necessary means to bring about Iraqi compliance. This, he argued, had not occurred in Resolution 707 (1991), which contained a reference to material breach and flagrant violations of the cease-fire terms.

Some years later, the United States would reject the original design of the material breach argument focused on the Security Council. The US Department of State Legal Adviser claimed in 1998, before Desert Fox, that it had always been the US position that it was entitled to act unilaterally:[63]

The United States has maintained that it is within its authority to take the necessary proportionate force to ensure that Iraq comply with and not violate any of the resolutions of the Security Council, but that it would be acceptable and useful to have the Security Council reiterate such authority. However, the United States does not consider that reiteration a precondition for its authority.

Whether there is a material breach is an objective fact. It is not necessary that it be the Council that determines or states that a material breach has occurred. If a material breach has occurred, under the normal rules the other side that agreed to the cease fire would have a right to use force to respond.

Again, this view reflects many of the conceptual confusions in the material breach argument in general. The United States appeared to see itself as a party to the cease-fire, despite the fact that the cease-fire resolution established legal relations between the UN and Iraq only. It claimed—incorrectly—that modern practice permitted forcible responses to cease-fire violations. And it reneged on the original proposition that this doctrine, in view of its potential virulence, would need to be administered exclusively by the Council. Even the United Kingdom, which supported the eventual invasion of Iraq, argued that at least a fresh finding by the Council as to a material breach, coupled with a threat of serious consequences, had to obtain, before the authority to use force might revive. It claimed that Resolution 1441 (2002), after the exhaustion of the final opportunity given to Iraq to comply with the arms inspections in 2002/3, furnished such additional authority.[64]

The material breach theory was put to the test in January 1993, when the Council warned Iraq once again of serious consequences in case of continued violations.[65] On 11 January, the Council adopted a lengthy presidential statement, addressing a number of recent developments. These concerned border incidents involving the United Nations Iraq-Kuwait Observation Mission (UNIKOM) and its flights, incursions into the demilitarized zone between Iraq and Kuwait

---

[63] Matheson (above n 48) 141.

[64] See the so-called 'Foreign Office Memorandum', *Iraq: Legal Basis for the Use of Force*, in (2003) 52 ICJQ 812, and Ch 6.

[65] UN Press Release, SC/5534, 8 January 1993, in Weller (above n 7) 736.

during which Iraq had removed missiles, and other equipment and incidents concerning UNSCOM. The statement added:[66]

These latest developments concerning the activities of UNIKOM and UNSCOM constitute further material breaches of resolution 687 (1991) which established the cease fire and provided the conditions essential for the restoration of peace and security in the region, as well as other relevant resolutions and agreements. The Council demands that Iraq cooperate fully with UNIKOM, UNSCOM and other United Nations agencies in carrying out their mandates, and again warns Iraq of the serious consequences that will flow from such continued defiance.

The Council had put in place all the requirements foreseen by the UN Legal Adviser. It had determined the existence of a material breach, it had linked this expressly to the conditions essential for the maintenance of the cease-fire, and it had threatened serious consequences.

   The developments that ensued were, however, somewhat confused. In January 1993, the coalition powers issued an ultimatum to Iraq, demanding the withdrawal of anti-air installations from the no-fly zones.[67] Iraq appeared at first to have complied with the terms of the ultimatum.[68] However, it then reneged and action was taken, according to the UK Government 'in self-defence to ensure the safety of coalition aircraft patrolling the No-Fly Zone'.[69] This was one of the issues that had not been addressed by the Council in its presidential statements. The no-fly zones were maintained outside of the context of Resolution 687 (1991).[70] The United States also emphasized that action had been taken to ensure that Iraq did not pose a threat to coalition aircraft patrolling the zones. However, the statement went on to indicate:[71]

The US government fully associates itself with the January 8 and January 11 statements by the President of the UN Security Council that declared Iraq in material breach of UN Security Council Resolution 687 (1991) and the cease-fire regime, and also that warned of the serious consequences of Iraq's actions. We stand ready to take additional forceful actions with our coalition partners if Iraq continues to flout the will of the international community and if it continues to disregard its international obligations. ...

The UN Secretary-General issued a statement shortly thereafter, indicating that this action had been 'undertaken under a mandate from the Council according to Resolution 678 (1990)' and 'the cause of the raid was the violation by Iraq of

[66] UN Press Release SC/5536, 11 January 1993, in Weller (above n 7) 736.
[67] US Press Release: 'Iraq Warned Move Missiles—Keep out of No-Fly-Zone', 7 January 1993, in Weller (above n 7) 734.
[68] White House Statement, 9 January 1993, in Weller (above n 7) 736.
[69] Press Statement from No 10 Downing Street, 13 January 1991, in Weller (above n 7) 738.
[70] Instead, Resolution 688 (1991) was sometimes invoked. That Resolution had demanded that Iraq must cease repressing its population and permit the operation of humanitarian agencies on its territory. However, the Resolution was not directly tied to the cease-fire and was not adopted with express reference to Chapter VII of the UN Charter: S/RES/688 (1991), 5 April 1991.
[71] US Press Statement, 13 January 1993, in Weller (above n 7) 739.

Resolution 687 (1990) concerning the cease-fire'.[72] However, once again, thus far the military operation undertaken by the coalition powers had only addressed the perceived missile threat in the no-fly zone imposed by way of humanitarian action—there had been no action connected with the enforcement of Resolution 687 (1991), although the United States had threatened such action. This is important, as the Secretary-General's statement would subsequently be invoked as authority in favour of the unilateral enforcement of the cease-fire in relation to the disarmament obligations.[73]

On 17–18 January 1993, there was a renewed wave of attacks, mainly directed again against Iraqi anti-air installations and justified once more with reference to self-defence.[74] However, US Tomahawk cruise missiles also attacked what the United States described as a nuclear fabricating plant near Baghdad. The US Government claimed that 'the strike was designed to help achieve the goals of United Nations Security Council Resolutions 787 (1992), 707 (1991), and 715 (1991). ... Today's action is designed to make clear to Iraq that non-compliance with UN Security Council resolutions will not be tolerated'.[75] The United Kingdom added that that action had been taken:[76]

.... to ensure that Iraq complies with its mandatory obligations under UNSCR 687 and related resolutions. Iraq has committed a number of material breaches of UNSCR 687 and wilfully ignored warnings given by the Security Council and the US, UK, France and Russia on 11 and 14 January respectively.

France, a fellow member of the coalition, appeared to distance itself from this part of the operation. According to agency reports, the French Foreign Minister argued that the US operation overstepped resolutions of the Security Council.[77] Russia emphasized that the reaction to Iraq's actions must be 'adequate and follow only agreed decisions'.[78] China felt it necessary to offer a public position on the matter. Referring specifically to the US cruise missile attack, China indicated that 'our consistent position is to peacefully settle international disputes'.[79]

Overall, the material breach argument initially appeared to have suited the Council, at least to the point of threatening force in order to bring Iraq back into compliance. In fact, however, force was mainly used within a self-defence argument connected to the no-fly zone and, therefore, the legal justification of humanitarian intervention that had not, in fact, been authorized by the Council.

---

[72] UN Press Release, 14 January 1993, reproduced in Weller (above n 7) 741. However, it is to be noted that this statement was made while the Secretary-General was travelling, and the next day his spokesman distanced himself from it: ibid, 742.   [73] See Chapter 5, 182.

[74] Statement in the House of Commons by the UK Secretary for Defence, 18 January 1993, in Weller (above n 7) 748–749.

[75] US Press Release, 17 January 1993, in Weller (above n 7) 746–747.

[76] Statement in the House of Commons by the UK Secretary for Defence, 18 January 1993, in Weller (above n 7) 748–749.

[77] Comment attributed to Roland Dumas, French Foreign Minister, 20 January 1993, in Weller (above n 7) 751.

[78] Russian Foreign Minister Statement on the situation around Iraq, 18 January 1993, in Weller (above n 7) 749.   [79] Reply by Chinese Foreign Ministry Spokesman, 18 January 1993.

It was only a separate, subsequent armed action by the United States against one Iraqi target that was specifically focused on its disarmament and connected with the aims of Resolution 687 (1991). The part of the operation that actually relied on the material breach argument was received with some hesitation, not only by France, but also by Russia and China. Hence, from the very beginning, the theory of the material breach was uncertain, both in terms of its legal persuasiveness and in terms of its actual implementation. Nevertheless, it served its purpose in the political sphere. It provided a means to legitimize, if not authorize, the threat of force to ensure Iraq's compliance with its disarmament obligations when this was still supported in the Council. At least up to the point of the threat of force, this proved acceptable to other states which were, on the other hand, politically unable or formally unwilling to adopt a new mandate.

However useful at the time, as was argued above, this approach nevertheless disregarded important principles of international law and introduced flexibility into a system where force was meant to be permitted only if specifically authorized by the Council. Even in 1993, governments voiced discomfort with this approach when it actually resulted in the use of force by the United States. This sense of discomfort increased among the members of the Council as the uses of force against Iraq continued over time, on the basis of a variety of more or less controversial legal grounds.[80] In June 1993, the US attacked the intelligence headquarters building in Baghdad with references to the attempted assassination of former President Bush while visiting Kuwait in April of that year.[81] In October 1994, the United States threatened to use force in relation to Iraqi troop movements near the Kuwait border. In 1996, the United States attacked Iraq with 44 cruise missiles after Iraqi units moved into northern Iraq, apparently at the invitation of one of the Kurdish parties exercising authority there. In January/February 1998, the United States and United Kingdom threatened to use force in response to Iraq's failure to cooperate with the arms inspections. In November 1998 they launched an attack which was recalled at the very last moment when Iraq appeared to offer cooperation.[82] Throughout this period, there were increasing incidents in relation to the no-fly zones imposed initially over northern Iraq, and subsequently also southern Iraq. The issue came to the fore when Operation Desert Fox was launched in December 1998.

III. Operation Desert Fox

A. The road towards Operation Desert Fox

In June 1997, Iraq began interfering with UNSCOM helicopter flights. In a presidential statement, the Council reminded Iraq of its obligations under the relevant

---

[80] See C Gray, 'From Unity to Polarization: International Law and the Use of Force Against Iraq' (2002) 13(1) *European Journal of International Law* 1.

[81] See D Kritsiotis, '1993 US Missile Strike on Iraq' (1995) 45 ICLQ 162.

[82] M Weller, 'The Threat or Use of Force in a Unipolar World: The Iraq Crisis of Winter 1997/98' (1998) 4(3–4) *International Peace-keeping* 63.

resolutions to permit the 'Commission to carry out its air operations anywhere in Iraq without interference of any kind'.[83] Iraq also precluded access of UNSCOM teams to certain sites designated for inspection. The Council responded by adopting Resolution 1115 (1997), condemning the action, and, acting under Chapter VII of the UN Charter, demanded unrestricted access to 'any and all areas, facilities, records and means of transportation which they wish to inspect'. At the time, there was mounting pressure on the Security Council to terminate or modify the sanctions regime against Iraq, which had been kept in place after the conclusion of the 1991 conflict. Resolution 687 (1991) envisaged such a step pending review of Iraqi compliance with the cease-fire terms. Now the Council decided to delay this review until after the publication of a further consolidated progress report by UNSCOM, due on 11 October 1997. Furthermore, the Council threatened the imposition of certain measures against 'categories of Iraqi officials responsible for non-compliance'.

In his report on Iraqi compliance, the Executive Chairman of the Special Commission noted progress towards the elimination of Iraq's programme of WMD. However, he was unable to certify substantial compliance by Iraq with Resolution 687 (1991) and other relevant resolutions.[84] Instead, he had to report on further Iraqi obstruction of UNSCOM's inspection activities and interference with freedom of movement and the right of over-flight—actions that were answered in another Chapter VII resolution demanding compliance. That resolution also designated individuals who could be targeted by any travel restrictions imposed in future.[85]

On 29 October 1997, Iraq demanded the removal of all UNSCOM personnel within one week and a cessation of over-flights of US-registered U-2 intelligence-gathering planes that had been placed at the disposal of UNSCOM.[86] This action prompted UNSCOM to suspend its operations and the Security Council to issue a further condemnatory statement.[87] The statement also announced that failure to comply immediately and fully would have 'serious consequences'.[88]

When Iraq maintained its position, removed dual-use equipment from UNSCOM-monitored sites, and interfered with monitoring equipment, the Council adopted a further Chapter VII resolution on 12 November 1997, imposing travel restrictions on Iraqi officials who were responsible for, or who had participated in, instances of non-compliance.[89]

---

[83] Statement by the President of the Security Council, S/PRST/1997/33, 18 June 1997.

[84] Note by the Secretary-General, S/1997/774, 6 October 1997.

[85] Resolution 1134 (1997).

[86] Letter from the Deputy Prime Minister of Iraq to the Security Council, S/1997/829, 29 October 1997 and Letter from the Permanent Representative of Iraq to the Executive Chairman of UNSCOM, S/1997/837, 2 November 1997, Annex.

[87] Press Briefing by Richard Butler, Executive Chairman of UNSCOM, 29 October 1997. Similarly, the IAEA suspended activities. Letter from the Director General of the IAEA addressed to the Secretary-General, S/1997/833, 31 October 1997.

[88] Statement by the President of the Security Council, S/PRST/1997/33, 18 June 1997.

[89] Resolution 1137 (1997).

UNSCOM then met in emergency session.[90] In a conciliatory gesture, UNSCOM reported that there were no indications that any weapons-usable nuclear materials were left in Iraq. It was also noted that considerable quantities of chemical weapons and related materials and equipment had been destroyed and that only a small but significant number of proscribed missiles and components remained to be accounted for. However, due to a lack of disclosure by Iraq, there had been no significant progress on the matter of biological weapons. In order to address the remaining issues, UNSCOM recommended a plan of action. This plan was endorsed by the Security Council, which expressly echoed the acknowledgement of UNSCOM of the need to respect the 'legitimate national security, sovereignty and dignity concerns of Iraq in the context of the need for full application of the mandate given to it by the Council'.[91] In this way, the Security Council went some way in acknowledging Iraq's concerns with a view to encouraging a resumption of cooperation with the inspection regime. However, Iraq persisted in its demands, in particular relating to so-called 'presidential' or 'sovereign' sites. It claimed that these should not be subjected to inspection or even over-flight. Iraq based this view that certain sensitive sites should be exempt on the apparent recognition by the Council of legitimate security interests and concerns about sovereignty. However, invoking the US threat of aerial bombardment, Baghdad was unwilling to provide maps or specific designations of sensitive sites, unless the Council President provided a written guarantee that such attacks would never take place.[92] These views and proposals were rejected in a further Presidential Statement of the Council.[93]

By the end of December 1997, it appeared that a *modus vivendi* relating to the 'presidential' and other sensitive sites had been achieved with the assistance of Russian mediation, and UNSCOM inspections resumed. However, on 12 January 1998, Iraq once again ceased to cooperate with UNSCOM, objecting to the perceived strong presence of US personnel as part of the inspection teams.[94] The Council, in a further Presidential Statement, rejected this attempt by 'Iraq to try to dictate the terms of its compliance with its obligations to cooperate with the Special Commission', demanded full access and compliance, and indicated that it might adopt an appropriate response on the basis of the relevant resolutions.[95]

---

[90] Report of UNSCOM Emergency Session, S/1997/992, 21 November 1997.

[91] Statement by the President of the Security Council, S/PRST/1997/54, 3 December 1997.

[92] Letter from the Executive Director of UNSCOM to the President of the Security Council, S/1997/987, 17 December 1997.

[93] Statement by the President of the Security Council, S/PRST/1997/56, 22 December 1997.

[94] Letter from the Executive Chairman of UNSCOM to the President of the Security Council, S/1998/27, Annex, and S/1998/28, 12 January 1998. Indeed, it was subsequently confirmed that the UNSCOM machinery contained and drew heavily on national intelligence resources, in particular from the United States, eg Scott Ritter.

[95] Statement by the President of the Security Council, S/PRST/1998/1, 14 January 1998.

In relation to the developments during 1997, the UK law officers reportedly advised the UK Prime Minister on the revival argument. They indicated that it was an essential precondition for the renewed use of force that the Security Council determine the existence of a breach of the cease-fire conditions, 'and that the Council considers the breach sufficiently grave to undermine the basis or effective operation of the cease fire'.[96]

B. The threat of the use of force in January/February 1998

The failure of Iraq to cooperate with UNSCOM triggered a strong response from the United States, backed up by the UK Government. While emphasizing that a diplomatic solution was to be preferred, the US Government declared its willingness to use substantial and sustained military force.[97] The aim of these 'strong measures—not pinpricks, but substantial strikes' was to 'reduce Saddam's capacity to reconstitute his weapons of mass destruction and diminish his ability to threaten Iraq's neighbors and the world'.[98] While US President Bill Clinton admitted that even such sustained strikes would not destroy all the WMD capability allegedly or potentially available to Iraq, US action 'can and will leave [Saddam Hussein] significantly worse off than he is now in terms of the ability to threaten the world with the weapons, or to attack his neighbours'.[99] Following the initial wave of attacks, it was envisaged that the United States would 'carefully monitor Iraq's activities with all the means at our disposal. If he seeks to rebuild his weapons of mass destruction we will be prepared to strike him again'.[100]

The claim for such broad authority to threaten or use force was not firmly rooted in any precise legal justification. The UK Prime Minister, supporting the US position, spoke of the need to 'enforce the Security Council's will'.[101] Bill Richardson, the US Permanent Representative to the United Nations, asserted that a finding by the Council as to a material breach of Resolution 687 (1991) might be desirable, although he added that 'no additional Security Council action to justify the use of force' was required.[102] As already noted above, the US Secretary of State referred to the need to avert, on the one hand, the threat to the international community at large, posed by Iraq's potential to develop WMD, and the threat posed by Iraq's military potential to regional states.[103]

---

[96] Quoted in Lord Goldsmith, Attorney General's Memorandum, 28 March 2002.

[97] US Secretary of State Albright, Interview with 'Face the Nation', Released by the Office of the Spokesman of the Department of State, 9 February 1998.

[98] US Secretary of State Albright, Statement before the Senate Foreign Relations Committee, Released by the Office of the Spokesman of the Department of State, 10 February 1998.

[99] Remarks by the President on Iraq to Pentagon Personnel, White House Press Release, 17 February 1998.   [100] Ibid.

[101] Extract from a speech by the UK Prime Minister, Tony Blair, at a Labour Party Policy Forum, Millbank, London, 31 January 1998.

[102] Press Conference by US Ambassador Richardson, Press Release 11/98, 30 January 1998.

[103] Above ns 97, 98.

The UN Secretary-General attempted to diffuse the crisis. He made himself available at UN Headquarters to monitor the situation and maintain high-level contacts with all relevant delegations. In the meantime, expert consultations between UNSCOM and the authorities in Baghdad continued, to identify the remaining compliance issues with greater precision. On 17 February 1998, the UN Secretary-General met with the permanent members of the Security Council before setting off for talks in Baghdad, where he arrived three days later. After extensive negotiations, the Secretary-General announced an agreement on 23 February. This Memorandum of Understanding, consisting of only seven short paragraphs, confirmed the principle of full compliance by Iraq with all relevant resolutions, including Resolution 687 (1991).[104] UNSCOM pledged to respect the legitimate concerns of Iraq relating to national security, sovereignty, and dignity, and a special inspection procedure was agreed for eight designated presidential sites. Moreover, UNSCOM would intensify efforts to complete its mandate, according to the plan of action adopted at its emergency session of 21 November 1997. The paramount importance to the people and Government of Iraq of the lifting of sanctions was also noted.

The Council endorsed the Memorandum of Understanding in Chapter VII Resolution 1154 (1998) of 2 March 1998. That Resolution stated that 'any violation would have severest consequences for Iraq'. While the United States maintained the position that unilateral forcible action in response to violations remained permissible, a significant number of delegations expressly rejected this view.[105] Brazil, for example, confirmed that only the Council enjoyed the authority to determine if, when, and under what conditions the formal cease-fire it had declared in 1991 held. There would be no automatic authorization of the use of force in the case of a possible violation by Iraq. Japan, a co-sponsor of the Resolution, also clarified that it had not introduced such automaticity. China expressly stated that, during negotiations on the draft text, agreement had been reached to the effect that there would be no automatic endorsement of the use of force. Gambia, France, and Russia also emphasized that the lack of reference to automaticity was of particular importance. France and Russia added that it was up to the Council to evaluate the conduct of a country and to take the necessary decisions. Sweden insisted that the Council's primary responsibility for international peace and security must not be circumvented and Slovenia pointedly explained that any future violation by Iraq would prompt the Council to consider other effective measures to ensure compliance. Pakistan and Malaysia rejected the possible use of force in this instance. Egypt expressly referred to the law on the non-use of force, emphasizing the limitations imposed upon the exercise of the right to self-defence.

---

[104] Letter dated 25 February 1998 from the Secretary-General addressed to the President of the Security Council, S/1998/166, 25 February 1998.
[105] Provisional Record of the Security Council, S/PV.3858, 2 March 1998, passim.

Overall, this *opinio juris* amounted to an extraordinarily strong rejection of the arguments put forward by the United States. There was very clear rejection of the view that the 'will' of the Council could, in circumstances other than humanitarian emergencies, be implemented forcibly in the absence of a mandate. The thesis that individual states can determine a material breach of a cease-fire which operates in relation to the Council, and that they can auto-determine the consequences of such a breach, was similarly rejected. Finally, opposition was expressed to an open-ended definition of self-defence.

C. The crisis of November 1998

On 14 May 1998, the Council noted reports from the IAEA and UNSCOM, and welcomed the 'increased access provided to the Special Commission and the IAEA by the Government of Iraq following the signature of the Memorandum of Understanding'.[106] However, the Council also noted that full disclosure had yet to be obtained from Iraq in several critical areas, in spite of repeated requests from the Special Commission.

Confidence in the effectiveness of UNSCOM was shaken somewhat when one of its prominent members, William S Ritter, resigned, indicating that the inspections were hamstrung by requests from the US Government and others to avoid provocation in relations with Iraq.[107] Moreover, Iraq once again restricted ongoing monitoring, disarmament, and verification activities. In a further Chapter VII resolution, the Council condemned this development and demanded that Iraq rescind its decisions in this respect. The Council once again determined that until that had occurred, there would be no review of Iraqi compliance, as provided for in paragraphs 21 and 28 of Resolution 687 (1991). Carefully avoiding any reference to the concept of material breach, Resolution 1194 (1998) identified the Iraqi action in deliberate, non-technical, non-legal language as 'a totally unacceptable contravention of its obligations' under Resolution 687 (1991) and other relevant resolutions.[108]

On 6 October 1998, UNSCOM presented its regular report to the Security Council. The suspension of cooperation by Iraq in several areas was noted again. There remained a few, not insignificant, outstanding issues in the area of missiles and chemical weapons, and bacteriological weapons, due to Iraq's failure to cooperate in the investigation. Of course, as we now know, no evidence has come to light indicating that such a weapons programme was in operation.[109] In addition, the Executive Chairman of UNSCOM indicated that concealment activities continued to occur, as did the unilateral destruction

106 Statement by the President of the Council, S/PRST/1998/11, 14 May 1998.
107 Press Briefing by UNSCOM Executive Chairman, 27 August 1998. See, at length, S Ritter, (2005) *Iraq Confidential*.   108 Para 1.
109 Iraq Survey Group, Final Report, 30 September 2004, available at <http://www.globalsecurity. org/wmd/library/report/2004/isg-final-report/>.

of items and the continued failure to provide requested documents.[110] On 31 October 1998, the Executive Chairman had to report to the Council that Iraq had further suspended cooperation with UNSCOM.[111] While some routine activities, such as transport flights and the maintenance of monitoring cameras, could continue, the Executive Chairman noted in a subsequent report that 'Iraq's decisions of 5 August and 31 October make it impossible for the Commission to implement its disarmament and monitoring rights and responsibilities'.[112]

The Council responded by adopting, on 5 November 1998, under Chapter VII of the UN Charter, Resolution 1205 (1998), condemning Iraq's actions as 'a flagrant violation of resolution 687 (1991) and other relevant resolutions' and demanding once again that Iraq rescind its obstructive decisions.[113] The Council added an unusual concluding paragraph, deciding 'in accordance with its primary responsibility for the maintenance of international peace and security, to remain actively seized of the matter'.[114] This was a reflection of a view widely expressed by a range of delegations in the Council that no authorization for the use of force had been granted and that there should be no unilateral action. Moreover, it was again specifically indicated that there would be no 'automaticity' of response.[115] Despite these clear indications, the United States stated (rather imperially) that it nevertheless claimed the right to military action if so required. Sir Jeremy Greenstock, the Permanent Representative of the United Kingdom, also asserted that the Council had just endorsed what in fact it had rejected:[116]

Certain speakers have given their views on the meaning of this Resolution as regards any possible use of force. Let me set out the UK view. It is well established that the authorization to use force given by the Security Council in 1990 may be revived if the Council decides that there has been a sufficiently serious breach of the conditions laid down by the Council for the ceasefire. In the resolution we have just adopted the Council had condemned the Iraqi decision to cease cooperation with UNSCOM as a flagrant violation of these obligations.

A few days later, the UK Government claimed that what had occurred was not 'a technical breach; it is a substantial breach of the agreement [of February]

---

[110] Note by the Secretary-General, S/1998/920, 6 October 1998.

[111] Letter dated 31 October 1998 from the Deputy Executive Chairman of the Special Commission established by the Secretary-General pursuant to paragraph 9(b)(i) of Security Council Resolution 687 (1991) address to the President of the Security Council, S/1998/1023, 31 October 1998.

[112] Letter dated 2 November 1998 from the Executive Chairman of the Special Commission established by the Secretary-General pursuant to paragraph 9(b)(i) of Security Council Resolution 687 (1991) addressed to the President of the Security Council, S/1998/1032, 4 November 1998.

[113] Resolution 1205, para 1.   [114] Ibid, para 6.

[115] Provisional Record of the Security Council, S/PV.3939, 5 November 1998.

[116] Statement by Sir Jeremy Greenstock, KCMG, issued by the UK Permanent Mission to the United Nations, 5 November 1998.

because it is clear from evidence that [Saddam Hussein] will, if unchecked, try to develop weapons of mass destruction'.[117] Military action might be necessary, it was added, and would be 'designed to make him comply and to ensure that he does not remain the threat to his neighbours and to the world that he does at the present moment'.[118]

On 15 November 1998, it emerged that the United States had launched a significant military strike against Iraq, which was recalled when Iraq communicated its intention to resume compliance.[119] It was announced, however, that in case of further non-compliance by Iraq with its obligations, 'there will be no further warning whatsoever'.[120] The United States and United Kingdom also declared that they would engage in overt means of supporting democratic forces working towards the overthrow of the Government of Iraq.[121]

The modalities of resumed cooperation with UNSCOM were set out in an exchange of letters with the Commission's Executive Chairman.[122] On 15 December 1998, the UN Secretary-General forwarded reports from UNSCOM and the IAEA respectively. In his covering letter, the Secretary-General noted that UNSCOM indicated that 'Iraq has provided the necessary level of cooperation to enable the above enumerated activities to be completed and effectively'. However, the Secretary-General found that the UNSCOM report 'presents a mixed picture and concludes that UNSCOM did not enjoy full cooperation from Iraq'.[123]

In fact, the UNSCOM report did refer to considerable cooperation from Iraq, including the toleration of unannounced inspections, even of so-called 'sovereign' and other special sites, and the facilitation of monitoring activities. Yet, there had been one incident of obstruction in relation to an inspection of one building (claimed to be the headquarters of the ruling political party) and there had been no significant improvement in Iraq's willingness to furnish the documentation requested.[124] The Secretary-General, in his covering letter, suggested

---

[117] UK Prime Minister, 11 November 1998.

[118] Statement by UK Defence Secretary George Robertson, 12 November 1998.

[119] Speech by US President Clinton, 15 November 1998.

[120] Interview with the UK Prime Minister, 15 November 1998.

[121] The US Government appointed a 'Special Representative to the Iraqi Opposition': USIA Report, 20 November 1998. The UK Foreign and Commonwealth Office officially hosted a gathering of Iraqi opposition figures to assist it in its work: Press Briefing by Minister of State Fatchett, 23 November 1998.

[122] Letter dated 26 October from the representative of Cyprus addressed to the Secretary-General, S/1998/1006, 20 November 1998, Annexes; Letter dated 30 November 1998 from the Executive Chairman of the Special Commission established by the Secretary-General pursuant to paragraph 9(b)(i) of Security Council Resolution 687 (1991) addressed to the President of the Security Council, S/1998/1127, 30 November 1998, Annexes.

[123] Letter dated 15 December 1998 from the Secretary-General addressed to the President of the Security Council, S/1998/1172, 15 December 1999.   [124] Ibid, Annex 2.

that there would be three possible options which the Council might consider in response:

- a finding that the experience over the period since 17 November did not provide the Council with a sufficient basis to move forward with a comprehensive review of Iraqi compliance at that time;
- a finding that Iraq had not provided full cooperation but that it should be permitted additional time to demonstrate its commitment to do so;
- a decision to proceed to the comprehensive review on the premise that it was sufficiently important to know precisely what had been achieved over the entire period since 1991.

The path proposed by the UN Secretary-General, therefore, was one of continued diplomacy, seeking to encourage further cooperation from Iraq. However, on the night of 15 December 1998, the Secretary-General received a telephone call from US Ambassador Burleigh, indicating that his government was asking US personnel in the region to leave, and that it had advised UNSCOM Executive Chairman Richard Butler to withdraw UNSCOM personnel from the country. Richard Butler immediately instructed his personnel to do just that, and the IAEA also withdrew its staff.[125] On 16 December 1998, the United States and United Kingdom launched significant aerial attacks against Iraq.

At 6pm Eastern Standard Time, US President Clinton announced that the Butler Report had concluded that Iraq had failed to comply with its obligations: 'This situation presents a clear and present danger to the stability of the Persian Gulf and the safety of people everywhere', which had made it necessary to launch a:

...strong, sustained series of air attacks against Iraq. They are designed to degrade Saddam's capacity to develop and deliver weapons of mass destruction, and to degrade his ability to threaten his neighbors. At the same time, we are delivering a powerful message to Saddam: If you act recklessly, you will pay a heavy price.

The President added that action had to be taken immediately:

...because, in the judgement of my military advisors, a swift response would provide the most surprise and the least opportunity for Saddam to prepare. If we had delayed for even a matter of days from Chairman Butler's report, we would have given Saddam more time to disperse forces and protect his weapons.[126]

The US Secretary of State added that the immediate goal of the campaign was to degrade Iraq's ability to develop and deploy WMD, and to degrade Iraqi command and control over some of its security areas in order to neutralize its capacity

---

[125] UN Press Briefing, 16 December 1998.
[126] Statement by the US President, 16 December 1998.

to threaten its neighbours. In the mid-term, the aim was to achieve full compliance with Security Council resolutions and to restore UNSCOM's full and unfettered operation:

We are now dealing with a threat, I think, that is probably harder for some to understand, because it is a threat of the future rather than a present threat or a present act, such as a border crossing, a border aggression. Here, . . . we are concerned about the threat posed by Saddam Hussein's ability to have, develop, deploy weapons of mass destruction and the threat that he poses to the neighbors, to the stability of the Middle East and, therefore ultimately to ourselves.[127]

The UK Prime Minister stated:[128]

Following the Butler report, after more than a year of obstruction and a catalogue of broken promises . . . we have no option but to act. Our objectives in this military action are clear: to degrade his capability to build and use weapons of mass destruction and to diminish the military threat he poses to his neighbours. The targets chosen, therefore, are targets connected with this military capability, his weapons of mass destruction capacity and his ability to threaten his neighbours.

The aerial campaign ended after 70 hours, on 19 December 1998. The US Government reported that 40,000 of its troops had been involved. There had been 600 aerial sorties and more than 40 ships performed strike and support roles, 10 of which had launched 300 cruise missiles. The United States claimed that Iraq's ballistic missile programme had been delayed by one or two years, and command and control facilities and highly visible symbols of the regime had been destroyed. Over 600 Republican Guards securing suspected weapons of mass destruction programmes had been killed, along with approximately 800 Revolutionary Guard troops. A large oil refinery supplying 30 per cent of Iraq's 'illegal' oil exports had also been destroyed.[129] The UK Government reported similar successes against weapons facilities and Republican Guard headquarters, and command and control facilities.[130]

   Once more, the US/UK legal position was strongly opposed in the Security Council. In fact, a meeting of the Council had been convened to discuss peaceful options, proposed by the UN Secretary-General. In adopting Resolution 1205 (1998), the Council had deliberately shied away from making a finding of material breach—the technical term from the law on treaties noted above—precisely in order to avoid giving credence to an argument based on a purported material breach. Instead, the Council referred to a 'flagrant violation' of Resolution 687 (1991), and it had specifically indicated that it would continue to address the situation 'in accordance with its primary responsibility under the Charter for the

[127] US Secretary of State Albright, Statement of 17 December 1997.
[128] Statement by the Prime Minister, 16 December 1998.
[129] Briefing by Army General Hugh Shelton, 5 January 1999.
[130] Operation Desert Fox: Battle Damage Assessment, 22 December 1998.

maintenance of international peace and security'. However, Sir Jeremy Greenstock, the UN Permanent Representative to the UN, later recounted rather proudly:

...my use of Resolution 1205 seriously annoyed my Russian counterpart, because he realized that I had succeeded in establishing in Resolution 1205 a declaration of material breach of Iraq which he hadn't intended should be allowed by the resolution, which then lay the basis for the use of force in December 1998.[131]

In fact, this statement confirms that Council delegations had not intended to authorize the use of force by means of this Resolution. The Foreign Office Legal Adviser involved in crafting the UK position at the time subsequently confirmed:[132]

...we recognized that it was rather a strained legal argument and it was sharply criticised thereafter by Security Council members....So that was a lesson we should have learned...

Criticism came from a significant range of states. Russia indicated that no state could act independently on behalf of the United Nations and assume the role of world policeman. China considered it an unprovoked military action by two states, which was completely groundless. Costa Rica emphasized that states were under an obligation to settle their disputes peacefully and that force, as an exceptional recourse, was the sole and exclusive power of the Council; only the United Nations could authorize such actions. Sweden, too, noted that action had been taken without a decision of the Council, at the very moment when it had been meeting in informal consultation about the issue of Iraq. Brazil added that the use of force should be a last resort, taken within a multilateral framework. The Council, Brazil added, remained the sole body with legal authority to mandate actions aimed at reinforcing compliance with its own resolution. Gambia also noted that action had been taken while reviewing the options proposed by the Secretary-General. It emphasized that it was the Council that exercised primary responsibility for the maintenance of international peace and security. Kenya expressed its concern about the fact that the strike had been launched during the time the Council had been considering the UNSCOM and IAEA reports. Given the content of the reports, it was difficult to understand the reason for the attacks. Kenya reminded the Council of its repeatedly stated view that any further action against Iraq remained the sole responsibility of the Council. Several other delegations expressed their regret at the turn of events in a more general way.[133]

Operation Desert Fox had three important consequences. First, Iraq terminated all cooperation with the UN arms inspection regime, arguing that the action demonstrated that inspections would only be used to prepare for further military action. Second, support for any further action by the Council resulted

---

[131] Sir Jeremy Greenstock, Chilcot Testimony, 27 November 2009, 35.
[132] Elisabeth Wilmshurst, Chilcot Testimony, 26 January 2010, 29.
[133] Provisional Record of the Security Council, S/PV.3955, 16 December 1998.

in a stalemate due to the 'breakdown in the Security Council' after the bombing campaign.[134] In particular, an attempt to convert the existing sanctions regime in relation to Iraq was much delayed as a result of the mistrust that had arisen in the Council, particularly in relation to Russia.[135] The new arms inspection regime, UNMOVIC, was narrowly agreed in Resolution 1284 (1999), a year after the bombardment, with France, China, and Russia abstaining. Given Iraq's refusal to cooperate, the Resolution never became fully operational and had to be administered from outside of the country. Finally, and most damaging for the negotiations leading up to Resolution 1441 (2002), several states resolved not to be lured again into the finding of a breach that might be invoked to justify the use of force, as had been the case with Resolution 1205 (1998).

IV. Conclusion

This chapter has traced the development of the theory of material breach. In view of its subsequent history, it is noteworthy that this concept was generated within the UN Secretariat. It was a way of legitimizing further use of force against Iraq while there was still a consensus in the Council that the disarmament obligations contained in Resolution 687 (1991) had to be enforced, even if an express mandate could not be adopted to that end. From the beginning, the theory was adventurous, inasmuch as it transposed a concept from the law of treaties to the context of the use of force. In that way, it offered a hint that, after all, international legal obligations can be enforced militarily—a highly controversial proposition. However, the original design of the doctrine left it for the Security Council to determine that (a) a breach had occurred, (b) the breach was of sufficient gravity to suspend the cease-fire and (c) the authority to use force revived in relation to certain former coalition powers. In this way, the doctrine was exclusively linked to the Council and its administration of the cease-fire conditions. It would not be available for invocation by states in other circumstances. Instead, the material breach argument merely furnished an indirect way for the Council to generate a mandate for the use of force. However, as it turned out, this approach was very risky. It only operated without controversy as long as all states concerned understood the underlying rules of the game articulated by the UN Legal Adviser and agreed to play by them. However, this consensus broke down on two fronts. As time progressed, more and more states expressed dissatisfaction with the ongoing disarmament process and the failure to conclude it through the review process envisaged in Resolution 687 (1991). While it was Iraq's own failure to comply in an unqualified way that had caused this delay, aspects of UNSCOM's performance, the fact that much of its mandate appeared to have been fulfilled, and

---

[134] Sir Jeremy Greenstock, Testimony, 27 November 2009, 3.
[135] It was eventually adopted in Resolution 1409 (2002).

the repeated use of force against Iraq turned opinion in favour of Baghdad. The initial consensus, favouring limited force to constrain compliance with the disarmament provisions, vanished.

At the same time, however, that initial consensus was also unravelled from the other end. The United States and United Kingdom invoked the material breach argument in circumstances that had not been foreseen. Even when the Council avoided determining the existence of material breach by using other formulations ('serious violation'), this was invoked by them as informal authorization for the use of force. However, by 1997 and early in 1998, other delegations to the Council began to challenge this view. Nevertheless, the United States and United Kingdom persisted in claiming a mandate to enforce the will of the Security Council, when the Council had not in fact been willing to have its will enforced. In December 1998, the majority of the Council members, the arms inspection team, and the UN Secretariat were all participating in an attempt to nurture the inspection process and to bring it to its conclusion (or at least to the stage of long-term monitoring). Instead, the United States and United Kingdom launched Operation Desert Fox—an action that was very clearly and unambiguously disowned by members of the Council as an impermissible arrogation of power by the two states. It is odd that, despite this clear rejection of the material breach doctrine at this point, it continued to be invoked as legal authority in the run-up to the invasion of Iraq in 2003.

5

Resolution 1441 (2002) and the
Invasion of Iraq

Throughout the 1990s relations between the United States and Iraq were tense, with the United States using force against Iraq in a variety of contexts.[1]

Iraq had persistently frustrated UN efforts to implement the terms of cease-fire Resolution 687 (1991) relating to weapons of mass destruction (WMD) and delivery vehicles (missiles of a range beyond 150km). The United States repeatedly struck weapons-related installations in Iraq, claiming authority to enforce the UN's demands militarily.[2] In response to the alleged plot by Iraqi intelligence to assassinate President Bush Senior during a visit to Kuwait, the United States bombed the Iraqi intelligence headquarters building in June 1993. The attack, which used 24 cruise missiles, was described by the United States as having been designed 'so that it would be proportionate to the attack on President Bush'.[3] In 1994, Iraq built up its armed forces on the Iraqi border, moving some 80,000 troops southwards. This led to a stern warning from the UN Security Council and the rapid reintroduction of US forces to the region amid threats of armed action.[4] The former US administration was at that time sharply criticized for failing to march on Baghdad in 1991 and dispose of Saddam Hussein—a factor that may have influenced the decision-making of the second Bush administration. Finally, there was a persistent pattern of armed action against Iraq with regard to the no-fly zones. Initially, Iraqi aircraft challenging coalition patrols were engaged, but over time the wider Iraqi military infrastructure, or at least its air defence network, became a running target, culminating in the 70-hour bombing campaign of Operation Desert Fox.[5]

In its Iraq Liberation Act of 1998, Congress had already determined that US policy should 'support efforts to remove the regime headed by Saddam Hussein

---

[1] SS Akermark, 'Storms, Foxes and Nebulous Legal Arguments: Twelve Years of Force Against Iraq, 1991–2003' (2005) 54 ICLQ 221; C Gray, 'From Unity to Polarization: International Law and the Use of Force against Iraq' (2002) 13 *European Journal of International Law* 1.

[2] See Ch 4.

[3] T Weiner, 'Raid on Baghdad', *New York Times*, 27 June 1993, available at <http://www.nytimes.com/1993/06/27/world/raid-on-baghdad-attack-is-aimed-at-the-heart-of-iraq-s-spy-network.html?pagewanted=1>. One missile failed to explode.   [4] Resolution 949 (1994).

[5] See Ch 4.

from power in Iraq and to promote the emergence of a democratic government to replace that regime'.[6] This included an appropriation of up to US$95 million in military assistance to the democratic opposition, although direct military action was not yet foreseen.

The prospect of using force against Iraq was raised in the United States immediately after the 9/11 attack. However, there was general agreement that Afghanistan should be the target of military action, given the intimate involvement of the Taliban regime with the Al Qaida movement. The Taliban were directly supporting Al Qaida, offering important training and operational facilities on its territory. In the wake of Al Qaida attacks on US targets, in particular its embassies in Tanzania and Kenya, the UN Security Council had clearly confirmed that link, imposed sanctions, and even demanded the surrender of Osama bin Laden.[7]

I. Self-defence and Preventative War

After 9/11, the UN Security Council recognized the right of the United States to self-defence in response.[8] NATO invoked its collective defence clause contained in Article 5 of its constitutive instrument.[9] The armed action against Afghanistan, conducted in cooperation with local opposition forces, led to the surprisingly rapid collapse of the Taliban regime. There was widespread international support for the operation, which lasted from 7 October to 13 November 2001. It was not seriously challenged in the UN Security Council and indirectly endorsed by it.[10] The lack of a challenge was due in part to the widespread sympathy for the United States and the trauma of 9/11.[11] In addition, much of the fighting on the ground, including the march on Kabul, was carried out by indigenous Afghan opposition forces. Hence, many observers felt that the question of whether the removal of the Afghan Government was a proportionate response to the 9/11 attack by the United States alone did not arise. Moreover, the Taliban had persistently ignored mandatory demands of the Security Council to remove the terrorist infrastructure from their territory. Sanctions had been employed, to no avail. It was, therefore, possible to argue that force had become 'necessary' in the legal sense of the word, all other avenues of action having been exhausted.

---

[6] Public Law 105–338, 105th Congress, 112 Stat 3178, 31 October 1988.

[7] For example UN Security Council Resolution 1267 (1999).

[8] Resolutions 1368 (2001) and 1373 (2001).

[9] North Atlantic Council, Press Release 124 (2001), 12 September 2001.

[10] Resolution 1378 (2001) noted the result of the operation in the Preamble in the context of its 'support for international efforts to root out terrorism'.

[11] For example M Williamson, (2009) *Terrorism, War and International Law: The Legality of the Use of Force Against Afghanistan in 2001* 195ff.

Afghanistan was, in fact, an example of forcible regime change. To the US administration, it must have appeared that regime change was militarily possible (indeed, relatively easy) and would not necessarily trigger international condemnation. In 2000, the Milosevic Government of Serbia had been removed from office. Although this had been a peaceful, internal process, it was thought that the result was a delayed consequence of NATO armed action against Kosovo in 1999. Moreover, in 2000, very limited UK intervention led to the restoration of a semblance of democratic governance in Sierra Leone. Again, there was no international resistance to this operation, and it appeared that regime change was indeed an option that might be pursued more broadly, and perhaps with only limited military involvement and political costs.[12]

A. The preventative war argument

The possibility of US military action against Iraq was raised again as soon as the Taliban regime had fallen. On 21 November 2001, President Bush reportedly gave instructions to his Secretary of Defence Donald Rumsfeld to review military plans for an invasion of Iraq.[13] This process continued with increasing intensity over the following months. On 29 January 2002, President Bush gave his State of the Union Address. In it, he described North Korea, Iran, and Iraq as elements of an 'axis of evil':[14]

By seeking weapons of mass destruction, these regimes pose a grave and growing danger. They could provide these arms to terrorists, giving them the means to match their hatred. They could attack our allies or attempt to blackmail the United States. In any of these cases, the price of indifference would be catastrophic. ... America will do what is necessary to ensure our national security.

As preparations for war continued, the President became more specific. Addressing the West Point Military Academy in June 2002, he attacked the previous international strategy of seeking to contain Iraq through a mixture of sanctions, arms limitation, and no-fly zones: 'Containment is not possible when unbalanced dictators with weapons of mass destruction can deliver those weapons on missiles or secretly provide them to terrorist allies', he claimed.[15] In addition to addressing the risks of WMD and future terrorism, it was believed that 'regime change in Iraq would bring about a number of benefits to the region'.[16]

---

[12] For a perceptive assessment of this background, see WM Reisman, 'Why Regime Change is (Almost Always) a Bad Idea' (2004) 98(3) AJIL 516.

[13] B Woodward, (2004) *Plan of Attack* 1.

[14] State of the Union Address, 29 January 2002, reproduced in J Ehrenberg et al., (2010) *The Iraq Papers* 59ff.

[15] Graduation Speech at West Point, 1 June 2002, reproduced in Ehrenberg et al. (above n 14) 65f.

[16] Dick Cheney, Speech at Veterans of Foreign Wars National Convention, 26 August 2002, reproduced in Ehrenberg et al. (above n 14) 75, 79.

This included freedom for the people of Iraq and the prospect of democratization and greater stability for the Middle East as a whole. These wider aims coincided with the neoconservative stream of foreign policy that was progressively taking hold of the administration. This was led by important figures, including in particular Vice President Dick Cheney, Secretary of Defence Donald Rumsfeld, and Deputy Secretary of Defence Paul Wolfowitz.[17]

The US Government believed that there was already sufficient legal authority to act against Iraq. However, that authority would be bolstered by the newly emerging doctrine of pre-emption.[18] This doctrine indicated that, in the age of the confluence of terrorism and WMD, and after the traumatic experience of 9/11, the United States would not sit idly by while threats to its security gathered force. Instead, it would strike first, according to its new National Security Strategy, issued by President Bush and his National Security Adviser Condoleezza Rice in September 2002. That document stated:[19]

For centuries, international law recognized that nations need not suffer an attack before they can lawfully take action to defend themselves against forces that present an imminent danger of attach. Legal scholars and international jurists often conditioned the legitimacy of pre-emption on the existence of an imminent threat—most often a visible mobilization of armies, navies and air forces preparing for attack.

We must adapt the concept of imminent threat to the capabilities and objectives of today's adversaries. Rogue states and terrorists do not seek to attack us using conventional means. They know such attacks would fail. Instead they rely on acts of terror and, potentially, the use of weapons of mass destruction—weapons that can be easily concealed, delivered covertly, and used without warning. ...

The United States has long maintained the option of pre-emptive actions to counter a sufficient threat to our national security. The greater the threat, the greater is the risk of inaction—and the more compelling the case for taking anticipatory action to defend ourselves, even if uncertainty remains as to the time and place of the enemy's attack. To forestall or present such hostile acts by our adversaries, the United States will, if necessary, act pre-emptively.

The United State will not use force in all cases to pre-empt emerging threats, nor should nations use pre-emption as a pretext for aggression. Yet in an age where the enemies of civilization openly and actively seek the world's most destructive technologies, the United States cannot remain idle while dangers gather.

In October 2002, while feverish attempts were underway in New York to agree new modalities for the completion of the disarmament process of Iraq through

---

[17] The various motivations for war have been assessed by many writers, most recently, for instance, by J Record, *Wanting War* (2010). He explains the action with reference to the wider neoconservative project that had gained hold of the US Administration.

[18] AD Sofaer, 'On the Necessity of Pre-emption' (2003) 14(2) *European Journal of International Law* 209; M Glennon, 'Pre-empting Terrorism: The Case for Anticipatory Self-Defense' (2002) 7(19) *The Weekly Standard* 24.

[19] The National Security Strategy of the United States of America, issued in September 2002, reproduced in Ehrenberg et al. (above n 14) 81, 84.

the UN, the US Congress adopted a Joint Resolution, authorizing the use of US armed forces against Iraq. The Resolution determined that Iraq 'posed a continuing threat to the national security of the United States and international peace and security in the Persian Gulf region'. Iraq had demonstrated its 'continued hostility toward, and willingness to attack, the United States, including by attempting in 1993 to assassinate former President Bush'. Moreover, it claimed that Al Qaida members responsible for the 9/11 attacks were present in Iraq. The 9/11 attacks, the document continued, underscored the gravity of the threat posed by the acquisition of WMD by international terrorist organizations. In view of its past use of WMD:[20]

...the risk that the current Iraqi regime will either employ those weapons to launch a surprise attack against the United States or its Armed forces or provide them to international terrorists who would do so, and the extreme magnitude of harm that would result to the United States and its citizens from such an attack, combine to justify action by the United States to defend itself.

At the commencement of the invasion of Iraq, US President Bush declared that action had been taken 'to defend the world from grave danger'. The United States and its allies would not 'live at the mercy of an outlaw regime that threatens the peace with weapons of mass murder'.[21] Immediately after the outbreak of hostilities, a number of legal commentators endorsed the thesis that legal authority for action could be based on self-defence.[22] They remained, however, isolated.

B. Self-defence and pre-emption in international law

The International Court of Justice (ICJ) has confirmed that self-defence is available 'only when the wrongful act provoking the response was an armed attack'.[23] The 2002 US National Security Strategy correctly claimed that self-defence can apply even before an armed attack—required by Article 51 of the UN Charter on self-defence—finds its target.[24] According to the classical formula established in the *Caroline* case, and widely accepted as being reflective of customary international law, self-defence can be invoked in cases of 'instant and overwhelming

---

[20] HJ Res 114, 207th Congress, 2nd Sess, available at <http://usgovinfo.about.com/library/weekly/bliraqreshouse.htm>.

[21] George W Bush, Announcement of the Start of Operation Iraqi Freedom, 19 March 2003, reproduced in Ehrenberg et al. (above n 14) 114.

[22] For instance, J Yoo, 'International Law and the War in Iraq' (2003) 97 AJIL 563, 571; R. Wedgwood, 'The Fall of Saddam Hussein: Security Council Mandates and Pre-emptive Self-Defence' (2003) 97 AJIL 576, 582; with the opposing position taken by M Shapiro, 'Iraq: The Shifting Sands of Pre-emptive Self-Defence' (2003) AJIL 599; TM Franck, 'What Happens Now? The United Nations after Iraq' (2003) AJIL 607, 611.

[23] *Military and Paramilitary Activities* (1986) ICJ Rep 14, 110.

[24] This is a very well-rehearsed issue in international law. See, eg TM Franck, (2002) *Recourse to Force: State Action against Threats and Armed Attacks*.

necessity' and 'leaving no choice of means and no moment of deliberation'.[25] The US doctrine sought to expand significantly upon the criteria for anticipatory self-defence by replacing the traditional criterion of imminence of a threat with that of a 'sufficient' threat.[26]

There has been debate about the point in time when the right of self-defence becomes available to counter an imminent threat.[27] Israel's first strike against Egypt in 1967 was found acceptable by some. Egypt had required the removal of the UN peace-keeping force in that instance, had placed its forces in readiness, and deployed them for attack. Intelligence clearly confirmed that the capacity to attack within a very short period of time was matched by an intention to do so.[28] On the other hand, when Israel launched an air attack against Iraqi nuclear installations in 1981, that action was strongly condemned. The Security Council unanimously declared (with the concurring vote of the United States) that the attack amounted to a 'clear violation of the Charter of the United Nations'.[29] Much like the United States in this instance, Israel argued that the Iraqi reactors posed a gathering threat that would, in the future, result in an Iraqi nuclear capacity capable of being deployed against Israel. While this contingency was still some way off, it was necessary to attack the reactors at this early point, before they became operational and could not be destroyed without posing a significant risk to the environment.[30]

International law balances the need to maintain the credibility of the prohibition of the use of force with the need to permit self-defensive action at a time when the state concerned can still effectively defend itself. In particular, in the missile age, it has been difficult to require a state under imminent threat of attack to await the first strike, as this might seriously impair its ability to mount an

---

[25] In fact, traditionally, there has been a huge debate on whether or not the UN Charter still permits this classical right of anticipatory self-defence enunciated in the *Caroline* case (1837) 2 *Moore's Digest* 409. Proponents of this view point to the fact that Art 51 on self-defence describes the right as an 'inherent' one. If it is inherent, it cannot be restricted by a new definition offered in the UN Charter, the argument goes. The opposing view holds the Art 51 requires that an armed attack 'occurs'. Hence, self-defence is only available in response to an actual, not an anticipated attack.

[26] For example AC Arend, 'International Law and the Preemptive Use of Military Force' (2003) 26 *Washington Quarterly* 89, who held the doctrine to be incompatible with anticipatory self-defence and argued that the United States should commit itself to the *Caroline* formula while working towards its adaptation to current circumstances in the Security Council.

[27] This debate is famously represented by I Brownlie in (1963) *International Law and the Use of Force by States* 259f, who cautioned that 'to permit anticipatory action may well be to accept a right which is wider than self-defence and akin to that of self-preservation', and by D Bowett in (1958) *Self-Defence in International Law* 192, who claimed that 'no state can be expected to await an initial attack which, in the present state of armaments, may well destroy the state's capacity for further resistance and so jeopardize its very existence'.

[28] See, with further references, SA Alexandrov, (1996) *Self-Defence against the Use of Force in International Law* 153.   [29] Resolution 487 (1981), para 1.

[30] WT Mallison and SV Mallison, 'The Israeli Aerial Attack of 7 June 1981' (1982) 17 *Vanderbilt Journal of Transnational Law* 417; A Contra, 'Israel's Air Strike against the Osiraq Reactor: A Retrospective' (1996) 10 *Temple International and Comparative Law Journal* 259.

effective defence. On the other hand, permitting armed action in response to less immediate threats of attack would result in a high degree of instability. Each state would be tempted to strike earlier than the other.

This balancing act is achieved by ruling out preventative or pre-emptive war, while permitting anticipatory self-defence. Preventive war is a matter of classical cabinet diplomacy of the nineteenth century. One state or alliance would attack another while it was in a position of military preponderance. There would be no point in waiting until the other side had strengthened its own military capability. That future prospect would be denied through preventative action. The prohibition of war as a means of national policy has clearly removed that prospect.

Pre-emptive war concerns a situation where armed conflict is likely. The other side has already amassed a significant, and perhaps superior military arsenal and may, in the future, consider mounting an attack: 'A claim for pre-emptive self-defence can point only to a possibility among a range of other possibilities, a contingency'.[31] In such a situation a first strike is undertaken in order to ensure victory that might be less certain, or indeed impossible, if the other side were to strike first. Both the wording of Article 51 of the UN Charter on self-defence (if an armed attack occurs), and the customary requirement of an 'instant of overwhelming necessity' rule out pre-emption.

Finally, there is anticipatory self-defence. Where an adversary has obtained the capacity to launch an imminent attack (deploying its forces in strike positions, fuelling up missiles, etc) and there is clear evidence of an intention to strike, action may be taken at the last possible moment to disrupt a chain of events that would otherwise inevitably result in the landing of the attack. Any such self-defence action must not only be absolutely necessary, but must also remain within the boundaries of proportionality.

However, the application of this balanced doctrine to the new circumstances of terrorism poses problems.[32] First, until 9/11, it was controversial whether the

---

[31] WM Reisman and A Armstrong, 'The Past and Future of the Claim of Pre-emptive Self-Defence' (2006) 100 AJIL 525, 527.

[32] D Brown, 'Use of Force Against Terrorism after September 11th: State Responsibility, Self-Defence, and Other Resources' (2003) 11 *Cardozo Journal of Comparative and International Law* 1; M Byers, 'Terrorism, the Use of Force, and International Law after 11 September' (2002) 51 ICLQ 401; A Cassese, 'Terrorism Is Also Disrupting Some Crucial Legal Categories of International Law' (2001) 12 *European Journal of International Law* 993; JI Charney, 'The Use of Force Against Terrorism and International Law' (2001) 95(4) AJIL 835; J Delbrück, 'The Fight Against Global Terrorism: Self-Defense or Collective Security as International Police Action? Some Comments on the International Legal Implications of the "War against Terrorism"' (2001) 44 *German Yearbook of International Law* 9; C Greenwood, 'International Law and the "War against Terrorism"' (2002) 78 *International Affairs* 301; G Guillaume, 'Terrorism and International Law' (2004) 53 ICLQ 537; WK Lietzau, 'Old Laws, New Wars: Jus Ad Bellum in an Age of Terrorism' (2004) 8 *Max Planck Yearbook of United Nations Law*, 383; R Müllerson, 'Jus Ad bellum and International Terrorism' (2002) 32 *Israel Yearbook on Human Rights* 1; J Paust, 'Use of Armed Force against Terrorists in Afghanistan, Iraq and Beyond' (2002) 35 *Cornell International Law Journal* 533; N Schrijver, 'Responding to International Terrorism: Moving the Frontiers of International Law for "Enduring Freedom"' (2001) 48 *Netherlands International Law Review* 271; J-A Romano, 'Combating

right of self-defence applied at all in the context of terrorism. It was previously assumed that Article 51 of the UN Charter on self-defence applied only in relations among states and did not extend to non-state actors.[33] However, the clear response of the Security Council to 9/11, along with NATO's uncontested invocation of Article 5 of the Washington Treaty, overturned that assumption.[34] Several difficult problems remain, however. First, it is hard to establish that a terrorist movement has the capacity and intent to launch a strike in the immediate future. Unless the organization in question has been penetrated by intelligence, it is impossible to observe any tangible infrastructure of warfare. Even if the organization is penetrated, it may not be possible to reveal publicly why an imminent attack is certain at the point of anticipatory action. This has led a group of distinguished international legal experts to conclude that, in the case of terrorist threats, self-defence should be permitted at the very last point when the threat can still be effectively engaged. At this point, the extent of the risk posed should be considered, and in particular whether WMD are involved. However, in view of the risk of abuse of that doctrine, 'force may be used only on a proper factual basis and after a good faith assessment of the facts'.[35]

Second, there is the issue of attribution. Unless an attack engages a target on the high seas in a vessel without national registration, it is inevitable that armed action against terrorists will take place on the territory of a third state. At what point is that state sufficiently entwined with the terrorist movement to attract the consequences of a strike against a target on its territory? Classical international law is very restrictive on this point, requiring a direct relationship of command and control between the state concerned and irregular armed forces, before the

Terrorism and Weapons of Mass Destruction: Reviving the Doctrine of State Necessity' (1999) 87 *Georgetown Law Journal* 1023; KA Felix, 'Weapons of Mass Destruction: The Changing Threat and the Evolving Solution' (2003) 34 *McGeorge Law Review* 391; S Gahlaut, 'The War on Terror and the Non-Proliferation Regime' (2004) 48(3) *Orbis* 489; A Kelle, 'Terrorism using biological and nuclear weapons: a critical analysis of risks after 11 September 2001', PRIF Research Report, No 64; GD Koblentz, 'Pathogens as Weapons: The International Security Implications of Biological Warfare' (2003) 28(3) *International* 84; J Parachini, 'Putting WMD Terrorism in Perspective' (2003) 26(4) *Washington Quarterly* 37; RS Litwak, 'Non-Proliferation and the Dilemmas of Regime Change' (2003/4) 45(4) *Survival* 7.

[33] See the extensive discussion in L Moir, (2010) *Reappraising the Resort to Force* 22ff; and the ICJ in the *Wall* Opinion (2004) ICJ Rep 135, 62.

[34] TM Franck, 'Terrorism and the Right of Self-Defense' (2001) 95(4) AJIL 839; C Stahn, 'Terrorist Acts as "Armed Attacks": The Right to Self-Defense, Article 51 of the UN Charter, and International Terrorism' (2003) 27 *Fletcher Forum of World Affairs* 35; SD Murphy, 'Self-Defense and the Israeli *Wall* Advisory Opinion: An *Ipse Dixit* from the ICJ?' (2005) 99 AJIL 62; R Wedgwood, 'The ICJ Advisory Opinion on the Israeli Security Fence and the Limits of Self-Defense' (2005) 99(1) AJIL 52.

[35] E Wilmshurst, (2005) *Chatham House Principles of International Law on the Use of Force by States* 8: 'Force may be used only when any further delay would result in an inability by the threatened state effectively to defend against or avert the attack against it. In assessing the imminence of the attack, reference may be made to the gravity of the attack, the capability of the attacker, and the nature of the threat, for example, if the attack is likely to come without warning'. See also V Lowe, 'Clear and Present Danger: Responses to Terrorism' (2005) 54 ICLQ 185, 192.

state itself can be subject to self-defence action.[36] More recently, it has been suggested that action can be taken if the host state of the terrorist group has proven persistently unwilling or unable to address the threat, and if there is no other means of engaging an imminent attack.[37]

A third problem concerns the reactive nature of counter-terrorism operations. Self-defence is not meant to be punitive. It is not to be confused with retaliation directed at the transgressing state, or an act of reprisal. Such action is clearly prohibited in international law.[38] Instead, self-defence is only permitted to prevent or terminate an actual or imminent armed attack. Its application ceases when the armed attack has been reversed. However, it will generally not be possible to engage a terrorist attack when it happens. In practice, action has to be taken subsequently, once the authors of the attack and the location of their infrastructure have been identified. In the earlier practice of the UN Security Council, such action (usually performed by the United States, and previously by Israel and South Africa) was generally condemned by other states.[39] However, in more recent instances, Security Council members have noted formal claims to self-defence in such instances with greater understanding.[40] There was still hesitancy in 1993 when the United States attacked the Iraqi intelligence headquarters in Baghdad in response to an alleged Iraqi intelligence plot against former US President Bush. But by 1998, when the United States attacked targets in Sudan and Afghanistan in connection with Al Qaida terrorist attacks, the operation was more sympathetically received by other states.[41] And, as already noted, the 2001 operation against Afghanistan was generally accepted as self-defence.

In all these instances, the United States formally invoked the right to self-defence. While the action taken was clearly triggered by a previous act of terrorism, it was necessary to argue that it was not mere retaliation. Instead, it was claimed to be preventing the next terrorist operation. Further operations would invariably follow unless the terrorism infrastructure that was uncovered was destroyed.[42]

---

[36] Further to the *Nicaragua* case (*Military and Paramilitary Activities in and against Nicaragua (Nicaragua v United States of America)*, Merits, judgment of 27 June 1986), see *Armed Activities (DRC v Uganda)* (2005) ICJ Rep 14, 146, and the useful survey of the case law in C Gray, (3rd edn, 2008) *International Law and the Use of Force* 75ff.

[37] See the significant body of writings on these issues, eg: Brown (above n 32); Byers (above n 32); Cassese (above n 32); Charney (above n 32), who argue against uses of force in response to terrorism without Chapter VII authorization; Delbrück (above n 32); Greenwood (above n 32); Guillaume (above n 32); Lietzau (above n 32); Müllerson (above n 32); Paust (n 32 above); Schrijver (above n 32).

[38] For example General Assembly Resolution 2625 (XXV), Principle 1: 'States have a duty to refrain from acts of reprisal involving the use of force'.

[39] For example, the 1986 US bombing of Libya in response to the terrorist attack against the La Belle Discotheque in Berlin, which was mainly frequented by US service members.

[40] For example Williamson (above n 11) 132–145.

[41] In fact, it later emerged that the claims against Sudan may well have been unfounded.

[42] This practice is supported, *inter alia*, by O Schachter, 'The Right of States to Use Armed Force' (1984) 82 *Michigan Law Review* 1620.

A fourth problem concerns the requirement of proportionality.[43] It is very difficult to assess what level of force is proportionate to an atrocity of the scale of the World Trade Centre attacks. Moreover, as self-defence is meant to aim at preventing the next, imminent attack, how does one judge what is proportionate to an attack that has not yet occurred, and about which little or nothing is known?

The United States had, in fact, moved towards a modest policy of pre-emption in relation to terrorism attacks during the previous period of conservative government under President Reagan. Under the so-called 'Schultz doctrine', it was asserted that 'a nation attacked by terrorists is permitted to use force to prevent or pre-empt future attacks, to seize terrorists, or to rescue its citizens when no other means is available'.[44] However, it was also clarified that this approach would concern tactical or surgical operations against specific and individual terrorist targets.[45] The new doctrine of prevention, it seemed, was potentially of far broader application, in particular where it concerned the use of force against the so-called 'rogue states', or members of the axis of evil for the purpose of regime change.

The reintroduction of the notion of pre-emption, or even of preventative wars aimed at regime change, into the diplomatic dictionary was widely resisted in international legal practice and scholarship.[46] The endorsement of prevention or pre-emption by the United States was noted at the time with increasing desperation even by Washington's closest allies.[47] For instance, the principal UK Legal Adviser wrote:

If state practice were to develop in the direction of a doctrine of 'pre-emption' or if 'regime change' became accepted as a proper objective, it would be open season for all States to attack those whom they perceive as threatening them (eg. India and Pakistan).[48]

---

[43] J Gardam, (2004) *Necessity, Proportionality and the Use of Force by States* 155ff.

[44] US Secretary of State Schultz, 15 January 1986, quoted in Reisman and Armstrong (above n 31) 528, and AD Sofaer, 'The Reagan and Bush Administrations' in MP Scharf and PR Williams, (2010) *Shaping Foreign Policy in Times of Crisis: The Role of International Law and the State Department Legal Adviser* 65, 85.   [45] Ibid.

[46] See, eg Gray (above n 36) 211ff; and at length the broader discussion, for instance in: WM Reisman, 'In Defense of World Public Order' (2001) 95(4) AJIL 833; WM Reisman, 'Assessing Claims to Revise the Laws of War' (2003) 97(1) AJIL 82; I Brownlie, 'International Law and the Use of Force by States Revisited' (2001) 21 *Australian Yearbook of International Law* 21; IH Daalder, 'The Use of Force in a Changing World—US and European Perspectives' (2003) 16(1) *Leiden Journal of International Law* 171; TM Franck, 'The Use of Force in International Law' (2003) 11 *Tulane Journal of International and Comparative Law* 7; J Brunnee and SJ Toope, 'The Use of Force: International Law After Iraq' (2004) 53(4) ICLQ 785; H Neuhold, 'Collective Security After "Operation Allied Force"' (2000) 4 *Max Planck Yearbook for United Nations Law* 73.

[47] The Australian Prime Minister John Howard had appeared to endorse pre-emptive strikes against terrorism, triggering a very strong rash of rejections of this proposition from his own opposition and from the states of the region. See 'Malaysia, Philippines Slam Howard's Pre-Emptive Strike Talks', *Sydney Morning Herald*, 2 December 2002, available at <http://www.smh.com.au/articles/2002/12/02/1038712877384.html>.   [48] Below, Chapter 6, 204.

As the prospect of war with Iraq drew closer, the UN Secretary-General himself found it necessary to remind the United States and others that:[49]

When states decide to use force, not in self-defence but to deal with broader threats to international peace and security, there is no substitute for the unique legitimacy provided by the United Nations Security Council. States and peoples around the world attach fundamental importance to such legitimacy, and to the international rule of law.

After the Iraq episode, the UN High Level Panel on Threats, Challenges, and Change ruled authoritatively on the matter. It confirmed that a threatened state can take military action 'as long as the threatened attack is *imminent*'. In respect to threats that are not imminent, but still 'claim to be real', such as the acquisition with allegedly hostile intent of nuclear weapons-making capability, the question would be whether a state could act without reference to the Security Council. According to the Panel:[50]

190. The short answer is that if there are good arguments for preventive military action, with good evidence to support them, they should be put to the Security Council, which can authorize such action if it chooses to. If it does not so choose, there will be, by definition, time to pursue other strategies, including persuasion, negotiation, deterrence and containment—and to visit again the military option.

191. For those impatient with such a response, the answer must be that, in a world full of perceived potential threats, the risk to the global order and the norm of non-intervention on which it continues to be based is simply too great for the legality of unilateral preventive action, as distinct from collectively endorsed action, to be accepted. Allowing one to so act is to allow all.

In his document 'In Larger Freedom' in 2005, the UN Secretary-General opined:[51]

124. Imminent threats are fully covered by Article 51, which safeguards the inherent right of sovereign States to defend themselves against armed attack. Lawyers have long recognized that this covers an imminent attack as well as one that has already happened.

At the 2005 UN World Summit, this view was authoritatively confirmed. The Summit expressly recognized a whole range of threats that required urgent, collective, and more determined responses. However, it found:[52]

We reaffirm that the relevant provisions of the Charter are sufficient to address the full range of threats to international peace and security. We further reaffirm the authority of the Security Council to mandate coercive action to maintain and restore international peace and security. We stress the importance of acting in accordance with the purposes and principles of the Charter.

---

[49] UN Information Service, 'Secretary-General Says United Nations Has Duty to Exhaust All Possibilities of Peaceful Settlement Before Resorting to Use of Force', SG/SM/8600, 10 February 2003.   [50] Note by the Secretary-General, A/59/565, 2 December 2004.
[51] Report of the Secretary-General, A/59/205, 21 March 2005.
[52] A/60/1, 24 October 2005.

Similarly, shortly after the invasion of Iraq the ICJ emphasized that:[53]

The prohibition of the use of force is a cornerstone of the United Nations Charter. ... Article 51 of the Charter may justify a use of force in self-defence only within the strict confines there laid down. It does not allow the use of force by a State to protect perceived security interests beyond these parameters. Other means are available to a concerned State, including, in particular, recourse to the Security Council.

The thesis of preventative or pre-emptive war therefore was widely rejected.[54] Nevertheless, the United States continued to place the proposed armed action against Iraq in the context of prevention.[55] After the invasion was launched, the United States informed the UN Security Council that it was a necessary step to 'defend the United States and the international community from the threat posed by Iraq'.[56] However, there was no specific indication as to the nature of the threat or, more particularly, its imminence.

These statements were mainly directed at the political arena. In reality no very serious attempt was made to pursue the argument of preventative or pre-emptive self-defence beyond this claim. While it may have been possible to consider Iraq a 'gathering' danger, it was not possible to place it in the category of an imminent threat. This applied to the United States itself, as it had been established at the time of the invasion that Iraq was not in fact involved with Al Qaida. There was also no claim from any state in the region that Iraq constituted an imminent threat. Instead, the official justification proffered by the United States to the Council was based on the fact that 'in view of Iraq's material breaches, the basis for the cease-fire has been removed and force is authorized under resolution 678 (1990)'.[57] Similarly, the US Department of State Legal Advisers found it necessary to entitle their justification for the war 'Pre-emption, Iraq and International Law'.[58] However, they actually based their argument entirely on the so-called 'revival argument', as in the US submission to the Council. That argument sought to establish legal authority for the use of force on the basis of previous Security Council authorizations. The US Legal Advisers merely claimed in their article that the legal justification offered by previous Council decisions was not undermined by the fact that the operation could also be characterized as pre-emption.

---

[53] *Armed Activities (DRC v Congo)* (2005) ICJ Rep 1, 53f.

[54] Again, see eg the debate between M Bothe, 'Terrorism and the Legality of Pre-emptive Force' (2003) 14(2) *European Journal of International Law* 227; M Sapiro, 'Agora—Future Implications of the Iraq Conflict: Iraq: The Shifting Sands of Pre-emptive Self-Defense' (2003) 97(3) AJIL 599; C Schaller, 'Massenvernichtungswaffen und Präventivkrieg—Möglichkeiten der Rechtfertigung einer militärischen Intervention im Irak aus völkerrechtlicher Sicht' (2002) 62 *Zeitschrift für öffentliches ausländisches Recht und Völkerrecht* 641.

[55] For example White House Spokesman Ari Fleisher, 15 October 2002, quoted in Reisman and Armstrong (above n 31) 531.

[56] US Letter to the President of the Security Council, S/2003/353, 20 March 2003.

[57] Ibid.

[58] WH Taft IV and TF Buchwald, 'Pre-Emption, Iraq and International Law' (2003) 97 AJIL 557.

Given the internationally controversial nature of the doctrine of pre-emption, and the fact that it was deemed unacceptable by Washington's close and critical ally, the United Kingdom, the battle for legal authority relating to Iraq turned on the question of possible UN authorization, in particular the revival argument, considered at some length in Chapter 4.[59] As Paul Wolfowitz put it, 'We settled on the one issue that everyone could agree on, which was weapons of mass destruction, as the core reason'.[60] After considerable internal debate and division, at the insistence of Secretary of State Colin Powell and the UK Prime Minister, the US administration also agreed to 'go the UN route' in seeking to strengthen the case for action against Iraq.[61] However, it maintained throughout that it had authority to act regardless.

II. Resolution 1441 (2002)

In his speech to the UN General Assembly in September 2002, US President Bush appeared to endorse the plan of 'going the UN route' in relation to Iraq. That speech, however, was not really reflective of a wholehearted endorsement of further UN involvement in the matter, but had a bellicose ring to it. The President noted that 'outlaw groups and regimes that accept no law of morality and have no limit in their violent ambitions' posed a major threat, and that 'our greatest fear is that terrorists will find a shortcut to their mad ambitions when an outlaw regime supplies them with the technologies enabling them to kill on a massive scale'.[62] He continued:[63]

In one place, in one regime, we find all these dangers, in their most lethal and aggressive forms—exactly the kind of aggressive threat the United Nations was born to confront. ...

Saddam Hussein's regime is a grave and gathering danger. ... Saddam Hussein attacked Iran in 1980 and Kuwait in 1990. He has fired ballistic missiles at Iran and Saudi Arabia, Bahrain and Israel. His regime once ordered the killing of every person between the ages of 15 and 70 in certain Kurdish villages in Northern Iraq. He has gassed many Iranians and 40 Iraqi villages. ...

My nation will work with the Security Council to meet our common challenge. If Iraq's regime defies us again, the world must move deliberately and decisively to hold Iraq to account. We will work with the Security Council for the necessary resolutions. But the purposes of the United States should not be doubted. The Security Council Resolutions

---

[59] Sean Murphy argues that the United States in fact formally abandoned the pre-emption argument: SD Murphy, 'Assessing the Legality of Invading Iraq' (2003–4) 92 *Georgetown Law Journal* 173, 175.

[60] The context of this statement was later disputed, but the correct attribution has been confirmed: S Tannenhaus, interview with *Vanity Fair*, 9 May 2003, available at <http://transcripts.cnn.com/TRANSCRIPTS/0305/30/se.08.html>.

[61] For example Woodward (above n 13) 156, 183. [62] A/57/PV.2, 12 September 2002, 6.

[63] Ibid.

will be enforced, and the just demands of peace and security will be met, or action will be unavoidable, and a regime that has lost its legitimacy will also lose its power.

President Bush established a series of conditions that would have to be fulfilled 'if Iraq wishes peace'. These included:

- Immediate destruction of all weapons of mass destruction, long-range missiles, and all related material.
- Ending all support for terrorism and action to suppress it.
- Ceasing persecution of its civilian population.
- Releasing or accounting for all personnel whose fate from the Kuwait war remained unknown.
- Returning all stolen or looted Kuwaiti property.
- Accepting liability for all losses resulting from the invasion of Kuwait.
- Terminating all illicit trade outside the Oil for Food programme.

This listing of requirements was extensive. They could all be based on demands made by the UN Security Council, although it is not clear how any other than the first two (disarmament and terrorism) were related to a gathering threat posed by Iraq that might require a forcible response.[64]

A. Elements of a possible resolution

Discussions at the UN on a possible fresh resolution to reignite international collective action relating to Iraq commenced almost immediately after President Bush's speech.[65] At the time, the applicable arms control regime was contained in Resolution 1284 (1999), which had been adopted after the collapse of the disarmament effort in the wake of Operation Desert Fox. In answer to Iraqi allegations that the UN Special Commission (UNSCOM), the previous UN inspection body, had acted as a spy for the United Kingdom and United States before the armed attack, the Commission had been replaced by the UN Monitoring, Verification and Inspection Commission (UNMOVIC), a new body also operating under the authority of the Security Council. However, UNMOVIC essentially took over the existing mandate, although it was also supposed to offer a 'reinforced system of ongoing monitoring and verification' after the task of accounting and destroying of proscribed items was completed. UNMOVIC was to have unrestricted access to any areas, facilities, records, etc. It would operate according to an accelerated work plan, with a view to facilitating the progressive lifting of sanctions 120 days after the ongoing monitoring system had been put into place.

However, this 'new beginning' did not materialize. After the 1998 bombing campaign, Iraq evidently judged that it had suffered the worst that was to come.

---

[64] Essentially, these were all outstanding issues from UN Security Council Resolutions 687 (1991) and 688 (1991).

[65] See Sir J Greenstock, (2009) *Development at the UN: Statement to the Iraq Enquiry* 7ff.

The strong opposition in the Council to the use of force made it unlikely that additional forcible measures would be applied.

Iraq calculated that Council members would not be willing to adopt another resolution which, like Resolution 1205 (1998), might be invoked by the United States and United Kingdom as authority to use force again, however controversially. And even if more force were to be used, its impact would be limited and could be survived, as in the case of Operation Desert Fox. Moreover, the international consensus on maintaining sanctions, the only remaining pressure point, would gradually diminish. There was significant concern about the impact of sanctions on the Iraqi civilian population, backed by several UN reports detailing the suffering of vulnerable groups, including children.[66] Russia opposed a change in the sanctions regime towards targeted or so-called 'smart' sanctions, believing that sanctions should be removed altogether.[67] Other states shared this hostility towards the sanctions operation, and the complex and expensive (and, as it emerged, corrupt) Oil for Food programme attached to it. Hence, Iraq simply refused to admit the arms inspectors onto its territory. The inspectors remained ensconced in Cyprus, from where they were supposed to monitor developments.

By this time, however, the situation had changed. In view of the bellicose attitude of the United States, and the grim determination of the Bush administration to act, Iraq changed its stance in response to the speech at the General Assembly. Baghdad immediately declared its willingness to resume arms inspections. After discussions with the UN Secretary-General's staff in New York on 14–15 September 2002, Iraq decided 'to allow the return of the United Nations weapons inspectors without conditions'.[68] It did so expressly in the context of the commitment of all UN members, including in particular members of the Security Council, to respect the sovereignty, territorial integrity, and political independence of Iraq, as stipulated in Article 2 of the UN Charter (prohibiting the use of force).

The original UK plan had been to present Saddam Hussein with an ultimatum demanding the return of the inspectors to Iraq.[69] If rebuffed, this would have provided the *casus belli*.[70] The Iraqi declaration rendered that plan inoperative. Indeed, there was a risk that Iraq, and UNMOVIC, would simply return to the previous pattern of cat-and-mouse games, allowing the inspection process to exist in name only. Hence, it was decided that new requirements for the arms

---

[66] See the very extensive collection of materials from the World Health Organization (WHO), the UN Education, Scientific and Cultural Organization (UNESCO), the Food and Agricultural Organization (FAO), and NGOs assembled by the Campaign against Sanctions on Iraq, available at <http://www.casi.org.uk/info/themes.html#hum>.   [67] Ibid, 6.

[68] A/2002/1034, 16 September 2002.   [69] See Ch 6.

[70] 'Here the inspectors were introduced, but as a means to create the missing *casus belli*. If the UN could be made to agree on an ultimatum that Saddam accept inspectors, and if Saddam then refused to accept them, the Americans and the British would be well on their way to having a legal justification to go to war...': M Danner, 'The Secret Way to War' (2005) 52(10) *The New York Review of Books* 70, 74, available at <http://www.nybooks.com/articles/18034>.

inspection process would be established. If Iraq failed to comply immediately and unconditionally, the use of force would be clearly authorized by the Council.

While the United States was interested in 'setting the bar very high' for Iraq, with a view to obtaining an unquestionable case for military action if conditions remained unfulfilled, the United Kingdom advocated a more modest approach.[71] Elements of a draft resolution began circulating on 25 September 2002.[72] This document proved very controversial, as it appeared to include several suggestions developed by the Carnegie Endowment for International Peace on so-called 'coercive inspections', which included the possible threat or actual use of force on the ground during the inspections process.[73] The proposal, publicized in the United States at the very beginning of the negotiations process, had provided:[74]

It is a new system of coercive inspections to replace the game of cat and mouse that Mr. Hussein has perfected. The Security Council would create a powerful, American-led multinational military force, the inspections implementation force, that would enable the inspection teams to carry out 'comply or else' inspections. If Iraq refused to accept, or obstructed the inspections, regime change (preferably under a United Nations mandate) would be back on the table.

This force would be strong enough to ensure that inspectors see what they want, when they want, including sites previously designated off limits, with full security for the inspectors. A key is establishment of both 'no flight' and 'no drive' zones in the region where an inspection is being conducted. Air and armored cavalry forces would provide the ground strength. Intelligence is crucial. The force would be provided with a complete range of reconnaissance, surveillance, listening, encryption and photo-interpretation capabilities. True surprise inspections and prompt entry would be the norm, not the lucky exception.

The deployment of a US-led force in Iraq under a UN arms inspection mandate would not have been realistic. Nevertheless, important parts of this proposal were included in the initial discussion paper offered by the United States and United Kingdom on elements of a possible draft resolution, and a few were eventually retained in what became Resolution 1441 (2002). As the UK Permanent Representative recalled, the tensions that were to dog the search for the first, and then the second, resolution were present from the beginning:[75]

The harsh terms which Washington introduced at the beginning of the debate in mid September 2002 produced a strong reaction from France, China and particularly Russia, when we presented them within the P5. There were some very difficult and depressing exchanges. The US and UK in fact avoided presenting a draft resolution text as such,

[71] See Chapter 6.

[72] Printed in 'Latest US-Britain Draft of Resolution in the UN', *The New York Times*, 2 October 2002. [73] H Blix, (2004) *Disarming Iraq* 77.

[74] JT Mathews and CG Boyd, 'Arming the Arms Inspectors', *The New York Times*, 19 September 2002, available at <http://www.carnegieendowment.org/publications/index.cfm?fa=view&id=1075&zoom_highlight=coercive+disarmament>.

[75] Sir Jeremy Greenstock, (2009) Statement to the Iraq Inquiry 10.

because the Russians and French threatened immediately to counter-present a text of their own, a situation which it is wise to avoid in the Security Council. We were therefore constantly talking about 'elements' and 'concepts'. Gradually Negroponte and I obtained instructions to make concessions here and there and chinks of hope returned that we could make some small progress. As we moved into October, the Russian opposition appeared to turn a little less virulent, while the French took over the lead adversarial role through their insistence that no resolution could be passed without specifying that, then or later, the Security Council had to be the place where the actual use of force was decided upon.

The draft elements that were eventually submitted for consultation declared that Iraq was still, and has been for a number of years, in material breach of its obligations under the relevant resolutions. This reference would open the door to the revival argument, which had lost credibility after Desert Fox.[76] That argument held that the authority granted to states cooperating with the Government of Kuwait in 1990 by the Security Council to liberate Kuwait and restore peace and security in the area could be revived if Iraq materially breached the cease-fire terms of Resolution 687 (1990).

In order to begin to comply, Iraq would have to offer, not later than 30 days after the adoption of the resolution, a full and complete declaration of all aspects of its WMD programme. There would be immediate and unconditional access for UNMOVIC to any and all areas, facilities, records, etc. Moreover, UNMOVIC would be able to conduct interviews with Iraqi personnel outside of Iraq. To minimize the risk of pressure against these personnel, they could be accompanied by family members. No Iraqi observers would be present.

The proposal then set out additional modalities for the operation of UNMOVIC. These included the obligation that Iraq name all personnel associated with its WMD programme. Moreover, UNSCOM had the immediate right 'at their sole discretion' to remove, destroy, or render harmless all proscribed items, and to impound or close any facilities or equipment for the production thereof. Thus far, the conditions represented a tightening-up of previous procedures for implementing the arms inspection demands established in 1992. With the possible exception of the list of personnel (which may have run into thousands of potential candidates), the list appeared reasonable.

However, a number of additions were bound to be highly controversial. First, there was a requirement that any permanent member of the Security Council could be represented on the inspections team with the same rights as the proper inspectors. In view of the well-founded allegation that UNSCOM had been riddled with (mainly US) spies, and the fact that UNMOVIC had been created in response, this was unusual. Moreover, the inspection teams would be accompanied by 'UN Security Forces'. The status of such forces was unclear. They would have the right to declare no-fly/no-drive zones, exclusion zones, and/or

---

[76] See Ch 4.

ground- and air-transit corridors. Again, these powers were open and potentially very broad. Moreover, the proposal provided that these zones would be enforced by UN Security Forces 'or by members of the Council'. Hence, this appeared to give fairly open-ended enforcement powers to UN Council members even during the inspection process, before it was clear whether or not there was full compliance.

The proposal concluded with the following:

Decides that false statements or omissions in the declaration submitted by Iraq to the Council and failure by Iraq at any time to comply and cooperate fully in accordance with the provisions laid out in this resolution, shall constitute a further material breach of Iraq's obligations, and that such breach authorizes member states to use all necessary means to restore international peace and security in the area.

This provision went beyond previous pronouncements of the Security Council that were deemed sufficient to revive the use of force authorized in 1990. Earlier practice was that there needed to be (1) a finding that Iraq was in non-compliance, (2) a determination that such non-compliance was sufficiently serious to materially breach the terms of the cease-fire, and (3) a threat that Iraq would face 'serious consequences', merely implying that forcible action might ensue.[77] The express authorization to use 'all necessary means' (that is, force) would have been far preferable to reliance on implied authorization, given the controversy attached to previous practice under the revival doctrine.

Shortly thereafter, this initial document was converted into a more complete draft, although this was never officially tabled.[78] That draft included a reference to Resolution 678 (1990), which contained the original authorization to use force, and the fact that Iraqi compliance with Resolution 687 (1991) was a necessary step towards restoring international peace and security. This implied that, in the absence of full compliance, peace and security had not been restored and that an element of the forceful mandate granted in 1990 remained unfulfilled. Moreover, the draft recalled that the 1991 cease-fire suspending the operation of that authority was based on acceptance by Iraq of the provisions of the cease-fire resolution. This was another step towards restoration of the material breach argument. If Iraq breached the disarmament obligations contained in Resolution 687 (1991), it would thereby remove the basis for the cease-fire and the authority to use force would revive.

In line with previous elements, the draft confirmed that Iraq had been, and was at that time, in material breach. This brought the revival argument into operation. Nevertheless, the text provided for steps that Iraq could take in order to 'begin to comply' with its disarmament obligations. Thus, the onus was on Iraq to remove the present status of 'material breach', and the attendant (claimed) authority to

---

[77] See Ch 4, 106.
[78] Draft Security Council Resolution of the US/UK, 2 October 2002, available at <http://www.casi.org.uk/info/usukdraftscr021002.html>.

use force, through active cooperation with the inspection effort. Again, a further material breach would authorize states to take all necessary measures.

The draft also added conditions to the modalities of operation of the arms inspectors. In particular, it held that the procedures agreed in 1988 relating to presidential and other sites would no longer operate.[79] Moreover, the most difficult part of the previous elements—the authority for a UN Security Force or Member States to enforce exclusion zones and transit corridors on Iraqi soil—was placed in square brackets, indicating that the matter might be discussed.

B. Initial draft resolutions

By 15 October 2002, three informal draft texts were emerging. Russia had put forward a short draft resolution.[80] The text did not refer to the conditioning of the cease-fire on Iraqi compliance with disarmament obligations. Instead, it noted the acceptance by Iraq of the return of inspectors without condition, and the fact that the UNMOVIC Chair and the Director General of the International Atomic Energy Agency (IAEA) had in the meantime reached agreement with Iraq for the modalities of the immediate resumption of inspections. There was no reference to a present state of material breach. Instead, Iraq was assured that compliance would open the way to ending the prohibitions referred to in Resolution 687 (1991).

In terms of substance, the text endorsed the obligation of unrestricted access to all sites, including to officials and other persons under the authority of the Iraqi Government whom the inspectors might wish to interview. Rather than overturning the 1988 modalities for inspections, it directed UNMOVIC to 'improve' them so as to facilitate immediate, unconditional, and unrestricted access. Iraq would be obliged to make a complete, detailed, and updated declaration concerning proscribed activities. The arms inspectors would immediately report to the Council any 'serious failure' by Iraq to comply. The Council would then convene immediately upon receipt of such a report 'in order to consider the situation and the needed steps to ensure full compliance with the relevant Security Council resolutions'.

While this draft did not contain the more exotic US requirements relating to coercive arms inspections, it did make an effort to incorporate some elements of the US position. However, it entirely omitted any reference to the revival argument relating to the use of force. Instead, it was left to the Security Council to determine what steps, if any, were needed in case of serious non-compliance.

France also presented an informal draft text.[81] It recognized the threat posed by Iraq's non-compliance to international peace and security, and deplored the obstacles to full access of the arms inspectors by Iraq. It also noted that in

---

[79] See Ch 4, 120–126.

[80] Draft Security Council Resolution of the Russian Federation, 23 October 2002, available at <http://www.casi.org.uk/info/russiadraftscr0210.pdf>.

[81] Draft Security Council Resolution of France, 23 October 2002, available at <http://www.casi.org.uk/info/francedraftscr0210.pdf>.

Resolution 687 (1991) the Council had decided upon a formal cease-fire between Iraq and the states cooperating with Kuwait in accordance with Resolution 678 (1990) upon official notification by Iraq of its acceptance of the provisions of that Resolution. The Council, it continued, had remained seized of the matter to take such further steps as may be required for the implementation of the Resolution and to secure peace and security in the region. Through this wording, France avoided any reference to a material breach. Moreover, it clarified that the relationship established in Resolution 687 (1991) existed between Iraq and the Security Council, and not individual Member States. Hence, it was the Council that would exercise its responsibility in the matter.

In terms of substance, the text also demanded a full declaration by Iraq on WMD issues within 30 days and unrestricted access, including to officials and other persons under Iraqi authority. This would include a listing of the names of the relevant officials and the possibility of interviewing them without the presence of Iraqi officials (although there was no reference to interviews outside of Iraq). It also restated most of the other requirements put forward by the United States and the United Kingdom, including the right to declare, for the purpose of freezing a site to be inspected, no-fly/no-drive zones, exclusion zones, and/or ground- and air-transit corridors. There was also provision for civilian UN security guards, but only at UN bases, and no enforcement powers were foreseen for them. Instead, Iraq would be held fully accountable for the safety of arms inspection teams.

The chief arms inspectors were instructed to report directly to the Council any serious failure by Iraq to comply with its disarmament obligations. The Council would convene immediately upon receipt of such a report in order to consider the situation and the 'needed' (rather than necessary) steps to ensure full compliance with all relevant Security Council resolutions in order to restore international peace and security. It also recalled that the Council had repeatedly warned Iraq that it would face serious consequences as a result of its continued violations of its obligations. As in the Russian proposal, there was no invocation of the terms that were previously associated with the revival doctrine, other than the threat of serious consequences. Instead, there was a strong emphasis on the further application of the collective security mechanism.

These informal drafts were answered by a formal US/UK draft resolution, published as a Security Council document,[82] in which some of the previous substantive requirements, such as the right of permanent members to join the inspection teams, were dropped. The security force accompanying the inspectors was abandoned; instead, there would only be UN security guards at UNMOVIC and IAEA facilities. No further mention was made of enforcing no-fly or no-drive zones, security corridors, etc. As negotiating theory would have it, where the

---

[82] United Kingdom of Great Britain and Northern Ireland and United States of America: Draft Resolution, S/2002/1198, 25 October 2002, available at <http://www.un.org/News/dh/iraq/iraq-blue-en-s-2002–1198.pdf>.

arms inspection process was concerned, the draft had entered the 'zone of possible agreement'.

In relation to the use of force, the draft formally recalled the authority granted to Member States in Resolution 678 (1990), and the fact that compliance by Iraq with the terms of Resolution 687 (1991) had been imposed as a necessary step for achieving the stated objective of restoring international peace and security in the area. As before, it was suggested that the aim of Resolution 687 (1991) to restore peace and security had not yet been fully achieved, and that its terms, therefore, remained in force. Moreover, the text again recalled that the cease-fire was based on Iraq's acceptance of the terms of Resolution 687 (1991). As before, there was a finding of past and continuing material breach of the terms of the cease-fire, paving the way for the revival of the use of force. In a new point, however, the draft added the threat of 'serious consequences'.

If the draft resolution had ended there, it would have satisfied at least the legal requirements for the potential use of force that had been deemed necessary by the United Kingdom in the context of Operation Desert Fox. There was a finding of material breach coupled with a warning of serious consequences. Individual states would be able to act to restore peace and security in the area and implement the UN's disarmament goals. However, in this instance, the Council members were no longer willing to countenance the application of that doctrine, in part precisely because of their experience of the previous military operation. The Russian and French drafts had carefully avoided any references that could be used in aid of that position. While France was not fundamentally opposed to the argument, it did not believe that the situation warranted its application. Russia, on the other hand, appeared to oppose the use of force against Iraq under any circumstances. Moreover, all delegations had observed the debate about regime change in the US administration, and few were willing to provide cover for the implementation of such a broad aim through the use of force.

Hence, what emerged was a two-step approach. Paragraph 4 of the text determined that further violations of Iraq's commitments under the resolution 'shall constitute a further material breach of Iraq's obligations'. The chief arms inspectors would report immediately to the Council any failure to comply, which would then be considered by the Council. While the majority of Council members could argue that military action would then ensue only once it had been authorized by the Council, the United Kingdom and United States could still rely on unilateral action following Council consideration.

However, to many members of the Council, this risk was ultimately too dangerous. Instead, in very arduous further negotiations, some additional changes were made which transformed the two-step approach into a three-step one.

C. Resolution 1441 (2002)

When the definitive text of Resolution 1441 (2002) emerged, the notion of Iraq's final chance to comply was introduced, along with certain provisions strengthening the role of the Security Council. In step one, in line with the revival argument, the Resolution confirmed the continued applicability of all previous resolutions on Iraq, including Resolution 678 (1990). It expressly recalled that:[83]

...its resolution 678 (1990) authorized Member States to use all necessary means to uphold and implement its resolution 660 (1990) of 2 August 1990 and all relevant resolutions subsequent to resolution 660 (1990) and to restore international peace and security in the area...

The Council also recalled that Resolution 687 (1991) imposed obligations on Iraq as a necessary step for achieving its stated objective of restoring international peace and security in the area, and that in Resolution 687 (1991) the Council declared that a cease-fire would be based on acceptance by Iraq of the provisions of that Resolution, including the obligations on Iraq contained therein. The Council then decided, in operative paragraph 1:

...Iraq has been and remains in material breach of its obligations under relevant resolutions, including resolution 687 (1991), in particular through Iraq's failure to cooperate with United Nations inspectors and the IAEA, and to complete the actions required under paragraphs 8 to 13 of resolution 687 (1991);

Moreover, the Council recalled in concluding paragraph 13 that 'the Council has repeatedly warned Iraq that it will face serious consequences as a result of its continued violations of its obligations'.

In a major achievement for the United States and United Kingdom, the material breach argument was now endorsed by the Council, despite its previous controversial nature. The cease-fire, it was now confirmed afresh, had been conditioned on Iraqi compliance. Iraq had been found to be in a state of non-compliance to a degree that amounted to material breach. There was also a reference to serious consequences, which previously had been thought sufficient (at least by the United States and United Kingdom) to hint at the authority to use force. Hence, the authority granted in Resolution 678 (1990) might revive. This could include the broader mandate to restore international peace and security in the area.

However, the Resolution then balanced this clear approach in favour of the revival argument by adding two additional steps. First it decided, notwithstanding the finding of material breach in paragraph 1:

...to afford Iraq, by this resolution, a final opportunity to comply with its disarmament obligations under relevant resolutions of the Council; and accordingly decides to set up an enhanced inspection regime with the aim of bringing to full and verified completion the disarmament process established by resolution 687 (1991) and subsequent resolutions of the Council;

Hence, the onus was on Iraq to neutralize the possible application of the revival argument by making use of this final opportunity and entering into full

---

[83] UN Security Council Resolution 1441 (2002), Preamble.

compliance. While Iraq was in compliance, there would thus be no authority to use force. The requirements for compliance were set out in line with the emerging consensus within the Council, noted above. First, there was the matter of the declaration. The Council decided in operative paragraph 3 that:

...in order to begin to comply with its disarmament obligations, in addition to submitting the required biannual declarations, the Government of Iraq shall provide to UNMOVIC, the IAEA, and the Council, not later than 30 days from the date of this resolution, a currently accurate, full, and complete declaration of all aspects of its programmes to develop chemical, biological, and nuclear weapons, ballistic missiles, and other delivery systems such as unmanned aerial vehicles and dispersal systems designed for use on aircraft, including any holdings and precise locations of such weapons, components, subcomponents, stocks of agents, and related material and equipment, the locations and work of its research, development and production facilities, as well as all other chemical, biological, and nuclear programmes, including any which it claims are for purposes not related to weapon production or material;

In addition to the declaration, paragraph 5 demanded full cooperation with the arms inspection process:

Iraq shall provide UNMOVIC and the IAEA immediate, unimpeded, unconditional, and unrestricted access to any and all, including underground, areas, facilities, buildings, equipment, records, and means of transport which they wish to inspect, as well as immediate, unimpeded, unrestricted, and private access to all officials and other persons whom UNMOVIC or the IAEA wish to interview in the mode or location of UNMOVIC's or the IAEA's choice pursuant to any aspect of their mandates; further decides that UNMOVIC and the IAEA may at their discretion conduct interviews inside or outside of Iraq, may facilitate the travel of those interviewed and family members outside of Iraq, and that, at the sole discretion of UNMOVIC and the IAEA, such interviews may occur without the presence of observers from the Iraqi Government; and instructs UNMOVIC and requests the IAEA to resume inspections no later than 45 days following adoption of this resolution and to update the Council 60 days thereafter;

This process was to be carried out in accordance with the modalities agreed by Iraq and the inspectors at their Vienna meeting, which were attached to the Resolution. Moreover, in view of the suspension of the inspection regime since 1999, additional, enhanced requirements were added in paragraph 7:

- UNMOVIC and the IAEA shall determine the composition of their inspection teams and ensure that these teams are composed of the most qualified and experienced experts available;
- All UNMOVIC and IAEA personnel shall enjoy the privileges and immunities, corresponding to those of experts on mission, provided in the Convention on Privileges and Immunities of the United Nations and the Agreement on the Privileges and Immunities of the IAEA;
- UNMOVIC and the IAEA shall have unrestricted rights of entry into and out of Iraq, the right to free, unrestricted, and immediate movement to and from inspection sites, and the right to inspect any sites and buildings, including immediate, unimpeded,

unconditional, and unrestricted access to Presidential sites equal to that at other sites, notwithstanding the provisions of resolution 1154 (1998) of 2 March 1998;

- UNMOVIC and the IAEA shall have the right to be provided by Iraq the names of all personnel currently and formerly associated with Iraq's chemical, biological, nuclear, and ballistic missile programmes and the associated research, development, and production facilities;
- Security of UNMOVIC and IAEA facilities shall be ensured by sufficient United Nations security guards;
- UNMOVIC and the IAEA shall have the right to declare, for the purposes of freezing a site to be inspected, exclusion zones, including surrounding areas and transit corridors, in which Iraq will suspend ground and aerial movement so that nothing is changed in or taken out of a site being inspected;
- UNMOVIC and the IAEA shall have the free and unrestricted use and landing of fixed- and rotary-winged aircraft, including manned and unmanned reconnaissance vehicles.
- UNMOVIC and the IAEA shall have the right at their sole discretion verifiably to remove, destroy, or render harmless all prohibited weapons, subsystems, components, records, materials, and other related items, and the right to impound or close any facilities or equipment for the production thereof; and
- UNMOVIC and the IAEA shall have the right to free import and use of equipment or materials for inspections and to seize and export any equipment, materials, or documents taken during inspections, without search of UNMOVIC or IAEA personnel or official or personal baggage;

Iraq faced a considerably beefed-up inspections regime, although administered by a team of inspectors who would be chosen according to competence, and who would not include additional representatives from the permanent members. The idea of occupying sensitive sites had been somewhat defanged, by declaring that the freezing of a site would merely serve the temporary purpose of preserving it during the inspections process. Still included was the possibility of interviewing Iraqi officials outside of Iraq. However, the nature and extent of its substantive obligations and of the powers of the inspectors had been carefully negotiated in the Council until consensus had been reached. They were not, in principle, unachievable, although they were considerably tougher than the modalities for the disarmament effort that had applied before.

The important question was, of course, what the standard of compliance would be. In paragraph 4, the Council had indicated that:

... false statements or omissions in the declarations submitted by Iraq pursuant to this resolution and failure by Iraq at any time to comply with, and cooperate fully in the implementation of, this resolution shall constitute a further material breach of Iraq's obligations ...

Iraq was concerned that the issue of the declaration in itself would constitute the 'hidden trigger': 'What if there is nothing to report?'[84] But it was clear that

---

[84] Recounted by Blix (above n 73) 89.

a deficient declaration alone would not suffice to constitute a further material breach. Instead, the word 'and' (inserted after much negotiation) indicated that it would need to be accompanied by a violation of the substantive arms inspections process. It was also thought that this would need to be a serious violation. As the UK Foreign Secretary, then much involved in the discussions, explained:[85] 'I personally was extremely happy about that because I wanted the test for further material breach to be a high bar, not to be a low bar'.

The third step concerned the mechanism for determining the breach and its consequences. Paragraph 4 added that false statements and omissions in the declaration and failure to cooperate with the arms inspectors 'will be reported to the Council for assessment in accordance with paragraphs 11 and 12 below'. Nearly every word in that half sentence was to gain immense importance in the legal debates that were to follow. First, the wording chosen did not in itself indicate who would make such a report to the Council. The United States and United Kingdom took the view that it might be Members States, in addition to the arms inspectors.

After the eventual use of force, the United States would claim that the conditions of the Resolution had been fulfilled, as violations of paragraph 4 were in fact reported by the US Secretary of State Colin Powell 'whose comprehensive reports drew on human intelligence, communications intercepts, and overhead imagery regarding Iraq's ongoing efforts to pursue WMD and missile programmes and conceal them from United Nations inspectors'.[86] This statement seemed to imply that US intelligence was in fact a more reliable means of establishing the basis of reporting of breaches.

However, according to the Resolution the reporting was to occur 'in accordance with paragraphs 11 and 12 below'. Paragraph 11 directed the UMOVIC Executive Chairman and the Director-General of the IAEA to report violations to the Council. This ran counter to the US/UK argument. The United Kingdom later accepted that the reports of the arms inspectors would, at least, be 'highly significant' in this respect.[87] Most other delegations, in their statements reproduced below, took the view that only the inspectors could report to the Council on violations.

The concluding paragraphs of the Resolution provided:

11. *Directs* the Executive Chairman of UNMOVIC and the Director-General of the IAEA to report immediately to the Council any interference by Iraq with inspection activities, as well as any failure by Iraq to comply with its disarmament obligations, including its obligations regarding inspections under this resolution;

12. *Decides* to convene immediately upon receipt of a report in accordance with paragraphs 4 or 11 above, in order to consider the situation and the need for full compliance

[85] Jack Straw, Chilcot Testimony, 8 February 2010, 54.
[86] Taft and Buchwald (above n 58) 562.
[87] Lord Goldsmith, Memorandum, 7 March 2003, para 29.

with all of the relevant Council resolutions in order to secure international peace and security;

13. *Recalls*, in that context, that the Council has repeatedly warned Iraq that it will face serious consequences as a result of its continued violations of its obligations;

14. *Decides* to remain seized of the matter.

It was clear that the Council would convene immediately once it received reports on violations by the inspectors. The major question that arose was what happened next. The UK Foreign Secretary confirmed that:[88]

...the French were profoundly concerned that there should, in the words of Dominic de Villepin, be no automaticity; in other words, that the first resolution that became 1441, should not provide approval or authority of itself for immediate military action as 687 had done. We accepted that...and the architecture of 1441 was without question one which had two stages.

In accordance with these stages, paragraph 12 indicated that the Council would then 'consider' the situation and the need for full compliance. A French proposal in favour of the word 'decide' instead of 'consider' was not adopted, due to opposition from the United States/United Kingdom.[89] It was argued that they would not have accepted a need for a formal Council decision before action could be taken. The United States argued subsequently:[90]

The fact that this language was not included in Resolution 1441 as ultimately adopted shows that the Council decided only that it would consider the matter, but not that it would be necessary for it, or even its purpose, to make a further decision. Rather, the Council had already made the decision that violations described in paragraph 4...would constitute a material breach of Iraq's obligations, and thus authorize the use of force to secure Iraqi compliance with its disarmament obligations.

The United Kingdom added:[91]

The choice of words was deliberate; a proposal that there should be a requirement for a decision by the Council, a position maintained by several Council members, was not adopted. Instead the members of the Council opted for the formula that the Council must consider the matter before any action is taken.

The key point was that while the word 'decide' was ultimately not used, this was devoid of much significance. As Alex Bellamy argues:[92]

The UN Charter contains in Art. 2(4) a *jus cogens* rule prohibiting the use or threat of force. The UN Charter allows only two exceptions to this rule: collective enforcement

---

[88] Jack Straw, Chilcot Testimony, 8 February 2010, 37.

[89] The final French text refers to 'd'examiner'.   [90] Taft and Buchwald (above n 58) 562.

[91] Foreign and Commonwealth Office Paper, 'Iraq: Legal Basis for the Use of Force (2003)', reproduced in (2003) 52 ICLQ 812, 814.

[92] AJ Bellamy, 'Legality of the Use of Force Against Iraq' (2003) *Melbourne Journal of International Law* 8.

action authoritized by the Security Council and the inherent right to self defence. In the absence of Security Council authorization to use force or good grounds for claiming a right of self-defence...a refusal to specifically repudiate force in a particular case does not constitute a decision to waive Art 2(4).

Moreover, in terms of the argument based on the negotiating history, the Netherlands inquiry into the war stated:[93]

An amendment to state clearly that the Security Council, if a violation took place, would meet again to take a decision on the next step was not included in the final text. It is not unusual in both politics and diplomacy to choose carefully considered ambiguous formulations in order to satisfy as many directly involved parties as possible and keep them on board. This and several other ambiguities in the resolution ... do not, however, delegate to individual states the authority of the Security Council to make an assessment of any violation nor to take any subsequent action.

In fact, when read in conjunction with paragraph 4, it becomes clear that in the text finally adopted, the breach was to be 'reported to the Council for assessment'. Assessment implies a finding of fact or law.[94] Hence, the position that the Council would merely consider, but not be expected to make a finding, is difficult to maintain. As the UN Legal Counsel found when considering the wording, 'any reported "material breach" of Iraq's obligation required the convening of the Council for assessment of the situation and did not therefore create automaticity with respect to the use of force'.[95] Moreover, the reference to consideration 'in order to secure international peace and security' has generally been read as a reference to the collective security powers of the Council in this context, rather than unilateral action.

In paragraph 4 of the Resolution, the Council had already decided 'in advance' that any false statements or omissions and failure to cooperate would amount to 'a further material breach'. However, it was agreed, even by the United Kingdom, that the trigger point for the material breach argument was supposed to be a 'high bar'. The UK Secretary of State for Foreign and Commonwealth affairs later clarified to the UK Parliament that:[96]

Material breach means something significant; some behaviour or pattern of behaviour that is serious. Among such breaches could be action by the Government of Iraq seriously to obstruct or impede the inspectors, to intimidate witnesses, or a pattern of behaviour where any single action appears relatively minor but the action as a whole adds up to something deliberate and more significant: something that shows Iraq's intention not to comply.

---

[93] 'Report of the Dutch Committee of Inquiry on the War in Iraq', (2010) NILR 57, 83–137.

[94] According to the *Oxford English Dictionary*, this includes 'to evaluate, to gauge, to judge'. See <http://dictionary.oed.com/cgi/entry/50013355?single=1&query_type=word&queryword=assess &first=1&max_to_show=10>.

[95] Reported in R Zacklin, (2010) *The United Nations Secretariat and the Use of Force in a Unipolar World* 140.

[96] HC Deb, cols 51–54, 25 November 2003; also quoted by Lord Goldsmith (above n 87).

A minor inaccuracy in the statement and insubstantial failure to cooperate would not suffice. Hence, it would not be obvious what kind of infraction would constitute a material breach and a finding as to the existence of a material breach would still be required. The Council would indeed need to assess the reported infraction.

In his initial legal thinking on the matter, the UK Attorney-General took the following view:[97]

It was very clear from Resolution 1441 (2002) that, in the event of Iraq's non-compliance, there would have to be further discussion in the Security Council. It seemed implicit in Resolution 1441 (2002) that, in that eventuality, it would be for the Security Council to decide whether Iraq were in fact in material breach. ... the position remained that only the Security Council could decide on whether there had been a material breach (and whether the breach was such as to undermine the conditions underpinning the cease-fire) and/or whether all necessary means were authorized. The question of whether there was a serious breach or not was for the Security Council alone.

He later amended that view, but considered that reducing the Council to mere discussion would render this 'a procedural formality'. In such a case:[98]

The Council would be required to meet, and all members of the Council would be under an obligation to participate in the discussion in good faith, but even if an overwhelming majority of the Council were opposed to the use of force, military action would proceed regardless.

If the natural meaning of the words used in a treaty or legal text leaves its meaning obscure, it is permissible to consider the negotiating history in order to discover the intent of its authors. This also applies to UN Security Council resolutions. The UK Attorney General had access to all negotiating documents on the position favouring force without further Council action, including the US materials. He noted 'the strength and sincerity of the view' of the US administration that they would never have accepted a process requiring a further Council pronouncement. But there was the problem of evidence in this instance:[99]

...we are reliant on their assertion for the view that the French (and others) knew and accepted that they were voting for a further discussion and no more. We have little hard evidence on this beyond a couple of telegrams recording admissions by French negotiators that they knew the US would not accept a resolution which required a further Council decision. The possibility remains that the French and others accepted OP 12 because in their view it gave them a sufficient basis to argue that a second resolution was required (even if that was not made expressly clear).

The UK Legal Adviser also took the view that the UK telegrams invoked would not likely be acceptable as *travaux preparatoires* of the Resolution, since they 'are not independent or agreed records'.[100]

---

[97] Lord Goldsmith (ibid) paras 7–8.   [98] Ibid, para 24.   [99] Ibid, para 23.
[100] Michael Wood, (2002) *Iraq: Security Council Resolution 1441* 3.

D. Statements made upon the adoption of Resolution 1441 (2002)

In the absence of a detailed negotiating history, either officially preserved or even unofficially recorded, it is particularly important to take account of the context of the adoption of legal instruments. This includes statements made by delegations upon adoption of the text. At the outset of the Council meeting, as agreed in prior consultations, Resolution 1441 (2002) was adopted unanimously. It was immediately apparent that a certain choreography had been agreed, to assuage the anxiety of Council members that they were being trapped into authorizing force when that had not been their intention, as had been the case with Resolution 1205 (1998) and Operation Desert Fox. Following a brief statement by the UN Secretary-General, the two sponsors of the Resolution spoke. The United States confirmed:[101]

As we have said on numerous occasions to Council members, this resolution contains no 'hidden triggers' and no 'automaticity' with respect to the use of force. If there is a further Iraqi breach, reported to the Council by UNMOVIC, the IAEA or a Member State, the matter will return to the Council for discussions as required in paragraph 12. The resolution makes clear that any Iraqi failure to comply is unacceptable and that Iraq must be disarmed. And, one way or another, Iraq will be disarmed. If the Security Council fails to act decisively in the event of further Iraqi violations, this resolution does not constrain any Member State from acting to defend itself against the threat posed by Iraq or to enforce relevant United Nations resolutions and protect world peace and security.

This statement confirmed expressly that the Resolution itself did not authorize the use of force—no hidden triggers, no automaticity. The United States also reserved its own legal position, relating to its claim to act in self-defence against the 'threat' posed by Iraq. Given that there was no evidence of any immediate threat posed by Iraq to the United States, this can only be understood as a reference to the claim to preventative action. However, as noted earlier, that claim has no basis in international law. The United States could not reserve a right it did not have. The United States also claimed authority to enforce UN resolutions and 'protect world peace and security'. Again, it did not have a general right to enforce the will of the Security Council, if the Council itself did not will it. Hence, the United States appeared to be claiming the very right that, in view of virtually all other Council members, had not been granted and did not exist outside of such a grant. The even wider claim to authority to protect world peace and security was also an abstract statement that had no basis in law.

The UK statement was somewhat more circumspect. In accordance with the agreed choreography, the United Kingdom was also constrained to join in the mantra of no-automaticity. It declared:[102]

We heard loud and clear during the negotiations the concerns about 'automaticity' and 'hidden triggers'—the concern that on a decision so crucial we should not rush into

---

[101] Record of the 4644th meeting of the United Nations Security Council, S/PV.4644, 8 November 2002, 3.   [102] Ibid, 4f.

military action; that on a decision so crucial any Iraqi violations should be discussed by the Council. Let me be equally clear in response, as a co-sponsor with the United States of the text we have just adopted. There is no 'automaticity' in this resolution. If there is a further Iraqi breach of its disarmament obligations, the matter will return to the Council for discussion as required in paragraph 12. We would expect the Security Council then to meet its responsibilities.

The United Kingdom, in its slightly more nuanced view, retained the view that the matter would return to the Council for discussion, rather than decision. There was a strong expectation that the Council would then meet its responsibilities. The United Kingdom, therefore, did not formally claim authority to use force unilaterally if the Council decision offered no further authorization.

In a statement of the Foreign Secretary made to the House Foreign Affairs Committee at a time when the Resolution had not yet been adopted, but its text was stabilizing, he claimed that the UK view on the two-stage process related to the possibility of a veto. The United Kingdom was concerned that 'military action is necessary and palpably obvious and yet the one or other member of the Security Council decides to veto it'.[103] This indicated a view that the United Kingdom only felt entitled to take action if a further mandate was precluded due to the application of a veto by one or two states acting in isolation—a position subsequently expressed by the UK Prime Minister. Of course, in the end, there was a threat of a veto from France. However, in reality two further Permanent Members, Russia and China, were also opposed. Moreover, as will be noted below, six other states were unlikely to vote in favour. Hence, this reserve of the UK position would not have covered the circumstances that ultimately arose. Apparently, at a political level it was believed that a second resolution would command widespread support, although there was a risk of veto that had to be contained.

Sir Jeremy Greenstock, the UK Permanent Representative, subsequently claimed that the United Kingdom had not relinquished authority to use force:[104]

...the UK accepted that the Security Council would be active in the case of Iraqi non-compliance, and that this was what non-automaticity meant. But the UK was not specific in saying that a new decision would not be necessary. ... the UK's actual position was that the whole corpus of resolutions, from SCR 678 and 687 onwards, substantiated the case for the use of force against Iraq, through the termination of the 1991 ceasefire, if Iraq was shown not to have complied with the relevant resolutions. In taking this position, we were using exactly the same approach as in justifying the bombing of Iraq in December 1988, which up to this time had never been contested on a legal basis by any other member state.

This statement reveals a fundamental confusion on the part of its author. It appears to endorse a view that the 'whole corpus of resolutions' from Resolution

---

[103] HC II96-iii, 30 October 2002, (2002) 73 BYIL 878.
[104] Sir Jeremy Greenstock, (2009) Written Statement to the Inquiry, 11.

678 (1990) onwards authorized force. However, in contrast to the United States, the UK view of the revival argument had always been that it did not operate unilaterally. A decision of the Council was necessary in all instances, including in December 1998 in relation to Desert Fox. After all, it was Sir Jeremy himself who had triumphantly declared that he had tricked Russia into adopting a resolution that ultimately permitted force on that occasion.[105] And it was clear that Resolution 1441 (2002) did not in itself amount to such a decision. This view was consistently maintained by Sir Jeremy's own FCO Legal Advisers.[106] Even Professor (now Judge Sir) Christopher Greenwood, the lead-author of the so-called 'Foreign Office Memorandum' that was generated to justify the use of force against this advice, notes 'Resolution 1441 (2002) did not, in and of itself, constitute such a fresh mandate'.[107]

If, however, no fresh mandate was obtained, no authority for the use of force could be derived from the Resolution. In that sense, Sir Jeremy Greenstock's argument operates the other way. As it is clear that the other delegations did not accept the proposal to authorize the use of force in Resolution 1441 (2002), at least the UK requirement for lawful action had not been met.

As was stated in an Advisory Memorandum to the Australian Leader of the Opposition:[108]

... nor is there any reason to conclude that Resolution 678 or Resolution 687 override the effect of Resolution 1441. Resolution 1441 is clear and unequivocal as to its intent: Iraq is given one final opportunity to comply—failing this the Security Council will decide what needs to be done in order to achieve compliance.

However, the United Kingdom sought to put a particular spin on the understanding of the terms 'automaticity' and 'hidden triggers'. By claiming that this was meant to prevent a 'rush into military action', the United Kingdom laid the ground for its subsequent argument that these references concerned only the timing of possible military action, not their legal authorization. According to this view, the sponsors of the Resolution merely promised not to launch military operations immediately after the adoption of the Resolution. Instead, the arms inspection process would be given the space to develop.

A UK Foreign and Commonwealth Office paper, intended to justify the war, adopted a different position on this matter. On automaticity, it accepted that there was a requirement to go through the process foreseen in paragraph 12—it was not merely a promise to delay action outside of the Council. However, according to the paper, once the Council had 'considered', that would not mean that no further action could be taken without a new resolution of the

---

[105]   See Ch 4, 129   .[106]   See Ch 6.
[107]   C Greenwood, 'Pre-emptive Use of Force' (2003) 4 *San Diego International Law Journal* 7, 33.
[108]   G Niemann, Legal Advisory Memorandum to the Australian Leader of the Opposition, reproduced in (2003) *Melbourn Journal of Intenational Law* 190, 193.

Council.[109] However, as the UK Permanent Representative himself had to admit:[110]

Most members of the Council, however, made an assumption that further discussion in the Security Council about Iraqi compliance would itself lead to a decision for or against the use of force.

Indeed, this admission is still something of an understatement. There had been a very clear understanding that 'automaticity' and 'hidden triggers' referred not only to a delay in taking military action, but to the substantive legal basis for taking such action. This is apparent in the whole series of statements, made with astonishing consistency by virtually all other members of the Council. Given the importance of this point, and the impressive nature of this evidence, it is necessary to rehearse it in somewhat fuller measure.

France indicated:[111]

The resolution strengthens the role and authority of the Security Council. That was the main and constant objective of France throughout the negotiations which have just concluded. That objective was reflected in our request that a two-stage approach be established and complied with, ensuring that the Security Council would maintain control of the process at each stage.

That objective has been attained: in the event that the Executive Chairman of the United Nations Monitoring, Verification and Inspection Commission (UNMOVIC) or the Director General of the International Atomic Energy Agency (IAEA) reports to the Security Council that Iraq has not complied with its obligations, the Council would meet immediately to evaluate the seriousness of the violations and draw the appropriate conclusions. France welcomes the fact that all ambiguity on this point and all elements of automaticity have disappeared from the resolution.

In the French view, the UN inspectors, and not the Member States, would be reporting breaches to the Council. In a further step, the Council would then meet to 'evaluate' and 'draw the appropriate conclusions'. The Russian Federation, the other key delegation in negotiations on the text, made a similarly clear submission:[112]

As a result of intensive negotiations, the resolution just adopted contains no provisions for the automatic use of force. It is important that the resolution's sponsors today officially confirmed in the Security Council that that is their understanding and that they provided an assurance that the resolution's objective is the implementation of existing Security Council decisions concerning Iraq through inspections by the United Nations Monitoring, Verification and Inspection Commission (UNMOVIC) and by the International Atomic Energy Agency (IAEA). That is an objective shared by all members of the Council. In that connection, it is of fundamental importance that the resolution

---

[109] Foreign and Commonwealth Office Paper (above n 91) 814.
[110] Sir Jeremy Greenstock, (2009) Statement to the Iraq Inquiry 11.
[111] Record of the 4644th meeting of the UNSC (above n 101) 5.   [112] Ibid, 8.

clearly confirms that all Members of the United Nations respect the sovereignty and territorial integrity of Iraq and of all other States in the region.

It is particularly important that—as many of my colleagues have said today—in the event of any kind of disagreement over disarmament matters, it is the heads of UNMOVIC and of the IAEA who will report that to the Security Council, and that it is the Council that will consider the situation that has developed. That is the sequence set forth clearly in paragraphs 4, 11 and 12 of the resolution.

Placing its statement in the context of the prohibition of the use of force (sovereignty and territorial integrity of Iraq), Russia emphasized that the sponsors of the Resolution had given an assurance as to the operation of the process envisaged in the resolution. The arms inspectors would report on breaches, and the Council would then consider the matter. Russia added a warning against yielding to the temptation of unilateral interpretation of the Resolution's provisions and pleaded for the preservation of the consensus and unity of all members of the Security Council.

China was similarly clear in its view:[113]

That would enable the Council to draw objective, fair and realistic conclusions and decide on the next steps in the light of the situation and the views of the various parties concerned. China supports the two-stage approach. The Chinese delegation actively participated at all stages of the consultations on the draft resolution, and put forward its views and suggestions in a constructive manner. We are pleased to note that, after many rounds of consultations, the sponsors of the draft resolution accommodated our concerns, and the Council members have finally reached consensus...

As the sponsors pointed out in their statements earlier, the purpose of the resolution is to achieve the disarmament of Iraq through effective inspections. The text no longer includes automaticity for authorizing the use of force. According to the resolution that has just been adopted, only upon receipt of a report by UNMOVIC and the IAEA on Iraq's non-compliance and failure to cooperate fully in the implementation of the resolution, will the Security Council consider the situation and take a position.

We are also pleased to note that, at the request of many members, including China, the resolution now includes other important elements, for example, reaffirming the commitment of all Member States to the sovereignty and territorial integrity of Iraq.

China very expressly indicated that 'no automaticity' meant that there was no authorization for force at this stage. Instead, there would be a two-step approach. 'Only' upon a report by the chief arms inspectors would the Council consider the situation and 'take a position'. Moreover, in referring to the sovereignty and territorial integrity of Iraq, the Council offered a reminder that the prohibition of the use of force contained in Article 2(4) of the UN Charter applied.

---

[113] Ibid, 12f.

In addition to the permanent members who had been principally involved in the drafting process, other members clearly expressed themselves in a similar vein. Mexico indicated:[114]

The resolution just adopted is the result of negotiations in which those who called for automatic recourse to the use of force agreed to give Iraq one last chance to voluntarily, immediately and unconditionally comply with Security Council resolutions. Iraq now has an obligation to the Council and to the international community to comply fully with its international obligations. Similarly, this resolution also constitutes progress, as it eliminates the concept of automaticity in the use of force in response to a serious violation without the explicit agreement of the Council. We welcome the fact that the two-stage approach has been accepted. ...

In effect, my country proposed that the Security Council's response should be based on two clearly differentiated stages. The first stage would entail a credible process to evaluate Iraq's true military capability and its intention to use its weapons or the ability of terrorist groups to have access to them. The second stage would entail the agreement of the Security Council and other States involved on the measures to be adopted if the evaluation process detects a threat to international peace and security.

Mexico here formally expressed its understanding that the sponsors of the Resolution had 'agreed' to abandon a claim to the automatic use of force. Instead, a two-stage approach would prevail. First, there would be evaluation of Iraq's compliance, followed by agreed action in the Council in response to a threat to peace and security emanating from possible non-compliance.

Ireland took a similar view:[115]

We have noted carefully and we welcome the assurances given by the sponsors that their purpose in presenting this resolution was to achieve disarmament through inspections, and not to establish a basis for the use of military force. The use of force is, and must remain, a matter of last resort. This is, therefore, a resolution about disarmament, not war. It is about removing all threat of war.

The resolution provides for a clear, sequential process, whereby the United Nations Monitoring, Verification and Inspection Commission (UNMOVIC) or the International Atomic Energy Agency (IAEA) will give the Council its assessment of any material breach or alleged material breach of Iraq's obligations under Security Council resolutions. The matter will then be fully examined by the Security Council itself. As far as Ireland is concerned, it is for the Council to decide on any ensuing action. Our debate on 17 and 18 October made it clear that this is the broadly held view within the United Nations. However, we are confident that, should it be necessary, the Council will, in the words of the Secretary-General, face its responsibilities.

Ireland expressly recorded the assurances that the Resolution would not be seen as 'a basis for the use of force'. Again, it would be the arms inspectors providing

---

[114] Ibid, 6.   [115] Ibid, 7.

the critical report to the Council, and it would then be for the Council to 'decide on any ensuing action'. Bulgaria was also express in its evaluation:[116]

This resolution is not a pretext for automatic recourse to the use of force. Rather, it attests to the international community's determination to work tirelessly for Iraq's disarmament through peaceful means. . . .

My country welcomes the fact that the resolution categorically reaffirms the centrality of the Security Council in our decision-making process. Resolution 1441 (2002) is in perfect harmony with my country's dedication to multilateralism as a governing principle of international relations.

Syria placed reliance on the assurances given by the United States and United Kingdom on the issue of legal authority:[117]

Syria voted in favour of the resolution, having received reassurances from its sponsors, the United States of America and the United Kingdom, and from France and Russia through high-level contacts, that it would not be used as a pretext for striking against Iraq and does not constitute a basis for any automatic strikes against Iraq. The resolution should not be interpreted, through certain paragraphs, as authorizing any State to use force. It reaffirms the central role of the Security Council in addressing all phases of the Iraqi issue.

Syria has also received reassurances from the permanent members of the Security Council that the resolution strengthens the mandate of the international inspectors; that it serves the objective of preserving Iraq's sovereignty, territorial integrity and inviolability; . . .

Norway, somewhat more obliquely, referred to the agreed procedure whereby the Security Council would convene immediately to ensure international peace and security in case of non-compliance.[118] Columbia 'insisted on preserving the central role of the Security Council, as clearly stipulated in paragraphs 4, 11 and 12. This resolution is not, nor could it be at this time, a resolution to authorize the use of force'.[119] Cameroon emphasized the 'centrality of the Security Council in the maintenance of international peace and security. Cameroon has always maintained and supported that. Let us trust in the Charter and abide by it'.[120] Guinea similarly reaffirmed the role of the Council as guarantor of international peace and security.[121] Finally, Mauritius saw in the Resolution an affirmation of 'the clear and unambiguous role of the Security Council'.[122]

The extraordinary energy invested in clarifying the understanding of the legal position generated by the Resolution, and by the assurance given by its sponsors, went even further. After the vote, China, France, and the Russian Federation sent a joint letter to the President of the Security Council, recording their understandings formally. They stated that, 'Resolution 1441 (2002) adopted today by the Security Council excludes any automaticity in the use of force'. In case of failure

---

[116] Ibid, 9.   [117] Ibid, 11.   [118] Ibid, 10.   [119] Ibid, 11.   [120] Ibid.
[121] Ibid, 12.   [122] Ibid.

by Iraq to comply, such failure would be reported to the Council by the arms inspectors: 'It will be then for the Council to take a position on the basis of that report'.[123]

The record reproduced here makes it difficult to dispute that the Council was clear on a number of points when voting on Resolution 1441 (2002):[124]

- The Resolution in itself did not grant fresh authority to use force.
- The Resolution provided for a finding of non-compliance by the UN arms inspectors, not individual states, in order to trigger the process.
- It would be up to the Council to determine the consequences of such violation, including the possibility of the use of force.

E. An underlying agreement on the US position?

The United States and United Kingdom nevertheless advanced the view that other delegations voted for Resolution 1441, having been appraised by its sponsors of their interpretation of it. However, in view of the overwhelming majority of states that expressed the above point, this proposition should be phrased the other way round. It is difficult to see how the United States and United Kingdom could have voted for the Resolution if they felt it imperative to safeguard the legal position they had advanced. Moreover, it is to be noted that the United Kingdom, in fact, was circumspect in the matter, referring merely to the expectation that the Council would exercise its responsibility. The Foreign and Commonwealth Office's own Legal Advisers argued instead that the Resolution did not grant authority to use force without a further decision by the Council, either in the form of a presidential statement or another resolution.[125] The UK Attorney General himself appeared to endorse that position consistently, until the very point of the invasion, when he appears to have undergone a change of view.[126]

The US practice of accepting a text, but then claiming that others had understood that the United States would interpret it differently from its ordinary meaning, had a precedent. In the Afghanistan peace agreement package of 1988, for instance, the United States pledged 'to invariably refrain from any form of

---

[123] Letter from the Representatives of China, France, and the Russian Federation, S/2002/1236, 8 November 2002, text available at <http://www.staff.city.ac.uk/p.willetts/IRAQ/FRRSCHST. HTM>.

[124] See also, eg R Hofmann, 'International Law and the Use of Military Force against Iraq' (2002) 45 *German Yearbook of International Law* 9; P McLain, 'Settling the Score with Saddam: Resolution 1441 and Parallel Justifications for the Use of Force against Iraq' (2003) 13(233) *Duke Journal of Comparative and International Law* 233; M Weisburd, 'The War in Iraq and the Dilemma of Controlling the International Use of Force' (2004) 39 *Texas International Law Journal* 521; Schaller (above n 54); G Simpson, 'The War in Iraq and International Law' (2005) 6 *Melbourne Journal of International Law* 1.   [125] This is covered in great detail in Ch 6 of this book.

[126] In fact, even then, in his formal advice of 7 March 2002, the Attorney General only claimed that the US position was 'reasonably arguable', without endorsing it. He held the alternative view to be the 'safer' one.

interference and intervention in the internal affairs' of Afghanistan.[127] This would have very clearly precluded the continuance of military and other support for the Mujahideen rebels. However, the United States then claimed a right, after all, to supply the rebels as long as the Soviet Union supplied the Afghan Government. Before signing, the US Secretary of State George Schultz declared[128] that 'they haven't chosen to go along with that idea [of continued support], and so we assert confidently our right to supply our friends in Afghanistan as we see the need to do so'.

If the other parties had not accepted the idea in the treaty, it is difficult to see how the United States could assert the right to act in accordance with it. Yet, upon signature, the United States indicated that it had 'advised' the Soviet Union that it retained the right to provide military assistance to the armed opposition.[129] There was no support for that assertion in the positions articulated by the other parties or in any other published documents. However, after US policy was challenged, the United States asserted that the statement had served to publicly record understandings on the military assistance issue arising from prior negotiations and written exchanges with the Soviets—an assertion that was eventually borne out by Moscow's failure to rely on the US guarantee of non-intervention.[130] In that instance, however, the United States had stated its position in an exchange of letters with the Soviet Union which, it could be said, signed the agreement on the basis of an understanding that had been reached.

In this instance, however, the situation was different. Negotiations had been carried out over some two months, moving towards the final agreed text. As the declarations quoted above confirm, there were underlying assurances and understandings. But these went the other way—they were assurances against the proposed interpretation of the Resolution as furnishing authority to use force. Hence, the argument that the text could not be interpreted in accordance with its natural meaning, because the other delegations were aware of the US view when they voted, failed.

F. Leaving the US position 'intact'

A variant of the above argument was put forward by the UK Secretary of State for Foreign and Commonwealth Affairs. He claimed that France and Russia were 'virtually' saying that they 'understood that there might well be a breach, but that

---

[127] Afghanistan Peace Accords, US-USSR Declaration of Guarantees, 14 April 1988.

[128] Statement of 11 April 1988, 88 Department of State Bulletin (June 1988), 54.

[129] US statement upon signature, 14 April 1988, 88 Department of State Bulletin (June 1988), 55.

[130] The Soviet Union instead relied on the US obligation not to push Pakistan, another treaty party that had not made a comparable declaration, towards violation by supplying the Mujahideen through Pakistani territory. See, at length, M Weller, 'The Afghanistan Peace Accords of 1988, 1991 and 1993' (1994/5) 5 *Finnish Yearbook of International Law* 505.

while they would in fact support the need for military action, they would not be able to support a resolution in terms authorizing the use of force'.[131] Hence, the matter was left open.[132] In the view of the Foreign Secretary, this confirmed an understanding that Resolution 1441 (2002) authorized force after all.

This claim cannot be dismissed out of hand, as Jack Straw had direct talks with both governments at a senior level during the drafting of the Resolution. But, again, the meaning of such a tacit acceptance of the possibility that force might be used is different from that attributed to it by the Foreign Secretary. What both governments may have indicated was that they understood that the United States had taken a position claiming to be entitled to act outside of the authority of the Council. This was also the understanding of the UN Legal Counsel of the relevant statements, believing them to refer to the fact that Resolution 1441 (2002) did not diminish the inherent right to self-defence.[133] However, states were unwilling or unable to extend UN legal authority to the action through the Resolution, as the Foreign Secretary himself noted. Hence, the essential message to take from this exchange was that both governments confirmed that they would not grant authority to act in the Resolution, rather than the opposite, whatever the additional purported entitlements to the use of force the United States might put forward.

This view was confirmed with regard to Russia through the detailed *Legal Assessment of the Use of Force Against Iraq* published by its Legal Advisers. They maintained that China, France, and Russia voted for the Resolution specifically on the understanding that it did not add to the authorization for the use of force.[134] The UK Government, on the other hand, pointed to a subsequent comment made by the French Permanent Representative to the Security Council, Jean Levitte, immediately after the outbreak of the conflict. At a US Council on Foreign Relations event, he was quoted as saying:[135]

One word about the second resolution in the Security Council. I think I can say it now on the record, you have to know that weeks before it was tabled, I went to the State Department and to the White House to say, don't do it. First, because you'll split the Council and second, because you don't need it. Let's agree between gentlemen, as we did on Kosovo, before the war in Kosovo.

This statement was taken as confirmation on the part of France that Resolution 1441 (2002) provided sufficient authority to act. One may be hesitant to attach overwhelming importance to an off-hand comment in a public discussion. Nevertheless, even if this comment could be taken as authoritative, it would prove the opposite. The French representative was here confirming again that there was no prospect of obtaining authority for the use of force against Iraq through a Council

[131] David Brummel, Chilcot Testimony, 12 November 2002, para 10.   [132] Ibid, para 6.
[133] Zacklin (above n 95) 142.   [134] Reproduced in English in (2003) 52 ICLQ 1059.
[135] Transcript of 25 March 2003, available at <http://www.cfr.org/publication/5774/france_germany_and_the_us.html>.

resolution, even at stage two of seeking to obtain a second resolution. Hence, it would be unwise to return to the Council to ask for that which was unobtainable. Instead, if action were to be taken, it would have to be taken on the basis of authority claimed outside UN authorization. This is what occurred in relation to Kosovo. There, no attempt was made to obtain a formal mandate for forcible action against Yugoslavia, as it was known that such an attempt would not succeed. Instead, the action was justified with reference to the doctrine of forcible action in the face of a grave humanitarian emergency. In this instance, the comment that 'you don't need' Council authorization, therefore, did not confirm that the Council had already authorized action in Resolution 1441 (2002). That would be entirely out of line with what France had in fact argued consistently throughout the episode, including its official reaction to the invasion of Iraq. Instead, France was pointing out that the United States was relying on alternative claims to the use of force that had not even been the subject of the negotiations on Resolution 1441 (2002).

As noted at the outset, the United States had indeed claimed that, in any event, it did not require Council authority. This was due either to the preventative self-defence claim, or to its view that it could, on its own, and without further Council action, enforce the will of the Security Council. While these arguments were not accepted by any state, it is argued that some at least were aware of them. As the former State Department Legal Adviser put it:[136]

This, in our view, left intact our authority to use force without further authorization from the UN Security Council if Iraq failed to comply. We stated that this was our understanding of the situation in our explanation of the vote on Resolution 1441. Other States expressed different understanding of what the resolution required at the same time. We felt that the language that we had drafted provided better support for our position than for theirs. What was important, we thought, was that no one could be in doubt about our interpretation and the basis of it.

In fact, therefore, the United States—in opposition to the United Kingdom—was not relying on additional or fresh legal authority derived from the Resolution. Instead, it merely claimed that its authority to use force was 'left intact'. Other states, the argument continued, were fully aware of that understanding and, therefore, accepted it when voting for the Resolution. There were three possible legal positions that may have been preserved in this way. First, there was the right to self-defence. Second, there was a broad right to enforce Council resolutions relating to Iraq. Third, there might conceivably have been an argument of an even wider right to enforce the will of the organized international community.

The first argument of preventative force has already been discussed above. While it attracted some support in US scholarship in the immediate wake of the operation, it was not seriously put forward on the legal plane and in any event was widely rejected.

---

[136] W H Taft IV, 'The Bush (43rd) Administration' in Scharf and Williams (above n 44) 133.

Second, the US relied on a more general application of the revival argument, holding that the authority provided in Resolution 678 (1990) to restore peace and security in the area persisted to this day. The cease-fire had merely temporarily suspended it. In cases of material breach, the United States would be free to react forcibly without reference to the Security Council. In relation to Operation Desert Fox, a senior US Legal Adviser had claimed that:[137]

The United States has maintained that it is within its authority to take the necessary proportionate force to ensure that Iraq comply with and not violate any resolutions of the Security Council, but that it would be acceptable and useful to have the Security Council reiterate such authority. However, the United States did not consider that reiteration a precondition of its authority.

This argument was restated by the then US Legal Advisers in their defence of the 2003 operation:[138]

As a legal matter, a material breach of the conditions that had been essential to the establishment of the cease-fire left responsibility to member states to enforce those conditions, operating consistently with Resolution 678 to use all necessary means to restore international peace and security in the area. ...

The US view was that whether there had been a material breach was an objective fact, and it was not necessary for the Council to so determine or state.

This view stepped outside the original revival doctrine established by the UN General Counsel and acted upon during the 1990s. As was recalled by the UN Legal Counsel when analysing the developments of 2002–2003, the revival argument was not immediately available to individual states:[139]

For that authorization to revive two steps would be necessary: the Council must determine that Iraq had violated the cease-fire in a manner that was sufficiently serious as to negate its basis, and the Council would have to make clear its view as an organ that Member States were justified in using all necessary means, up to and including armed force, to bring Iraq into compliance with 687 (1991).

The administration of the revival doctrine through the Council was a crucial element in its creation and initial application—it was never seen as an open-ended invitation to any state to enforce disarmament obligations at will.[140] This fact was certainly appreciated by the United Kingdom from beginning to end of this episode and impelled its quest initially for a first resolution and then, when it transpired that that had not in fact offered sufficient authorization, for a second.[141]

Moreover, even if the material breach/revival argument could still have operated, and operated outside of Council control, this did not really resolve the legal

---

[137] M Matheson (1998) 92 *American Society of International Law Proceedings* 136, 141.
[138] Taft and Buchwald (above n 58) 560.   [139] Reproduced in Zacklin (above n 95) 146.
[140] See Ch 4.   [141] See Ch 6.

dilemma for the United States and the United Kingdom. As Mark Weisburg points out:

> ... if one assumes that breaches of Resolution 687 might justify four days of air strikes directed against military targets, it does not follow that such breaches could justify what the United States and the United Kingdom actually did in 2003—conquering Iraq and assuming total control of the country.[142]

Moreover, the requirement of necessity and proportionality would still operate.[143] The armed action would have had to be specifically and exclusively targeted towards the destruction of whatever WMD potential both states could reliably demonstrate that Iraq still possessed at the time.

In any event, it would ordinarily have to be accepted that the process instituted by Resolution 1441 (2002) would regulate the modalities of application of the revival doctrine. That was essentially the compromise that had been agreed. According to paragraphs 4, 11, and 12 of the Resolution, the tough new inspections regime was balanced by the assessment mechanism. But even if the United States could be judged to have succeeded in avoiding this effect by reserving its previous stance, this was not much help. That stance was not accepted by states other than the United States (and possibly Australia, although not on the Council), and was rejected by both the UN and even the UK Legal Advisers.[144]

Thirdly, there was the possible argument that the United States had reserved a very wide right to implement the will of the organized international community more generally. That is to say, the UN Security Council had expressed on behalf of the global community certain clear aims (the disarmament of Iraq). The United States would be entitled to implement these aims on behalf of the organized international community. After all, it had not only demanded Iraq's disarmament but, acting under Chapter VII of the UN Charter, had found that the present state of affairs amounted to a threat to international peace and security.[145]

This would, however, mean that any state could claim authority to use force in pursuit of the aims the UN Security Council expressed in a Chapter VII resolution. But, in that case, the Council might no longer be willing to adopt any decision under Chapter VII, if it implied a mandate of states unilaterally to adopt

---

[142] Weisburd (above n 124) 536.

[143] See Gardam (above n 43) Ch 6, on the application of necessity and proportionality in the context of UN authorized actions.

[144] The Australian Attorney General's Department and Foreign Affairs and Trade Department Legal Adviser offered a rather cryptic advisory note to the government that offered an extreme rendering of the revival theory. It simply held that 'the cease fire is not effective and the authorization for the use of force in SCR 678 is reactivated'. This result was not overturned by any subsequent Council resolution, including Resolution 1441 (2002): 'Advice on the Use of Force against Iraq', reproduced in (2003) 4(1) *Melbourne Journal of International Law* 181, 178ff. That advice was, however, opposed by two legal opinions commissioned by the Leader of the Opposition. Those two more detailed opinions came to the opposite view: see ibid, 183ff.

[145] In this direction, see C Stahn, 'Enforcement of the Collective Will After Iraq' (2003) 97 AJIL 804.

whichever enforcement action they deemed appropriate. Again, this argument was not seriously pursued.[146]

In truth, therefore, the United States was unable to rely on any justification for the use of force outside of a possible UN mandate granted through Resolution 1441 (2002). However, as Sean Murphy puts it:[147] 'The result,...was a new regime under Resolution 1441 (2002) that did not contain an authorization to use force, such that the default rule—no use of force—remained intact'.

III. The Operation of the Inspection Regime

The implementation process for Resolution 1441 (2002) did not have an auspicious start. Four days after its adoption, Iraq sent a letter to the UN Secretary-General, claiming, in a lengthy tirade, that the allegations concerning WMD advanced by the United States and United Kingdom were lies and slander. The letter concluded somewhat prophetically:

So let the inspectors come to Baghdad to perform their duty in accordance with the law, whereupon we shall hear and see, together with those who hear, see and act, each in accordance with his obligations and rights as established in the Charter of the United Nations and international law.[148]

This was followed by a more technical communication, challenging the factual assumptions underlying Resolution 1441 (2002) and its terms.[149] However, in essence, the modalities for the resumption of inspections had already been settled by the Resolution, which contained in an annex further requirements agreed by the parties during their earlier meetings in Vienna. Moreover, the overall regime established in Resolution 1284 (1999) relating to UNMOVIC remained in place, as amended by these subsequent texts.

After a preliminary visit by the UNMOVIC Executive Chairman to Baghdad on 18–19 November 2002, the inspections resumed on 27 November. On 7 December 2002, Iraq provided what it considered the full declaration of its weapons programme as required by Resolution 1441 (2002). On 28 December, Iraq also provided a list of its personnel associated with its weapons programme.

A. The inspection process

An initial informal assessment by UNMOVIC indicated that the 12,000-page dossier did not contain much that was new.[150] Instead, it appeared to bundle

---

[146] See Murphy (above n 59), and, on the earlier incarnation of this argument, N Kirsch, 'Unilateral Enforcement of the Collective Will: Kosovo, Iraq and the Security Council' (1999) 3 *Max Planck Yearbook of United Nations Law* 59.   [147] Murphy (above n 59) 227.

[148] Letter, S/2002/1242, 12 November 2002.

[149] Letter to the Secretary General, S/2002/1294, 25 November 2002.

[150] Blix (above n 73) 106ff.

together materials that had been offered previously. In particular, there was little evidence on the issues of chemical and, in particular, biological weapons, or on alleged Iraqi attempts to reconstitute its nuclear potential. US Secretary of State Colin Powell declared even then that, 'These are material omissions that, in our view, constitute another material breach'.[151] However, there was no formal move at the time to act on that thesis.

In his first full report to an open Council meeting, the head of UNMOVIC, Hans Blix, found that Iraq had in principle cooperated in the process, notably in relation to access to sensitive sites.[152] But there were also outstanding matters concerning guarantees of safety for the use of US U-2 aerial imaging planes, and the use of helicopters in the no-fly zones. A large batch of documents had been found in the private home of an Iraqi scientist, raising the prospect of further concealment of such documentary evidence throughout Iraq. Iraq had provided a list of some 480 individuals involved in weapons programmes. A small number had been requested by UNMOVIC to present themselves for interview, but these had insisted on being accompanied by Iraqi officials.

Some issues remained unresolved. A possible 1,000 tonnes of chemical weapons had not been accounted for, along with 8,500 litres of anthrax biological warfare agents. Iraq claimed to have destroyed its chemical and biological capacity in 1991, but this was not supported by documentation. Moreover, Iraq had developed the Al Samoud and Al Fatah missiles which had been tested at a range of over 150km. If that range were confirmed, these could also be liable for destruction.

Hans Blix did not characterize the overall state of compliance. Neither did Mr ElBaradei, the Director General of the IAEA, who merely indicated good progress in the inspection process,[153] which had included a significant number of interviews with scientists and others. However, once again, individuals had been reluctant to make themselves available unless accompanied by Iraqi officials. In terms of substance, the inspections had revealed that the aluminium tubes that Western sources claimed had been imported to support nuclear weapons-related work would probably not be suitable for that purpose. Other outstanding issues were due to be investigated over the following weeks and months.

The Council debated the issue on 5 February 2003. The meeting opened with a dramatic presentation by US Secretary of State Colin Powell. Supported by video, satellite imagery, and radio intercepts, he sought to demonstrate the extent and danger posed by clandestine Iraqi activities in all areas of WMD, nuclear, chemical, and biological. He claimed that there were serious infractions where delivery vehicles were concerned, including unmanned aerial vehicles. Secretary

---

[151] Quoted in SD Murphy, 'Contemporary Practice of the United States Relating to International Law' (2003) 97 AJIL 419.
[152] Record of the 4692nd UN Security Council meeting, S/PV.4692, 27 January 2003, 2.
[153] Ibid, 9.

Powell also sought to establish links between Iraq and terrorism, including a 'sinister nexus between Iraq and the Al Qaeda terrorist network'.[154] Thus far, it was held, Iraq had failed to take advantage of its final opportunity of compliance. The UK Foreign Minister also asserted that the only possible conclusion was that Iraq was in material breach of Resolution 1441 (2002). Other delegations, however, noted the progress that had been made in the inspections process and urged Iraq to improve its compliance further.

At a subsequent meeting two weeks later, Hans Blix stated that some 400 inspections covering 300 sites had taken place throughout Iraq. Those inspections had not revealed the proscribed items. The problem was certainty; for instance, with respect to the possibility that Iraq might have retained 1,000 tonnes of chemical agents, 'One must not jump to the conclusion that they exist. However, that possibility is also not excluded'. Blix added that, 'credible evidence to that effect must be presented'.[155] As later become apparent, however, Iraq was simply not in a position to offer evidence of that which it did not have.

In substantive terms, there was progress. The issue of the Al-Samoud missiles had been addressed by experts. They were found to have been in excess of the agreed maximum range. Iraq offered to present witnesses in support of its claims that it had destroyed chemical and biological agents in 1991. A few interviews had been held in private. The IAEA also reported on progress. The Director General indicated there was 'no evidence of ongoing prohibited nuclear-related activities in Iraq'.[156] During the ensuing Council debate, there was considerable unease about the division that was emerging among its members. Several delegations warned against precipitate action and emphasized the controlling role of the Council.

On 18 February 2003, the Council met again, this time at the request of the 115 Members of the Non-Aligned Movement, who had considered the issue at the initiative of South Africa. It was declared that, 'The message that has emanated from the 14 February debate in the Security Council is that the inspection process in Iraq is working and that Iraq is showing clear signs of cooperating more proactively with the inspectors'.[157] The wide range of non-members of the Council who addressed the gathering spoke overwhelmingly in support of that view.

At the end of February, UNMOVIC presented its regular quarterly report to the Council. The report emphasized once again that the Iraqi declaration of December had not presented significant fresh information relating to earlier activities, but did offer new insight into activities performed since the interruption of the inspections process in 1998. In its concluding paragraph, it found that 'Iraq could have made greater efforts to find any remaining proscribed items or provide credible evidence showing the absence of such items'.[158] UNSCOM was also

[154] Record of 4701st UN Security Council meeting, S/PV.4701, 5 February 2003, 14.
[155] Record of 4707th UN Security Council meeting, S/PV.4707, 14 February 2003, 3.
[156] Ibid, 9.   [157] Ibid, 4.   [158] A/2003/232, 28 February 2003, 13.

assembling a 173-page dossier that listed outstanding disarmament issues. That document—often referred to as the 'cluster document'—was presented to the Council shortly after a further meeting on 7 March 2003.[159] As indicated by its size, the dossier contained a detailed list of issues still to be addressed. Hans Blix subsequently suggested that his finding that Iraq could be making 'greater efforts' was an urgent warning to Iraq to accelerate compliance in view of the threat of force. The cluster document was meant to inform UNSCOM's future work plan. However, both UNMOVIC's quarterly report and the cluster document were taken by the United States and the United Kingdom as strong evidence that Iraq was not in full and unconditional compliance.

B. The attempt to obtain a second resolution

At this point, it was becoming clear that time was running out for the inspection process. It was widely expected that force would be used by mid-March.[160] At a meeting of 31 January 2003 between President Bush and Prime Minister Blair, the prospect of force was reportedly found to be unavoidable—despite the fact that both leaders were now no longer confident that a 'smoking gun', in the shape of proscribed weapons, would actually be found.[161]

At this point, a different kind of trigger was constructed. It took the shape of the famous, so-called 'second resolution'. After some consultation, on 24 February 2003, Spain, the United Kingdom and the United States put forward a joint draft resolution. The draft stated in its preamble that:[162]

Iraq has submitted a declaration pursuant to its resolution 1441 (2002) containing false statements and omissions and has failed to comply with, and cooperate fully in the implementation of, that resolution.

It further stated that, recognizing the threat that Iraq's non-compliance posed to international peace and security, the Council would decide 'that Iraq has failed to take the final opportunity afforded to it by resolution 1441 (2002)'. This text, therefore, put in place the authority required for the operation of the revival argument under Resolution 1441 (2002).

Given the strong sense in the Council at that time that the inspections process was producing results, it is difficult to see how the draft could have expected to attract the necessary support. It was answered, on the same day, by a memorandum from France, Germany, and the Russian Federation, which confirmed that

---

[159] UNMOVIC Working Document, *Unresolved Disarmament Issues: Iraq's Proscribed Weapons Programmes*, 6 March 2003. The document was made available in draft to certain key Council delegations, but was only issued after the meeting of 7 March 2003.

[160] Sir Jeremy Greenstock, (2009) Written Statement, 16.

[161] 'Bush Was Set on Path to War, UK Memo Says', *The New York Times*, 27 March 2007, available at <http://www.nytimes.com/2006/03/27/international/europe/27memo.html>.

[162] Spain, United Kingdom of Great Britain and Northern Ireland and United States of America: Draft Resolution, S/2003/215, 7 March 2003.

'so far the conditions for using force against Iraq have not been fulfilled'.[163] This was due to the fact that the inspections had not in fact revealed that Iraq possessed prohibited weapons. They were only then working at full pace and Iraqi cooperation was improving. The document proposed a programme of action, including in particular the accelerated presentation of the inspectors' work plan. The work plan would focus on priority areas, which would make it easier for Iraq to cooperate actively, and would provide a clear mechanism for the Council to assess cooperation. Moreover, in accordance with a French non-paper circulated previously, the inspections regime could be strengthened yet further. This could include additional staff, more aerial surveillance, and the use of mobile units to check trucks on Iraqi roads (in answer to the US/UK allegation that Iraq possessed mobile biological weapons factories).

The timeline for this proposal foresaw adoption of the work plan by 1 March 2003, followed by intensive inspections and a report after 120 days. The memorandum admitted that the inspections process could not continue indefinitely. However, 'the combination of a clear programme of action, reinforced inspections, a clear timeline and the military build-up provide a realistic means to reunite the Security Council and to exert maximum pressure on Iraq'.[164]

When the Council met on 7 March 2003 to consider the report of UNSCOM, there was a sense of high drama. Blix chose his words carefully, in view of the reception of the tone of his written report. He claimed that the initial difficulties indicated previously had been overcome. The U-2 flights had commenced, supplemented by French Mirage jets and German drones. The destruction of Al-Samoud 2 missiles had commenced. Blix emphasized that the state of active compliance by Iraq had now improved, in contrast to the period covered in his written report: 'There is a significant Iraqi effort under way to clarify a major source of uncertainty as to the quantities of biological and chemical weapons that were unilaterally destroyed in 1991'.[165] On other issues, Iraq had offered explanations and was proposing ways and means to verify its claims.

Overall, Blix avoided a clear answer on whether or not Iraq had cooperated immediately, actively, and unconditionally in accordance with Resolution 1441 (2002). While Iraq had on occasion attempted to attach conditions to its cooperation, it had not persisted in so doing: 'If it did, we would report it'.[166] In view of the trend towards more proactive cooperation, it would be hard to find in this statement a report by the arms inspectors of material breach. Instead, Blix indicated that the work programme of UNMOVIC would be presented in March, and would include priority areas of further work. It was expected to take some months to carry out.

---

[163] Letter dated 24 February 2003 from the Permanent Representatives of France, Germany, and the Russian Federation to the United Nations addressed to the President of the Security Council, S/2003/214, 24 February 2003.   [164] Ibid.
[165] Record of the 4714th meeting of the UN Security Council, S/PV.4714, 4.
[166] Ibid, 5.

The IAEA Director General reported that several of the allegations levelled against Iraq had turned out to be false. Aluminium tubes and magnets purportedly used for nuclear centrifuges had not in fact been acquired for that purpose. Claims that Iraq had sought to obtain uranium from Niger were based on documents found to be 'not authentic', that is, forgeries: 'After three months of intrusive inspections, we have to date found no evidence or plausible indication of the revival of a nuclear-weapons programme in Iraq'.[167]

Germany, introducing the joint initiative in favour of enhanced, continued inspections according to a clearly focused work programme, indicated that war could only be a last resort and that peaceful means had not yet been exhausted.[168] The United States, by contrast, faced with the failure of the inspections process to produce evidence indicating serious violation by Iraq, indicated that 'we must not allow Iraq to shift the burden of proof onto the inspectors'.[169] Hence, it would be up to Iraq to prove compliance rather than the other way around. Accordingly, the United States supported a new version of the draft resolution that had been circulated but not yet tabled. This draft again noted that Iraq had failed to comply with the terms of Resolution 1441 (2002). However, in its substantive part it now provided:[170]

Decides that Iraq will have failed to take the final opportunity afforded by resolution 1441 (2002) unless, on or before 17 March 2003, the Council concludes that Iraq has demonstrated full, unconditional, immediate and active cooperation in accordance with its disarmament obligations under resolution 1441 (2002) and previous relevant resolutions, and is yielding possession to UNMOVIC and the IAEA of all weapons, weapon delivery and support systems and structures, prohibited by resolution 687 (1991) and all subsequent relevant resolutions, and all information regarding prior destruction of such items.

This text reversed the possibility of a veto in relation to an authorization to use force. The previous version contained a simple finding of non-compliance, paving the way for use of force in accordance with Resolution 1441 (2002). This version, by contrast, required an affirmative vote, including that of the United Kingdom and United States as permanent members of the Council, to prevent the automatic occurrence of a finding of non-compliance by a clearly specified date.

There was no majority in the Council either to authorize war directly, or to do so by requiring the Council to muster a vote against it. Hence, the amendment to the Resolution did not make much difference. Nevertheless, in the days that followed, the United Kingdom proceeded to work on the draft with a view to obtaining a majority in favour. This was backed by the application of very strong pressure to the 'middleground six' Council members that were believed to be persuadable in favour of the Resolution. On the side of the United States/United

---

[167] Ibid, 8.   [168] Ibid, 19.   [169] Ibid, 14.
[170] Spain, United Kingdom of Great Britain and Northern Ireland and United States of America: Draft Resolution, S/2003/215, 7 March 2003.

Kingdom were Spain and Bulgaria. It was clear that Russia, China, and France were in opposition, along with Syria. This left Angola, Cameroon, Chile, Mexico, Pakistan and, possibly, Germany.[171]

On 10 March 2003, the French President stated in an interview that 'regardless of the circumstances, France will vote "no" because she considers this evening that there are no grounds for waging war in order to achieve the goal we have set ourselves, i.e., to disarm Iraq'.[172] A day later, the Council held a further meeting attended by a very large number of non-members, who spoke overwhelmingly against the impending use of force.[173] That meeting had, again, been requested by the Non-Aligned Movement, professing to represent 'two thirds of humanity'.[174] The Movement adopted a declaration opposing unilateral action.[175]

In the meantime, the United Kingdom was developing a proposal for an objective test of Iraqi compliance, with a view to making the ultimatum more acceptable. This consisted of the following:[176]

- A statement by Saddam Hussein undertaking to cooperate fully with UNMOVIC and the IAEA in immediately addressing and resolving all outstanding questions.
- An undertaking to make 30 Iraqi scientist available for interview outside Iraq.
- An undertaking to surrender all remaining anthrax and anthrax production capability.
- An undertaking to surrender all mobile bio-production laboratories for destruction.
- An undertaking to destroy Al-Samoud II missiles and components.
- An undertaking to account for unmanned aerial vehicles and remotely piloted vehicles.

These six points had been developed by the UK Prime Minister, and were to be used to assess whether Saddam Hussein had, after all, had a change of heart, or had taken a strategic decision in favour of compliance. The former had been a UK requirement from the outset, and meant that war could only be avoided if Saddam Hussein fundamentally changed his attitude in respect to the arms issue.[177] The strategic decision requirement had replaced the US hope of finding

---

[171] In fact, Germany turned out to be solidly opposed and was ultimately represented by its Foreign Minister, a flamboyant former peace activist and now leading member of the Green Party, in the Security Council. See D Dettke, (2009) *Germany says No* Ch 6.

[172] 'Iraq—Interview given by M. Jacques Chirac, President of the Republic, to TF1 and France 2, Paris', website of the French Embassy in the United Kingdom, available at <http://www.ambafrance-uk.org/Iraq-Interview-given-by-M-Jacques.html>.

[173] Record of the 4717th UN Security Council meeting, S/PV.4717, 11 March 2003. In fact, the debate lasted two days, given the strong interest.   [174] Ibid, 7.

[175] Reproduced in Ehrenberg et al. (above n 14) 140.

[176] Jack Straw, Written Statement, 8 February 2010, 17.   [177] See Ch 6.

decisive evidence of WMD. Instead, much like the British stance, Iraq would now need to present positive evidence of fundamental change.[178]

Prime Minister Blair claimed that the six requirements had been created in direct consultation between himself and Blix, in order to gain international legitimacy and possible support in the vote on the Resolution.[179] They were in part reflective of elements noted for further investigation in the cluster document. However, as is now known, they also contained elements that Iraq could not conceivably fulfil, such as the surrender of the non-existent anthrax or mobile bio-laboratories.

The UK's campaign to muster votes was eventually abandoned amid severe recriminations against France. The earlier statement of the French President was now invoked as a ground for pulling the draft resolution, arguing that the prospect of a veto had removed any chance of building consensus around the text. In fact, the French statement did not really threaten a veto under 'any circumstance' in general terms. Instead, when read in context, the statement related exclusively to the UK/US/Spanish draft as it then was. Given the hawks' intent of forcing a decision in favour of war, when the wider view was that the inspections regime was now functioning, that was not an unreasonable attitude.

France expended some effort in clarifying that it had not meant to preclude a vote in favour of force under any circumstance, for instance if there were indications of serious non-compliance.[180] Diplomatic telegrams reportedly confirmed that this was understood by the United Kingdom.[181] Peter Rickets, the Political Director of the Foreign Office, later reportedly described the French statement as a 'gift',[182] in that it gave cover to the Prime Minister, who had previously declared that he would only join in the armed action if a second resolution were adopted, unless such a resolution were to be blocked by an unreasonable veto.[183]

Moreover, at the time, the United States and United Kingdom had not managed to persuade the 'middleground six' to support the resolution, although efforts to that end were ongoing. However, the allegation by the United Kingdom that the French announcement had removed all prospect of agreement was not true. Instead, the other delegations were simply not persuaded of the case for war. Nevertheless, it was thought that it would still be preferable to have a majority in favour of the action, even if the ultimatum was ultimately vetoed by France, Russia, and/or China. This, it was thought, would at least have accorded the operation political legitimacy.[184] While he claimed that the French declaration had cut away the ground for further discussion with unfortunate incisiveness,

[178] Blix (above n 73) 238.

[179] Tony Blair, Chilcot Testimony, 29 January 2010, 121. Blix indicated that he was rushed in surprise to the UK Mission at the UN at 8am and acquainted with the proposal: Blix (above n 73) 245.   [180] Jack Straw, Chilcot Testimony, 8 February 2010, 91.

[181] C Short, *An Honourable Deception?* (2004) 183.

[182] S Kettell, *Dirty Politics?* (2006) 101.   [183] See Ch 6, 215.

[184] Murphy (above n 151) 424.

Sir Jeremy Greenstock, the UK Permanent Representative, admitted that there was ultimately no such majority:[185]

At that stage, too, the approaches to the capitals of the middleground six became more intensive, without hitting success. Around 13/14 March there were signs that Mexico and Chile might inspire a counterresolution, requiring a delay on any military action, but Washington managed to turn this off. On Friday 14 March Security Council discussions faded away into an eerie silence, while the countries favouring military action prepared to attend a final summit meeting in the Azores. The most important factors, therefore, in all this saga were first, the absence of irrefutable evidence that Iraq was pursuing an active programme of WMD; and second, the determination of the United States to proceed with military action whatever the state of the evidence produced at the UN.

By that time, Canada was proposing a modest extension of the inspection process until the end of March. The middleground six were in fact indicating a readiness to contemplate the UK ultimatum, but proposed 45 days of additional inspections.[186] However, by then the timing of the invasion was already fixed:[187]

Timing was indeed a crucial consideration. There appeared to be an assumption in the military planning of the invasion of Iraq that the heat of the summer months had to be avoided. I was not part of the discussions in London about our own military preparation or about our own preferred timing for military action. The UK had started by planning an attack on Iraq through Turkey, by agreement with the US, but the Turks declined to cooperate in this. London was therefore preoccupied with hasty preparations for the alternative, an attack from Kuwait into the south of Iraq. It seemed to me that the option of invading Iraq in, say, October 2003 deserved much greater consideration. But the momentum for earlier action in the United States was much too strong for us to counter. The Prime Minister's arguments for more time, as I observed them from New York, appeared to win two weeks or so of delay, but no more. The 'second resolution' as we designed it for March 2003 might have taken on a different shape and character on a different timing. Nevertheless, with hindsight, my judgement is that a majority of members of the Security Council would have opposed the use of force against Iraq by the US and the UK on almost any timing, unless the inspectors had succeeded in exposing Iraq's deception with the discovery of an active chemical or biological weapon.

At a summit of supporters of the war held on the Azores Islands on 16 March 2003, President Bush issued a final ultimatum. He indicated that Saddam Hussein had one day to go into exile if he wanted to avoid the armed invasion.[188] In an Address to the Nation of Iraq on 17 March, he indicated that Saddam Hussein and his sons had 48 hours to leave Iraq.[189] He also indicated that, 'It is too late for Saddam Hussein to remain in power', encouraging Saddam's military

---

[185] Jeremy Greenstock, (2009) Statement to the Iraq Inquiry, 16.   [186] Ibid, 15.
[187] Ibid.
[188] 'President Bush: Monday "Moment of Truth" for World on Iraq', White House Official website, available at <http://georgewbush-whitehouse.archives.gov/news/releases/2003/03/20030316–3.html>.
[189] SD Murphy, (2006) 2 *United States Practice in International Law* 340, n 39.

instead to permit the 'peaceful entry of coalition forces to eliminate weapons of mass destruction'.[190]

On the same day, Hans Blix presented to the Council his proposals for an accelerated work programme for the completion of the inspection tasks.[191] By that time, however, UNMOVIC inspectors had already been withdrawn from Iraq in expectation of the onset of hostilities. As the US Permanent Representative informed the Council, 'considering a work programme at this time is quite simply out of touch with the realities we confront'.[192]

IV. Responses to the Use of Force

On 19 March 2003, President Bush announced the beginning of Operation Iraqi Freedom, which commenced the next day with an attempt to decapitate the Iraqi leadership through a decisive 'shock and awe' first strike. Major combat operations were terminated on 14 April. The United States claimed that the invasion was supported by around 44 states. In reality, only Australia and, to a very limited extent, Poland directly participated in hostilities along with the UK.[193]

The coalition states put forward formal justifications for the operation to the Council. The United States emphasized that the actions taken 'are authorized under existing Council resolutions, including its resolutions 678 (1990) and 687 (1991)'. Resolution 687 (1991) imposed a series of obligations on Iraq, including, most importantly, extensive disarmament obligations, which were conditions of the cease-fire established under it:[194]

It has been long recognized and understood that a material breach of these obligations removes the basis of the ceasefire and revives the authority to use force under resolution 678 (1990). This has been the basis for coalition use of force in the past and has been accepted by the Council, as evidenced, for example, by the Secretary-General's public announcement in January 1993 following Iraq's material breach of resolution 687 (1991) that coalition forces had received a mandate from the Council to use force according to resolution 678 (1990).

Iraq continues to be in material breach of its disarmament obligations under resolution 687 (1991), as the Council affirmed in its resolution 1441 (2002). Acting under the authority of Chapter VII of the Charter of the United Nations, the Council unanimously decided that Iraq has been and remained in material breach of its obligations and recalled

---

[190] Reproduced in Ehrenberg (above n 14) 112.
[191] Record of the 4721st UN Security Council meeting, S/PV.4721, 19 March 2003, 1.
[192] Ibid, 13.
[193] Others made symbolic contributions. Denmark, for instance, dispatched a submarine—not normally seen as a vessel ideally suited for desert warfare (although it was claimed that it played a role in bottling-up the (non-existent) Iraqi Navy).
[194] Letter dated 20 March 2003 from the Permanent Representative of the United States of America to the United Nations addressed to the President of the Security Council, S/2003/351, 21 March 2002.

its repeated warnings to Iraq that it will face serious consequences as a result of its continued violations of its obligations. The resolution then provided Iraq a 'final opportunity'
to comply, but stated specifically that violations by Iraq of its obligations under resolution
1441 (2002) to present a currently accurate, full and complete declaration of all aspects
of its weapons of mass destruction programmes and to comply with and cooperate fully
in the implementation of the resolution would constitute a further material breach. The
Government of Iraq decided not to avail itself of its final opportunity under resolution
1441 (2002) and has clearly committed additional violations. In view of Iraq's material
breaches, the basis for the ceasefire has been removed and use of force is authorized under
resolution 678 (1990).

The United States added that the operation was an 'appropriate' response.
Moreover, it was a 'necessary step' to defend the United States and the international community from the threat posed by Iraq and to 'restore international
peace and security in the area'.[195] The United Kingdom, in its submission, also
based its claim on the revival argument:

The action follows a long history of non-cooperation by Iraq with the United Nations
Special Commission (UNSCOM), the United Nations Monitoring, Verification and
Inspection Commission (UNMOVIC) and the International Atomic Energy Agency
(IAEA) and numerous findings by the Security Council that Iraq has failed to comply
with the disarmament obligations imposed on it by the Council, including in resolutions
678 (1990), 687 (1991) and 1441 (2002). In its resolution 1441 (2002), the Council reiterated that Iraq's possession of weapons of mass destruction constitutes a threat to international peace and security; that Iraq has failed, in clear violation of its obligations, to
disarm; and that in consequence Iraq is in material breach of the conditions for the cease-
fire at the end of hostilities in 1991 laid down by the Council in its resolution 687 (1991).
Military action was undertaken only when it became apparent that there was no other
way of achieving compliance by Iraq. The objective of the action is to secure compliance
by Iraq with its disarmament obligations as laid down by the Council. All military action
will be limited to the minimum measures necessary to secure this objective.

Both states confirmed to the Security Council that the armed action was not
directed against Iraq or its people, but against its regime.[196] Australia also
offered a legal justification for its participation in the operation, again invoking
Resolution 1441 and the revival argument:[197]

In its resolution 1441 (2002), the Council recognized that Iraq's possession of weapons
of mass destruction constitutes a threat to international peace and security, that Iraq
has failed, in clear violation of its obligations, to disarm and that in consequence Iraq
is in material breach of the conditions for the ceasefire at the end of hostilities in 1991
laid down by the Council in its resolution 687 (1991). Military action was undertaken

---

[195] Ibid.

[196] Record of the 4726th UN Security Council meeting, S/PV/4726, Resumption, 27 March
2003, UK, 23, US, 25.

[197] Letter dated 5 March 2003 from the Chargé d'affaires a.i. of the Permanent Mission of Israel
to the United Nations addressed to the Secretary-General, S/2003/352, 21 March 2003.

consistent with resolutions 678 (1990), 687 (1991) and 1441 (2002) only when it became apparent that there was no other way of achieving compliance by Iraq.

Russia put forward a detailed legal memorandum, arguing that the operation could not be justified under UN law or general international law. It rejected both the general application of the revival theory, and its attempted application through Resolution 1441 (2002).[198] In the Council debate following the commencement of hostilities, Russia found that:[199]

An unprovoked military action has been undertaken, in violation of international law and in circumvention of the Charter... The military action... cannot be justified in any way. In fact, those countries were unable to provide any proof to support their allegations regarding Iraq's possession of weapons of mass destruction and Baghdad's support for international terrorism...

It is clear to everyone that the use of force against Iraq in an effort to change the political regime of a sovereign State runs totally counter to the fundamental principles contained in the Charter.

China added:[200]

Such an action constitutes a violation of the basic principles of the Charter of the United Nations and of International law. ...

Security Council Resolution 1441 (2002), which was adopted unanimously last November, is an important basis for the political settlement of the question of Iraq. It is the universal view of the international community that achieving the goal of peacefully disarming Iraq of its weapons of mass destruction is possible through the strict implementation of that resolution. ... However, to our profound regret, the weapons inspections being carried out by the United Nations inspectors were suspended at a time when they had been making steady progress.

France indicated that the 'military action has been engaged in Iraq without the endorsement of the United Nations'.[201] Perhaps in deference to the view that the United States remained free to mount an argument outside of the context of Resolution 1441 (2002), and that it had been made aware of this prior to the adoption of the Resolution 1441 (2002), it did not expand at that time on the legal issues. In fact, very few of the middleground six offered express views on that issue. Even Germany, which had previously vigorously attacked the possible use of force as unlawful, expressed itself in fairly moderate tones in the Council. The view was that these states had offered their positions opposing force and seeking to preserve the controlling role of the Council in earlier debates. Their position had been made known when they failed to accept the proposed ultimatum carrying with it the authorization to use force. Now, as they all indicated, it was necessary to look to the future and avoid a further collapse of action in the Council, in

---

[198] Russian Memorandum, reproduced in (2003) 52 ICLQ 1059.
[199] Record of the 4726th UN Security Council meeting, S/PV.4726, 26 March 2003, 27.
[200] Ibid, Resumption R-28.   [201] Ibid.

particular in view of the developing humanitarian situation on the ground, and the difficult challenges that would lie ahead.[202]

The Non-Aligned Movement, on the other hand, expressly declared that the war against Iraq 'is being carried out in violation of the principles of international law and the Charter'.[203] The League of Arab States considered the 'aggression a violation of the Charter of the United Nations and the principles of international law'.[204] Others deplored the action as a clear violation of international law.[205] Algeria, along with others, asked:[206]

How can the use of such extreme, disproportionate and definitive measures be justified when no present and immediate danger was threatening international peace and Security and when the inspections instituted by the Security Council of the peaceful disarmament of Iraq were proceeding in the right direction?

Many other delegations expressed regret over the operation. This included states listed by the United States as supporting it.[207] In fact, only a few supportive states expressly endorsed the US/UK legal position, while a number of its allies expressed political support without offering legal reasons.[208]

Bearing in mind that the Non-Aligned Movement, which had requested the debate, represented some 115 states, the legal justification of the invasion of Iraq was, therefore, overwhelmingly rejected. The UN Secretary-General later confirmed the view of the UN that the action would have required a second resolution and was illegal: 'I have stated clearly that it was not in conformity ... with the UN Charter'.[209]

V. Conclusion

'Going the UN route' in order to achieve US and UK objectives proved a difficult process, even in the very first phase of defining that route through a Security Council resolution. Over a period of seven weeks, the initial US/UK draft elements for a resolution were changed considerably. Those elements that would have been impossible for Iraq to accept (enforcement on the ground by UN or

---

[202] See throughout the debate, ibid, and Resumption 1.   [203] Ibid, 7.   [204] Ibid, 8.

[205] Ibid. For example, Indonesia, 19; Brazil, 28; Switzerland, 30; Vietnam, 32; Iran, 33; Lebanon, 35; Argentina, 37; Belarus, 38; Morocco, 44; Venezuela, 45; Laos, 47; Liechtenstein, Resumption, 2; Uruguay (referring to its previous statement), R-4; Saudi Arabia, R-7; Ethiopia, R-15; Kyrgyzstan, R-16; Slovenia, R-17; Mexico, R-19; Pakistan, R-20; Syria, R-32; Germany, R-34 (but more clearly in the meeting of 7 March).

[206] Ibid, 10, also South Africa, 20; Jamaica, 32; Mauritius, 27; Tanzania, 9; Kenya, R-17; Cameroon, R-24; Chile, R-30;   [207] For instance, New Zealand, ibid, 23.

[208] Ibid, Poland, 24; Australia, 27, an exception perhaps; Singapore, 26. Other states offering support to the United States/United Kingdom in a more general way included Albania, Bulgaria, Georgia, Macedonia, Nicaragua, Uzbekistan, Iceland, Latvia, Mongolia, El Salvador, Micronesia, Uganda, Spain.

[209] Kofi Annan, Interview, 16 September 2004, reproduced in Ehrenberg (above n 14) 161f.

Council Member States) were dropped. Overall, the new inspection modalities that emerged were tough, but could be implemented.

The legal effect of Resolution 1441 (2002) in relation to the possible use of force was somewhat ironic, at least from the UK perspective. Originally, a simple ultimatum by the Council was envisaged. This would have expressly authorized force upon the expiry of a certain deadline. This proved unobtainable. Then, an attempt was made to lay the groundwork for the operation of the revival document. This required a new finding by the Council of a serious violation capable of suspending the cease-fire, coupled with a threat of serious consequences.

The Council was just as unwilling to issue an indirect authorization of the use of force in this way as it had been to do so through a simple ultimatum. This was the lesson learnt from the experience of Operation Desert Fox. Hence, Resolution 1441 (2002) resulted in a compromise. It restored the possibility of using the revival argument, but attached procedural strings. The argument could only operate once the Council had considered whether Iraq had taken its final opportunity to comply. It would be for the Council to control that process. Hence, the legal position, at least from the perspective of the United Kingdom, was diminished as a result of going the UN route. The revival argument of old could no longer be deployed. It was now dependent on the Council's administration of the arms inspection process and on the Council meeting its 'responsibility', as the United Kingdom had indicated. In consequence, the United Kingdom would later frantically work towards a 'second resolution', in an effort to obtain the legal authority that was still missing, at a point when it was clear that the United States was going to use force regardless, and that the United Kingdom would participate in that venture.

The UK Representative to the UN, Sir Jeremy Greenstock, subsequently claimed with great vigour that the United Kingdom had not in fact accepted a text that diminished whatever authority might have existed prior to Resolution 1441 (2002), and this would have been in conflict with his instructions. However, the record reviewed in this chapter reveals that this was a self-serving statement not borne out by the realities of the result of the negotiations, and one that was denied by Sir Jeremy's own Legal Advisers in the Foreign Office. It is clear that Resolution 1441 (2002) did not in itself offer fresh legal authority for the use of force. In contrast to the United States, the United Kingdom could not argue that action could be taken in the absence of such fresh authority. Hence, the UK statement made on the adoption of the Resolution did not contain such a claim.

The United States had gone the UN route reluctantly and was in no mood to subject its claimed freedom of action to a further decision by the Security Council. Hence, it reserved its position, claiming that the authority to use force that already existed had not been diminished by the Resolution. However, it is difficult to reserve that which one does not have. There were no good grounds for the use of force available to the United States. Self-defence did not apply—no real case had been made that there was an imminent threat of attack emanating from

Iraq. Instead, President Bush referred to 'sovereignt authority to use force in assuring its own national security'.[210] This statement was reminiscent of assertions of the powers of self-preservation before the advent of the UN Charter. There was no overwhelming humanitarian emergency. There was no international acceptance of the US claim to a general right either to administer the revival argument outside the Council, or to implement what it perceived to be the will of the Council unilaterally. In those circumstances, the situation reverted to the operation of general international law, which does not admit the use of force unless justified by self-defence, possibly forcible humanitarian action, and UN authorization. In addition, it had been made abundantly clear that there was no fresh authorization for the unilateral use of force that could be drawn from Resolution 1441 (2002).

Another issue concerned the proportionality of the operation. Even if there had been authority to enforce the terms of Resolution 687 (1991), forcible action would have had to be limited to what was strictly necessary and proportionate to that aim. Although the United States and United Kingdom attempted to place regime change within the context of this limited aim, such an argument was not persuasive. Instead, limited armed action directed against the suspected weapons sites would have been expected.

There is no room to argue that regime change was produced as an incidental result of such a limited operation. It was clear throughout that regime change was the goal of the operation, and its conduct confirmed this. Moreover, even if such a result had occurred by accident, the United States/United Kingdom would still have been held to account for the result that obtained objectively in consequence of a use of force.[211]

By the time the operation was launched, there was an increasing sense resulting from the inspections process that claims relating to Iraqi WMD capabilities were unfounded. In addition to questions about proportionality, the issue of necessity, therefore, also arose. Even if Resolution 1441 (2002) could have been taken to offer in itself an authorization to use force, or if authority existed outside of it, there were no indications that forcible action at that point would have been legally necessary, given the viability of the inspection effort as a peaceful alternative. Even if there were still doubts about Iraq's WMD activities, the continuation of the inspection process would have made it possible to confirm this. However, this would have required the United States/United Kingdom to maintain the threat of force, and their troops, in place for a period of several months. The subsequent revelation by the US Iraq survey team that there were in fact none of the suspected WMD further undermined any possible legal justification for the act.[212]

---

[210] Address to the Nation, 17 March 2003, quoted in Murphy (above n 189) 340.

[211] C Gray, (3rd edn, 2008) *International Law and the Use of Force* 233.

[212] The Duelfer Report concluded that there was no weapons capacity, but still claimed that Iraq maintained 'strategic intent' in this respect. See <http://www.globalsecurity.org/wmd/library/report/2004/isg-final-report/>.

Despite the drama at the time, the overall impact of this episode on the international system and the rules on the use of force were, perhaps, rather overstated. There was considerable debate about the reconfiguration of international law in the face of one single super- (or hyper-) power,[213] debate about the Security Council's future credibility,[214] and some soul-searching about the future of the prohibition of the use of force.[215] In fact, the longer-term consequences of this episode have been more limited than might have been expected. The Council has not been precluded from ever again adopting Chapter VII resolutions that might conceivably attract unilateral claims for military enforcement. Instead, the Council has responded pragmatically. It now routinely confirms in resolutions of this kind the specific basis of legal authority used, and reserves expressly the right of the Council to control further steps. Moreover, in addition to refining the substance of any mandate granted, more thought is being devoted to its extension in time. Where the substance of the rules governing the use of force is concerned, there have been several important attempts to restore a consensus around the traditional rules governing self-defence, as they apply in non-traditional contexts.[216] The United States, under the new Obama administration, has engaged in a major campaign to emphasize its own, renewed commitment to these rules. As President Obama proclaimed in his acceptance speech for the Nobel Peace Prize:[217]

To begin with, I believe that all nations—strong and weak alike—must adhere to standards that govern the use of force. I—like any head of state—reserve the right to act unilaterally if necessary to defend my nation. Nevertheless, I am convinced that adhering to standards, international standards, strengthens those who do, and isolates and weakens those who don't. ... Furthermore, America—in fact, no nation—can insist that others follow the rules of the road if we refuse to follow them ourselves. For when we don't, our actions appear arbitrary and undercut the legitimacy of future interventions, no matter how justified.

---

[213] For example M Byers and G Nolte, (2003) *United States Hegemony and the Foundations of International Law*; G Simpson, (2004) *Great Powers and Outlaw States*.

[214] For example ND White, 'The Will and Authority of the Security Council after Iraq' (2004) 17 *Leiden Journal of International Law* 645.

[215] For example J Brunee and SJ Toope, 'The Use of Force: International Law after Iraq' (2004) 53 ICLQ 785; V Lowe, 'The Iraq Crisis: What Now?' (2003) 52 ICLQ 859.

[216] For example 'Chatham House Principles of International Law on the Use of Force by States in Self-defence', available at <http://www.chathamhouse.org.uk/research/international_law/papers/view/-/id/308/>.

[217] Available at <http://nobelprize.org/nobel_prizes/peace/laureates/2009/obama-lecture_en.html>; see also the new national security strategy published in 2010: 'The United States must reserve the right to act unilaterally if necessary to defend our nation and our interests, yet we will also seek to adhere to standards that govern the use of force. Doing so strengthens those who act in line with international standards, while isolating and weakening those who do not', available at <http://www.whitehouse.gov/sites/default/files/rss_viewer/national_security_strategy.pdf> 22.

6

The Role of International Law in
UK Decision-making

Hugo Grotius, a Dutchman, is the father of early modern international law. However, the United Kingdom is indisputably the ancestral home of international law as we now know it. While France retained control of the language of diplomacy well into the twentieth century, the UK played a key part in shaping the rules of the global system during its period of imperial domination. This was due in part to its common law tradition based on the application of reason, common sense, and human experience. This approach was more suited to the new exigencies at the dawn of the age of technology that shrank distances around the globe and required a legal framework for cooperation. On the continent, learned doctors of civil law were hotly disputing the existence of international law. Their denial of the legal quality of international law was based on the metaphysical doctrine of super-sovereignty of the Hegelian nation state, or later on ultra-positivist doctrinal definitions of the necessary elements of a legal system. In the UK, on the other hand, the towering legal figures of the age were pragmatically adapting international law from Grotian tradition to administer the needs of a global system of commerce and communication.[1]

After the First World War,[2] and even after the end of empire in the wake of the Second World War,[3] the UK retained its scholarly dominance over the field of

---

[1] In fact, the initial early modern work of great import was authored by the US scholar/practitioner Henry Wheaton, (1836) *Elements of International Law*, who had been trained in the Anglo-American tradition. The book was re-edited virtually throughout the nineteenth century. However, the establishment of the Chichele Chair in Oxford (1859) and the Whewell Chair in Cambridge (1868) very firmly moved the discipline's centre of gravity to the UK, being associated with names such as Harcourt, Holland, Maine, and Westlake. Somewhat ironically, this process reached its apogee at the turn of the nineteenth/twentieth century with the works of Lassa Oppenheim and later his successor in editing his major treatise, Sir Hersh Lauterpacht, both Whewell professors at Cambridge. Both came from the heart of the positivist, civil law tradition, Germany and the Austro-Hungarian Empire respectively. Nevertheless, as Oppenheim pragmatically put it in his famous treatise, 'In practice, international law is constantly recognized as law': L Oppenheim, (1905) *International Law: A Treatise* 13. Of course, there were contributions from the continent, such as those of Heffter and de Martens, but overall, the subject established its true home in the cloisters of Oxford and Cambridge.

[2] For example (AP) Higgins, Brierly, McNair, Lauterpacht.

[3] For example Waldock, Jennings, and their more contemporary successors.

international law.[4] This position was reinforced by the reputation of UK foreign policy as being generally informed by international legal advice of the highest quality and the consistently high impact of the Legal Advisers in the Foreign and Commonwealth Office (FCO) on policy.[5] Indeed, some of the great names in international law during the inter- and post-war years were active both as leading scholars and as Legal Advisers to the FCO, either formally or informally (Waldock, Fitzmaurice, Lauterpacht).

The unlawful UK armed action in relation to Suez in 1956 was profoundly shocking to the foreign policy establishment, in part precisely because it violated this tradition of seeking to strengthen the international rule of law.[6] This sense of shock persisted, even into the new millennium. Elizabeth Wilmshurst, Deputy Legal Adviser to the FCO, who left following the invasion of Iraq, explained:[7]

Certainly that was the lesson I draw from Suez: that it is in the UK's interests to keep within international law and within the UN Charter... that it is in our interests that we should go about international peace and security in a collective way.

I. The Role of Legal Advice in UK Foreign Policy

The traditional commitment of the UK to international law does not mean that its foreign policy has been lacking in robustness due to an excessive reliance on idealist, legalist views. On the contrary, due to the more flexible common law approach bred into its lawyers, the UK has generally been able to draw on its experience of international law as an intensely practice-driven subject and deploy it in the national interest. Using its reputation in the field, along with its technical legal expertise, in many areas the UK has been able to develop the law in line with its long-term national and international interests. Hence, the ability to draw authoritatively on the legal system, partially of its own making, to justify its policy aims, represents an important element of UK soft power. Beyond this longer-term phenomenon, the UK has also been able to deploy its credibility and authority in interpreting the law where most immediate circumstances so demand. For instance, when mounting an armed action to recapture the Falkland/Malvinas Islands in 1982, the persuasive strength of the UK legal case, based on self-defence, displaced the competing claims to the territory put forward by Argentina.

---

[4] Indeed, even today Oxford and Cambridge retain their pre-eminence in the field, along with a handful of key law schools in the United States.

[5] See, eg A Carty, (2000) *Sir Gerald Fitzmaurice and the World Crisis: A Legal Adviser in the Foreign Office 1930–1945*.

[6] L Johnman, 'Playing the Role of Cassandra: Sir Gerald Fitzmaurice, Senior Legal Advisor to the Foreign Office' (1999) 13(2) *Contemporary British History* 46; see also A Gorst and S Kelley (eds), (2000) *Whitehall and the Suez Crisis* 46.

[7] Elizabeth Wilmshurst, Chilcot Testimony, 26 January 2010, 10. All evidence relating to the Iraq Inquiry is available at <http://www.iraqinquiry.org.uk/>.

As noted in Chapter 3, the UK also had courage of conviction when it came to legal innovation, even concerning the use of force. It acted as the principal norm entrepreneur in relation to the doctrine of humanitarian intervention in Iraq, north and south, and in relation to Kosovo. True, this action was somewhat daring; but the UK's reputation for a commitment to the international rule of law turned what might otherwise have been seen as an opportunistic argument into a reasoned position that required serious engagement as a matter of legal debate—a debate that led many to reassess the law on forcible humanitarian action.

In the instance of Suez, FCO Legal Advisers and Law Officers both consistently rejected proposals for the use of force against Egypt as unlawful. But at the crucial moment, when the decision to use force was taken, they were simply not consulted.[8] Instead, the Government relied on the Lord Chancellor and his more accommodating (and misguided) advice. However, according to UK constitutional practice, the Law Officers (the Attorney General and his or her Deputy, the Solicitor General, supported by the Attorney General's Office), are the chief advisers to the Government on key issues of domestic and international law. Ultimately it is for the Law Officers alone to offer definite legal advice on the lawfulness or otherwise of potential government action.

In formulating that advice, the Law Officers are supported in various ways. First, there is frequent consultation with the relevant departments and their legal advisers. In this instance, there was close cooperation with the FCO, and its team of around 35 international law experts based in London and in key international missions. Indeed, one of these had been seconded to the Attorney General's office in order to support work on international legal issues. The Ministry of Defence also maintains a staff of legal experts and was involved in consultations about Iraq.

According to the Ministerial Code, ministers must 'comply with the law, including international law and treaty obligations'.[9] This includes the obligation to consult the Law Officers 'in good time before the Government is committed to critical decisions involving legal considerations'.[10] This includes cases where 'the legal consequences of action by the government might have important repercussions in the foreign, European Union or domestic field'.[11]

It could hardly be doubted that there would be important repercussions arising from UK involvement in the large-scale invasion of Iraq. These included the immediate question of whether or not the action being contemplated was lawful, that is, whether the UK would render itself a very serious transgressor of international law, and extended to consequential issues such as reparations or individual

---

[8] See the magnificent study by the late G Marston, 'Armed Intervention in the 1956 Suez Canal Crisis: The Legal Advice Tendered to the British Government' (1988) 37 ICLQ 773.

[9] Ministerial Code, here used in the version of July 2001 applicable during the period in question, available at <http://www.cabinetoffice.gov.uk/media/cabinetoffice/propriety_and_ethics/assets/ministerial_code_2001.pdf>, para 1.   [10] Ibid, para 22.

[11] Ibid.

criminal responsibility on the part of the political leadership ordering the action or the military executing it. There were also considerable wider implications for the credibility of UK foreign policy, worldwide and in particular in relation to the Middle East. Finally, the action would have important consequences for the way the organized international community operated, particularly in relation to the credibility of international law and of the United Nations.

It is also clear that the decision would involve legal considerations, as required by the Ministerial Code. Although policy issues were clearly important, the requirement that the action comply with international law meant that the question of the use of force hinged directly and immediately upon legal considerations. The law in this instance was not an incidental issue but a principal one, and the acquisition of an authoritative legal determination on the lawfulness of the proposed action was accorded overwhelming importance in UK policy-making.

In this context, the strong commitment of New Labour under Tony Blair to an 'ethical foreign policy' may be recalled. This required transparent decision-making in relation to foreign affairs, and stipulated that the UK would act as a strong pillar of the international legal order.[12] Using force unlawfully, and on such a massive scale, would have posed a challenge to the Government that would probably have broken it. Hence, the legal debate also became a matter of life and death for Tony Blair and his Labour Government. Indeed, its importance was highlighted by the February 2003 march in London of upwards of one million anti-war protesters.[13]

Based on the analysis of international law presented in preceding chapters, it may be thought that the chances of finding in favour of invasion were slim. Indeed, as revealed by the following discussion, the advice given by the FCO international law experts throughout the run-up to the war, including by the Attorney General himself, excluded participation in the invasion. Nevertheless, the Attorney General ultimately certified that there was sufficient legal authority for war. This chapter reviews the legal advice as it developed in the prelude to hostilities. It does so on the basis of highly sensitive documents that were previously classified and the testimony of the principal protagonists in the UK. These materials have now been made available by the UK Chilcot Inquiry into the Iraq War. Further documents remain unavailable and there may be more revelations to come. However, this new information already provides valuable insights into the role of international law in UK decision-making.

This chapter will briefly review the UK-specific political context of the Iraq debate. It will then track the flow of legal advice up to the point of the invasion.

---

[12] See NJ Wheeler and T Dunne, 'Good International Citizenship: A Third Way for British Foreign Policy' (1998) 74(4) *International Affairs* 847; D Chandler, 'Rhetoric without Responsibility: The Attraction of "Ethical" Foreign Policy' (2003) 5(3) *British Journal of Politics and International Relations* 295.

[13] BBC News, '"Million" March against Iraq War', 17 February 2003, available at <http://news.bbc.co.uk/1/hi/2765041.stm>.

There follows an analysis of particular issues relating to the way this advice was managed and acted upon (or not) by the Government.

II. The Development of UK Policy on Iraq

Operation Desert Fox froze developments relating to Iraq. A new resolution replacing the UN Special Commission (UNSCOM) arms inspection effort with a new mechanism, now called the UN Monitoring, Verification and Inspection Commission (UNMOVIC), had been adopted by the Security Council in 1999. According to Resolution 1284 (1999) UNMOVIC would establish a 'reinforced system of ongoing monitoring and verification... and address unresolved disarmament issues'.[14] The Resolution was in fact encouraging to Iraq, promising removal of the sanctions regime after a relatively short period of continued disarmament, and the immediate lifting of elements of the sanctions having important humanitarian implications. However, the disarmament provisions remained largely unimplemented. Iraq asserted that the UN arms inspection effort was riddled with US spies, and maintained that information gathered had actually been used for targeting during the Desert Fox bombing campaign. Hence, Iraq could hardly be expected to cooperate once again with a similar inspection regime, even a rebranded one. In view of this situation, the arms inspectors had to attempt to monitor events in Iraq from abroad. The first pillar of international policy vis-a-vis Iraq—arms inspection—was gradually collapsing.

At the same time, the second pillar was also becoming increasingly difficult to sustain, as international support for the sanctions regime was gradually eroded. Iraqi claims that sanctions had led to the deaths of hundreds of thousands of civilians, in particular children, gained greater resonance over time. The argument of Western governments that the Iraqi Government was itself responsible for the deteriorating humanitarian situation became less persuasive to a liberal, democratic audience, and the technical and complicated nature of the 'Oil for Food' programme made it difficult for the wider public to understand where responsibility actually lay.

In addition to arms inspections and sanctions, the third pillar of the policy of containment of Iraq was also beginning to crumble. Developments, not least the passage of time, had undermined the credibility of operating the no-fly zones that were still covering most of Iraqi airspace. Keeping the no-fly zones in place for close to a decade did not appear consistent with their justification as a temporary measure designed to avert an imminent humanitarian emergency. Indeed, for the public there was little evidence of an ongoing emergency of significant dimensions. Instead, the situation appeared relatively stable. Moreover, a sense was emerging that the no-fly zones were being used as cover for a wider campaign

---

[14] Resolution 1284 (1999), para 2.

to diminish and degrade Iraqi military potential, and occasional attacks against the Iraqi military infrastructure outside the zones appeared to confirm this. Moreover, Iraq continued to challenge military over-flights on its territory. While US/UK aircraft had thus far eluded Iraqi ground-to-air missiles, it seemed inevitable that at some point there would be casualties or captured pilots.

In view of these difficulties, by March 2001 a new policy framework was being discussed at No 10 Downing Street. This framework balanced steps towards normalization of relations with Iraq with a continuation of the policy of containment. It proposed terminating sanctions on civilian trade, restoring civil air traffic to Iraq, and unfreezing assets on non-regime members in Iraq. Sanctions would be targeted against Iraqi officials. Increased trade with Iraq would be monitored at a limited number of border crossings, with Iraqi oil revenues remaining under UN control. The no-fly zones would remain in place but, in order to make the practice more sustainable, patrolling levels would be at higher altitudes to minimize risk to UK aircrew, and the territorial scope of the zone would be reduced.

In relation to weapons of mass destruction (WMD), the document accepted that the new regime under Resolution 1284 (1999) might remain unimplemented by Iraq. UNMOVIC would probably continue to operate from outside Iraq. There did not appear to be any particular urgency in relation to implementation of the original disarmament requirements imposed by Resolution 687 (1991). Rather, the status quo appeared acceptable.

A red line was nevertheless drawn in relation to a possible 'material breach' that might trigger 'direct action' once the necessary regional support 'and legal base' were in place.[15] However, while implementation of the inspection regime under Resolution 1284 (1999) remained the 'stated objective', the red line did not really apply to it. Instead, it concerned the reconstitution by Iraq of a military capacity threatening its neighbours, or the development of a new WMD and missile capability. Hence, the assumption within the Government appeared to have been that Iraq did not at that time possess such weapons or posed an unacceptable threat to its neighbours. The option of force was reserved for the event of an active increase in Iraq's WMD potential, rather than a failure to complete the destruction and monitoring process originally demanded by the UN.

The UK policy framework paper of March 2001 also introduced the objective of 'regime change'. This was to be consistent with the territorial integrity of Iraq, that is, presumably without the use of overt military force.[16] By December 2001, however, it was sufficiently clear that elements in the US Government were considering military action against Iraq to secure a change of regime.[17] At this point, the atrocities of 9/11 had already occurred. Regime change was put forward to address (incorrect) claims that Iraq had close connections to the attackers

---

[15] Letter from John Sawers (Prime Minister's Private Secretary) to Sherard Cowper-Coles (FCO) re Iraq: New Policy Framework, 7 March 2001, paras 8–9.   [16] Ibid, para 10.
[17] Jack Straw, Chilcot Inquiry, Written Statement, 21 January 2010, 3.

of the World Trade Centre and the Pentagon. The policy was also proposed as an answer to Iraq's continued ability to destabilize the region. Moreover, it was seen as a way of inaugurating a 'New American Century' by securing a liberal democratic foothold in the region that would (in theory) act as a beacon for the political transformation of the Arab world.[18]

Initially, the UK FCO sought to restrain the application of the doctrine of forcible regime change to Iraq in two ways. First, it emphasized that Baghdad had not been connected with the 9/11 attacks or with the Al Qaida organization. Second, it addressed the claim that Iraq represented a gathering threat that needed to be dealt with under the emerging US doctrine of pre-emption. This threat would either consist of Iraq's potential to mount further acts of aggression in its own neighbourhood, or might lie in its actual or potential possession of WMD that could be passed on to terrorist organizations targeting the West. The FCO continued to argue that containment would be the most appropriate way of countering this threat. Should offensive military action be contemplated, it was argued, this would 'almost certainly' require new Security Council authority.[19]

However, by this point, the UK Prime Minister had undergone a significant shift in his strategic thinking. In his view, 9/11 had fundamentally altered the global security environment. It had demonstrated that non-state actors could mount armed attacks on a par with governments, a capacity that would be multiplied many-fold if they ever acquired significant WMD. In this context, Iraq appeared persistent in its campaign to reconstitute its WMD capability. Faced with international pressure, and acting in the manner of a rogue state, it might be tempted to share this capacity with terrorist actors. The prospect of WMD falling into the hands of a movement like Al Qaida posed unacceptable risks. Moreover, Iraq had a history of launching aggressive wars against its neighbours, and had even attacked its own population. This included the use of chemical weapons against the mainly Kurdish inhabited village of Halabja, where some 5,000 civilians had been killed. To the Prime Minister, these factors combined indicated that Iraq would have to be dealt with in a more fundamental way, essentially through regime change:[20]

I think there is a danger that we end up with a very sort of binary distinction between regime change here and WMD here. The truth of the matter is that a regime that is brutal and oppressive, that, for example, has used WMD against its own people, such as Saddam did, and had [sic] killed tens of thousands of people by the use of chemical weapons, such a regime is a bigger threat, if it has WMD, than one that is otherwise benign.

The Prime Minister expanded on this point:[21]

. . . my assessment of the security threat was intimately connected with the nature of the regime. I don't know whether the members of the Committee understand this, but when

---

[18] See Ch 5.　　[19] Jack Straw (above n 17).
[20] Tony Blair, Chilcot Testimony, 29 January 2010, 28f.　　[21] Ibid, 65.

you actually read the descriptions of what happened when Saddam Hussein used chemical weapons in the Halabja village, and by some accounts as many as 5,000 people died through chemical weapons, there are people in Iraq today still suffering the consequence of that... to me that indicated a mindset that was horrific.

It is horrific whether or not he then uses weapons of mass destruction, but if there is any possibility of him ever acquiring them or using them, it is a mindset that indicates this is a profoundly wicked—I would say almost psychopathic—man. We were obviously worried that, after him, his two sons seemed to be as bad, if not worse. So yes, it is absolutely true, this definitely impacted on our thinking.

In the Prime Minister's view, there were two options for regime change. First, the regime would change fundamentally of its own accord. As he put it, Saddam might do 'a Colonel Gaddafi, and completely "reposition" himself vis-a-vis the international community'.[22] However, in the absence of such a sea change in attitude, the forcible removal of the Iraqi regime from the outside would be necessary. Secondly, although it was widely accepted in the UK that pro-democratic intervention would not be internationally lawful,[23] the Prime Minister considered that the issues of regime change and of Iraqi performance relating to its UN disarmament obligations were virtually indistinguishable. To leave the Iraqi regime in place and risk that it might gain access to WMD posed an unacceptable risk in the post-9/11 world.

At this point, therefore, Downing Street policy began to regard regime change as a necessary means of addressing Iraq, come what may. In that sense, there was a strong confluence with US policy which, although driven in part by different motivations, also favoured forcible regime change in Iraq. The famous visit of the Prime Minister to President Bush's ranch in Crawford, Texas, of April 2002, was therefore not an occasion where the UK signed up to the US agenda of regime change for the sake of alliance solidarity alone. Tony Blair was indeed mindful of the need to reassure the United States that the UK would stand by it, even to the point of going to war, in the interest of maintaining their close transatlantic relationship. However, the Prime Minister had apparently come to his own very strongly held view that Iraq had to be addressed through regime change. As he put it, 'if we couldn't resolve it through the UN inspectors, we had to resolve it by removing Saddam'.[24]

III. The Emerging Legal Strategy

In accordance with this thinking, on 8 March 2002 a detailed 'Options Paper' for UK policy on Iraq was produced. It is noteworthy that this paper did not

---

[22] Ibid, 103.
[23] For example Jack Straw, Supplementary Memorandum to the Chilcot Inquiry, 8 February 2010, 2.   [24] Tony Blair, Chilcot Testimony, 29 January 2010, 101–102.

emanate from the lead department in the matter, the FCO. Instead, in line with the Prime Minister's style of leadership, which concentrated power in a few individuals operating around him ('sofa government'), it was put forward by the Overseas and Defence Secretariat of the Cabinet Office, although others also contributed.

The paper noted that the United States appeared to have lost faith in the policy of containment relating to Iraq and was now considering regime change through the use of force. However, this was only an emerging requirement from the US side. The paper also found that the UK's own objective of reintegrating a 'law-abiding Iraq which does not possess WMD or threaten its neighbours, into the international community...cannot occur with Saddam Hussein in power'.[25]

It was noted that regime change might be achieved by encouraging opposition groups to mount an uprising, or providing air assistance in support of such a venture. However, the paper concluded that the use of overriding force in a ground campaign was the only option capable of removing Saddam Hussein and bringing Iraq back into the international community. Lesser means might risk the replacement of Saddam Hussein with another 'Sunni military strongman'.[26] The paper, therefore, concluded that 'the only certain means to remove Saddam and his elite is to invade and impose a new government'.[27] This, it was thought, would require a ground force of around 200,000–400,000 troops and sufficient air assets. It would take some five months to prepare for the invasion, ie until autumn 2002, with the 'optimal times to take action [being] early spring'.[28]

However, at the same time the paper acknowledged that 'regime change has no basis in international law'. Nevertheless 'a legal justification of the invasion would be needed. Subject to Law Officers advice, none currently exists. This makes moving quickly to invade legally very difficult'.[29]

In order to overcome this difficulty and satisfy the requirement of legality, it was necessary to adopt a staggered approach. First, there would be stricter implementation of sanctions. This would be flanked by military build-up. In the meantime, a legal basis could be established for the use of force outside the context of regime change. Referring to the revival argument based on the suspension of cease-fire Resolution 687 (1991), and renewed activation of the mandate granted in Resolution 678 (1990), the document cautioned that '[a]s the ceasefire was proclaimed by the Security Council in 687 (1991), it is for the Council to decide whether a breach of obligations has occurred'.[30] However, refusal to admit UN

---

[25] Overseas and Defence Secretariat, Cabinet Office, 8 March 2002, Summary Page. This is one of eight papers that were already publicly available before the Chilcot Inquiry, often referred to as the 'Downing Street Memos'. While these have not been officially acknowledged, their authenticity has not been disputed and indeed was confirmed through Chilcot Inquiry testimony. The documents are available at <http://downingstreetmemo.com/>. Official documents drawn from this source, instead of the Chilcot Inquiry, will be designated 'DSM' in the footnotes that follow.

[26] Ibid, para 11.   [27] Ibid, Summary Page.   [28] Ibid, para 23.

[29] Ibid, Summary Page, para 28.   [30] Ibid, para 31.

inspectors, or their admission and subsequent likely frustration, could result in new findings by the Security Council that justified military action, in parallel with the justification for Operation Desert Fox of 1998.[31]

The origin of, and defects in, the doctrine of material breach were discussed at length in Chapter 4. The doctrine assumed that the authority granted to members of the coalition to use all necessary means to liberate Kuwait and to restore peace and security in the area had only been suspended by the cease-fire terms imposed upon Iraq in Resolution 687 (1991). If these terms were materially breached, the authority to use force would thus be revived. However, the Council would at least have to determine the existence of such a breach and confirm that serious conse-quences would flow henceforth.

The paper foresaw active measures intended to manoeuvre Iraq and the inter-national community into a position where force would become lawful as a means of addressing Iraqi WMD on the basis of the material breach argument. In line with the Prime Minister's approach, the paper placed this strategy directly at the service of a policy of regime change in Iraq—an approach that was deemed unlawful by the paper itself.[32]

While the paper had originated in the Cabinet Office, it was accompanied by a Foreign Office memorandum entitled *Iraq: Legal Background*. The document explained at some length why no legal justification for the use of force against Iraq could be drawn from the doctrines of self-defence or humanitarian action. It also considered the application of the revival argument, seeking to reactivate the authority to use all necessary means against Iraq that had been granted by the Security Council shortly after its invasion of Kuwait. The memorandum empha-sized that, in contrast to the position of the United States, it was indeed for the Security Council to assess whether a breach of the obligation terminating or sus-pending the cease-fire at the end of the Kuwait conflict had occurred. Individual states had no such authority.

The *Legal Background* memorandum confirmed that the finding of a breach invoked in relation to Operation Desert Fox in 1998 could now no longer be relied upon:[33]

There has not been any significant decision by the Council since 1998. Our interpreta-tion of resolution 1205 was controversial anyway; many of our partners did not think the legal basis was sufficient as the authority to use force was not explicit. Reliance on it now would be unlikely to receive support.

While the memorandum did not spell out additional requirements for reactiva-tion of the use of force under this doctrine, it offered a reminder of a difficult

---

[31] Ibid, para 34.
[32] Ibid, para 28, 'REGIME CHANGE has no basis in international law' (emphasis in original).
[33] Foreign and Commonwealth Office, *Iraq: Legal Background*, 8 March 2002, para 4 (DSM, above n 25).

kind. In 1998, the UK sent a letter to the President of the Security Council defending Desert Fox:[34]

...we stated that the objective of that operation was to seek compliance by Iraq with the obligations laid down by the Council, that the operation was undertaken only when it became apparent that there was no other way of achieving compliance by Iraq, and that the action was limited to what was necessary to secure this objective.

This position of the UK at the time accepted strong limitations on the right to use force, even in the event of the revival argument being realized. The armed action could only aim to constrain compliance with the terms of the arms inspection regime. No other aims or goals could be pursued. Second, there had to be no other remedy. For instance, there could be no chance of pursuing this limited objective through means other than the use of force, such as a continuation of the arms inspection process. Finally, force could only be used to the extent that it was strictly necessary to achieve its stated, limited objective. That is to say, the doctrine of minimum force would need to be applied.

This reminder should in itself have excluded the application of the revival argument in relation to the aim of removing Saddam Hussein. That campaign would have failed all three of the criteria provided by the UK in 1998. It would have pursued an aim far broader than that established by the Security Council (regime change instead of compliance with disarmament requirements). As emerged in March 2003, there did appear to be other remedies available (continuing the arms inspections). In addition, even if force were an option, it could only be targeted against Iraq's prohibited armament and purported WMD capacity, and not against the state *per se*.

Nevertheless, in the absence of any other legal strategy, at this early stage the Government settled on the revival argument. It may have been assumed by the protagonists at this point that such action would merely require a fresh Security Council resolution demanding compliance with the arms inspection regime and threatening severe consequences or something similar in the event of non-compliance. If Iraq then failed to comply, as might be expected, military action might ensue.

One week after the Options Paper was presented, in preparation for the Prime Minister's celebrated visit with President Bush at his Ranch in Crawford, Texas, his principal foreign affairs adviser Sir David Manning was dispatched to Washington. There, he confirmed to US interlocutors that the Prime Minister would not budge in his support for regime change. However, 'it must be very carefully done and produce the right result'.[35] In this context a number of concerns needed to be addressed. These included the question of how international opinion could be made to understand that military action against Iraq was politically necessary and justified. Moreover, many states were insisting on the need for

---

[34] Ibid.
[35] Sir David Manning, Memorandum for the Prime Minister, 14 March 2002 (DSM, above n 25).

a legal basis, which should be attained through the UN dimension and the issue of weapons inspectors.

In parallel, in a discussion with US Deputy Secretary of Defence Paul Wolfowitz—a neoconservative who strongly supported invading Iraq—the UK Ambassador in Washington, Sir Christopher Meyer, confirmed that 'we backed regime change, but the plan had to be clever and failure was not an option'. He then 'went through the need to wrongfoot Saddam on the inspectors and the UNSCRs'.[36] In this discussion, therefore, the UN route was presented as a necessary step in the process of essentially manufacturing a legal basis for military action that, it was agreed, would ultimately follow.

The Foreign Secretary, in his briefing to the Prime Minister, noted that there was at that time no majority support for war inside the Parliamentary Labour Party, on which the survival of the Government depended.[37] There would be a long way to go to convince them as to, *inter alia*, 'the justification of any military action in terms of international law'.[38]

He then spelt out the strategy for achieving regime change in the context of the debate on WMD in greater detail. He noted that Iraq's flagrant breach of international legal obligations imposed upon it by the Security Council:[39]

...provides us with the core of a strategy, and one which is based on international law. Indeed if the argument is to be won, the whole case against Iraq and in favour (if necessary) of military action, needs to be narrated with reference to the international rule of law.

'Narrating' the story with reference to international law sounds like spinning it. As the Foreign Secretary explained, this strategy of gaining legitimacy for regime change would consist of making operational a new sanctions regime and demanding the readmission of weapons inspectors, but this time operating in a free and unfettered way.[40] This he regarded as essential in terms of public explanation and in terms of 'legal sanction for any subsequent military action'.[41] The Foreign Secretary added:[42]

9. Legally there are two potential elephant traps:
    (i) regime change per se is no justification for military action; it could form part of the method of any strategy, but not a goal. Of course, we may want credibly to assert that regime change is an essential part of the strategy by which we have to achieve our ends—that of the elimination of Iraq's WMD capacity; but the latter has to be the goal;

---

[36] Christopher Meyer, Iraq and Afghanistan: Conversation with Wolfowitz, Note to Sir David Manning, 18 March 2002, para 2 (DSM, above n 25); see also PF Ricketts, FCO Political Director, to the Secretary of State, 22 March 2002 (DSM, above n 25).

[37] Jack Straw, Memorandum to the Chilcot Inquiry, 21 January 2010, 24, where he claims that without his direct and personal support for the war, it could not have happened in view of the position in the Labour Party.

[38] Jack Straw, Personal Briefing Note for the Prime Minister, Crawford/Iraq, 25 March 2002 (DSM, above n 25), para 1.   [39] Ibid, para 6.

[40] Ibid, para 7.   [41] Ibid, para 8.   [42] Ibid, para 9.

(ii) on whether any military action would require a fresh UNSC mandate (Desert Fox did not). The US are likely to oppose any idea of a fresh mandate. On the other side, the weight of legal advice here is that a fresh mandate may well be required. ...

Similar to the merger of the issues of regime change with the enforcement of WMD restrictions in the mind of the Prime Minister, the two issues were now also intertwined in the emerging legal strategy. Regime change could be explained merely as a 'method' for obtaining compliance with the disarmament requirements. It would also be possible to obtain legal authority, at least in relation to the latter aim, which had UN endorsement.

Ordinarily it may be thought that the means of action must not be broader than the political aim that is to be achieved. Or, in legal terms, if force is used, this must only be done to the extent strictly necessary to obtain the legitimate aim (in this case, compliance with the arms inspection regime), for instance further targeted attacks against Iraq's military infrastructure and suspected weapons production facilities. Here, the limited aim of implementing what remained of the UN disarmament agenda for Iraq was to be implemented through the far broader 'method' of invading the country with a view to overthrowing its government and reconstituting a new system of governance. The aim of regime change—in itself unlawful—would be semantically downgraded to a mere 'method' of achieving the legitimate aim of disarmament.

In reality, regime change was indeed the desired end, as the Prime Minister and others made clear. The arms issue seemed to offer a way of 'wrongfooting Saddam'. This would require what became known as 'going the UN route' in order to lay down the necessary trigger for the use of force. That trigger would consist of a new UN resolution that would allow the revival argument to operate again.[43]

By this point, the FCO Legal Adviser Michael Wood (now Sir Michael Wood QC) had intervened in discussions on deploying the revival argument in the context of arms inspections. He noted a diplomatic telegram to the US Secretary of State Colin Powell indicating that the Foreign Secretary appeared to have committed himself to supporting military action to address Iraq's WMD. The Foreign Secretary had emphasized that this would need to be in compliance with international law, even if not explicitly endorsed by the Security Council.

The Legal Adviser confirmed again that, in the absence of a further Council decision that Iraq was in flagrant violation of its obligations under the cease-fire Resolution, there would be no support for the use of force based on the original 1990 Resolution, which authorized the use of force in the liberation of Kuwait.[44] As was the case with the Legal Memorandum of March 2002, this position chimed with the revival argument, as expressed in relation to Operation Desert Fox in 1998. It applied a relaxed trigger for the use of force when compared to the original concept of material breach generated by the UN Secretariat in 1991/2.[45] Instead

[43] Sir Christopher Meyer (above n 36).
[44] Michael Wood, Memorandum, 20 March 2002.   [45] See Ch 4, 107–122.

of a finding of 'material breach' by the Council, a 'flagrant violation' would be sufficient, as had been argued against much international opposition in 1998. There was also no reference at that point to the need for the Council to spell out the consequences of such a violation (a threat of 'serious consequences' or even the authorization of 'all necessary means' to be employed by states in response). On the other hand, the memorandum was very short and condensed and was not intended to spell out in detail the conditions for application of the revival argument.

The Attorney General also began to voice his views, which were fully in accordance with the advice offered by the FCO Legal Adviser. He responded to a press interview given by Defence Secretary Geoffrey Hoon, in which the latter appeared to have suggested that the UK would be perfectly entitled to use force without going back to the United Nations. The Attorney General countered with a statement that, pending submissions on the issue, he saw 'considerable difficulties in justifying reliance on the original authorization to use force'.[46] The Attorney General referred in this context to advice given by the Law Officers to the Prime Minister a year before Desert Fox. That advice had indicated that it was an essential precondition for the renewed use of force that the Security Council determined the existence of a breach of the cease-fire conditions, 'and that the Council considers the breach sufficiently grave to undermine the basis or effective operation of the cease fire'.[47] This view would, therefore, require a twofold test: first, the Council would have to determine the existence of a breach; second, it would have to find that the breach was so serious that it would suspend the cease-fire.[48]

IV. Legal Advice up to the Adoption of Resolution 1441 (2002)

Following the meeting between Prime Minister Blair and President Bush at the Crawford ranch in Texas between 5 and 7 April, the issue of the possible use of force became more prominent. The Prime Minister had assured the President that 'if it came to military action because there was no way of dealing with this diplomatically, we would be with him'.[49] The Prime Minister succeeded in confirming with the President that action in the UN before the possible use of force was a priority.[50] This was in line with the Prime Minister's understanding of the legal issues based on the advice given thus far—that further action by the Council would be required—although at that stage it may have seemed that a mere finding of a further significant violation of the cease-fire would suffice.

The issue was raised again in a high-level meeting attended by the Prime Minister, the Foreign Secretary, the Defence Secretary, the Attorney General, and others in July 2002. At that meeting, it was reported that the United States saw military

[46] Lord Goldsmith, Memorandum, 28 March 2002.   [47] Quoted in ibid, 2.
[48] As noted above, the view of the UN Legal Advisers required a third step, which was a threat of severe consequences in case of further non-compliance issued by the Security Council.
[49] Tony Blair, Chilcot Testimony, 29 January 2010, 48.
[50] UK Diptel 73 of 101727Z, April 2002.

action to remove Saddam Hussein as 'inevitable'.[51] There was no patience with the UN route; instead, facts and intelligence were 'being fixed around this policy'.[52]

At the meeting, the Attorney General reiterated that regime change 'was not a legal base for military action'. With reference to the alternative revival argument and the WMD issue, he cautioned that relying on Council Resolution 1205 (1998) would also be difficult, given the amount of time that had elapsed and interim developments.[53] The Prime Minister noted that it would make a big difference politically and legally if Saddam refused to allow in the UN inspectors, stating that:

Regime change and WMD were linked in the sense that it was the regime that was producing the WMD... If the political context were right, people would support regime change. The two key issues were whether the military plan worked and whether we had a political strategy to give the military plan space to work.[54]

This discussion led the Government to strive even harder to obtain an adverse UN finding relating to Iraqi compliance on the arms issue. According to the meeting note, it was agreed that the Foreign Secretary would 'discreetly work up the ultimatum to Saddam'.[55] In the meantime, 'we must not ignore the legal issues: the Attorney-General would consider legal advice with the FCO/MOD legal advisors'.[56]

At this point there was agreement at the highest levels of government on a policy of armed action in favour of regime change in Iraq. It was accepted, however, that this campaign was to be presented ('narrated') as being focused on Iraq's purported WMD capacity, delivering regime change incidentally.[57] There is little evidence in the records published at that time that the plan to 'go the UN route' was seen as anything other than presenting an 'ultimatum' to Iraq as part of a political strategy aimed at giving the military option 'space to develop' and covering it with a mantle of legality. The possibility of Iraqi compliance was not given prominence in this scheme. However, it that this attitude may have changed later, as the nature of the renewed disarmament process was defined in Resolution 1441.

The Attorney General was present while this plan was being put together. However, he confirmed then, as subsequently, that at the time no legal authority for the action was being contemplated.[58] This did not seem to impact on the preparations for military action that were to be put into place. Instead, there was an unrealistic sense that the UN route would deliver the necessary legal authority. In fact, there was no prospect of a direct finding by the Council that would revive the authority to use force, and even if one had been forthcoming this would have required a considerable stretch to cover the aim of regime change.

[51] Matthew Rycroft, Iraq, Prime Minister's Meeting, 23 July 2003 (DSM, above n 25).
[52] Ibid.
[53] Ibid; expanded upon in Lord Goldsmith, Chilcot Testimony, 27 January 2010, 22, 25 on the need that a new resolution would need to make 'a clear determination that there was a material breach'.
[54] Matthew Rycroft, Iraq, Prime Minister's Meeting, 23 July 2003 (DSM, above n 25).
[55] Ibid.   [56] Ibid.   [57] Jonathan Powell, Chilcot Testimony, 18 January 2010, 102.
[58] Lord Goldsmith, Chilcot Testimony, 27 January 2010, 16.

Following this meeting, the Attorney General produced a four-page memo-randum to the Prime Minister in advance of a further meeting with President Bush. This advice once again emphasized that the revival argument was possible, but confirmed that from the UK perspective a further decision of the Security Council would be required.[59] Moreover, he was now more specific in his asser-tions that it would be necessary to obtain 'the right' resolution that would actu-ally authorize force or activate the revival document.[60] Noting that the revival argument had been controversial, the Attorney General added that 'even if there were such a resolution, but one which did not explicitly authorize the use of force, it would remain highly debatable whether it legitimized military action...'. Moreover, a simple ultimatum, issued unilaterally or by the Council, would not strengthen the legal position. While he suggested that his advice had not been particularly welcome, the Prime Minister indicated that he 'was dealing with an already difficult situation. Now I had another issue to take account of. I had to take account of it, rightly...because it made a big difference to the way we approached 1441'.[61]

The result of the Attorney General's intervention was to refocus efforts on the UN route, returning to the requirements that had originally been part of the revival argument as articulated by the UN Secretary-General's Legal Advisers in 1991/2. Hence, in addition to a fresh finding of a material breach, there would also have to be a reference to serious consequences that would follow.

By August 2002, the discussion concerning the use of force had sufficiently matured to compel the FCO Legal Adviser Michael Wood to submit a further memorandum, stating bluntly that 'I am not, at present, aware of facts which would provide a respectable legal basis for military action, though further action by the Security Council could provide such a basis'.[62] He noted once more that there was no basis in international law for the doctrine of pre-emption advanced by the United States, or for regime change as a lawful objective in and of itself:

If state practice were to develop in the direction of a doctrine of 'preemption' or if 'regime change' became accepted as a proper objective, it would be open season for all States to attack those whom they perceive as threatening them (e.g. India and Pakistan).[63]

He added that it would be important for the Government to act in accordance with international law, and not merely as a requirement of the Ministerial Code:

Compliance with international law matters for its own sake. The rule of law is as impor-tant internationally as it is at home. To act in flagrant disregard of the law would do lasting damage to the United Kingdom's international reputation (cf Suez).[64]

---

[59] Ibid, 23, and Lord Goldsmith's Memorandum to the Prime Minister, 30 July, 2002.
[60] Tony Blair, Chilcot Testimony, 29 January 2010, 148.   [61] Ibid, 231.
[62] Letter from Michael Wood (FCO Legal Adviser) to Stephen Wright re Iraq: legality on the use of force, Chilcot Inquiry, 15 August 2002, para 4.   [63] Ibid, para 5.
[64] Ibid.

He warned of potential criminal responsibility of UK service members and civil servants for murder. He concluded his memorandum starkly: 'To advocate the use of force without a proper legal basis is to advocate the commission of the crime of aggression, one of the most serious offences under international law'.[65]

On 12 September 2002, President Bush announced to the UN General Assembly his intention to try the UN route. However, the President also issued a list of demands that Saddam Hussein would have to fulfil 'if he wishes peace', that went significantly beyond cooperation with the arms inspectors.[66] Similar to Tony Blair's view of the interrelationship of all the sins of the Iraqi leadership beyond the WMD issue, these included support for terrorism, cessation of repression of its civilian population, release of individuals still held by Iraq in the wake of the Kuwait conflict, return of all stolen property to Kuwait and acceptance of liability for damages, and full compliance with UN sanctions. Such action would open up the possibility of the UN helping to build a democratic Iraq, complete with internationally supervised elections. Essentially, the President was demanding not only implementation of the cease-fire terms relating to disarmament issues, but of all elements of Resolution 687 (1991). Moreover, he added the requirements of Resolution 688 (1991). That Resolution, addressing repression of Iraqi citizens by their own government, was not part of the cease-fire deal and had not been adopted under Chapter VII of the UN Charter. Moreover, even if all of these demands were fulfilled, the regime was still expected to work towards its own abolition through UN-supervised democratic elections.

By embracing the UN route, the President demanded that the world move deliberately and decisively towards holding Iraq to account should its regime remain defiant: 'We will work with the Security Council for the necessary resolutions', he declared. He added, however, that the intentions of the United States should not be doubted, and that Saddam Hussein would be removed from office in any event:[67]

The Security Council resolutions will be enforced, and the just demands of peace and security will be met, or action will be unavoidable, and a regime that has lost its legitimacy will also lose its power.

In his speech before the UN General Assembly, the President accidentally referred to his wish to obtain UN Security Council resolutions, in the plural.[68] In a discussion with the Foreign Secretary the Attorney General warned that 'too much emphasis on a second resolution would cause him problems' concerning whether or not the first resolution allowed the use of force.[69] It was necessary to see the final shape of any resolution before coming to a view. While reserving his view on legal authority the Attorney General moved closer to the view of the Prime

[65] Ibid, para 7.
[66] Provisional Verbatim Record of the General Assembly, A/57/PV.2, 12 September 2002, 8.
[67] Ibid, 9.   [68] See Ch 5, 144.
[69] Simon McDonald, note with relevant extract about a meeting between Foreign Secretary Jack Straw and Attorney General Lord Goldsmith on 23 September 2002.

Minister by stating that regime change could serve as a means, if not as an end in itself: 'Although regime change could not be the objective, it would possibly be the means by which an objective was achieved [if the only way to disarm Iraq of its WMD were to change the regime]'.[70]

Two days later, the UK Foreign Secretary stated publicly that:

...we do not regard [the existing SCR] as an inadequate basis... if you go through the existing resolutions, there is ample power there and also ample evidence of a material breach.[71]

This statement appeared to suggest that the only requirement for rendering the revival argument operational was a finding of material breach by the very states seeking to use force, without the need for a further finding by the Council. This prompted the FCO Legal Adviser to intervene yet again. He reiterated that revival of the authorization to use force in Resolution 678 (1990) would require a further decision by the Council, such as a finding of 'material breach'. As previously, this appeared to suggest that a finding of a breach by the Council would of itself suffice to allow revival of the authority to use force on the part of individual states, without further reference to the consequences of such a breach.

By this time, negotiations on such a finding, in what was to become Resolution 1441 (2002), were well underway. However, the Legal Adviser added a much more demanding and specific requirement. He noted that:

...the law and practice of the United Nations is quite clear that the fact that a Security Council resolution is adopted under Chapter VII, and is therefore mandatory, does not mean that States are therefore authorized to use force to ensure compliance with it. The use of force requires express authorization.[72]

This statement served as a further warning to officials that legal requirements would not be fulfilled simply by obtaining a further resolution of any description. This advice related to the argument that had been floated in Whitehall that armed action against Yugoslavia in relation to Kosovo could be used as a precedent here. In that conflict the Council had adopted mandatory demands in relation to Belgrade's policy, acting under Chapter VII of the UN Charter. It had not authorized military means in order to enforce these aims. Nevertheless, NATO had launched a sizeable and sustained military operation against Yugoslavia. However, in that instance, the action was not taken simply in furtherance of aims that had been expressed in a Chapter VII Security Council resolution, albeit one that did not contain an express mandate to enforce these aims militarily. In the Kosovo case, the UK Government had instead relied on the controversial justification of humanitarian intervention in general international law. Such an independent legal justification was absent in relation to Iraq. There was no argument that an armed intervention was the only possible means of averting actual or imminent humanitarian disaster faced by the people of Iraq.

---

[70] Ibid.
[71] Quoted in Note from Michael Wood (FCO Legal Adviser) to the Foreign Secretary's Private Secretary re Iraq, 4 October 2002, para 4.　　　　　　[72] Ibid, para 6.

In clarifying this point by requiring express legal authorization for the use of force in a Chapter VII resolution, the FCO Legal Adviser now seemed to be insisting on the very thing that had been unobtainable during negotiations on the resolution on Iraq in the Security Council—express authorization for the use of force.[73]

The Legal Adviser also returned to an issue he had introduced earlier, through his reference to the formal justification for Operation Desert Fox made by the UK to the Security Council. This concerned the extent of the force used that was 'critical to its justifiability':

Force may be used only if and to the extent that it is necessary and proportionate to achieve the objective, which is likely to be compliance with the WMD requirements of the SCRs. The nature and extent of any force used will need to be related to the breach. Any military planning that may be going on (of which I have no knowledge) will need to be tailored to the particular circumstances.[74]

In this passage, the Legal Adviser appeared to take issue with the thesis that regime change might be justified by legal authority relating to the need to control WMD. The use of force beyond that which was necessary for enforcing the disarmament obligations would not comply with the requirements of necessity and proportionality. Hence, even if the UN route did produce fresh authority to use force, this would not necessarily extend to the policy of regime change being discussed. However, this point was made only obliquely and was, according to the published record, not pursued later. The Legal Adviser apparently came to the view that armed action, if justified by a further decision of the Council according to Resolution 1441 (2002), might extend to regime change or he decided to abandon the point.

Somewhat disconcertingly in view of the advice given, on 15 October 2002 the Legal Adviser received an urgent request from the Foreign Secretary regarding the practical consequences of the UK acting without international legal authority in using force against Iraq, including potential court cases against the Government or individual service personnel.[75] In his reply, the Legal Adviser noted that such a request raised an extremely theoretical prospect: 'It would be inconceivable that a Government which has on numerous occasions made clear its intention to comply with international law would order troops into a conflict without justification in international law'.[76] Instead, there would at least need to be a case based on 'respectable legal arguments'.[77]

The Legal Advisor noted that the Ministerial Code required ministers to comply with international law. Moreover, ministers were not able to ask civil servants to act in a way that would conflict with the Civil Service Code or the Diplomatic Service Code, again requiring compliance with international law. A requirement by ministers to plan and execute actions conflicting with international law had to

---

[73] Ibid.　　[74] Ibid.

[75] Simon McDonald, Memorandum, 15 October 2002, note from the Foreign Secretary's Private Secretary to Michael Wood (FCO Legal Adviser) re Iraq.

[76] Michael Wood, 15 October 2002, note from Michael Wood (FCO Legal Adviser) to the Foreign Secretary's Private Secretary re Iraq, para 2.　　[77] Ibid, para 1.

be referred to the Permanent Secretary for further guidance. Moreover, ministers and civil servants needed to 'be honest' in their dealings with Parliament—'to act knowingly against international law could not be hidden from Parliament'.[78]

In an extraordinary passage, the memorandum noted that under international law 'use of force of the kind envisaged, if not legally justified by Security Council resolutions or as self-defence, would constitute an act of aggression'. The document added, with reference to the Charter of the Nuremberg Tribunal, that under customary international law the planning or waging of wars of aggression constituted an international crime.[79] This point was a very serious one. It was obvious that self-defence was not really applicable in this case. But at this time it also became clear to the Legal Advisers that the text of what was to become Resolution 1441 (2002) did not justify the invasion of Iraq either.

In a further memorandum produced two days later, the FCO Legal Adviser clearly noted that the draft resolution as it then stood would provide neither express authorization for use of force, nor offer implied authorization based on revival of the authority to use force contained in Resolution 678 (1990). He concluded that:[80]

...a finding of material breach on OP1 of the current text, followed by a long list of provisions detailing the action which the Council expects Iraq to take, together with a final paragraph which indicates that the Council would need to meet in the case of a further breach by Iraq, or some such, would not permit the revival argument. Rather it would point to further action to be taken by Iraq, and then by the Council, if Iraq were not to cooperate.

The Legal Adviser was sufficiently concerned about this issue that he suggested an urgent démarche to the Prime Minister.[81] When the wording of Resolution 1441 (2002) had stabilized further, the Legal Adviser also indicated to the Foreign Secretary that a further Security Council decision would still be necessary if the use of force were to be lawful.[82]

In a similar vein, on 18 October 2002, the Attorney General warned the Foreign Secretary that the drafts for what was to become Resolution 1441 (2002) did not appear to 'be enough' to satisfy the requirement of a legal basis for the use of force.[83] Interestingly, in view of his subsequent position, the Foreign Secretary confirmed that under present circumstances he 'accepted that we would need a second resolution' to authorize the use of force. He noted, however, that 'tactically, we should not commit ourselves to this externally yet'. Hence, even the Foreign Secretary took the view that the draft text, then nearly the same as that eventually adopted, did not authorize the use of force. Moreover, the Foreign Secretary suggested that the Attorney General's view stating this finding very clearly should

---

[78] Ibid, para 3.   [79] Ibid, para 8.

[80] Michael Wood, Memorandum, 17 October 2002, para 3.

[81] Ibid, para 4. It was then proposed that this information be presented to him via his Foreign Affairs Adviser, Sir David Manning, according to a hand-written note on this memorandum.

[82] Submission of 6 November 2002, not published, but referred to in Michael Wood, 24 January 2002.

[83] Lord Goldsmith, Chilcot Testimony, 27 January 2010, 27 and Foreign Secretary's conversation with the Attorney General Memorandum, 18 October 2002, and 21 October 2002.

not be recorded 'on paper', despite the express wish of Lord Goldsmith to place his advice 'clearly on the record'. He restated this legal position in a meeting with the Prime Minister on 22 October. On 7 November, immediately before the adoption of Resolution 1441 (2002), when the text was in its final form, the Attorney General indicated to the Foreign Secretary that they 'shouldn't take it for granted that, when it came to it and definite legal advice was given, it was going to be that we are in a position to take military action'.[84]

V. Resolution 1441 (2002)

The adoption of Resolution 1441 (2002) occasioned a detailed telephone conversation between the Attorney General and the Foreign Secretary, Jack Straw. The Attorney General was keen to counter the impression that he was persuaded that there was now sufficient legal authority for the use of force. Jack Straw advanced the view that France and Russia, in negotiations on the text of the Resolution, had had to abandon express preclusion of the use of force unless authorized by the Council. He claimed that both counties were 'virtually' saying that they 'understood that there might well be a breach, but that while they would in fact support the need for military action, they would not be able to support a resolution in terms authorizing the use of force'.[85] Hence, the matter had been left open.[86] The Attorney General, on the other hand, indicated that:

It was very clear from Resolution 1441 (2002) that, in the event of Iraq's non-compliance, there would have to be further discussion in the Security Council. It seemed implicit in Resolution 1441 (2002) that, in that eventuality, it would be for the Security Council to decide whether Iraq were in fact in material breach ... [T]he position remained that only the Security Council could decide on whether there had been a material breach (and whether the breach was such as to undermine the conditions underpinning the cease-fire) and/or whether all necessary means were authorized. The question of whether there was a serious breach or not was for the Security Council alone.

Interestingly, therefore, after the actual terms of Resolution 1441 (2002) had become known, the Attorney General adopted a position that was far more restrictive than his previous view. Initial efforts seemed to have focused on obtaining from the Council a further finding of serious violation as sufficient grounds for the operation of the revival argument. Now, it was clear that not only did there have to be such a finding, but it had to be a finding of material breach in the sense of being sufficiently serious to suspend the cease-fire, and even then there would need to be authorization for the use of force ('all necessary means'). This view accorded with overwhelming consensus in the interpretation of the Resolution.[87] The Attorney

General subsequently restated this view in discussions with the Foreign Secretary and the Office of the Prime Minister—the latter discussion following rumours that his views had been misrepresented in relation to the Prime Minister.[88]

On 25 November 2002, the House of Commons carried a motion supporting Resolution 1441 (2002) and agreeing that the Security Council should meet in the event of Iraq's failure to comply fully with it. The motion, therefore, appeared to assign to the Council the key role in taking further decisions. However, before the vote, the Foreign Secretary indicated that the UK would need to reserve its position on the matter. This, he indicated, was necessary in order to demonstrate to Saddam Hussein that the UN would act in case of non-compliance. A considerable element of faith was placed in the Council by its members, including the United States, in discharging a high level of responsibility in the matter: 'So the discussion that will take place in the Security Council in the event of a material breach will be on the understanding that action will follow'. This statement was highly refined, holding out, at least indirectly, the possibility of unilateral action if the Council failed to live up to what the UK considered its responsibility. On the other hand, the UK did not formally commit itself to a position on the underlying legal issues.[89]

Resolution 1441 (2002) required that Iraq make a full declaration of its weapons-related activities within 30 days. Hence, 8 December 2002, one month after the adoption of the Resolution, was seen as a critical date. Upon expiry of the deadline, the FCO Legal Adviser, under instruction from the Foreign Secretary, prepared a memorandum to the Legal Secretariat to the Law Officers.

In that memorandum, the Legal Adviser set out the two alternative views that might be advanced, without indicating a preference. The first would leave it to the Council to determine whether a material breach had occurred and what the consequences of such a breach might be. This would require a further decision by the Council before force could be used. The second assumed that Resolution 1441 (2002) already confirmed the existence of a material breach and indicated that individual states would be entitled to act in case of a further material breach, provided the Council had at least been able to meet to consider the situation.[90] While the Legal Adviser had only recently stated his legal analysis of these rival positions, and clearly expressed a preference for the first, he was now specifically instructed by the Foreign Secretary to state the alternatives without evaluating their relative merit.[91]

In introducing his memorandum, the FCO Legal Adviser noted that 'no advice is required now', as much would depend on future action of the Security Council, in

---

[88] Lord Goldsmith, Chilcot Testimony, 27 January 2010, 57, 61 and note of telephone conversation between the Attorney General and Jonathan Powell, 11 November 2002, where Powell assured the Attorney General that No. 10 were 'under no illusion as to the Attorney's view', rejecting the lawfulness of the use of force under the terms of Resolution 1441 (2002).
[89] See Sir Michael Wood, Chilcot Testimony, 22 January 2010, 26.
[90] Sir Michael Wood, Memorandum, 9 December 2002.
[91] Jack Straw, Chilcot Testimony, 8 February 2010, 11–17.

particular if it were to be seized with a report on Iraqi non-compliance.[92] He added that for the time being it would be wiser, at least in public, to avoid taking a position on the matter: 'if it is our view that a further decision by the Council is needed before force may lawfully be used, it would not be wise to say so publicly, since this may lead Saddam Hussein to believe that he might be protected by a veto'.[93]

Apparently at the political level the expectation remained that France, which maintained important commercial interests in relation to Iraq and was in any event keen to preserve an air of independence in its foreign policy, or Russia might ultimately veto a second resolution, or at least that the Iraqi Government might expect such a turn of events.[94] If the UK Government had committed itself clearly to the view that force might not be used in the absence of a further decision that attracted such a veto, the threat of the use of force would be obsolete.

To threaten force without condition was something of a gamble. Such action may have been necessary to achieve compliance on the basis of a credible threat, but if there was ultimately no compliance, then the use of force, however undesirable, would be inevitable.

It is interesting to note that the Legal Adviser felt constrained to participate in the game of raised stakes and credible threats by explaining this policy background to the Law Officers. It can be presumed that he had been instructed to act in this way. After all, the same logic applies to the legal issues as to the policy considerations. If no legal requirements are inserted into policy at an early stage, it may not be possible to introduce them subsequently. Hence, further delay in articulating a firm legal position to guide policy carries considerable risks. Moreover, the issue appeared to be one of secrecy, rather than one relating to the authoritative establishment of a legal position. Generating a legal position at this point would not have undermined the credibility of the threat against Iraq, even if the advice turned out to be adverse to the prospect of using force. The advice of the Law Officers has by convention always been treated as highly confidential.[95] The relevant materials had not been prone to the leaks that seem to occur in other instances.[96]

Second, as a matter of law, the threat of the use of force may be as unlawful as the use of force—or, to put it the other way around, if the use of force is itself unlawful,

---

[92] 'It had been made clear to me that I should say we didn't need legal advice at that stage': Michael Wood, Chilcot Testimony, 26 January 2010, 38.

[93] Michael Wood, Memorandum, 9 December 2002.

[94] It may have been presumed that Russia or China would pose such a risk, but it was apparently felt that they would acquiesce in further Council action. See R Cook, (2004) *The Point of Departure* 206f.

[95] Prior to this instance, there were only three cases of disclosure, two of which were obtained in legal proceedings. The third also concerned legal action, but was leaked after the event: Butler Report, House of Commons, (2004) *Review of Intelligence on Weapons of Mass Destruction*, 94.

[96] Indeed, while a number of key policy documents were leaked after the invasion had taken place, the Attorney General's eventual advice remained confidential until the Government itself, under tremendous political pressure, decided to release it.

it is similarly unlawful to threaten that use of force.[97] Hence, if the use of force is threatened, UK policy ordinarily requires that the threat is similarly consistent with international law. Hence, even at this point, legal guidance is required.

The exact function of the memorandum is also puzzling. On the one hand, the memorandum has been regarded by protagonists as the document that actually requested the issuing of legal advice on the use of force by the Law Officers.[98] Indeed, as is usual when formal advice is requested, this document was addressed to the Legal Secretariat, whereas other correspondence or interaction was conducted directly among the principals involved.[99] On the other hand, the memorandum begins by stating that no advice was required for at that time.

The most likely explanation is that Iraqi non-compliance could have arisen at any moment (given the expiry of the deadline for the full declaration). This would then have triggered consideration by the Security Council according to Resolution 1441 (2002). A decision on the use of force—either with or without a further decision of the Council, depending on developments—might then have been required very quickly. Hence, it was essential that the Law Officers had all the materials necessary to make their findings to hand. Alternatively, in view of the unpredictable nature of potential action by the Council, it was not possible to offer a definite view.

While this approach made sense at one level, it contained certain risks at another. If the Attorney General was not requested to form his view at the moment of the request, he might be subjected to a rolling campaign to shape and modify his views in accordance with policy, rather than the law. This, it appears, is exactly what happened.

In preparing his advice, the Attorney General began a prolonged process of refining his position by presenting it repeatedly to 'his client'—the Prime Minister, his officials, and the Foreign Secretary. The Attorney General invited them to dispute the arguments in favour of a requirement for a further Council decision.[100] This process began 10 days after the FCO memorandum had been received when, on 19 December, the Attorney General attended a meeting with officials at No 10 Downing Street, setting out his initial views, arguing: 'what could the phrase "for assessment" mean if it did not mean an assessment as to whether the breach was sufficiently material to justify resort to the use of force? Sir David Manning, the Prime Minister's key foreign policy advisor, confirmed that 'it would then be for the SC [Security Council] ... to decide what action should be taken. It was noted that this would suggest that it was expected that the SC would have to express its view'. Hence, by that stage, both the Foreign Secretary [on 18 October] and the Prime Minister's Office, had initially confirmed the

---

[97] Nuclear Weapons Advisory Opinion (1996) ICJ Rep 66, para 47. See, at length, N Stuerchler, *The Threat of Force in International Law* (2007) 38ff.

[98] Lord Goldsmith, Chilcot Testimony, 27 January 2010, 64.

[99] The process of requesting advice is detailed in the Butler Report (above n 95) 93f.

[100] Lord Goldsmith, Chilcot Testimony, 27 January 2010, 68, and Note of Meeting at No.10 Downing Street, 19 December 2002.

Attorney's restrictive interpretation of Resolution 1441 (2002), excluding the use of force in the absence of a further Council decision.

On 14 January 2003, the Attorney General submitted his draft advice in written form to the Prime Minister. He found it 'hard not to read these words [Ops 4, 11, 12] as indicating that it is for the Council [to] assess if an Iraqi breach is sufficiently significant in light of all the circumstances to constitute a material breach and thus revive the authorization to use of force.' He concluded very clearly and unambiguously: 'my opinion is that Resolution 1441 (2002) does not revive the authorization to use of force contained in Resolution 678 (1990) in the absence of a further decision of the Security Council.' This was followed by intensive further discussions, including a visit by Sir Jeremy Greenstock, who disputed some of the points made in the document.[101] Subsequently, the Attorney General discussed the matter with the Prime Minister, indicating that 'he hadn't got me there, if you like, yet'.[102] In fact, at the end of January, the Attorney General sent a short minute to the Prime Minister, indicating that he was 'unpersuaded' and that his view remained that a second decision would be required from the Council.[103] He wrote unambiguously: 'I remain of the view that the correct legal interpretation of Resolution 1441 (2002) is that it does not authorize the use of military force without a further determination by the Council.'

The FCO Legal Adviser, in a clearly worded démarche to the Foreign Secretary dated 24 January 2003, also restated his view that no force could be used unless the Council took a further 'decision', that is, it adopted a second resolution or at least a presidential statement: 'To use force without Security Council authority would amount to the crime of aggression', he re-emphasized.[104]

In an extraordinary act, the Foreign Secretary replied that he noted the advice, 'but I do not accept it'. He claimed that the issue was an arguable one, capable of honestly and reasonably held differences of view.[105] It is questionable how the Foreign Secretary could assert that the alternative view was reasonably arguable, given the repeated, clear advice to the contrary from his Legal Advisers. He argued that an alternative view had been set out by the Legal Adviser himself, in his briefing note to the Attorney General. However, the Foreign Secretary had to accept that this had been done at his own express instruction.[106]

The Foreign Secretary then took the unusual step of representing his own legal analysis of the situation to the Attorney General in a detailed memorandum answering the Attorney General's draft advice. That advice had been in line with the view of the FCO Legal Advisers that a further decision by the Council was

---

[101] Ibid, 75–76. Attorney General, Draft, Iraq: Interpretation of Resolution 1441, 14 January 2003, paras 6, 13. [102] Ibid, 89.
[103] David Brummell, Chilcot Testimony, 26 January 2010, 14; Lord Goldsmith, Chilcot Testimony, 27 January 2010, 90. Memorandum to the Prime Minister, 30 January 2003.
[104] Sir Michael Wood, Memorandum, 24 January 2003.
[105] Jack Straw, 29 January 2003, a note from Foreign Secretary to Sir Michael Wood (FCO Legal Adviser) re Iraq: legal basis for the use of force, 1.
[106] Jack Straw, Chilcot Testimony, 8 February 2010, 11–17.

required.[107] Thus, the Foreign Secretary was personally arguing against the position of his own expert advisers. He asserted that on the basis of the negotiating history of the Resolution 'the better interpretation of the scheme laid out in 1441 (2002) is that (i) the fact of a material breach, (ii) (possibly) a further UNMOVIC report and (iii) "consideration" in the Council together revive 678'.[108] This position, coupled with the argument that the Council had already determined that any further violation by Iraq of its obligations would automatically amount to a material breach, permitted unilateral action.

In the meantime, the Prime Minister visited the United States, seeking agreement to attempt to obtain a second UN resolution. At this stage, the Prime Minister was acting on the informal advice of the Attorney General, which indicated that a second resolution or decision by the Security Council would be required before force could lawfully be used.[109] Moreover, it appeared that the Parliamentary Labour Party would insist on a second resolution if force were to be used, reflecting a widespread sense in the country to that effect and Tony Blair's own pledge on the issue.[110]

While the Prime Minister succeeded in obtaining agreement on a campaign for a second resolution in Washington, it was also clear that the United States would be committed to the use of force even if that campaign failed and no resolution was forthcoming.[111] The Prime Minister noted subsequently that 'we were going to be faced with a choice I never wanted to be faced with: did you go then without a second resolution?'.[112] He added that in that case there would be 'the legal question, which was very important, because Peter [Goldsmith, the Attorney General] had drawn my attention to that'.[113] The Prime Minister was, therefore, in significant difficulty. He had promised the United States unwavering military support, provided the UN route had been taken. Now, it appeared that the UN route required a second resolution that might never come. According to the advice received, taking military steps in such a situation would be unlawful. Nevertheless, action would, in his view, be politically necessary.

VI. The Second Resolution and the Initial Advice of the Attorney General

Despite the divergence of views in the Security Council, by early February 2003 the Prime Minister proclaimed optimism in relation to the second resolution. In

---

[107] The draft memorandum has not been released, but its contents can be gleaned from Jack Straw's answer to it, which in part also quotes from it: Jack Straw, Memorandum, 6 February 2003.
[108] Ibid.   [109] Tony Blair, Chilcot Testimony, 29 January 2010, 96.
[110] The Prime Minister added the caveat of the 'unreasonable veto' (see below). In the end, his change of view in this respect resulted in the resignation of the Leader of the House of Commons and former Foreign Secretary, Robin Cook. See Cook (above n 94) 207, and his resignation speech at 378.   [111] Tony Blair, Chilcot Testimony, 29 January 2010, 121–122.
[112] Ibid, 98.   [113] Ibid, 99.

an extensive television interview, he pledged, again, that force would not be used unless there was a second resolution. However, he noted a qualification:[114]

If the inspectors do report that they can't do their work properly because Iraq is not co-operating there's no doubt that under the terms of the existing United Nations Resolution that's a breach of the Resolution. In those circumstances there should be a further Resolution. If, however, a country were to issue a veto because there has to be unanimity amongst the permanent members of the Security Council. If a country unreasonably in those circumstances put down a veto then I would consider action outside of that. ...

But supposing in circumstances where there plainly was a breach of Resolution 1441 and everyone else wished to take action, one of them put down a veto. In those circumstances it would be unreasonable.

Then I think it would be wrong because otherwise you couldn't uphold the UN. Because you'd have passed your Resolution and then you'd have failed to act on it.

Of course, this proposition is not consistent with the provisions of the UN Charter.[115] States are expected to vote in accordance with their Charter obligations and to do so in good faith. However, ultimately their vote is a matter of political discretion as much as it is a matter of implementing the law. After all, the Council's principal role is not to act as a court. Instead, its principal function is to take effective measures to maintain or restore international peace and security. To determine what action is best capable of achieving this aim tends to be a political decision. Even if it is a minority view, that would not turn the exercise of political judgment in such an instance into an 'unreasonable' exercise or abuse of powers.[116]

The idea of an unreasonable veto had been raised in another instance involving the controversial use of force in the absence of a Security Council mandate. When debating NATO's armed action against Yugoslavia in 1999, the Netherlands, for instance, had argued:[117]

The [UN] Secretary General is right when he observes in his press statement that the Council should be involved in any decision to resort to the use of force. If, however, due to one or two permanent members' rigid interpretation of the concept of domestic jurisdiction, such a resolution is not attainable, we cannot sit back and simply let the humanitarian catastrophe occur. In such a situation we will act on the legal basis we have available, and what we have available in this case is more than adequate.

---

[114] BBC Newsnight Interview with Jeremy Paxman, 6 February 2003, available at <http://www.bbc.co.uk/pressoffice/pressreleases/stories/2003/02_february/07/blair.pdf>.

[115] UN Charter, Art 27.

[116] In fact the International Court of Justice (ICJ) confirmed the decisive effect of the veto, even if that veto would be entirely isolated, in the context of Admissions Decisions: see *Competence of Assembly regarding Admission to the United Nations* (1950) ICJ Rep 4, 10. Bosnia and Herzegovina failed in its attempt to bring an action in the ICJ against the UK, arguing that its voting behaviour in the Security Council had unreasonably or even unlawfully deprived Bosnia of the right to self-defence. An attempt in the wake of the Bosnia and Rwanda episodes to persuade permanent members of the Council voluntarily to agree to refrain from using their veto powers when the Council was addressing the most severe instances calling for armed intervention (genocide) was similarly unsuccessful.   [117] Verbatim Record of the Security Council, S/PV.3988, 24 March 1991, 8.

However, that situation was different. First, the NATO action could be based on a legal justification that operated independently of a Council mandate—that of forcible humanitarian action. Second, in that instance, there was evidence of an actual overwhelming humanitarian emergency, which was answered through the use of force. There was no such urgency of action in this instance. Finally, no Security Council endorsement had been sought in that instance. Hence, the argument of a reasonable veto was not fully applied.

In this more specific context, however, the theory of the unreasonable veto was meant to construct a certain kind of highly qualified automaticity, rooted in Resolution 1441 (2002) rather than in the UN Charter more generally. If there were reports of a failure by Iraq to comply, and if all members but one permanent member of the Council were in favour of military action in consequence, then the view of that one permanent members might be disregarded and action taken in the absence of the (otherwise vetoed) second resolution. The reason for this negation of a veto would presumably be the argument that all Council members had pledged in Resolution 1441 (2002) to attach 'serious consequences' to a material breach. Failing to do so in circumstances where such a breach was manifest would amount to a breach of their responsibility as Council members.[118]

In the event, the Attorney General later dismissed this proposition in his detailed legal advice of 7 March 2003 and it was subsequently disowned by the Government.[119] However, the fact that the Prime Minister had invested considerable energy into making the argument indicated two things. First, the Government assumed that the Attorney General's final advice might ultimately require a second decision by the Council. Second, there was a sense that such a decision might be forthcoming, although there was a risk that one permanent member of the Council might oppose it. The unreasonable veto argument provided a bulwark against that fairly narrow possibility.

In accordance with this view a strong campaign was launched in New York and other Council member capital cities to facilitate a second resolution authorizing the use of force. However, in the event that this strategy failed, efforts to change the view of the Attorney General were also redoubled. In consequence of further persuasion from the Foreign Secretary and others, the Attorney General agreed to review again the negotiating history of the Resolution, this time in consultation with his US colleagues.

During his visit to the United States on 10–11 February 2003 the Attorney General had detailed discussions with the Department of State Legal Adviser and a range of other senior persons involved in the issue, including the National Security Adviser.[120] The Attorney General later recounted that they all spoke with

---

[118] UK statements in Parliament and to the Security Council repeatedly emphasized the expectation that the Council would need to meet its responsibilities. See Ch 5.

[119] See the memorandum of the Attorney General of 7 March 2003, below, and Jack Straw, Chilcot Testimony, 8 February 2010, 47.

[120] Lord Goldsmith, Chilcot Testimony, 27 January 2010, 110.

one voice on the question of the interpretation of Resolution 1441 (2002), down to the last minutiae of detailed textual questions.[121] In fact, the US side had carefully prepared for what was widely understood as a very crucial and important visit. It was clear that a failure to persuade the Attorney General might have dramatic consequences for the UK's position on the impending war. All involved did in fact ensure, through inter-office coordination, that they spoke with one voice. Hence, for example, it was agreed not to raise the more controversial point of the right to pre-emption. Instead, a clear focus was placed on the US analysis of Resolution 1441 (2002). As William H Taft IV, the US Legal Adviser, later recalled:[122]

Talking points were prepared by our office and shared with the White House counsel, the Attorney General, and the General Counsel of the Department of Defence. Lord Goldsmith met with each of these officials separately and heard the same analysis of the situation each time.

The US presentation addressed principally the fact that the United States would never have agreed to a requirement for a second resolution, given its view that it had legal authority to act even without the first one. Taking the UN route had been very controversial within the administration. Hence, instructions had been very clear on the need to draw a red line on this point. Others in the Council also understood this, including the French. Looking at the text of the Resolution, which had previously suggested the need for a further decision by the Council, the Attorney General now wondered: 'Ultimately, can they really have made a mess of this?'.[123] Hence, the key element in persuading the Attorney General was the proposition that the agreed text must have reflected the US position, since the US negotiators would otherwise not have agreed to it. Of course, the same could have been be said of the French, Russians, and Chinese on the other side, who could have argued that the wording chosen for the final text of the resolution had only been agreed to because it reflected their understanding of the legal requirements for future action.

In subsequent testimony, the Attorney General freely acknowledged that he was relying on a one-sided view. There was little evidence of an 'understanding' having been reached on the US view, or in relation to the French, as had been claimed, although such an implication could be read into some telegrams summarizing discussions from the US/UK point of view. The views of the United States on the legal issues were already widely known, and the negotiating record was similarly available to the Attorney General for weeks, while he maintained his negative attitude in relation to the use of force. Nevertheless, the strong presentation by his US colleagues proved a tipping point. Previously, the Attorney General had followed the position of the UK Legal Advisers, who had indicated that the actual wording of the text of Resolution 1441 (2002) had to be decisive. While the negotiating history of the Resolution could be considered, only the objective accounts

---

[121] Ibid.
[122] MP Scharf and PR Williams, (2010) *Shaping Foreign Policy in Times of Crisis, The Role of International Law and the State Department Legal Adviser* 133.   [123] Ibid, 113.

approved by both sides, and the public statements of the delegations at the time of voting, could actually be relied upon. This part of the evidence supported the view that a further decision by the Council was required before force could be used. Moreover, the FCO Legal Adviser later testified that both the informal negotiating record and the public record were 'pretty heavily weighted towards the view that it was for the Council to take the decision on whether force could be used'.[124]

However, the Attorney General now attributed decisive weight to the recollection of the US Legal Advisers, backed by the submissions of Sir Jeremy Greenstock and the Foreign Secretary on the UK side. He thought that their interpretation of such a key and important point could not be informed purely by wishful thinking. Hence, even if the record did not fully bear out their views, these had to be taken seriously into account.

The day following his return from Washington, the Attorney General revised his draft opinion, believing that an argument could be made in favour of action without a further resolution.[125] He now wrote that 'having regard to the arguments of our co-sponsors which I heard in Washington, I am prepared to accept that a reasonable case can be made that Resolution 1441 revives the authorization to use force in Resolution 678'. This view was diametrically opposed to his previous draft opinion presented four weeks earlier, and to his firm view formally communicated to the Prime Minister in writing on 30 January, after he had considered the views and recollections of the Foreign Secretary and Sir Jeremy Greenstock on the negotiating history. The only intervening event has been his visit to the US. The Attorney General added, however: 'if action were taken without a further Security Council decision, particularly if the UK tried and failed to secure adoption of a second resolution, I would expect the government to be accused of acting unlawfully.'

By 27 February 2003 the Attorney General was ready to indicate to the Prime Minister's office that he thought that a reasonable case could be made in favour of using force in the absence of a further Council decision:[126] 'I had given them, therefore, as I saw it, and as I believe they saw it... the green light, if you will, that it was lawful to take military action, should there not be a second resolution and should it be politically decided that this was the right course to take'.[127] At a meeting of 28 February 2003, the Attorney General communicated his view to the Prime Minister's Chief of Staff, Jonathan Powell, his Foreign Policy Adviser, Sir David Manning, and Baroness Morgan. He was then asked to put these views into writing.[128]

Previously, the Attorney General's Office had been asked to delay giving formal advice, in view of the need to await a possible report to the Security Council on Iraqi non-compliance in accordance with Resolution 1441 (2002) and the response of the Council. However, at this time discussion about a possible second resolution was progressing in the Council. This project was abandoned only two weeks later. In the absence of any intervening event that made this the appropriate

---

[124] Sir Michael Wood, Chilcot Testimony, 26 January 2010, 26.
[125] Lord Goldsmith, Chilcot Testimony, 27 January 2010, 130; Iraq Interpretation of Resolution 1441, Draft, 12 February 2003.   [126] Ibid, 71.
[127] Ibid, 131.   [128] Butler Report (above n 97) 95.

moment to tender advice, it could have been argued that the Attorney General was not formally requested to offer his opinion in definitive form until he had reached 'the right one'.

The draft for a second resolution put forward by the United Kingdom gave Iraq only a very short period to commence full compliance—around one week from the time of the adoption of the resolution. Full compliance was to be assessed through an agreed list of six tests or criteria developed in coordination with the arms inspectors, which included making available a certain number of Iraqi scientists for interview abroad, revealing information concerning anthrax production, etc.[129] This 'ultimatum' was backed by an endorsement, directly or indirectly, of the use of force after its expiry.[130] The plan to 'work up an ultimatum' to Saddam Hussein at the UN had already been formed six months earlier, over the summer.[131] In view of the lack of appetite for authorizing the use of force on the part of other members, Resolution 1441 (2002) had emerged as the result of intensive negotiations. It was difficult to see why such an ultimatum would be available, now that the inspections process was appearing to bear fruit.

Nevertheless, there were at that point a significant number of outstanding disarmament issues, although it appeared that in the main only the United States and UK considered these to amount to a further material breach.[132] Moreover, the reports of the chief arms inspectors to the Council were more encouraging, noting acceleration in Iraqi efforts to comply. Now that implementation of the Resolution appeared to be progressing (although not in an unqualified way) there was strong pressure in the Security Council in favour of continuing the arms inspections for a longer period. Rival proposals sought a period of between 45 and 90 days for the inspectors to continue their work.

In view of this situation, on 10 March 2003 France announced that it would veto a resolution authorizing the use of force. After further efforts to gain support for the ultimatum failed to yield results, the UK seized upon the words of President Chirac, who appeared to oppose the use of force 'under any circumstances', arguing that this had rendered any further attempt to obtain a second resolution futile.[133]

As discussed in Chapter 5, the French position was actually more nuanced. However, at this point, the basic tension that had existed throughout the entire episode was brought starkly into relief. The Council had given some credence to the application of the revival argument in this instance by permitting the language of material breach to be reflected in Resolution 1441 (2002). However, in exchange, the French also felt that they had reasserted control over the application of the Council's decision. This consisted of the process requirements for Council consideration (and,

[129] See Ch 5, 146–147.
[130] Sir Jeremy Greenstock, Written Statement to the Chilcot Inquiry, 27 November, 2009, 14.
[131] See Ch 5, 146.
[132] See Ch 5. The UK attempted to reverse this by indicating that none of the members of the Council had declared that known infractions did not amount to a material breach.
[133] These events are detailed in Sir Jeremy Greenstock's Written Statement to the Chilcot Inquiry, 27 November, 2009.

in the view of the French, action) after an allegation of non-compliance. Even then, before it was known whether Iraq would resume cooperation with the UN disarmament effort, automaticity in generating legal authority for the use of force had been expressly rejected. Now that the arms inspection process appeared to be by and large back on track, the UK proposal to generate such automaticity through its draft resolution (the 'ultimatum') seemed out of step with developments.

By this time military preparations for action had advanced significantly. The Chief of the Defence Staff and senior civil servants were now urgently seeking clarification of the legal authority to proceed. The Permanent Under-Secretary of State in the Ministry of Defence, Sir Kevin Tebbit, indicated that 'the call to action from President Bush could come at quite short notice and . . . we need to be prepared to handle the legalities so that we can deliver on our side'.[134]

The Attorney General then submitted his formal advice on the use of force on 7 March 2003. That advice had changed from his earlier submissions, although in fact the change was less pronounced than appeared at first reading.

The document drew on the paper provided by the FCO Legal Adviser, which had merely set out the two alternative arguments without deciding between them. There remained two alternatives: that Resolution 1441 (2002) either allowed for action without a further decision of the Council, or that it required a further decision of the Council. The Attorney General reiterated that previously it had been the Government's view that a violation of Iraq's obligations under Resolution 687 (1991), which was sufficiently serious to undermine the basis of the cease-fire, could revive the authorization to use force in Resolution 678 (1990). He added, however, that in opposition to the US position, and in consonance with a 1992 opinion of then UN Legal Adviser Carl-August Fleischhauer, it had been consistently maintained that it would be for the Council to assess whether any such breach of those obligations had occurred.[135] The question to be determined remained, therefore, whether the Council had already made such a determination in Resolution 1441 (2002).

The Attorney General recalled the proposition that any further failure by Iraq to comply would, according to the Resolution, constitute a further material breach: 'the argument is that the Council's determination *in advance* that particular conduct would constitute a material breach (thus reviving the authorisation to use force) is as good as its determination *after* the event'.[136] Hence, according to that view, a failure to comply would trigger the suspension of the cease-fire, without the need for further Council action, as the Council had already qualified such a potential failure as a material breach in Resolution 1441 (2002). According to this argument, the only element added by the Resolution would be a meeting of the Council to consider the situation, without a requirement to take a decision.

[134] Sir Kevin Tebbit, 5 March 2003, letter from Permanent Secretary, Ministry of Defence to Sir Andrew Turnbull (Cabinet Secretary).   [135] Ibid, paras 7, 8.
[136] Lord Goldsmith, Memorandum, 7 March 2003 (emphasis in original).

While the Attorney General professed that he had been impressed with the recollection of the negotiating history presented by Sir Jeremy Greenstock and the US Government in support of this proposition, he also acknowledged that this was a one-sided account that ultimately might not be fully persuasive. It needed to be balanced against the public statements of other delegations that generally opposed this perspective. Moreover, the Attorney General stuck to his view, previously expressed and then strongly disputed by the Foreign Secretary, that it would not be logical to assign to the Council merely the procedural function of permitting a discussion, if the decision on the revival of the use of force was already in hand. Summing up his analysis, he noted:

> ... the language of resolution 1441 leaves the position unclear and the statements made on adoption of the resolution suggest that there were differences of view within the Council as to the legal effect of the resolution. Arguments can be made on both sides. A key question is whether there is in truth a need for an assessment of whether Iraq's conduct constitutes a failure to take the final opportunity or has constituted a failure fully to cooperate within the meaning of OP [operative paragraph] 4 such that the basis of the cease-fire is destroyed. If an assessment is needed of that sort, it would be for the Council to make it. A narrow textual reading of the resolution suggests that sort of assessment is not needed, because the Council has pre-determined the issue. Public statements, on the other hand, say otherwise.[137]

Despite the public record, the Attorney General recalled that it was 'an essential negotiating point for the US that the resolution should not concede the need for a second resolution. They are convinced that they will succeed'. The Attorney General once again noted 'the strength and sincerity of the views' of the US administration he had heard in Washington on this point. Nevertheless, there was the problem of evidence:[138]

> ... we are reliant on their assertion for the view that the French (and others) knew and accepted that they were voting for a further discussion and no more. We have little hard evidence on this beyond a couple of telegrams recording admissions by French negotiators that they know the US would not accept a resolution which required a further Council decision. The possibility remains that the French and others accepted OP 12 because in their view it gave them a sufficient basis to argue that a second resolution was required (even if that was not made expressly clear).

The Attorney General then referred to the method of interpretation of international legal texts. He noted that it was very uncertain to what extent a court would accept evidence of the negotiating history to support a particular interpretation as there were no agreed or official records. Instead, the public statements of Council members would be considered upon the adoption of the Resolution. But these, too, were inconclusive. Only the United States had made an express statement claiming to preserve the right to use force in any event. Others had taken the opposite view or made more oblique statements.

---

[137] Ibid, para 26.   [138] Ibid, para 23.

However, the entire argument of being persuaded by the sincerity of the US position was fundamentally misplaced and reveals an astonishing error of law. The essence of the US position, which it sought to preserve throughout the negotiations, and in its statement made upon the adoption of the Resolution, was to ensure that its *own* legal position would not be overturned by the Resolution. As has been demonstrated at length in Chapter 5, that position was not actually based on Resolution 1441 (2002).[139] It held that there was ample legal authority to use force both by virtue of the new doctrine of pre-emption, and through a revival of previous UN Charter Chapter VII authority, which could occur without the need for any further pronouncements by the Council. This position itself was rejected by the other states. Even the UK did not agree with either of those propositions, and neither did the Attorney General.

It is difficult to see how the Attorney General was impressed by the argument that Resolution 1441 (2002) had not infringed upon the very authority that he believed did not exist in the first place. But the more fundamental point is that this was a position held outside of the terms of Resolution 1441 (2002), while the UK needed to find authority within the terms of the Resolution. The US attitude was, therefore, not an element that could be considered in the interpretation of the Resolution as it affected the other states, which had not taken this position or opposed it. Hence, it was not possible to draw conclusions from the US statement seeking to leave its position in general international law 'intact' for the way the Resolution operated generally, let alone to take it as the decisive tipping point in favour of reversing the Attorney General's understanding of the Resolution.

When the Attorney General reached his overall conclusion he remained of the opinion 'that the safest legal course would be to secure the adoption of a further resolution to authorise the use of force'.[140] This suggests that he retained the legal view that he had held since the text of Resolution 1441 (2002) became known— that the Resolution did not in itself authorize force. He added, however, in reflection of the confusion over the content of the US position:

Nevertheless, having regard to the information on the negotiating history which I have been given and to the arguments of the Administration which I heard in Washington, I accept that a reasonable case can be made that resolution 1441 (2002) is capable in principle of reviving the authorization in 678 (1990) without a further resolution.

Overall, therefore, it was not until 7 March 2003 that formal, detailed, and written advice was provided by the Attorney General. That advice did not, in fact, actually endorse either one view or the other. If anything, it tended towards the view that a further decision by the Council would be necessary, or at least strongly preferable. However, in contrast with earlier views, the memorandum no longer rejected the alternative position, finding instead that it could at least be reasonably argued. This finding, based on the misunderstanding of the relevance of the US position, was in fact wrong in law. It is not clear in any event why the fact that

---

[139] See, at greater length, Ch 5, 171.
[140] Lord Goldsmith, Memorandum, 7 March 2003, para 27.

a view could reasonable be put forward means that it becomes one upon which action should be based. Rather, the overall tone and analysis of the substantive paper appears to lean the other way. However, the Attorney General noted that on a number of previous occasions, 'UK forces have participated in military action on the basis of advice from my predecessors that the legality of the action under international law was no more than reasonably arguable'. This seemed to lower the threshold from the 'respectable case' required in earlier advice from the FCO Legal Advisers. The Attorney General indicated that this threshold had been suggested to him by his staff. He had initially felt uncomfortable about this test, which apparently informed the Government in the Kosovo case, and had not applied it in his earlier pronouncements. However, at this point, finding that the case could reasonably be made appeared to offer a way out of the dilemma faced by the Attorney General.[141]

There was one important difference, however, in relation to the precedent the Attorney General's staff had invoked. In the instance of Kosovo, the UK was content to make what it felt was a reasonably arguable case in favour of the invasion as a matter of law. In fact, the UK uniquely invested in providing a solid legal claim to act on the basis of a legal doctrine relating to humanitarian emergencies. This doctrine would apply equally to other cases—it was not put forward in relation to one case only. Instead, it drew on UK practice and pronouncements that had consolidated over a decade, commencing with the initial armed action to establish safe havens in northern Iraq. While this doctrine had not been universally accepted by the time of the Kosovo operation, there was a good chance that it might have been. Hence, when taking the position of a norm entrepreneur, seeking to advance the law in general terms, it is inherently necessary to make a case that is at first merely reasonable and arguable in good faith.

In contrast, in this instance, the Attorney General, was merely dealing with a single specific instance of the interpretation of a Security Council resolution. It was not a matter of detecting an emerging new rule of international law of general application. In such a case, the standard of evidence would not be that a case could be reasonably argued. Instead, what would be expected would be a clear finding as to the meaning of the text adopted and the intent of the drafters of the resolution. The tools of legal analysis had led the Foreign Office Legal Advisers to the correct finding in the matter—a position they maintained from beginning to end. The Attorney General had shared that interpretation, and still seemed to hold to it as the better, or at least safer, view. Hence, that would need to have become the UK position, rather than an alternative view which might be reasonably arguable, but which had been found to be less persuasive or unpersuasive.

The Attorney General himself warned the Prime Minister in his advice that making a reasonably arguable case might not be sufficient, should the matter come before a court. Instead, he advised that a court might well conclude that a further decision would be necessary to revive the authority to use force, just as it

[141] Lord Goldsmith, Chilcot Testimony, 27 January 2010, 126.

might arrive at the opposite conclusion. Moreover, he noted that in the previous instances, the level of legal and parliamentary scrutiny was nothing like as great as in the present instance.[142]

The advice also addressed the question of how a material breach might be reported to the Council. The Attorney General held that the revival argument could only be sustained:[143]

...if there are strong factual grounds for concluding that Iraq has failed to take the final opportunity. In other words, we would need to be able to demonstrate hard evidence of non-compliance and non cooperation. Given the structure of the resolution as a whole, the views of UNMOVIC and the IAEA will be highly significant in this respect.

Writing on the very day the Council was hearing further evidence from the arms inspectors, the Attorney General added:[144]

In the light of the latest reporting by UNMOVIC, you will need to consider extremely carefully whether the evidence of non-cooperation and non-compliance by Iraq is sufficiently compelling to justify the conclusion that Iraq has failed to take its final opportunity.

VII. The 'View' of the Attorney General

Despite the finely balanced views put forward, and the fact that the Attorney General had not endorsed the view in favour of force beyond asserting that it might be reasonably agued, this advice nevertheless came to be seen as confirmation of authority to use force. The Attorney General himself considered it 'the green light'.[145]

In a meeting of 11 March 2003 with the Attorney General, the Defence Secretary, the Foreign Secretary, and the Chief of the Defence Staff, the Prime Minister simply indicated that Lord Goldsmith had made it clear that a reasonable case could be made that Resolution 1441 (2002) was capable of reviving the previous authorization.[146] This seemed to suffice. However, in the meantime, and at that meeting, there were demands that the legal views of the Attorney General be heard in Cabinet, making the use of force conditional on 'a *clear legal opinion* about the circumstances under which military action without a further resolution could meet the UK Government's commitment to respect international law'.[147] There was also the requirement of the Chief of the Defence Staff and the Civil Service to give

---

[142] Memorandum, 7 March 2003, para 30.   [143] Ibid, para 29.   [144] Ibid.

[145] For instance, the Defence Secretary saw in the opinion a clear confirmation of legal authority: Geoffrey Hoon, Chilcot Testimony, 19 January 2010, 67.

[146] Matthew Rycroft, 11 March 2003, letter from Prime Minister's Private Secretary to Simon McDonald (FCO) re Iraq: legal and military aspects.

[147] Suma Chakrabati, 11 March 2003, letter from Permanent Secretary (DfID) to Sir Andrew Turnbull (Cabinet Secretary) re Iraq, para i.

clear confirmation that the contemplated action was indeed lawful, and to ensure compliance with the relevant codes and international law.[148] Hence, there was considerable pressure on the Attorney General to turn his cautious advice into what sounded like a definite determination without hesitation, contradiction, or doubt.

On 12 March 2003, the Attorney General abandoned his previous cautious position of merely reporting two views and claiming that both could be reasonably argued. He now 'had come to the clear view that on balance the better view was that the conditions for the operation of the revival argument were met in this case, i.e. that there was a lawful basis for the use of force without a further resolution beyond resolution 1441'.[149] In justifying this change of position, he relied again on the arguments drawn from the negotiating history of the Resolution. However, these very arguments had been discussed in full in his advice of 7 March 2003 and were found to be inconclusive at best.[150] He added that by the time of coming down in favour of the 'better' view, it had become clear that no second resolution would be forthcoming. However, the advice of 7 March specifically addressed the question of authority in the absence of a second resolution. Hence, the change remained unexplained, other than by reference to the need to give a clear position at this point:[151]

... then I very quickly saw that actually this wasn't satisfactory from their point of view. They deserved more, our troops deserved more, our civil servants who might be on the line deserved more, than my saying there was a reasonable case. So, therefore, it was important for me to come down clearly on one side of the argument or the other, which is what I proceeded to do.

The Attorney General responded on 13 March 2003, informing Lord Falconer and Baroness Morgan that 'his clear view' was that it would be lawful under Resolution 1441 (2002) to use force without a further resolution.[152] The following day, he also transmitted this assessment to the Ministry of Defence in answer to their request for confirmation of the legal position before the Chief of the Defence Staff could order forces into action.[153] Moreover, on 13 March his Legal Secretary had requested confirmation from the Private Secretary to the Prime Minister that 'it is unequivocally the Prime Minister's view that Iraq has committed further material breaches as specified in paragraph 4 of resolution 1441 (2002)'.

The Attorney General had at this point already confirmed that there existed a clear case for the use of force, even in the absence of this formal finding, apparently on the basis of oral assurance from the Prime Minister. However, his original

---

[148] Geoffrey Hoon, Chilcot Testimony, 19 January 2010, 69. Lord Goldsmith, Chilcot Testimony, 27 January 2010, 184, 191.

[149] David Brummel, 13 March 2003, note from Legal Sectretariat to the Law Officers about a discussion with the Attorney General on Iraq the legal basis for the use of force.

[150] In particular the acceptance by France of the word 'consideration' instead of 'decision' in operative paragraph 12: ibid, para 6.

[151] Lord Goldsmith, Chilcot Testimony, 27 January 2010, 171.

[152] Butler Report (above n 95) 95.   [153] Ibid.

advice had referred to the need to consider the discussion on the second draft resolution: 'If we fail to achieve the adoption of a second resolution, we would need to consider urgently at that stage the strength of our legal case in the light of circumstances at the time'.[154] Nevertheless, Lord Goldsmith had come to a 'clear' view in favour of force in the absence of a second resolution without the benefit of such a reassessment. Moreover, at that point, it appears at least from the available record that the FCO Legal Advisers were no longer involved in offering advice on the situation in the light of developments. The important Security Council debate was not considered, and nor was a subsequent meeting where a significant number of states opposed the use of force,[155] or the intervening pronouncements of the arms inspectors. This was in spite of the fact that the reports of the arms inspectors in the Council had been more optimistic.

This leads to the next issue. The Attorney General found in his advice of 7 March 2003 that the argument that Resolution 1441 (2002) alone had revived the right to use force required strong factual grounds for concluding that Iraq had not taken the final opportunity to cooperate, requiring 'hard evidence' of non-compliance and non-cooperation. He took the view that it would be for the Prime Minister to make such a determination, although he would need to evaluate 'extremely carefully' whether the evidence was sufficiently compelling. It might be asked whether it would not have been part of the Attorney General's remit to make this finding himself. When considering the continued legality of the no-fly zones, Lord Goldsmith's conclusions were very much contingent on his own evaluation of the factual circumstances:[156]

We sought a continuous review from the Cabinet Office of the factual basis for the evidence as to whether or not there would be a continuing or a repetition of a humanitarian catastrophe if the No Fly Zones were to cease. So we had regular reviews and we received updates from the Cabinet office of the factual position for justification of the No Fly Zones.

The information provided regularly by the Cabinet office was 'probed' and it fell to the Attorney General to determine whether or not the standard had been met to trigger the proposed legal justification for the military operation in Iraq.[157] Here, too, it might have been expected that the final part of the evaluation of the lawfulness of action would include an assessment of whether or not the criteria in Resolution 1441 (2002), even according to the 'reasonably arguable' alternative, were fulfilled (ie the report of non-compliance and non-cooperation followed by an inconclusive Council discussion). According to his own advice, the views of the arms inspectors would have been 'highly significant' even in this respect. However, instead of reviewing the record of events in New York, the Attorney General now merely sought the view of the UK Prime Minister.

---

[154] Lord Goldsmith, Iraq: Resolution 1441, 7 March 2002, para 31.
[155] See Ch 5, 163–167.   [156] David Brummell, Chilcot Testimony, 26 January 2010, 3.
[157] Ibid.

On 14 March 2003, the Private Secretary replied:[158]

...it is indeed the Prime Minister's unequivocal view that Iraq is in further material breach of its obligations, as in OP4 of UNSCR 1441, because of 'false statements or omissions in the declarations submitted by Iraq pursuant to this resolution and failure by Iraq to comply with, and co-operate fully in the implementation of, this resolution'.

No reasons were given for this finding. It is an extraordinary power transferred in this instance to the Prime Minister in two senses. First, the power originally lay with the UN arms inspectors and the UN Security Council. Second, it was now vested in one person only in terms of the UK constitutional position. There were no checks and balances of any kind applying to this finding. While it was indeed a political finding, it was given without the involvement of Cabinet, and, as it was not a reasoned finding, it could not be checked by the Attorney General against the legal standards he was meant to apply.

Given the risk of legal challenges, it was decided on 13 March 2003 to instruct Counsel, Christopher (now Sir Christopher) Greenwood, QC, then Professor of International Law at the London School of Economics, for the purpose of assisting in the development of the necessary legal arguments.[159] Professor Greenwood, now a judge at the ICJ, was indeed an authority on the law governing the use of force. Before the adoption of Resolution 1441 (2002) he had given evidence to the House of Commons supporting a wide reading of the revival argument.[160] His contribution was thought useful both in the preparation of the public statement of the legal position and in terms of being ready to meet legal challenges. In a preliminary discussion with the Attorney General, he confirmed that his views accorded with the legal advice that was now emerging.[161]

In a lengthy meeting with the Foreign Secretary on the same day, the Attorney General confirmed that, having decided to come down on one side (that Resolution 1441 (2002) was sufficient), he had also decided that he needed to explain his case in public as strongly and unambiguously as possible. He had a legal team under Professor Greenwood working on that explanation.[162] Over the weekend of 15–16 March 2003, this led to the drafting of a so-called 'Foreign Office paper' on the legality of the use of force, and a shorter document in answer to parliamentary questions, plus a paper with questions and answers on the issue.[163]

The involvement of Professor Greenwood, QC has since given rise to some controversy.[164] In particular, it was alleged that the Attorney General's own judgment had been replaced with that of a hired gun. This allegation was firmly denied,

---

[158] Reproduced in the Butler Report (above n 95) 96.

[159] David Brummel, Memorandum, 13 March 2003.

[160] 24 October 2002, available at <http://www.publications.parliament.uk/pa/cm200203/cmselect/cmfaff/196/2102409.htm>. His views were opposed by Professor Ian Brownlie, Chichele Professor at Oxford.   [161] David Brummell, Memorandum, 13 March 2003.

[162] Simon McDonald, Memorandum, 17 March 2003.

[163] David Brummell, Chilcot Testimony, 26 January 2010, 27; Michael Wood, Chilcot Testimony, 26 January 2010, 60.   [164] HC Deb. 8 March 2005 c 1636W.

and the record does not bear it out. Professor Greenwood had been involved in assisting the Government in a large number of cases involving international law. It was not unusual that he was called upon to prepare a possible defence against challenges to the decision that had been taken. Given his previous view on the issue, which was very isolated among the legal community, but accorded with the new, clear view of the Attorney General, and his recognized expertise on use of force issues, retaining him was a natural choice. What was perhaps unusual was that the drafting group was developing arguments that ran counter to the clear advice from the Foreign Office Legal Advisers, who were somewhat aghast at the *volte-face* of the Attorney General. More controversial still was the use to which the documents generated by this drafting group were put. Instead of advising, the Attorney General had signed up with the Foreign Minister, and moved into advocacy mode.[165] With the support of the legal team, the mission was no longer to analyse and determine the correct legal view. Now, the position that had previously been thought of as misguided, or later only reasonably arguable, was to be established as the clearly dominant one.[166]

However, in addition to the public argument, or a possible defence against a court challenge, the output of this work was still required for two important reasons of constitutional significance. First, there was the matter of providing the Cabinet with the necessary advice when discussing the matter. Second, it was necessary to put the legal view to Parliament.[167] It might be questioned whether the advocacy role in which the drafting team was thrust was in fact consistent with these important tasks—tasks that would, it could be argued, warrant an objective assessment.

On 17 March 2003, 10 days after the submission of his detailed legal advice, the Attorney General made a statement in the House of Lords, in which he claimed:[168]

7. It is plain that Iraq has failed so to comply and therefore Iraq was at the time of Resolution 1441 and continues to be in material breach.

8. Thus, the authority to use force under Resolution 678 has revived and so continues today.

9. Resolution 1441 would in terms have provided that a further decision of the Security Council to sanction force was required if that had been intended. Thus, all that Resolution 1441 requires is reporting to and discussion by the Security Council of Iraq's failures, but not an express further decision to authorize force.

This view contradicted all the earlier pronouncements of the Attorney General, including his opinion of 7 March 2003. Now, it was the UK Prime Minister, and

---

[165] David Brummell, Chilcot Testimony, 26 January 2010, 29; Michael Wood, Chilcot Testimony, 26 January 2010, 60.

[166] Michael Wood, Chilcot Testimony, 26 January 2010, 60, indicates that he was present, read drafts but remained on the sidelines, given his well-known position in the matter.

[167] In a Parliamentary Answer, the Solicitor General confirmed that Professor Greenwood was instructed to assist in the preparation of the Attorney General's statement to Parliament of 17 March 2003: above, n 164.

[168] The statement was also published by No 10 Downing Street on that date in answer to the persistent questions about the legal basis for the use of force, which was at that time becoming imminent. It is also reproduced in the Butler Report (above n 95) 96f.

not the Security Council who determined the existence of a breach, and whether it was sufficiently grave as to constitute a material breach that would suspend the cease-fire. The argument that the Council would have expressly required a further decision in favour of force, if that had been its intention, was also spurious and had been previously rejected. The default position in law was that the authority to use force (short of self-defence and humanitarian action) had to be granted positively by the Council. It is not necessary for the Council to reserve for itself a power that it already exclusively enjoys. That exclusive power is based in the UN Charter and the law on the use of force.[169]

There was no mention in the short memorandum of 17 March of the view advanced only 10 days earlier that the best that could be said in favour of this approach was that it was a reasonably arguable case, and one that might be overturned in court, or of the advice in favour of a second resolution as the 'safer' course of action. Against the background of all the previous incarnations of the legal advice of the Attorney General, this statement certainly had the air of advocacy, rather than of objective advice reflecting the actual legal position.

In a discussion with the Foreign Secretary, the Attorney General indicated that 'he might need to tell Cabinet when it met on 17 March that the legal issues were finely balanced'. Hence, even when the Attorney General claimed to regard the view that force could be used without a second resolution as the better one, he still admitted that the issue was finely balanced. However, the Foreign Secretary persuaded the Attorney General that in view of possible leaks from the Cabinet, it should only be acquainted with a shorter memorandum.[170] Hence, in the crucial Cabinet meeting preceding the use of force, the changed and condensed 'view' was presented as a clear and unambiguous conclusion, 'the complexities of and the history were omitted'.[171] In fact, at the meeting, the new, short document prepared for Parliamentary Questions was placed in front of participants. The Attorney General proceeded to read it out, expecting possible questions in relation to it. However, there was no significant debate. In fact, he did not even get to read out the short memorandum, since it was the sense of the meeting that each person could equally as well read it himself.[172] The clear impression among senior members of government was that the legal position was unambiguous, despite what had been observed in terms of academic debate surrounding the issue at the time.[173]

In subsequent parliamentary testimony it was argued that 'this was not a summary of the Attorney-General's confidential legal advice to Government, but went beyond what previous governments have done by setting out the Attorney-General's conclusions regarding the legality of proposed military action in Iraq'.[174]

---

[169] For more detail on these arguments, see Ch 5, 133–144.

[170] Simon McDonald, Memorandum, 17 March 2003, para 3.

[171] Lord Turnbull, Chilcot Testimony, 13 January 2010, 67.

[172] Lord Goldsmith, Chilcot Testimony, 27 January 2010, 214.

[173] Claire Short, Chilcot Testimony, 2 February 2010, 25, claiming to be misled by the Attorney General.

[174] Baroness Symons of Verham Dean, 14 March 2004, available at <http://hansard.millbank systems.com/written_answers/2005/mar/14/iraq-legality-of-armed-force>.

This view was later contested by the Attorney General, who did regard it as a summary, although only in the sense that it stated the legal position rather than offering detailed considerations of the legal issues.[175] Nevertheless, considerable effort was subsequently invested in claiming that the submission of the Attorney General to Parliament and Cabinet was the 'view' of the Attorney General, but not his 'advice'.[176]

The reasons for this rather arcane distinction between advice and view were threefold. First, there was the need to avoid a precedent in favour of publishing the actual advice given by the Law Officers. This would have been contrary to the convention reaching back for over a century, which aimed at enabling the Government to obtain legal advice confidentially. Hence, the parliamentary question that triggered the Attorney General's statement did not enquire after his advice, but instead asked about 'the Attorney General's view of the legal basis for the use of force against Iraq'.[177] Second, the Ministerial Code requires that:[178]

When advice from the Law Officers is included in correspondence between Ministers, or in papers for the Cabinet or Ministerial Committees, the conclusion may if necessary be summarized but, if this is done, the complete text of the advice should be attached.

Thus, if it was admitted that the document circulated in Cabinet was a summary of the advice of the Attorney General, the failure also to supply the full text of the original opinion at the request of the Foreign Secretary would have constituted a breach of the Ministerial Code. The Attorney General has answered this point by indicating that the original advice did not need to be attached if he himself was available in Cabinet.[179] However, such an exception was not provided for in the Code.

Third, the view offered by the Attorney General was in fact manifestly different from the advice given on 7 March 2003. Hence, it would be difficult to describe the short document as a summary of the long one. The fact that the 'advice' of the Attorney General and his 'view' were different would in any event have been difficult to understand at the time. Rather, the very fact of making the Attorney General available to Cabinet, and offering his statement to Parliament, must have appeared to the relevant audiences as an assurance that they were being offered an authoritative rendering of his advice before taking a decision on peace and war.

The same applies to the so-called 'Foreign Office Memorandum' that was presented to Parliament on the same day. That document set out the argument in favour of force in the absence of a second resolution in greater detail. It did not actually reflect the view of the Foreign Office legal experts. The Principal Foreign Office Legal Adviser had been left to linger on the sidelines while the document

---

[175] Lord Goldsmith, Chilcot Testimony, 27 January 2010, 220.

[176] See P Sands, (2005) *Lawless World* 261.

[177] Available at <http://www.fco.gov.uk/resources/en/news/2003/03/fco_not_180303_legal advice>.   [178] Ministerial Code (above n 9) para 23.

[179] Lord Goldsmith, Chilcot Testimony, 27 January 2010, 218.

was drafted under the guidance of Professor Greenwood over the weekend of 15/16 March 2003.

The memorandum recalled the justifications put forward by the Government in relation to the uses of force against Iraq in 1993 and 1998, based on the revival argument. It declared that the use of the term 'material breach' in Resolution 1441 (2002) 'is of the utmost importance because the practice of the Security Council during the 1990s shows that it was just such a finding of material breach by Iraq which served to revive the authorization of force in SCR 678'.[180] The memorandum reiterated the view that no express requirement for a further decision of the Council was included in Resolution 1441 (2002). Instead, the Council merely had to consider the issue of further material breaches, as had occurred regularly since the adoption of the Resolution. UNMOVIC's statements to the Council, its quarterly report, and the so-called 'Clusters Document', which reviewed Iraq's overall state of compliance, made it plain that Iraq had not complied with its disarmament obligations:[181]

No member of the Council has questioned this conclusion. It therefore follows that Iraq has not taken the final opportunity offered to it and remains in material breach of the disarmament obligations which, for twelve years, the Council has insisted are essential for the restoration of peace and security. In these circumstances, the authorization to use force contained in SCR 678 revives.

Through this final argument, the UK reversed the expectation that there should at least be a finding by the Council that a further material breach had occurred. Alternatively, if the Council refused to offer such a conclusion, the UN arms inspectors or some other neutral agency could be expected to report non-compliance in terms of a material breach. In this instance, the inspectors had carefully avoided any such determination in their reports on compliance. Hence, the UK was arguing that its position was strengthened by an absence of opposition to a finding that had not, in fact, been made at the UN. Instead, the UK Prime Minister had arrogated that power to himself when adopting his 'unequivocal view' on noncompliance in a private communication to the Attorney General.

The Prime Minister addressed the House of Commons on 18 March 2003. He found that there had been 'minor concessions, but there has been no fundamental change of heart and mind' on the part of the Iraqi Government.[182] Following a debate the House of Commons endorsed, by a vote of 412 to 149, the following motion in which it:[183]

... regrets that despite sustained diplomatic effort by Her Majesty's Government it has not proved possible to secure a second Resolution in the UN because one Permanent Member of the Security Council made plain in public its intention to use its veto

---

[180] Reproduced in the Butler Report (above n 95) 185f.   [181] Ibid, 186.

[182] *Hansard*, col 763, 18 March 2003, col. 763.

[183] Ibid, col 907, available at <http://www.publications.parliament.uk/pa/cm200203/cmhansrd/vo030318/debtext/30318-48.htm#30318-48_div118>.

whatever the circumstances; notes the opinion of the Attorney General that, Iraq having failed to comply and Iraq being at the time of Resolution 1441 and continuing to be in material breach, the authority to use force under Resolution 678 has revived and so continues today; believes that the United Kingdom must uphold the authority of the United Nations as set out in Resolution 1441 and many Resolutions preceding it, and therefore supports the decision of Her Majesty's Government that the United Kingdom should use all means necessary to ensure the disarmament of Iraq's weapons of mass destruction....

On the same day, Elizabeth Wilmshurst, the FCO Deputy Legal Adviser, indicated her decision to leave the FCO asserting that she could not agree that it would be lawful to use force against Iraq without a second Security Council resolution to revive the authorization given in Resolution 678 (1990). As subsequent testimony confirmed, all the Legal Advisers at the FCO who were dealing with the matter had a consistent view. Ms Wilmshurst added that an unlawful use of force on the scale that was about to be launched 'amounts to a crime of aggression'.[184] However, her letter and reasoning were not made public at the time.

The UK Government, on the other hand, set out its campaign objectives relating to Iraq. Its overall objective was 'to create conditions in which Iraq disarms in accordance with its obligations under [UN Security Council resolutions] and remains so disarmed in the long term'. From this overall objective, several 'tasks' would flow. These included the task to 'remove the Iraqi regime, given its clear and unyielding refusal to comply with the UN Security Council's demands'.[185]

However, in a small triumph for the FCO and its Legal Advisers, these wider aims were not restated officially when the UK gave formal notification of its use of force to the Security Council. In a curt letter to the Council President, the UK noted that:[186]

The objective of the action is to secure compliance by Iraq with its disarmament obligations as laid down by the Council. All military action will be limited to the minimum measures necessary to secure this objective.

Having considered the flow of events leading up to the launch of the war against Iraq, Chapter 7 will consider a number of issues that have arisen from this extraordinary story and offer some conclusions in relation to them.

---

[184] Elizabeth Wilmshurst, 18 March 2003.

[185] Reproduced in the Butler Report (above n 95) 177f. Letter from FCO Deputy Legal Adviser to Michael Wood (FCO Legal Adviser) on early retirement resignation.

[186] Letter dated 20 March 2003 from the Permanent Representative of the United Kingdom of Great Britain and Northern Ireland to the United Nations addressed to the President of the Security Council, S/2003/350, 21 March 2003.

7

The Legal Advisory Process in the United Kingdom

The United Kingdom (UK) went into a major war, intending to invade another state in order to overthrow its government. However desirable the removal of Saddam Hussein and his regime might have appeared in political terms, the international legal system was not, and is not, geared towards facilitating such a venture. It was clearly unlawful, and it was known to be unlawful at the time. The UK's legal position had been consistently rejected by many of its partners in the UN Security Council, by the wider community of states, and by the academy of international legal scholars speaking (uncharacteristically) with virtually one voice.[1] This view was consistently and unambiguously stated, even shouted, by the Government's own Legal Advisers—arguably the world's most refined machinery for offering authoritative guidance on international law. It was held for most of the period in question by the Attorney General, who was ultimately called upon to offer decisive advice. Even his final advice (of 7 March 2003), which held the case for war to be reasonably arguable, was carefully hedged, and cautioned that the legally safer alternative would be to obtain the second resolution that never came. In the largest demonstration ever seen in UK history, upwards of one million people marched against the use of force. Nevertheless, the UK Government, claiming to be firmly committed to an ethical foreign policy and the international rule of law, joined the United States in launching what elsewhere was perceived as an unlawful war.

I. The Institutions of Government

Chapter 6 traced the development of the UK Government's legal position in the matter. However, it may not be possible fully to understand how these

---

[1] For instance, the day the advice of the Attorney General was given, a group of international lawyers published a letter setting out the actual legal position in a very condensed view in the *Guardian* newspaper, 7 March 2003, available at <http://www.guardian.co.uk/politics/2003/mar/07/highereducation.iraq>. For some critical reflections by a number of its authors, see M Craven *et al.*, 'We are Teachers of International Law' (2004) 17 *Leiden Journal of International Law* 363. The principal issue they raised concerned the implication of their letter that the legal dimension of the debate would be the only, or the decisive, one.

developments took place without considering the human element in politics. The country was led by a Prime Minister who was a man of deep conviction. He believed that he could determine what was right and what must be done. He also possessed the power to persuade others of his views. Even where this was not possible (as was the case with the general public on the issue of the invasion of Iraq), he believed that it was his duty to act regardless, in the expectation that the success of the mission would eventually generate popular support. He could look back on his international leadership role in the Kosovo crisis, which provided some support for his conviction. There, too, force had been used in the face of at least some international and domestic resistance. The legal basis of the operation was subjected to much scrutiny and some doubt. But a humanitarian disaster was averted and, after a brief interval, peaceful regime change ensued. The Prime Minister felt that moral leadership had prevailed and generated the right result in the end.

The style of government at the time has been described as a 'sofa cabinet'. Decisions were prepared and taken by a small circle of trusted ministers and advisers at No 10 Downing Street:[2] 'The whole crisis was handled by Tony Blair and his entourage with considerable informality', one participant noted.[3] As the Butler Report found:[4]

... we are concerned that the informality and circumscribed character of the Government's procedures which we saw in the context of policy-making towards Iraq risks reducing the scope for informed collective political judgement.

The decisions prepared by this small group were hardly resisted in Cabinet. Those few who opposed were shunted aside,[5] but generally there was little opposition. Tony Blair's premiership, which had begun with the rebranding of Labour as New Labour, had been brilliantly successful thus far. Strict party discipline and loyalty to the party leader had been part of the secret of success. Few were willing to step outside of this pattern when it would have mattered.

Nor did the institutions of government offer much by way of counterweight.[6] The relevant Cabinet committees were at times either inactive or circumvented. The Cabinet Office was reorganized, focusing its work ever more closely on

---

[2] C Meyer, (2005) *DC Confidential* 239.

[3] C Short, (2004) *An Honourable Deception?* 147, adding (at 187): 'the tension was considerable across Whitehall on the question of legality, yet no note of the Prime Minister's meeting with the Attorney was made available. This was a considerable change in Whitehall practice. Blair controlled the Iraq policy personally and very informally and normal information-sharing systems were closed down'.

[4] Butler Report, House of Commons, (2004) *Review of Intelligence on Weapons of Mass Destruction* 148.

[5] Most notably, Clare Short, representing the Department for International Development (DfID), was isolated and treated as a troublemaker. Robin Cook, the more reflective critic (and prophet) of what was to come, had already been moved from the FCO to the post of Leader of the House of Commons.   [6] P Towle, (2009) *Going to War* 147.

the Prime Minister and his preferences, rather than the Cabinet as a whole.[7] Intelligence was no longer widely circulated but available only to a small number of key people around the Prime Minister.[8] The Joint Intelligence Committee in the Cabinet Office, rather than managing incoming information, took on the policy role of coordinating the drafting of the controversial dossier of September 2002, which dramatically highlighted the dangers of Iraq's failure to comply with the arms inspections.[9] Dissent from within the intelligence community was not encouraged.[10]

The Foreign and Commonwealth Office (FCO) did have strong reservations in relation to emerging policy concerning Iraq.[11] To some extent, however, the Office had been politically sidelined since the days of Margaret Thatcher, who viewed it mistrustfully as housing appeasers unwilling to stand up for British interests. Although its influence rose again during the Blair years, this was largely due to, and contingent upon, the standing of the Secretary of State for Foreign and Commonwealth Affairs within the Labour Party, and notably in relation to the Prime Minister. This particular feature posed a difficulty in the present episode. As the Foreign Secretary saw himself as a key member of the sofa cabinet, he would at times be prone to toe the Cabinet Office line rather than follow the advice of his own officials. Moreover, like the Prime Minister, he was a conviction politician who, in his past role as Home Secretary had taken on and, in his view rightly, overruled, his own bureaucracy. In this instance, he turned against his own advisers, rejecting their views on the legal aspects and acting in their stead, negotiating the terms of the Attorney General's advice with him.

Finally, Tony Blair did face a House of Commons revolt over Iraq, but it was defeated.[12] The stakes were too high for the Labour Party. Resisting the Prime Minister in this instance would have meant the collapse of the Government. Given the strong support of the opposition Conservative Party for armed action against Iraq, there was no viable opposition that could challenge the Government other than the stalwart, but tiny, Liberal Democratic Party. Overall, therefore, neither the Government, the civil service, nor Parliament could resist the powerful drive towards action. The course for action leading to war, with some sense of inevitability, had already been set one year earlier.

---

[7] Butler Report (above n 4) 147.   [8] S Kettell, (2006) *Dirty Politics?* 62.

[9] Alastair Campbell to John Scarlett (Chair of the Joint Intelligence Commission, and later head of the Secret Intelligence Service), 9 September 2002; Lord Hutton, (2004) *Report of the Inquiry into the Circumstances Surrounding the Death of Dr David Kelly*, 411.

[10] Again, the affair of Dr David Kelly, tragically exemplifies this.

[11] Meyer (above n 2) 241.

[12] See R Ramesh, (2003) *The War We Could not Stop* 43ff. The opposing amendment to the motion in favour of war was defeated 217 to 396: HC Deb, cols 902FF, 18 March 2003, available at <http://www.publications.parliament.uk/pa/cm200203/cmhansrd/vo030318/debtext/30318–47.htm#30318–47_div117>.

II. From Containment to Regime Change

Before 9/11, the policy of containment had remained dominant in relation to Iraq. In fact, there were moves to lessen pressure on the Iraqi regime. While it was clear to most that Iraq had not itself been implicated in 9/11, the atrocity vividly highlighted the capacity for destruction of terrorist movements. Should Iraq attain weapons of mass destruction (WMD) capacity, even more dramatic consequences were feared.

There is no reason to doubt that the UK Prime Minister and other key actors, including the Secretary of State for Foreign and Commonwealth Affairs, were genuinely concerned by the issue of WMD and the threat supposedly posed by Iraq.[13] This included the threat to the stability of the region should Iraq gain or regain a WMD arsenal and delivery capability, and the risk of proliferation of terrorist movements. The Prime Minister, in particular, was deeply impressed by Saddam Hussein's past actions. These included launching aggressive wars against Iran and Kuwait, and assaults on his own minority populations. In those instances, chemical weapons had been used.

Conflating into one the threats of terrorism using WMD to the Western World, the risks to stability of the Middle East due to a military resurgence of Iraq, and the threat posed to the Iraqi population by its own Government, appeared logical to the Prime Minister, and undoubtedly many others.[14] However, in terms of the international scene this approach posed certain difficulties. To the Prime Minister, all three factors, when taken together, turned Saddam Hussein (and, incidentally, his two sons) into 'monsters' that had to be dealt with.[15] However, the international system did not operate in a way that was conducive to managing amalgamated but distinct threats, and instead considered each of the alleged acts of Iraq on their own terms.

First, there was the threat to international peace and security posed by the risk of renewed Iraqi aggression. The UN Security Council had adopted arms limitation as the appropriate means of managing that risk. It had kept the sanctions regime in place against Iraq in order to obtain compliance. At the time, there did not appear to be any specific risk emanating from Iraq for the immediate, or even the wider, region. Second, on the issue of WMD and their possible proliferation, there had been no evidence of Iraqi involvement with terrorist movements. This appeared to be a serious, but principally speculative threat. As it later transpired, the threat was actually non-existent at the time. Moreover, its emergence in the future would be managed through the arms inspection process, which

---

[13] See, eg D Coates and J Krieger, (2004) *Blair's War* 9–59.
[14] C Bluth, The British Road to War (2004) 80 *International Affairs* 871, 890.
[15] Tony Blair, Chilcot Testimony, 29 January 2010, 246. All evidence relating to the Iraq Inquiry is available at <http://www.iraqinquiry.org.uk/>.

was of course targeted precisely with the aim of preventing Iraq from acquiring or reacquiring a WMD capacity. Finally, in relation to the threat to Iraq's own population, the Security Council had, in Resolution 688 (1991), demanded an end to repression inside Iraq. However, it had not been able to authorize military action to protect the threatened Kurdish population in the north, and the so-called 'Marsh Arabs' in the south. Nevertheless, there had been an element of acquiescence in the coalition operation to maintain the no-fly zones on behalf of the endangered populations, although there was a growing sense that this threat had subsided.

Overall, therefore, the UN system had managed to adopt what, in the view of the majority of members of the UN Security Council, were the necessary and appropriate steps for tackling Iraq. It could be argued that these steps did not guarantee that Iraq might not be involved in further aggression or terrorist outrages. Indeed, as noted in the Introduction to this book, the Security Council, uniquely, has the power to take 'effective collective measures for the prevention and removals of threats to the peace'.[16] This may include the use of force. However, in view of the risks to the stability of the system that are inherent in granting the power to use force preventatively, the emphasis is on 'collective measures' administered through the Security Council. This requires the consent of the requisite number of Council Members, including the Permanent Members.

After the shock of 9/11, the United States was moving towards a doctrine of prevention, claiming the authority to act against 'gathering' threats outside of the Security Council. Its 2002 national security strategy proclaimed that the United States would act to 'forestall or prevent' hostile acts by its adversaries.[17] However, while self-defence is available to counter an imminent attack, there is no room in international law for a broad doctrine of pre-emption against future threats that may materialize.[18] Certainly the UK, informed as it was on the law of self-defence by its FCO Legal Advisers, did not support such a vast expansion of the right to self-defence.[19]

The UK also did not share the view that there existed an open-ended right to use force against Iraq in consequence of Resolution 678 (1990) that had authorized force to remove Iraq from Kuwait and restore peace and security in the area. Instead, in the UK view, the revival of such authority also required action by the Security Council.

Hence, the UK was in a difficult position. It was clear that it would want to remain associated with the United States. In addition to solidarity demanded by the US-UK special relationship, the Prime Minister himself was persuaded of the need to act against Saddam Hussein. He also shared the view that such action

---

[16] UN Charter, Art 1(1).
[17] *The National Security Strategy of the United States of America*, September 2002, reproduced in J Ehrenbert et al., (2010) *The Iraq Papers* 81.   [18] See Ch 1.
[19] See the treatment of the subject by the then UK Legal Adviser, M Wood, 'The Law on the Use of Force: Current Challenges' (2007) 11 SYBIL 1.

would need to be decisive, addressing the issue fundamentally. Nothing short of the removal of Saddam Hussein and his Government would neutralize the future threat of the use of WMD or of their proliferation, and terminate the risks of future atrocities against Iraq's population. The UK appears to have been as committed to regime change in Iraq as the United States, albeit for different reasons and despite the clear knowledge of all involved that regime change would not be internationally lawful.

III. Regime Change and the Revival Argument

It was clear from the outset that regime change through the use of force was not lawful in this instance.[20] This was made evident in the very early legal advice tendered to the Prime Minister in the spring of 2002. There was also no sufficiently imminent threat emanating from Iraq to the UK or her allies that would warrant the deployment of self-defence as justification for the use of force. Moreover, there was no overwhelming humanitarian emergency requiring further armed action. Indeed, by that time, the Attorney General was carefully evaluating whether the no-fly zones could even be credibly maintained, not to speak of massive additional force.

Hence, it rapidly became clear that the only avenue of lawful forcible action against Iraq lay in a Security Council mandate to that effect. However, it was equally clear that there was no prospect of obtaining a mandate for the invasion of Iraq. There was little international support for the regime change agenda of the United States and the UK. Hence, the only remaining source of legal authority lay in the revival argument.

The revival argument held that force could be used to constrain Iraqi compliance with its UN disarmament obligations. However, the Council would first have to make a fresh finding, determining that Iraq had committed a material breach of its 1991 cease-fire obligations. Given the absence of any other avenue, the UK settled very early on the legal strategy of obtaining such a finding to justify the intended action against Iraq.

In strictly legal terms, there were several problems with this strategy. First, the revival argument itself was dubious.[21] It had been deployed in 1992–1993 with the support of the UN Secretariat and was regarded as reckless by some delegations in the Council. The United States, backed mainly by the UK, used force against Iraq on several occasions during the 1990s in circumstances that were not authorized, even indirectly, by the Council. The situation came to a head in 1998. Although Resolution 1205 (1998) had deliberately referred to a 'flagrant violation'

---

[20] 'Regime change in itself was plainly unlawful': Jack Straw, Supplementary Memorandum submitted to the Iraq Inquiry, February 2010, 8.
[21] See Ch 4, and Elisabeth Wilmshurst, Chilcot Testimony, 26 January 2010, 30.

by Iraq of the terms of the cease-fire rather than a 'material breach', precisely in order to avoid an argument in favour of the use of force by individual states, Operation Desert Fox was launched. The operation not only removed any prospect of the resumption of arms inspection activities for a considerable period, but also gave rise to significant opposition and protest from members of the Security Council. They insisted very strongly that only the Council could determine the existence of a material breach, and that it was for the Council to authorize the use of force if that were deemed necessary. As a result, other UN members were unlikely simply to offer an unqualified finding of a material breach by Iraq of its cease-fire obligations. If they were unwilling to grant a fresh mandate expressly, they would be similarly unlikely to do so by clearing the way towards deployment of the revival argument.

Second, the revival argument related to force used to support implementation of UN disarmament demands. It had been invoked to cover limited uses of force that had been specifically targeted at Iraq's weapons capability. It was difficult to see how the wholesale invasion of Iraq and the removal of its Government could be justified on that basis. As the UK Legal Adviser pointed out, the use of force, even under the revived UN authority, had to be necessary and proportionate in relation to the professed aim of supporting the UN's requirements. The view that Iraq's past record of non-compliance was such that nothing less than the removal of its Government could secure compliance stands in tension with these requirements.

In his advice of 7 March 2003, the Attorney General affirmed that the objective of any military operation could only be focused on the terms of the cease-fire, and had to be necessary and proportionate in relation to that end. However, he added:[22]

That is not to say that action may not be taken to remove Saddam Hussein from power if it can be demonstrated that such action is a necessary and proportionate measure to secure the disarmament of Iraq. But regime change cannot be the objective of military action. This should be borne in mind in considering the list of military targets and in making public statements about any campaign.

The UN would not commit itself to the position that compliance with its disarmament demands could only be achieved through regime change. Herein lay a tension within the UK position. If a fundamental change in governance of Iraq was indeed necessary to address the weapons issue, the UN route would never have been able to deliver. In addition to adherence to the principle of non-intervention for its own sake, a number of states represented on the UN Security Council (including, at the time, for example, Syria) would hardly encourage such a precedent for their own reasons. This tension seemed to make the unilateral use of force inevitable, whatever action was ultimately adopted at the UN.

[22] Attorney General, Chilcot Testimony, 7 March 2003, para 36.

Nevertheless, the UK Prime Minister and the Foreign Secretary persuaded themselves that conflating the aim of regime change with the goal of securing Iraqi compliance with the UN arms inspection regime would generate sufficient legal cover. The actual aim of regime change was semantically converted into the means or modality of action towards the subordinated goal of disarmament. But, as Tony Blair explained after it became clear that Iraq did not in fact possess any of the proscribed items, 'what influenced me was that my judgement ultimately was that Saddam was going to remain a threat and that in this change in the perception of risk after September 11 it was important that we were prepared to act'.[23]

Ultimately, the regime was the problem, and the real target of action, not its weapons potential. Oddly, the presumption that the use of force, even if available in relation to WMD, would also cover regime change, was not seriously questioned.

Tony Blair managed to persuade the United States to 'go the UN route', arguing that at least for the UK, a legal basis for participating in the invasion of Iraq would be required. The most fundamental problem with this strategy turned out to be the meaning of the concept of 'going the UN route'. On the one hand, this was very clearly seen, or at least sold to the United States, as a ploy to enhance legitimacy for forcible action. As the UK Ambassador to the United States, Sir Christopher Meyer, had explained to his US interlocutors:[24]

There had to be a strategy for building international support. So what was needed was a clever plan which convinced people that there was a legal basis for toppling Saddam and that the US was taking to account international opinion. The UN had to be at the heart of such a strategy. We would need to wrongfoot Saddam in the eyes of the Security Council. This, anyway, was long overdue. One way was to demand the readmission of the UN weapons inspectors into Iraq. If he refused, this would not only put him in the wrong but also turn the searchlight onto the multiple Security Council Resolutions of which he remained in breach.

Hence, it was a matter of 'wrongfooting' Saddam Hussein. On the other hand, going the UN route would take on its own meaning, as the UN became active again in relation to Iraqi WMD. Once it had been decided to go the UN route, this problem emerged with greater clarity.[25] As Robin Cook, who had been involved in some of the debates at the time, noted:[26]

Tony is entitled to full credit for persuading President Bush to delay the attack long enough for the UN inspectors to go in. But since both Tony Blair and George Bush were determined that the confrontation should end in invasion it is a puzzle what point they saw in resuming inspections. I suspect Tony promised Bush that the inspections would come up with the evidence that Saddam was a threat and thereby strengthen the case for war. If Tony himself believed half the allegations he included in the September dossier [on Iraq's WMD programme], he must have expected the inspectors to find some of

---

[23] Tony Blair, Chilcot Testimony, 29 January 2010, 130.   [24] Meyer (above n 2) 243.
[25] Ibid, 255.   [26] R Cook, (2004) *The Point of Departure* 311f.

the chemical weapons he claimed were ready to be fired in forty-five minutes, or at least some of the chemical weapons plants he claimed had been built. He sounded completely confident when he said in January that it was only a matter of time before the inspectors found something.

In that sense, it would be inappropriate to deny the commitment of the UK Government to the disarmament process according to the terms of Resolution 1441 (2002). It was committed to it, but in the expectation that it would most likely yield the evidence necessary to revive the authority to use force.[27] When the UN process failed to deliver this result with the necessary clarity within the required timeframe, the United States and the UK took it upon themselves to rule on the issue of Iraqi compliance.

IV. Going the UN Route

Having decided to go the UN route, the first problem concerned the operation of the legal basis that was meant to be generated. UK legal advice added increasingly to the specific elements needed in a new resolution to facilitate the operation of the revival argument. Initial FCO legal advice had been brief, suggesting that merely a finding by the Council of a further flagrant violation by Iraq might suffice. Subsequently, however, the Attorney General and the FCO Legal Adviser added to these conditions. There would have to be a confirmation that the violation was such as to render inoperative the cease-fire (that is, a material breach). Moreover, there would also need to be a reference to the authority of Member States to use 'all necessary measures', or at least to the 'serious consequences' that would flow from non-compliance. These increasing demands were noted by the Prime Minister and the Foreign Secretary, down to their negotiators in New York.

What had been foreseen as a swift 'ultimatum' to Iraq to comply was progressively converted into a complex resolution. Predictably, UN members were unwilling simply to endorse the use of force. Instead, a compromise emerged. Resolution 1441 (2002) confirmed that Iraq was at that time in a state of material breach of its disarmament obligations, an essential element of the cease-fire terms. In so doing, they restored credence to the discredited revival argument based on material breach. Iraq was given one final chance to demonstrate compliance with

---

[27] 'Thus, the idea of UN inspectors was introduced not as a means to avoid war, as President Bush repeatedly assured Americans, but as a means to make war possible. War had been decided on; the problem under discussion here was how to make, in the prime minister's words, "the political context ... right." The "political strategy"—at the center of which, as with the Americans, was weapons of mass destruction, for "it was the regime that was producing the WMD"—must be strong enough to give "the military plan the space to work." Which is to say, once the allies were victorious the war would justify itself. The demand that Iraq accept UN inspectors, especially if refused, could form the political bridge by which the allies could reach their goal: "regime change" through "military action"': Marc Danner, 'The Secret Way to War' (2005) 52(10) *The New York Review of Books,* available at <http://www.nybooks.com/articles/18034>.

a fortified inspections regime. In a further concession to the requirements of UK lawyers, the Resolution also threatened serious consequences if Iraq failed to take advantage of that final opportunity.

In the view of the other Council delegations, the Council would determine whether a material breach had occurred, and which of the serious consequences might ensue. The reference in the text of Resolution 1441 (2002) to 'assessment' of the situation by the Council made it difficult to accept that mere consideration of the issue would have been deemed sufficient.[28] While the United States and UK reserved their positions (to a somewhat different degree), they nevertheless joined in the mantra of 'no automaticity and no hidden triggers' during the process of adopting the Resolution. To the other delegations, this confirmed the view that Resolution 1441 (2002) was not meant to grant authorization to use force in the absence of a further decision by the Council. Indeed, once force became imminent, and also after the invasion commenced, the submissions of other governments expressly confirmed this point, rejecting the US/UK argument. The official Netherlands Inquiry into the Iraq war concluded that this reflected the actual legal position.[29]

The next issue was the question of Iraqi compliance. The attempt by the United States and the UK to build legitimacy for the eventual use of force would backfire if Iraq complied with the very tough new disarmament regime imposed by Resolution 1441 (2002). However, the Prime Minister indicated that all parties were ready to take a 'Yes' from Iraq as an answer.[30] The Foreign Secretary argued:[31]

Although the political and legal environment in the United States was very different from that of the United Kingdom, if the 'UN route' to which the US had now committed itself proved successful in securing Iraqi compliance there would be no case for UK military involvement, and it might also make unilateral military action by the United States much less likely.

It would be unfair to claim that all those involved in the arms inspection issue, including on the British side, were engaged in a cynical game of seeking to trap Saddam Hussein into war throughout this episode. There would have been moments when the UN Monitoring, Verification and Inspection Commission (UNMOVIC) and the International Atomic Energy Agency (IAEA) effort offered a promise of success in their eyes. The trouble was that success of the UN route in securing Iraqi compliance may have made US military action less likely, or it may

[28] See Ch 5, 156.
[29] Iraq Commission of Enquiry, The Hague, 12 January 2010, press release: 'Despite the existence of certain ambiguities, the wording of Resolution 1441 (2002) cannot reasonably be interpreted (as the Dutch government did) as authorizing individual Member States to use military force to compel Iraq to comply with the Security Council Resolutions, without authorization from the Security Council'. The full section addressing the international legal dimension has been published in English as 'The Basis in International Law for the Military Intervention in Iraq' (2010) NILR 81.
[30] Tony Blair, Chilcot Testimony, 29 January 2010.
[31] Jack Straw, Written Statement to the Chilcot Inquiry, 21 January 2010, 9.

not.[32] As Sir Christopher Meyer has noted, 'exhausting the UN route was going to mean different things in Washington and London. The timetables for war and for the inspections programme would not be made to synchronize'.[33]

The UK had committed itself to stay close to the United States and would probably be persuaded to follow its lead. As it turned out, most states on the Security Council took the view that Iraq was at least on the road to compliance. In relation to WMD, none of the arms inspection reports revealed a 'smoking gun'. Although there were a number of outstanding issues, they had not determined the existence of a material breach and compliance appeared to be becoming more proactive. The aims of the UN in relation to Iraq may well have been achieved had the inspection process been allowed to continue.

On the other hand, in military terms, time was running out. As in the case of the military operation to evict Iraq from Kuwait in 1991, the imminent onset of very hot weather supposedly required action before the end of March or effectively a delay of the operation for some six months. Indeed, given the commencement of Ramadan, the delay might be even longer.[34] In that situation, the UK was unable to resist the pressure from the United States for action.[35] Instead of finding that there was 'no case for UK military involvement' under those circumstances, the UK became one of the principal advocates of action. In fact, ultimately, the UK Prime Minister arrogated to himself the powers of the Security Council when, on 14 March 2003, he transmitted to the Attorney General his unequivocal conviction that Iraq had failed to take up its final opportunity to comply.

This result was preordained by the different understanding of compliance of the United States and the UK, on the one hand, and most other UN members, on the other. President Bush announced that compliance would have to result in the end of Saddam Hussein's rule. Similarly, Tony Blair announced his conviction that either a fundamental change in the attitude of the Iraqi Government, beyond the arms issue, would have to take place, or the regime would be removed. Hence, when Tony Blair addressed the UK Parliament before its vote on war, he acknowledged some progress in the arms inspection effort. The reports of the arms inspectors were inconclusive, but 'did it really indicate that this was someone who had had a change of heart?'.[36] It is difficult to see how the arms inspection effort in itself could have delivered those wider aims.

V. Legal Advice

Informal or operational legal advice was rendered proactively by both the FCO Legal Advisers and the Attorney General throughout this episode. However, the

---

[32] Meyer (above n 2) 255.   [33] Ibid, 261.

[34] In 2003, the festival of Eid-ul-Fitr marking the end of Ramadan fell on 25–26 November.

[35] Sir Jeremy Greenstock, Statement to the Iraq Inquiry, 27 November 2009, 15.

[36] Tony Blair, Chilcot Testimony, 29 January 2010, 115.

Prime Minister himself had indicated that it would be a mistake to seek formal legal advice too early: 'The time to debate the legal base for our action should be when we take that action'.[37] The Attorney General repeatedly voiced his wish to offer formal advice to the Foreign Secretary and No 10 Downing Street, for instance when Resolution 1441 (2002) had emerged but was rebuffed.[38] Indeed, the timing of the formal advice, presented at a very late stage, turned out to be critical.

From the beginning to (nearly) the end, it emerges that the consistent position of both the FCO Legal Advisers and the Attorney General was that there was, in fact, no authority to use force. This situation did not change with the adoption of Resolution 1441 (2002), despite the best and very protracted efforts of the US and UK negotiators. However, the absence of a legal basis does not appear to have constrained policy planning or its implementation. Instead, the Government committed itself to a course of action from which it would have been hard to withdraw, in the face of constant and consistent advice, including from the Attorney General, that legal authority did not exist.

It may have been hoped that a further resolution was possible. But, failing that, the country faced either considerable embarrassment and a significant international crisis, having deployed a very strong UK contingent along with a substantial US force ready to invade, or participation in a major unlawful use of force.[39] As the Prime Minister indicated, 'if Peter [Lord Goldsmith] in the end had said, "this cannot be justified lawfully", we would have been unable to take action'.[40] Both alternatives were hardly thinkable at the time the Attorney General reconsidered his views.

The only possible legal argument in favour of force was the revival argument. In discussions on the proposed invasion of Iraq in 2002, the Government's lawyers based their arguments on the revival argument without questioning it. In fact, senior politicians took the view that if action had been lawful in 1998 (Operation Desert Fox), then it was also lawful now.[41] It was only later that reference to the revival argument was regarded as unfortunate by legal advisers.[42] In fact, the material breach doctrine had been flawed from the beginning.

The Legal Advisers and the Attorney General were also hesitant in noting that, even if the revival argument could be applied in principle, it could not be used to justify regime change. In the record that is now in the public domain, this issue was raised indirectly by the FCO Legal Adviser on two occasions. However, the point is not addressed expressly in relation to regime change. Moreover, controversially, the Attorney General not only failed to challenge this view but signed

---

[37] Quoted by Robin Cook (above n 26) 135.
[38] David Brummell, Chilcot Testimony, 26 January 2010, 10, 12.
[39] This was clearly ruled out in testimony: see, eg Geoffrey Hoon, Chilcot Testimony, 19 January 2010, 69.   [40] Tony Blair, Chilcot Testimony, 29 January 2010, 150.
[41] Ibid, 151.   [42] Elisabeth Wilmshurst, Chilcot Testimony, 26 January 2010, 30.

on to the view of the Prime Minister and Foreign Secretary that regime change might be the lawful by-product of a campaign to address the weapons issue.

Much effort was expended in seeking to meet the test of the revival argument in the first resolution of the Council. These requirements appeared to become more stringent with time, as the FCO Legal Adviser and the Attorney General considered the revival argument and its origins in greater detail. The UK Prime Minister has confirmed that this operational advice shaped the UK (and with it the US) strategy at the United Nations very significantly.[43] Enormous effort was invested in obtaining a new determination of material breach of the cease-fire by Iraq. This tactical focus may somehow have obscured the broader fact that the revival argument was in itself heavily contested among the UN membership, and that it could hardly justify regime change. Moreover, Sir Jeremy Greenstock, the head of the UK delegation in New York, formed the view that he had achieved his mandate in the negotiations. This was more self-serving than accurate and rejected by his own Legal Advisers. The argument that the removal of the word 'decides' in the negotiations indicated that the Council would not need to pronounce itself on the question of material breach and its consequences reflected a misunderstanding. The powers of the Council existed and did not need establishing in the Resolution through an express reminder of its power to 'decide'. The shoe was on the other foot. The proponents of the use of force had to demonstrate that the Council had already granted authority in the Resolution to use force. But this was precisely what all other delegations refused.

Warnings from the Legal Advisers relating to the missing legal basis, even after the adoption of Resolution 1441 (2002), became steadily more audible. Clearly, they were heard from the outset, although the Foreign Office Legal Advisers were increasingly isolated from the policy process as the decision to go to war came closer. In fact, it appears that the regular channels in the Foreign Office were increasingly closed off in the run-up to the war. The Foreign Secretary indicated that he had noted the advice of the Legal Advisers, but disagreed with it.

This raised an important constitutional issue. Jack Straw claimed that as a minister, the ultimate decision on issues of this kind would need to rest with him, not with the civil servants advising him. However, according to the Ministerial Code,[44] his decision had to comply with law, including international law. His expert international Legal Advisers had presented him with what would appear to be reasoned, clear, and authoritative advice on the issue. The Foreign Secretary disregarded the advice.

The Foreign Secretary argued that, while he was not actually an international lawyer, he *was* a lawyer. Moreover, he had been privy to the negotiating history

---

[43] Tony Blair, Chilcot Testimony, 29 January 2010, 148.

[44] Ministerial Code, here used in the version of July 2001 applicable during the period in question, available at <http://www.cabinetoffice.gov.uk/media/cabinetoffice/propriety_and_ethics/assets/ministerial_code_2001.pdf>, para 1.

of Resolution 1441 (2002) and was, therefore, in a position to appreciate the legal position himself. In addition, his principal Legal Adviser, Michael Wood, had set out in a previous memorandum addressed to the Attorney General a 'balanced' position offering not one but two alternative views. Hence, contrary to the findings of the Legal Adviser that 'there is no doubt in anyone's mind' that a further resolution would be required, there was in fact room for doubt in any independent view he could form on the issue.

This statement appears somewhat disingenuous. Testimony revealed that Jack Straw himself instructed Michael Wood to present two views in the memorandum in question. This was taken as a request to the Attorney General to start developing his legal advice. At the specific request of the Foreign Secretary the memorandum did not offer an evaluation of the relative value of the two opposing views:[45] 'It had been made clear to me in the office that I should leave the matter open in that paper', the Legal Adviser recalled.[46] However, in the démarche from Michael Wood to the Foreign Secretary that triggered his rebuke, the Legal Adviser very clearly stated his own position, that only one of those two views was persuasive, and his conclusion that 'there is no doubt' in relation to the interpretation of Resolution 1441 (2002).

This finding cannot be characterized as unbalanced merely by virtue of the fact that it comes to a clear conclusion. Instead, throughout, the Legal Adviser generated well-reasoned assessments that carefully weighed both sides of the argument. In the application of the international legal method and reasoning, he then decided in favour of one of these, a view shared by all of his colleagues who were dealing with the matter.[47] That view, of course, was also shared by the wider international legal community.

This result is not undermined by the reference of the Foreign Secretary to his own direct knowledge of the negotiating history.[48] This information was very much available to the FCO Legal Advisers, who had been involved in all stages of the negotiations through daily exchanges of telegrams with New York, and their own Legal Adviser in the UK Permanent Mission to the UN.[49] The Legal Advisers had considered in detail the *travaux preparatoires*, and come to the conclusion that they did not displace the prevailing interpretation of Resolution 1441 (2002).

In view of these circumstances, it could be questioned whether the Foreign Secretary was entitled to reject the clear and unambiguous legal advice he received from his senior legal experts, apparently precisely because it was clear and unambiguous (and hence, in his view, 'unbalanced'). The Ministerial Code requires compliance with international law. The minister had received clear guidance of

---

[45] Jack Straw, Chilcot Testimony, 8 February 2010, 11–17.
[46] Michael Wood, Chilcot Testimony, 26 January 2010, 38.
[47] Elizabeth Wilmshurst, Chilcot Testimony, 26 January 2010, 5.
[48] Jack Straw, Supplementary Memorandum to the Chilcot Inquiry, 8 February 2010, 4.
[49] Michael Wood, Chilcot Testimony, 26 January 2010, 10.

the requirements of international law on this issue from those best placed to offer it: the Foreign Secretary's own Legal Advisers speaking with one voice, and leaving no room for doubt. Disregarding that guidance would certainly expose the minister to considerable risks. The arrogance of his persuasion might have turned into a lack of diligence in this instance.

The Foreign Secretary's principal Legal Adviser agreed that, ultimately, convention required that it would be the Attorney General who would furnish the decisive legal opinion. As the Foreign Secretary put it, '[i]t would be wholly improper of any Minister to challenge, or not accept, such an Attorney General decision'.[50] But this argument is again rather disingenuous. As the record has since revealed, the Foreign Secretary himself directly intervened with the Attorney General on numerous occasions, seeking to change his legal advice as it was developing. In fact, he himself penned and sent detailed legal arguments to the Attorney General that ran counter to the advice he had received from his own officials. Hence, the situation arose in which the Secretary of State for Foreign and Commonwealth affairs made use of the constitutional feature of the UK system, leaving the final determination of lawfulness to one person alone. And, in opposition to the FCO Legal Advisers who defended their role very strongly, it was thought that that person could be subjected to politically minded persuasion.

VI. Seeking to Influence the Attorney General

Up to February 2003 the Attorney General had taken the view that there existed no legal authority to use force. His view changed, in increments, thereafter. Nothing had changed in terms of the legal basis for action. The second resolution never materialized. The legal situation was, therefore, the same as it had been at the time of the adoption of Resolution 1441 (2002). If anything, the claim to use force as a necessary measure appeared to have diminished, given the progress of the arms inspection effort.

The Attorney General related to the Chilcot Inquiry his sense that his advice at earlier stages appeared positively unwelcome—a comment that was answered by the Prime Minister with the view that no advice was needed until it was needed.[51] Indeed, the Attorney General suggested that in the future, such advice should be sought throughout the development of policy and in line with developments. In particular, it might have been useful to seek his advice on the implications of Resolution 1441 (2002) before it was finally adopted. There are also indications that the Foreign Office Legal Advisers were progressively frozen out of the decision to launch the armed campaign after they had committed themselves to an

---

[50] Jack Straw, Supplementary Memorandum to the Chilcot Inquiry, 8 February 2010, 5.
[51] Tony Blair, Chilcot Testimony, 29 January 2010, 149.

interpretation of Resolution 1441 (2002) that was not in support of the aims of the Government.

The process of how the Attorney General reached and then changed his view was unorthodox. First, there was the issue of the instruction to give legal advice, 'but not just yet'. This seemed to leave the timing of the advice in abeyance, while it opened the process of negotiation with the Attorney General. While the latter has repeatedly claimed that he arrived at his conclusions entirely independently, he has also himself offered insights into this negotiating process.

Over the final critical period from December 2002 to March 2003, he began sharing his emerging legal analysis with the Prime Minister, the Foreign Secretary, and a few other dedicated supporters of military action. At each stage, he invited challenges and counter-arguments to his view advanced by 'his client', as he put it. The Foreign Secretary began to develop detailed arguments, and Sir Jeremy Greenstock put forward what the Attorney General saw as a dangerously one-sided negotiation history in order to help shift his views.

When the Attorney General remained unpersuaded only a short time before the launch of the invasion, he went to the United States to be presented with Washington's view of the negotiating history. The FCO Legal Adviser had warned with reference to the one-sided consideration of this material that 'if the matter were ever brought to a court, none of these records would be likely to be acceptable as *travaux préparatoires* of the resolution, since they are not independent or agreed records'.[52]

When the Attorney General changed his mind in view of the strongly held conviction that the United States would not have relinquished its claimed rights in the negotiations, he overturned his previous advice in error. He took the US position as indicative of the interpretation of the Resolution 1441 (2002). In reality, the United States merely undertook to preserve its position outside of the Resolution through the statement relating to self-defence and a broad reading of the revival argument that did not require any Council involvement. However, that position was not shared by any of the delegations of the Council, and it was not part of, or directly relevant to, the interpretation of the text. Even the UK did not accept either the US's prevention argument, or the claim that there existed an open-ended authority inherent in individual states to revive the authority granted in the Resolution without further Council action.

Even if its position had been relevant to the interpretation of the Resolution, the United States was hardly a disinterested party in the matter, and had maintained an isolated and strongly contested view throughout. After having heard the recollections of the negotiating record of Sir Jeremy Greenstock and of his own Secretary of State, the Attorney General remained unconvinced. However, during this visit to the United States, the Attorney General was persuaded by evidence that he had previously dismissed, or by the 'sincerity' of the US belief in its own position. However, that position was internationally isolated and not

---

[52] Sir Michael Wood, Memorandum, 9 December 2002, para 10.

shared by the UK. Moreover, this happened at the very moment when important states in the Security Council, which had also participated in the negotiations, were arguing very strongly against the lawfulness of the use of force and in favour of further inspections.

Clearly, the Attorney General was free to seek information and enlightenment from a variety of sources, in addition to governmental legal advisers. But the decision of the Attorney General to expose himself to such a one-sided argument from the very strongest advocates of the use of force, and essentially to negotiate his opinion with his 'clients' over a prolonged period of time, strains the understanding of his role in circumstances of this kind. It may be presumed that his task would be to study all the evidence and then arrive at his own view, without having that view constantly challenged and 'developed' through dialogue with one side. His client, in that sense, would be the nation, rather than the Prime Minister. Ultimately, there was an uncomfortable merging of his role as 'one of the team' and as the objective arbiter of the law.

The somewhat odd process of first discouraging advice, and then commissioning it but requesting that it should not be presented until further notice, made it possible for the political actors to request the Attorney General's formal advice only at a point in time when it became known that it now chimed with their political requirements.

Although the Attorney General's view changed, his legal advice of 7 March 2003 was a cautious document. The advice itself did not decide in favour of one view or the other. Instead, it merely declared both views 'reasonably arguable', although it warned that obtaining a second resolution would be the safer option. Nevertheless, he saw this finding as giving 'the green light' for the use of force in the absence of a second resolution. As the document did not elevate one view above the other, it appeared to be his less-formal communications with the Prime Minister's Office and others that gave such a signal. However, once it was given, the Attorney General came under immediate pressure to articulate this advice in writing and in a highly condensed form clearly favouring the position that Resolution 1441 (2002) did after all, authorize the use of force. This, it was argued, was necessary in order to provide the military and the civil service with the necessary assurance that they were not contributing to the unlawful launching of an aggressive war.

The original, hedged advice was, therefore, condensed into a few sentences, stating clearly and unambiguously that the international legal authority existed for the use of force. The Attorney General may have felt it appropriate to issue such a clear determination, if he really had meant his own, longer advice to give the green light for action.[53] However, having expressed this entirely unqualified position for that limited purpose, it was decided to build upon it for the purposes of public presentation.

---

[53] As noted above, he claimed that precedent indicated that it was merely necessary to find that a reasonable argument could be made in favour of action in order to allow the Government to proceed.

VII. Presenting the Legal Position

With the assistance of Christopher Greenwood, QC, a small team, composed of Harriet Harman, the Solicitor General, two officers from the Attorney General's office, the Lord Chancellor, Lord Irvine of Lairg, and three FCO officials, three documents were drafted. These were a short, two-page statement to Parliament on the Attorney General's 'view' on the use of force, the longer so-called 'Foreign Office Memorandum' supporting this view, and a question-and-answer paper for use with the press and others.[54] The documents did not reflect the uncertainties of the previous advice. Michael Wood, the FCO Legal Adviser, was present, but remained on the sidelines, given his known opposition to the view being developed. But it was clear that 'by that stage, we were in the advocacy mode as opposed to the advisory decision-making mode. This was a matter of presentation: how is this to be presented in public?'.[55]

The Attorney General had proposed to share his fuller considerations of 7 March 2003 with the Cabinet. However, at the suggestion of the Foreign Secretary the Cabinet was instead presented with the two-page statement, which formed the basis of its decision to support the war. It cannot have been apparent to the Cabinet that this was not a full rendering of his advice, or a fair summary of it, but rather an advocacy document intended for public consumption. Similarly, the document was issued to Parliament, along with the Foreign Office memorandum, immediately before the crucial debate in Parliament about the war. In fact, in contrast to previous parliamentary practice, a formal decision approving the war was sought. The Government claimed that it was particularly open in this instance to making available the views of the Attorney General which, by previous convention, has always been kept strictly confidential. It was obvious that the question of the legality of the action was a crucial element, if not perhaps *the* crucial element, in the decision to follow.

Like Cabinet, Parliament cannot have been aware that the 'view' of the Attorney General did not accord with the more lengthy formal 'advice', and that the Foreign Office legal experts were in fundamental disagreement with the Foreign Office memorandum. Robin Cook reportedly took the view that this amounted to misleading Parliament.[56] After seeing the full document, Clare Short, the former International Development Secretary, made that claim publicly.[57]

---

[54] See the Written Answer of Lord Goldsmith, HL Deb, Vol 670, cols 106–1099WA, 14 March 2005.   [55] Michael Wood, Chilcot Testimony, 26 January 2010, 60.

[56] BBC News, Goldsmith Denies War Advice Claim, 25 February 2005, available at <http://news.bbc.co.uk/1/hi/uk_politics/4296887.stm>.

[57] Nicola Boden, 'Blair Misled Parliament over Iraq', *Daily Mail*, 2 February 2010, available at <http://www.dailymail.co.uk/news/article-1247910/Iraq-war-inquiry-Clare-Short-claims-Lord-Goldsmith-misled-Government.html>.

While it is legitimate for the Government to produce arguments to defend a position it has taken, in this instance the advocacy approach prevailed one stage too soon—when the constitutional organs of the state, the Government (Cabinet), and Parliament were supposedly being informed of the objective advice emanating from the Attorney General. It is unfortunate that the Cabinet did not even listen to this advice, or challenge it, given the notoriety of the alternative view in the public debate.[58] It is, however, even more unfortunate that the Government sought to benefit from this confusion of advice and advocacy.

The Attorney General has indicated very credibly that he earnestly struggled with the issues involved. In the end, however, he seems to have abdicated the responsibility of making his own determination of the law, accepting that all he had to do was find that an argument in favour of force could reasonably be put forward, without embracing that argument himself. However, in a sense he was then trapped by the needs of the situation, having to offer a clear finding for the military and the civil service. The arguable case was clear for that purpose alone. But that finding was neither borne out by the advice he had so carefully given, nor by subsequent developments.

Having accepted the argument he had previously rejected, in favour of unilateral action under Resolution 1441 (2002), the Attorney General then went one step further by allowing the Prime Minister alone to determine whether the factual circumstances triggered its application and, with it, the use of force. This determination would ordinarily have had an important legal element to it—to apply the law to the facts. Equally as important, however, was the legal dimension. In simply requiring a 'yes' or 'no' determination from the Prime Minister, the Attorney General denied himself the opportunity to evaluate the reasons for the decision in the light of the applicable legal standard. Within the Cabinet there was an expectation that the Attorney General had undertaken this evaluation himself before coming to a clear view in favour of force.[59]

In the light of all these failings, should the role of providing authoritative advice on matters of international law, and of peace or war, have remained concentrated in one single person, who was part of the political process? The fact that, in the words of one of the protagonists, Lord Turnbull, 'the Attorney General is, in effect, the last court of appeal, because, once the Attorney General has ruled, then we all agree to stop arguing at that point, and that is, with one or two exceptions, what happened', may have led to unfortunate outcomes in this instance.[60]

The Attorney General is a political, ministerial appointment. There are clear advantages in retaining close contact between emerging policy and the Attorney General, if indeed his or her advice is consistently sought and acted upon. Direct

---

[58] A group of leading UK international lawyers had published their views in a letter to the Prime Minister, reprinted in the *Guardian* newspaper, 'War Would be Illegal', *Guardian*, 7 March 2003, available at <http://www.guardian.co.uk/politics/2003/mar/07/highereducation.iraq>, see also above n 1. [59] Cook (above n 26) 345.

[60] Lord Turnbull, Chilcot Testimony, 13 January 2010, 66.

access to Cabinet members, including the Prime Minister, is one such advantage. However, such access operates both ways. The credibility of the process can only be maintained if no suggestion is made that the incumbent should bow to political pressures, which can be immense. In this instance, the assurance lay in the professionalism and personal ethics of the Attorney General. However, in order to retain public confidence in performing what, in this case, turned out to be an absolutely decisive legal function, it was essential that decisions could be demonstrated to have been arrived at through legal reasoning alone, excluding policy considerations. Opening up the process of generating the legal advice to constant challenge and advice from No 10 Downing Street, and permitting repeated direct interventions in the process from the Foreign Secretary, was not consistent with that demand. Similarly, reliance on unbalanced evidence, in this case in the shape of the recollections of the US/UK side about the negotiations, did not accord with this standard.

Previously, the reliance on Law Officer's opinions had served well, in accordance with the UK's tradition of compliance with international law. The lesson from Suez had been that it was necessary to insist on the unipolar authority of the Attorney General in this respect. In that instance, the Government had circumvented the Attorney General (and also the FCO Legal Adviser) and had instead obtained advice from the Lord Chancellor.[61] However, in this instance, the exclusive reliance on one figure proved problematic. The Attorney General was clearly exposed to a very persistent and powerful campaign to assist him in coming to a view in line with governmental policy. The civil service governmental lawyers in the Foreign Office proved entirely resilient to such pressures, even when directly challenged by their minister.

To renew confidence in the system of legal advice, a number of steps could be considered. One would be to require the Attorney General to take account of the advice rendered to him by senior governmental lawyers representing the lead department in question. If his final advice conflicts with that advice, the department's view could be appended to his own, and he would need to offer reasons for overruling it. Another option would be to broaden the basis for the definite advice, requiring a joint view of both the lead department's legal advisers and the Attorney General. A third option would be to follow the practice of other governments, which have established small, Olympian groups of the top international law experts available in the country. On particularly contested issues, their opinion could be required and fed into the decision-making process of the Attorney General and/or the Government.

Whichever model is followed, it is necessary to operate a clear standard indicating when such advice must be sought. The Netherlands Inquiry into the Iraq war found that the expert advisory committee was circumvented when the

---

[61] L Johnman, 'Playing the Role of Cassandra, Sir Gerald Fitzmaurice, Senior Legal Adviser to the Foreign Office' in S Kelly and A Gorst, (2000) *Whitehall and the Suez Crisis* 46, 61.

Government decided to support the war politically. The relevant provision in the UK Ministerial Code is broad and could be supplemented with a more particular clause concerning decisions involving the application of military force.

The convention that final, decisive advice comes from one source only has the advantage that it produces a very clear result, as was the case here. It could be argued that such clarity of guidance is required for governmental decision-making. However, that is not necessarily the case. Where the position in law is unclear, or where, on balance, the law stands in opposition to the Government's proposed conduct, it is necessary for those who decide policy to be aware of this. Otherwise, no reasoned decision, based on the law but also on other considera-tions, can ensue. Hence, it is not strictly necessary that only one view be pre-sented. The actual advice of the Attorney General of 7 March 2003 was in that tradition. While it emanated from one person only, it reflected divergent views. It is perhaps attributable to the sofa style of cabinet that that advice was not, in fact, available to those who exercised collective responsibility for decisions in Cabinet.

It is true that had the full advice been available, the position of the Prime Minister and his Foreign Secretary would have become more difficult. Cabinet may have considered the matter with greater care. But this would ordinarily be seen as an advantage, rather than a disadvantage.

Another question concerns the publication of the advice. The Government took the view that Parliament should be involved in the decision to go to war and that it should do so in the knowledge of the legal position. This represented something of an innovation, and one that can only be endorsed. However, if the decision-making role of Parliament is to be enhanced in this way, it may not be possible to stick to the confidentiality rule relating to legal advice. If the Government had offered a fair summary of legal advice to Parliament in this instance, the option of a shorter rendering of the advice to Parliament might have been retained. However, the Iraq experience highlights the risks of a biased presentation by gov-ernment. Accordingly, where the Government decides to make evidence as to the legal position available, it will need either to issue the full advice or to commit itself more formally to ensuring that any summary it offers fully reflects the legal position as stated in the advisory document.

The House of Lords' Select Committee on the Constitution has considered the issue of the publication of the advice in some detail and concluded that such a step would be detrimental to the functioning of government.[62] If the full advice were to be published, it might be written in a way that anticipates scrutiny from outside the circle of the decision-makers to whom it has been tendered. In such a case, it could lose its character of candid guidance offered in confidence. However, where matters of peace and war are concerned, it is reasonable to expect that military action will only be taken in the future where there is a clear legal case in support.

---

[62] House of Lords, Select Committee on the Constitution, Fifteenth Report of Session 2005/6, HL Paper 236-I, 29.

As the Iraq case demonstrates, if the initial advice of the Attorney General had been published, the case for war might well have collapsed. Such a result would not amount to undue hindrance of the governmental function. It would be an element of transparent decision-making in a parliamentary democracy.

The House of Lords' Select Committee suggests that Parliament at least might equip itself with its own legal advisory service, in lieu of obtaining knowledge of the Attorney-General's advice.[63] Clearly, Parliament is free at all times to seek advice from a variety of sources. However, this does not overcome the constitutional problem encountered in this case. Parliament was fully aware of the opposing legal arguments put by government and scholars. Nevertheless, in the light of the categorical assurance of lawfulness given by the Attorney General in his 'view', instead of the full advice, this otherwise overwhelming evidence was swept aside. As long as the decisive value of the Attorney General's opinion is retained when expressing a view on international law, it will remain necessary to make it available. After all, this view can only be critically examined by those who hold democratic mandates if it is known. This requirement is also inherent in the ministerial-type appointment to the post of Attorney General. An appointment of this kind implies accountability to Parliament and the public. Public accountability does not function in secret.

A final point concerns the Ministerial Code. This is an informal document, being issued by the Prime Minister of the day. Consideration might be given to improving on its substance in line with the suggestions made here. In addition, however, it may be necessary to consider whether the obligations contained in such an improved document should be anchored more firmly in the UK's constitutional order.

VIII. International Law as an 'Uncertain Field' and the Standard of Evidence

In his letter rejecting the advice from his principal Legal Adviser, the Foreign Secretary argued that international law 'is an uncertain field,' and one permitting honestly and reasonably held differences of view.[64] However, in this instance, there was near unanimity on what the correct view actually was, not only within the UK Government, but also among the other governments concerned, within the UN Secretariat and among academics. The UK Government was aware that its eventual position would be isolated and internationally rejected. Against that background, it is difficult to see why that view was considered 'reasonably arguable'. However, even if that was the case, it may be questioned whether it constituted an appropriate test for legal justification of major use of force.

---

[63] Ibid, 30.

[64] Note from Foreign Secretary Jack Straw to Michael Wood (FCO Legal Adviser) re Iraq: legal basis for the use of force, 29 January 2003, 2.

In this instance, the Attorney General was guided by previous practice. The continued maintenance of the no-fly zones in Iraq had been subjected to periodic review by the UK Attorney General. He found that the Law Officers had previously accepted that a 'respectable legal argument' could be made in relation to the use of force. In his view, it was becoming 'more questionable whether a respectable legal argument can be maintained that force is justified on grounds of overwhelming humanitarian necessity' in Iraq. He concluded that 'it is still *possible* to argue that the maintenance of the No Fly Zones is justified', adding that this judgment was a 'very fine one'.[65] The Attorney General reiterated that this legal basis could not justify military action for other, ulterior motives, such as action to punish Saddam Hussein, or to enforce other UK or US objectives in the area. Moreover, it would be 'vitally important to keep constantly in view the precarious nature of the legal basis for the UK and US action in the No Fly Zones'.[66]

It is surprising that the formal advice of the Attorney General appears to have moved the standard of evidence necessary to justify the use of force from a 'respectable legal argument' to a 'very fine one' that was in fact 'precarious'. It is not clear why such a change should have occurred, other than the need not to disrupt what was by then a long-established UK policy relating to the no-fly zones.

In his subsequent advice, the Attorney General found, despite arguments to the contrary, that 'a reasonable case can be made that resolution 1441 (2002) is capable in principle of reviving the authorization in 678 (1990) without a further resolution'.[67] He added:[68]

In reaching my conclusions, I have taken account of the fact that on a number of previous occasions, including in relation to Operation Desert Fox in December 1998 and Kosovo in 1999, UK forces have participated in military action on the basis of advice from my predecessors that the legality of the action under international law was no more than reasonably arguable. But a 'reasonable case' does not mean that if the matter ever came before a court I would be confident that the court would agree with this view.

Jack Straw appeared to maintain that in the absence of clarification through a court there was greater leeway for argument. However, the contrary approach seems more appropriate here. In the absence of legal clarification by a centralized, authoritative mechanism like a court, states determine or develop international law through their own conduct. Hence, they should be mindful not only of their own, immediate interests triggered by a given situation, but by the impact of their actions on the development of the law. Accordingly, special care should be taken when weighing immediate national interests against the need to maintain the stability of rules that are highly important to the system as a whole.[69]

---

[65] David Brummell to Tom McKane, Memorandum, 12 February 2001, para 13 (emphasis in original). [66] Ibid, para 15.
[67] Attorney General, Memorandum, 7 March 2003, para 27. [68] Ibid, para 30.
[69] See Sir Michael Wood, Chilcot Testimony, 26 January 2010, 34.

Clearly, issues relating to the use of force concern international legal rules of the highest status. The prohibition of the use of force is part of the corpus of international *jus cogens*, from which there must never be derogation whatever the countervailing political considerations. A serious violation of such a rule triggers an obligation on the part of the rest of the international community not to recognize the result, not to assist the perpetrator of the violation in maintaining its consequences, and to consult through collective bodies on steps that can be taken to overturn it. There may also be individual criminal responsibility for launching an aggressive war.

The strong presumption against war in the international system must influence the standard applied when determining whether it can be lawfully waged. In that sense, it is hardly sufficient to wage war when it is merely possible to conceive of an argument that might reasonably be made in favour of it. Instead, a clear preponderance of evidence in favour of the authority to use force in a given instance would be necessary—the standard of 'beyond reasonable doubt' for example. Such an evaluation would have to be made in accordance with the international legal requirement of good faith, and through the application of international legal method (as opposed to the use of policy prescription or preferences in order to decide between competing views). It would also need to be in accordance with the longer-term view on the legal rules in question. That is to say, the rationale applied in favour of the action for which authority is sought must also be capable of being applied in other instances.

The UK's guiding principles concerning forcible humanitarian action exclude unilateral action: 'No individual country can reserve to itself the right to act on behalf of international community'.[70] Where action is taken that is not in strict self-defence or forcible humanitarian action, this requires authorization from the Security Council. When assessing whether such authority exists, it is necessary to be particularly mindful of the views of other governments and international agencies that can pronounce themselves on the issue with particular authority. In the case of Iraq, that would have included the other delegations in the Security Council, the UN Secretariat, and other bodies with expert knowledge of the issues and the law.

It would also be necessary to give an assurance that the finding of lawfulness of the use of force was obtained in a procedurally clean way. That would exclude the exertion of political influence on the process of identifying the law and compliance with an enhanced legal advisory process, as is outlined below.

In this instance, however, international practice relating to Iraq was lax. Throughout the early part of the 1990s, the multiple use of force against Iraq was widely tolerated and led to very few, if any, challenges in the Security Council. The revival argument generated within the UN reflected a convenient relaxation of the strict law of the UN Charter in order to address the refusal of Iraq to comply with its disarmament obligations. When the use of force against Iraq became

---

[70] The full guideline is cited in Ch 3, 87 and in (2000) 71 BYIL 646.

more controversial towards the end of the decade, it was difficult to contain that argument. Moreover, the practice of humanitarian intervention against Iraq also undermined the hitherto clear understanding of the prohibition of the use of force in relation to that state. The UK itself served as the principal norm entrepreneur in this instance. While this policy also became more controversial as time progressed, it was initially not resisted.

The UK also took the lead in presenting humanitarian intervention as formal legal justification for the use of force against Yugoslavia in 1999. While practice in Iraq re-introduced the doctrine into the international legal lexicon (before 1991, humanitarian intervention was widely believed to be unlawful), this development was not yet consolidated. Nevertheless, action was deemed necessary to avert an overwhelming humanitarian emergency. In that situation, the standard of advancing a legal justification for war that was merely 'arguable' was apparently introduced. Despite doubts, the UK Government felt confident in doing so, as it believed that it was contributing to the development of a new doctrine of general application, rather than merely putting forward a view to meet the exigencies of the situation. While the UK view also engendered controversy, it was nevertheless treated as a serious legal proposition. That proposition was later picked up in subsequent international practice and led to the adoption of the doctrine of 'responsibility to protect'. While that doctrine is not in fact identical to humanitarian intervention, the reception of UK-led practice into international law demonstrates a critical difference from the Iraq issue of 2003.

The UK never intended to create a proposal in favour of the auto-enforcement of Security Council aims or decisions. Indeed, it worked very hard to base its actions in 2003 in the very specific circumstances generated by the adoption of Resolutions 678 (1990) and 1441 (2002). However, as this attempt was ultimately unpersuasive, confidence in the UK's commitment to the international rule of law was shaken.

Clearly, the legal dimension is not the only consideration that informs a decision about peace or war. Legal authority is necessary but not sufficient. War cannot be waged merely because it may be legally possible to do so. Moral and other considerations of the highest order also apply. But the legal dimension is certainly a necessary requirement. If it is not clearly fulfilled, war cannot be an option.

In view of this consideration, the question of the final advice, or 'view', tendered by the Attorney General is of primary importance. Given the rarefied nature of international legal debate, it is impossible for the non-expert in Parliament, in Cabinet, or among the general public, to determine which view is correct. However, in this instance, the overwhelming majority of governmental lawyers and academic experts had expressed opposition to the use of force.

The answer to this problem traditionally has two elements. On the one hand, there is considerable confidence in the FCO's Legal Advisers and their ability to inform the Government of the legal position from the outset. However, in the critical period after the adoption of Resolution 1441 (2002), their advice was replaced by the amateurish and politically motivated legal investigation conducted by the Foreign Secretary himself. Second, the process by which the Attorney-General reaches his or her views must be transparent and beyond reproach. In this instance, the system failed on both counts.

Interestingly, the Attorney General's short and misguided memorandum had another, unintended effect. As the Netherlands Inquiry into the war has revealed, the document was presented by its government to Cabinet as critical evidence of the legal position when it decided to support the armed action politically. The legal position was similarly controversial in the Netherlands, and the finding of the UK Attorney General was taken as an unqualified and definite ruling on the issue.[71] The Australian Government also invoked the Attorney General's advice when its own, rather brief and unpersuasive brief on the matter was challenged by legal authority obtained by the Leader of the Opposition.[72]

IX. The Problem of Facts and Accountability

The UK Government relied on intelligence reports to support its view that Iraq possessed WMD capacity. Most Western governments had similar reports and relied on them in adopting their views. These have since proven inaccurate. The very extensive Iraq Survey conducted after the conclusion of the 2003 hostilities found that there was no such capability.

The UK was instrumental in attempting to make the case that Iraq posed a danger on account of its WMD potential. It published the famed September 2002 dossier, signed by the Prime Minister, which presented the purported evidence. The dossier was the result of an unprecedented influx of information from the secret intelligence services into a public relations document generated, in part, under the stewardship of the Prime Minister's powerful Director of Communications, Alastair Campbell. It was followed in February 2002 by what became known as the 'dodgy dossier'. That document appeared to offer new intelligence findings relating to Iraq's attempts to conceal its WMD capability. However, it later emerged that elements of the dossier had been plagiarized from an academic publication that had been in the public domain for some time.

The use and misuse of intelligence in this instance was the subject of several important inquiries in the UK and elsewhere, and it is not necessary to expand on this issue here.[73] In view of the Prime Minister's unequivocal finding of Iraq's

---

[71] See above n 29, 133.

[72] See the memoranda reproduced in (2003) 4 *Melbourne Journal of International Law* 183, and (2005) 24 *Australian Yearbook of International Law* 417.

[73] In addition to the Butler Report (above n 4), see the Hutton Report, (2004) *Report of the Inquiry into the Circumstances Surrounding the Death of Dr David Kelly CMG*, and the House of Commons Foreign Affairs Committee, *The Decision to Go to War in Iraq*, Ninth Report of Session 2002–03 (2003), HC 813–1.

failure to comply with the terms of Resolution 1441 (2002), it suffices to note the following conclusion of the Butler Report:[74]

Despite its importance to the determination of whether Iraq was in further material breach of its obligations under Resolution 1441, the JIC made no further assessment of the Iraqi declaration beyond its 'Initial Assessment'. We have also recorded our surprise that policy-makers and the intelligence community did not, as the generally negative results of UNMOVIC inspections became increasingly apparent, re-evaluate in early 2003 the quality of the intelligence.

It is, therefore, not entirely clear what the basis of the Prime Minister's finding of 14 March 2003 on Iraqi non-compliance was, other than a recollection of the claims made previously in his own dossier (at the time increasingly difficult to substantiate) and selective references to reports of the UN inspectors. The inspectors had also indicated that they had found no 'smoking gun', although they did identify a number of issues that warranted further investigation. Indeed, in fairness to the Prime Minister and the Foreign Secretary, it must be noted that the UNMOVIC cluster document of 6–7 March 2003 did raise a significant number of areas where further clarification was required.[75] However, that document sought to establish a focus for further inspection, not to give the green light for invasion on account of material breach. In fact, at that very time, the inspectors were increasingly emphasizing the progressively constructive attitude of the Iraqi authorities. The UK's own approach for benchmarking progress as part of its campaign for a second resolution confirmed that it would have been possible to assess compliance more objectively. It was not a matter of standards and their application, however. Instead, it was a matter of time available in the light of the schedule for military operation that was by then firmly fixed.

If the Prime Minister had reason to reconsider the state of the evidence in favour or against compliance on the point of going to war, the same was true of the Attorney General. As Robin Cook put it, 'how could Sir Peter Goldsmith be certain as a matter of fact that Iraq was in breach of its obligations? Or had Downing Street not shared with him the emerging doubts on intelligence that was available to the Prime Minister?'.[76] In fact, it emerged that the Attorney General had been given a number of intelligence briefings, but chose to shift responsibility for making a determination on compliance to the Prime Minister.

Robin Cook also asked another pertinent question:[77]

The Attorney General's legal advice is founded entirely on the failure of Saddam to comply with the 'obligations of Iraq to eliminate its weapons of mass destruction'. I am no

---

[74] Above n 4, 116.

[75] UNMOVIC, *Unresolved Disarmament Issues: Iraq's Proscribed Weapons Programmes* (2003). The Prime Minster heavily relied on this document when making his speech to the Commons in advance of the vote on war.   [76] Cook (above n 26) 345.

[77] R Cook, Memorandum, House of Commons, 17 June 2003, Select Committee on Foreign Affairs, Written Evidence, para 20, available at <http://www.publications.parliament.uk/pa/cm200203/cmselect/cmfaff/813/813we02.htm>.

lawyer, but it does appear arguable that if Iraq had no weapons of mass destruction there could in logic be no legal basis for a war to eliminate them.

It is tempting to consider whether the wrongfulness of launching an aggressive war may be legally precluded due to an error of fact on the part of the invading state. However, the International Law Commission Articles on State Responsibility do not contain error as a possible preclusion of wrongfulness.[78] Moreover, even if error could be pleaded for that purpose, it would not apply in relation to the launching of an aggressive war—perhaps the most serious transgression of the international legal order, which strongly privileges the maintenance and effectiveness of the prohibition of the use of force over other considerations. Admitting error as a circumstance precluding wrongfulness would dangerously undermine the prohibition of the use of force. Any state might claim after the event that it was in error of its assessment, say, of whether or not the conditions of self-defence had been met. Instead, the standard of state responsibility for unlawful uses of force is a strict one. Any state contemplating force must be certain of the facts justifying the action and of its legal basis. The consequences of a misidentification of the facts or law cannot be attributed to the victim state. Instead, a state contemplating the use of force must bear the full consequences of such a momentous decision. This has now just been confirmed by the Kampala Review Conference of the Statute of the International Criminal Court.

Even if the doctrine of error could be applied in the context of the use of force, it would probably not assist the UK in this instance. Error has been addressed in the context of the law of treaties. There, it is made clear that an error of law cannot itself be admitted as legal justification.[79] A state bears full responsibility for ensuring that its conduct is based on the correct identification of applicable international legal rules. Hence, the failure to interpret Resolution 1441 (2002) correctly did not furnish an excuse. Moreover, in terms of errors of fact, such a defence is not available where 'the state in question contributed by its own conduct to the error or if the circumstances were such as to put that state on notice of a possible error'.[80] Here, the failings in obtaining accurate information through the intelligence process, and the selective reliance on reports from the UN arms inspectors, amounted to a contribution to the error. Moreover, the controversial nature of the factual claims underpinning the action was notorious at the time, as was borne out by the Butler Inquiry.

The issue of facts raises another important problem. What are the implications of the use of force against the advice of the objective, best-placed agencies

---

[78] Reproduced in full with the Commission's commentary in J Crawford, (2002) *The International Law Commission's Articles on State Responsibility.*

[79] 'Nevertheless, it considered that to introduce into the article a provision appearing to admit an error of law as a ground for invalidating consent would dangerously weaken the stability of treaties. Accordingly, the paragraphs speaks only of errors relating to a 'fact' or 'situation': Vienna Convention on the Law of Treaties, ILC Final Draft with Commentary, para 6, reproduced in RG Wetzel and D Rauschnig, (1978) *Travaux Preparatoires* 349.

[80] Vienna Convention on the Law of Treaties, Art 48(2).

in terms of individual responsibility for launching an aggressive war? As this book is handed over to the press, the Review Conference of the Rome Statute has addressed this very issue. The Conference defined the crime of aggression as follows:[81]

For the purpose of this Statute, 'crime of aggression' means the planning, preparation, initiation or execution, by a person in a position effectively to exercise control over or to direct the political or military action of a State, of an act of aggression which, by its character, gravity and scale, constitutes a manifest violation of the Charter of the United Nations.

The text adds that there is no requirement to prove that the perpetrator has made a legal evaluation as to whether the use of armed force would be consistent with the UN Charter. Instead, the question of whether there would be a 'manifest' violation would be an entirely objective one.[82] Hence, even if the accused can point to legal advice arguing in favour of the lawfulness of the proposed action, this in itself does not provide legal cover in terms of individual responsibility.

Of course, even if this provision enters into force, it will not be applied retroactively to the case of Iraq. However, the question remains whether in an instance like the present one, the violation of international law would have been sufficiently 'manifest' in the sense of the draft. One position holds that, as long as legal opinion can be advanced on both sides, a violation would not be manifest. That view expressly refers to the fact that at least one senior legal scholar, then Professor Christopher Greenwood, supported the use of force.[83] The opposing position argues that such an approach would entirely undermine the very essence of the attempt to criminalize aggression, as it will always be possible to find a supporter of the use of force among academia or government lawyers.[84]

In this sense, the Iraq case offers a very interesting example. The overwhelming majority of states and of legal scholars had very clearly formed the view that the action was unlawful. Even governments that previously argued in favour of force have had to accept that their position was not well founded. Following its own inquiry process, including a very detailed consideration of the legal advice given, the Netherlands Government has accepted that its support for the war required a 'more adequate' basis in international law.[85] Moreover, in this instance, the principal legal advisers in the Foreign Office took a very clear stance against the use of force and expressly warned that a crime of aggression would be committed. The opinion of the Attorney-General itself admitted, at least in its original form, that the view favouring force was not 'safe' in the sense that it might be overturned by

---

[81] RC/Res.4, 17 June 2010, advance version.   [82] Ibid, Annex II.

[83] C Kress, 'Strafrecht und Angriffskrieg im Licht des "Falles Iraq"' (2003) 115 *Zeitschrift fuer die gesamte Strafrechtswissenschaft* 294.

[84] A Paulus, 'Second Thoughts on the Crime of Aggression' (2009) 20 *European Journal of International Law* 1117, 1124; cf C Kress, 'Time for Decisions: Some Thoughts on the Immediate Future of the Crime of Aggression: Re Reply to Andreas Paulus' in Paulus (ibid) 1129ff.

[85] Quoted in the Introduction to the published English version of the Inquiry Report in (2010) 58 NILR 71, 81.

a court. In those circumstances, senior politicians, however well-meaning, may not in future escape accountability for commissioning the use of force that subsequently turns out to amount to an international act of aggression. This factor in itself may contribute to a higher standard of due diligence in decision-making about the use of force in the future.

X. Conclusion

When invited to reflect upon this entire episode, the Prime Minister noted his responsibility, but no regret for removing Saddam Hussein:[86]

I think that he was a monster, I believe he threatened, not just the region but the world, and in the circumstances that we faced then, ... it was better to deal with this threat, to deal with it, to remove him from office, and I do genuinely believe that the world is safer as a result.

After having heard the evidence in relation to what was described as a 'lamentable failure' of the legal advisory process in this instance, the Prime Minister nevertheless maintained the view that the operation against Iraq was fully in line with UN resolutions, in particular Resolution 1441 (2002).[87] He argued that 'as a matter of common sense':[88]

The whole spirit of it was: we have been through ten years of Saddam Hussein breaching UN Resolutions. We finally decide that he is going to be given one last chance. This is the moment when, if he takes that last chance, there is no conflict, we resolve the matter, but if he doesn't take that chance and starts messing around again, as he started to do, then that's it.

The Prime Minister added:[89]

So, in my view, there had to be at least a strong prima facie case if you could show material breach, that this justified the revival argument, since, otherwise, you know, you couldn't have justified it in respect of 1998.

In this episode, therefore, it seems that the Prime Minister, supported by his Secretary of State for Foreign and Commonwealth Affairs, swept away the correct, technical legal advice that would have inhibited what they regarded as an overriding policy aim. They did so on the basis of their assessment of the relevant resolutions of the Security Council. This assessment was based on their own understanding, and that of their US counterpart, of what was essential and necessary when dealing with Saddam Hussein and his regime. However, their assessment turned out to be manifestly deficient, both in terms of its basis in

---

[86] Tony Blair, Chilcot Testimony, 29 January 2010, 247.
[87] Elisabeth Wilmshurst, Chilcot Testimony, 26 January 2010, 35.
[88] Tony Blair, Chilcot Testimony, 29 January 2010, 157.   [89] Ibid, 151.

law and, as it later transpired, in terms of fact. Where the law was concerned, the sophisticated machinery for rendering legal advice available within the FCO was ignored when its view opposed that of the Government. In accordance with constitutional convention it was left to a political figure, the Attorney General, to present a final legal determination on the issue. This determination originally opposed action in the absence of a second resolution. After accepting that the alternative view might at least be arguable, this hesitant acknowledgement was then transformed into a definite finding of lawfulness without any further justification in fact or law. The unique position of the Attorney General's advice foreclosed any further legal debate, and action was taken.

The UK Government claimed to have acted with particular openness, having published for the first time much of its intelligence-based knowledge of the facts, and having offered up for public debate the Law Officers' views on the legality of the proposed war. However, it transpired that the information provided on both counts more closely resembled a targeted advocacy effort than a balanced assessment from which the Cabinet, Parliament, and the general public could draw their own informed conclusions.

International law in itself would not be the only factor determining questions of peace or war. However, the legal rules concerned furnish a basic standard that must be fulfilled, in addition to moral and political considerations. Given the divergence of moral precepts and political interests around the world, the legal rules provide the only agreed, universally held basis for such decisions. In this instance, a small number of key actors in the United States and the UK determined, however, that exceptional, new factors had emerged. These were the new threat of WMD and their possible proliferation to terrorists, which required decisive action. But even this argument failed to justify action in this instance. First, the legal system did in fact provide for avenues of action. In case of a genuine, overwhelming, and imminent threat, states can act unilaterally. If there is merely a gathering danger, as was perceived in this instance, this can also be addressed, but it is then necessary to persuade others of the need to action. The United States and the UK failed to make that case in the UN Security Council, but chose to act nevertheless. They cannot claim to have done so in order to vindicate the values and demands articulated by the Council in relation to Iraq when the Council itself was broadly unwilling to authorize force towards that end.

8

Conclusion: The Thirty-year War and its Impact on the International System

Iraq and its immediate neighbourhood has been the scene of immense violence. On 22 September 1980 the first Gulf conflict erupted with the invasion of Iran by Iraq. That conflict combined practices of World War I (gas attacks and stagnant trench warfare) with those of World War II (the war of the cities, the tanker war), resulting in appalling casualties. It was fought over territory. Iraq wanted to reclaim what it had given up in a boundary agreement five years earlier. Moreover, after the Islamic Revolution, Iran had ambitions to export the doctrine of religious governance to the Shia population in the south. Iraq claimed to have been forced to resort to arms to terminate an underground and subversive terrorist campaign.

The conflict continued until 1988, when the Soviet withdrawal from Afghanistan brought an end to the Cold War. In this changed environment, the UN Security Council managed to flex some muscle in relation to both sides, threatening sanctions if hostilities continued. But the ensuing cease-fire left Iraq unsated. Bled dry by the war, Saddam Hussein looked towards Kuwait for economic salvation. Iraq owed the small sheikhdom billions of dollars. While it contained vast oil resources, it was virtually undefended and could be taken in a matter of days, if not hours. It was anticipated that although the organized international community would condemn and complain from the sidelines, the facts, although brought about by force, would ultimately prevail. As cover for its action, Iraq claimed that the intervention had been invited by the very government its tanks had brought into Kuwait City. Moreover, Baghdad pointed to its long-standing historical claim to the territory, as it had done in relation to Iran. How could Iraq be condemned for deploying its forces in an area that was legally its own?

However, the invasion was based on a serious miscalculation. First, Iraq had underestimated the strategic interest in Kuwait. Its advance on the sheikhdom was seen as a first step towards a potential march on neighbouring Saudi Arabia. Together, the two countries held a sizeable proportion of the world's known oil reserves. To leave this resource in the control of Saddam Hussein would have been unacceptable, not only to the United States, the world's vast oil consumer, but also to others. But there was more at stake. With the end of the Cold War, the soft power concept of a functioning World Order had once again gained credence. Collective opposition to aggression was the very first element of any concept of global order. The purported vindication of Iraq's territorial claims, or the defence of its rights to the Rumeila oil fields through force, smacked of pre-League of Nations practice. Up until then, states had invoked their legal rights and vital national interests as justification for war. The purported 'invitation' by Kuwaiti revolutionaries was reminiscent of similarly intolerable Cold War practice by the superpowers (Hungary, Czechoslovakia, Afghanistan, and, arguably, Panama), which, it was thought, had been overcome.

Thus, the Kuwait conflict became a conflict not about oil, but about order in the international system, addressing the central question of how this order was to be administered. The design of a system of UN collective security was premised on close cooperation among the key victorious allies of World War II. At its inception, it was anticipated that these states would continue to dominate the globe in the long term. But by 1990, France and the United Kingdom had lost their global empires and were mere middle powers, however much they sought to capitalize on the glory of the past and the nuclear weapons they had developed. At that time, China was focusing on emerging from the status of a developing nation, and was only just able to feed its vast population; then, there was little risk of it dominating the system. The Soviet Union was on the brink of implosion. Its crisis-riddled leadership sought status and reassurance in attempts to play a major international role, but its potential to exercise real power was severely diminished. That left only the United States, which was about to enjoy its unipolar moment in world history.

At the time, the United States was led by a patrician President, George HW Bush, who had been schooled in international affairs through decades of high-level experience. He had been UN Ambassador and was aware of the unique legitimacy the world organization could bestow on national and international action. His calm and stable stewardship of international affairs contributed much to the administration of the dangerous transition from the Cold War, in particular the dissolution of the Warsaw Pact and the unification of Germany. To him, multilateralism was an asset. While not averse to unilateral action when the national interest so demanded, he was keen to manage instances of the application of power as a building block towards a more stable international order. The liberation of Kuwait was his key achievement in that respect.

However, while the Kuwait episode appeared at first glance to be a triumphant vindication of UN principles and the doctrine of collective security, in fact the balance sheet was not so clear. The United States, which was to bear the brunt of the conflict with Iraq, trod cautiously. The Bush (Senior) administration cleverly used the UN as an enabling device, all the while ensuring that it would not restrict US options if it failed to deliver on its promise of collective security. This dual approach led to tension within the UN. When the United States and United

Kingdom announced the imposition of a naval blockade (interdiction) purportedly to enforce UN sanctions, there was much opposition. The Security Council
had not granted a mandate for the conduct of such an operation. Although it
could be justified as an exercise of the continuing right of Kuwait to collective
self-defence, it was seen as a betrayal of the spirit of collective action that had
characterized the response in the Council thus far.

The United States and United Kingdom backtracked and obtained a fresh
mandate, although the unilateral option of self-defence was always kept close
to hand. They did not make use of the invitation by the Council to coordinate
the interdiction collectively through the UN's Military Staff Committee (incidentally, chaired by a Russian Admiral during that month). In something of
a diplomatic triumph, they managed to achieve Resolution 678 (1990), which
authorized the use of force for the liberation of Kuwait. That Resolution was
ambiguous in some respects. It was not entirely clear whether it merely confirmed the right of Kuwait to continuing self-defence, and encouraged other
states to cooperate with it, or whether it offered independent authority towards
that end through collective security. This ambiguity was deliberate. It left the
coalition powers the option to claim the legitimacy that flowed from collective security, and possibly a broader mandate to use force than might have been
available under self-defence. However, there were no strings attached. While
the Resolution granted or confirmed authority, it did not impose the process
requirements for the administration of collective security foreseen in the UN
Charter.

Some of these requirements had in fact fallen into disuse (Article 43 agreements, for instance). But there remained the essential requirement that granting
collective security authority would need to be balanced by some form of supervision of the conduct of armed action by the Council. However, when hostilities
commenced the United States took the clear view that from that point onwards it
alone, with its allies, was in charge. There could be no second-guessing of military
strategy in the conduct of the operations. The Council was kept out of the action,
to the point of being precluded even from meeting during the initial phases of
aerial operations. When the conflict intensified, and questions arose about the
need to continue using force in view of a Soviet mediation attempt, only closed,
confidential meetings were allowed. At the point of the massive land invasion,
Cuba sought to bring forward a resolution calling for a cease-fire, or at least a
pause in fighting to allow the UN Secretary-General to test the various peace ini-
tiatives that were then being proposed. However, in view of Iraq's still ambiguous
attitude, the launch of the land offensive was justified. Nevertheless, the massive
application of force under the Powell Doctrine raised questions. More controversial still was the inability of the Council to reassert itself towards the conclusion
of the campaign. Sustained attacks continued at a point when Iraq had unconditionally accepted the UN demand for a full withdrawal, and while Iraqi forces
were in the process of withdrawing.

The UN managed to gain ground when it converted the suspension of hostilities, agreed by US General Norman Schwarzkopf with the Iraqi leadership, into a temporary cease-fire. However, the conditions of that cease-fire were unusual, appearing to enlarge the mandate to use force at the conclusion of hostilities rather than restricting it. Authority to use force was, however, then rapidly terminated according to the terms of Resolution 687 (1991), which established a definite, formal cease-fire. The elements of the cease-fire terms were unprecedented. While the fighting had taken place under exclusive US and coalition control, the administration of the cease-fire was left to the UN, functioning as a collective security organization. This included the demarcation of the Iraq–Kuwait Boundary by an international commission, the establishment of very wide-ranging mechanisms for awarding war reparations ('compensation'), and provision for Iraqi disarmament in relation to weapons of mass destruction (WMD) and their delivery vehicles. While the United States had initially pressed for assembling evidence against Saddam Hussein, his Government, and his armed forces during the period of Kuwait's occupation, there was no longer much appetite for international prosecution of the relevant individuals. It was left to subsequent cases in the former Yugoslavia and Rwanda, and the eventual establishment of the Rome Statute of the International Criminal Court, to break ground in that respect. In view of subsequent US and UK assertions that Saddam Hussein was a 'monster', who some years later had to be dealt with in the most extreme terms, that result is perhaps surprising.

The Iraqi Government certainly appeared to adopt a business-as-usual approach to the cease-fire terms. It forcibly repressed the revolt of Kurds in the north and Shia in the south. Despite doubt in the Council about the application of UN Charter, Chapter VII powers to essentially domestic matters, the Council managed to adopt a resolution demanding the cessation of repression and the granting of humanitarian access. No forcible mandate was attached. However, informally, it appears that there was an unexpressed consensus within the Council that the use of force might be appropriate after all, given the now overwhelming humanitarian emergency. The deployment of coalition forces on the ground in northern Iraq, the establishment by coalition forces of a no-fly zone, and humanitarian air drops in Iraqi air space without Iraqi consent, were generally not challenged in the Council.

This practice signalled the start of the Council's own, subsequent interventions in the domestic affairs of other states. On occasion, these were conducted by forces operating directly under the authority of the Council, and the command of the UN Secretariat (although generally also informally under national lines of command on the part of force-contributing states). In other cases, the Council authorized a lead state to form a 'coalition of the willing' to mount an interventionist action. This practice prevailed for some time after the disasters of Rwanda, Somalia, and Srebrenica, which were unfairly attributed to the cumbersome nature of the management of complex peace support by the UN.

As already noted, however, coalition action in northern Iraq, and the operation that followed in relation to the south, was not accorded a formal mandate.
Rather, it was seen by commentators as evidence of the existence, or revival, of a
right to so-called 'humanitarian intervention' in international law. It was argued
that, together with practice relating to Liberia and Sierra Leone, a doctrine of forcible humanitarian action was establishing itself in international customary law,
in derogation of an otherwise comprehensive prohibition on the use of force. UK
pronouncements, in particular, contributed to the view that some governments
were willing to act formally as norm entrepreneurs in this respect. This involved
holding with great confidence the view they were still seeking to advance, as
though it had already been established in custom. If successful, the practice and
opinio juris of other states would then crystallize around that view and generate a
new rule.

However, other states were unwilling to embrace a doctrine of humanitarian
intervention. While they tolerated coalition action in Iraq, and involvement by the
Economic Community of West African States (ECOWAS) in Liberia and Sierra
Leone, there was little enthusiasm for the proposed new rule, and states were hesitant to offer views on the legal basis of such operations. The NATO intervention
relating to Kosovo in 1999 highlighted this reluctance. With the exception of the
United Kingdom and Belgium (then advised by the present Legal Adviser at the
Foreign and Commonwealth Office), not even NATO states appeared to invoke
the doctrine of humanitarian action. Others referred to humanitarian circumstances and to the fact that action had, again, been undertaken in pursuit of aims
established by the UN Security Council. However, a significant number of states
also objected as a matter of law, denying that the prohibition of the use of force
admitted intervention in cases of humanitarian emergency. In view of this divergence of opinion, it would be difficult to establish a new exception to the prohibition of the use of force in international custom.

In fact, it was later clarified that even the United Kingdom, the proposed norm
entrepreneur, was itself not convinced of the existence of the rule it had so confidently proclaimed. Refining its statements over time, it was noted that action in
Iraq had been taken 'in accordance with' UN resolutions. In more general terms,
it was clarified that forcible humanitarian action should not take place unilaterally, but required collective action. Where the Security Council was unable to
act in the face of an overwhelming humanitarian emergency, others might then
do so, but only if the Council had determined the existence of a threat to peace
and security, and identified the minimum action necessary to prevent or avert it.
Moreover, the action taken would have to be necessary, there would have to be no
other means available, and it would have to be proportionate to the humanitarian
aim pursued.

This view was far narrower than the one initially proposed. If it hinged exclusively on a finding by the Security Council as to a threat to the peace (that is, a
Chapter VII determination) constituted by an internal emergency, it remained

closely connected to the collective security dimension of the UN Charter, although not strictly based in it. However, it could be argued that in extreme cases there can be collective action if other, best-placed, objective bodies authoritatively determine the extent of the emergency and the immediate requirements of action. If that is accepted, it is still necessary to find a legal basis for humanitarian emergency, to which there is then added the process requirement of objective identification of the need for action and the extent of permissibility. Rather than searching for an unobtainable new justification in customary law, one such basis could be provided via the doctrine of representation. There are clear cases where the government of a state or an effective authority within it can no longer claim to exclusively represent the population it controls. This includes instances where it exterminates or forcibly displaces a significant segment of the population or denies to it that which is necessary for its survival. In such instances, international action can be taken directly on behalf of the population, at the minimum level necessary, to act on its inherent desire to ensure its survival. Ordinarily, this process would be best administered by the Security Council, but regional organizations and others could also act where no other avenues present themselves.

Kofi Annan, the UN Secretary-General, sought to transform divergent views on the proposed rule of forcible humanitarian action into an international consensus. Impossible though that task appeared, especially in view of a General Assembly debate he himself had initiated in 1999, progress was nevertheless made. Deploying a high-level expert panel, sponsored by Canada, the doctrine of 'Responsibility to Protect' emerged, which claimed that governments had an obligation to provide for the well-being and protection of their citizens. When they failed to deliver, international action could be taken. The panel once again strongly favoured collective measures taken through the UN Security Council, although it did not expressly rule out individual action. However, when this doctrine was translated into international consensus during the 2005 UN World Summit, the possibility of unilateral action appeared to have been removed entirely.

The legal situation has thus remained unclear. Very few would accept that 'another Rwanda' should be allowed to occur if the Council fails to address a similar situation. The principle of 'overwhelming humanitarian emergency' pioneered by the United Kingdom might apply in such circumstances. But if it is not backed by a new exception in international custom, what then is it? One explanation is that circumstances of this kind are covered by the doctrine of necessity. The use of force would be *prima facie* inconsistent with the prohibition of the use of force, as there would be no justification exempting it from application of that rule. But the 'wrongfulness' of the action would nevertheless be precluded according to the rules of international state responsibility. A third view is that forcible humanitarian action remain unlawful, while nevertheless widely regarded as politically legitimate.

The somewhat loose assumption that unlawful action may nevertheless be legitimate may also have informed other aspects of the Iraq episode. In addition to initial humanitarian action, force continued to be used when the humanitarian emergency was less visible. Moreover, the continued maintenance of the no-fly zones was increasingly enmeshed with another aspect of US and UK action relating to Iraq. This concerned the implementation of the disarmament requirements for Iraq.

When it emerged that Iraq continued to obstruct the UN disarmament process, the question of remedies arose. Economic sanctions were still in place and could not have been strengthened further. Hence, only the use of force was left. But there was no majority in the Council in favour of authorizing the use of force outright.

In response to this dilemma, the UN Secretariat accepted the application of the doctrine of material breach in relation to cease-fire Resolution 687 (1991). It was argued that the cease-fire was predicated on Iraq's acceptance of all its terms, including disarmament provisions. If Iraq violated those terms in a serious way, a material breach would occur and the cease-fire could be suspended. The original authority to use force granted in Resolution 678 (1991) would then revive. However, in the view of the UN, which was initially generally accepted, only the Security Council could (a) determine the existence of a violation, (b) find that it was sufficiently serious to constitute a material breach, and (c) make the option of the use of force available. This would be furnished by Council condemnation of a material breach and the threat of serious consequences in either formal resolutions or less-formal statements agreed by the Council President.

This doctrine represented a convenient way out of the dilemma in the Council, where action was broadly thought to be necessary, but a mandate was unobtainable. It facilitated an informal consensus in favour of action and offered some sort of legal explanation for the use of force by the United States and United Kingdom. However, it was rooted in several serious legal uncertainties. It appeared to make the use of force available to ensure compliance with international legal obligations, rather than strictly as a last resort, in self-defence, or in the face of an overwhelming humanitarian emergency. It was also based on a sudden and unexpected reading of the 1990 mandate to liberate Kuwait, thought to have expired upon conclusion of the cease-fire. Now, this mandate appeared to have a potentially open-ended and very wide application. The original action to liberate Kuwait was based primarily on the authority to enforce Iraq's withdrawal in accordance with the Council's first resolution in the matter, Resolution 660 (1990). However, reference was now made to a procedural provision in Resolution 678 (1990), referring to authority to 'maintain international peace and security in the area'.

The Council has the authority to authorize whatever it regards as essential to restore peace and security. Hence, it would ordinarily not have been necessary to construct the complex argument based on the revival of Resolution 678 (1990). But the political circumstances of 1991–1993 made this approach attractive. Limited force in favour of disarmament could be used by the UN to increase pressure towards completion of the disarmament process based on the revival argument, but this pragmatic approach would soon have its price. When consensus in the Council crumbled over the continued use of force, it was difficult to put the genie back in the bottle. The United States argued that it could administer the revival argument by itself, without having to rely on pronouncements by the Council.

The United Kingdom still persisted in its view that the revival argument could only operate if administered according to the collective security process. In accordance with previous practice, at a minimum, the Council had to determine the existence of a breach and threaten serious consequences. Its Ambassador to the UN took some pride in having seduced the other delegations into making such a pronouncement before the launch of Operation Desert Fox. The relevant Council resolution had in fact been carefully crafted not to make a formal finding of material breach. The subsequent use of force invoking it as a legal basis led to serious confrontation in the Council. By that point, the consensus underpinning the revival approach had definitively collapsed.

The issue arose again, however, when in 2002 it appeared that the United States was determined to use force against Iraq in pursuit of its new doctrine of preventative war and strategy of regime change. The United Kingdom, impressed by the impact of 9/11 on the United States, and on international security more generally, had subscribed to this agenda for some time. However, it was unable to do so without an appropriate legal basis. This basis was then sought through the revival argument. The United States was persuaded to 'go the UN route' in part in deference to UK pressure. However, that process was doomed from the beginning, as it was underpinned by different expectations.

A larger segment of UN membership saw the ensuing action in the Security Council as a means of ensuring Iraqi compliance with the disarmament obligations established in 1991. The arms inspections process had been disrupted in 1998, as a result of Operation Desert Fox. At that time, it was thought that there were only a limited number of outstanding issues. The nuclear disarmament process had been virtually completed and most issues concerning chemical weapons had also been cleared up, although there remained questions about Iraq's biological weapons capacity.

When addressing these issues after Operation Desert Fox, the Council had offered Iraq an accelerated programme of completing the disarmament tasks and instituting long-term monitoring. This would have led to an expedited review of sanctions and the promise of their suspension. However, Iraq refused to admit the arms inspectors, arguing that these had been unmasked as US spies intent on identifying targets for future air assaults. From the perspective of the UN Secretariat and the majority on the Council, the increasingly serious threat of the use of force, manifested in the policy of President George W Bush, might have been deployed to facilitate resumption of the arms inspection process and, finally, its rapid conclusion. This would have led to the reintegration of Iraq into the international community.

However, the view adopted by the United States and United Kingdom was different. Their analysis of the threat posed conflated fears that Iraq was a threat to the region, that it possessed WMD, that it might transfer these to terrorists, and that it had been engaged in the most horrendous atrocities against its own population. Taken together, this meant that peace and security in the region could really only be maintained if the Saddam Hussein regime was removed. The arms inspection process was a means towards that end.

This meant that, from the perspective of the UN members, Iraq had to engage genuinely in the disarmament effort. From the US perspective, Saddam Hussein had to demonstrate a 'strategic change' covering a broader range of issues, or, as the UK Prime Minister indicated, he had to exhibit a fundamental 'change of heart'.

If the aims were divergent, there was also a lack of agreement about the process. The majority of UN members were unwilling to grant to the United States and United Kingdom advance authorization for the use of force. It was widely understood that such a use of force would not be focused on WMD, but would instead be far broader, involving the invasion and occupation of Iraq. Legally the United Kingdom still required a Council pronouncement before it could participate in the armed action. Without an express mandate, the United Kingdom sought to put in place the elements that had previously allowed it, so it argued, to apply the revival doctrine. Of course, even if that doctrine had been applicable, it would again have focused on the arms inspections, rather than regime change. However, the United Kingdom argued internally that the only way of achieving compliance with the disarmament obligations would be through regime change. Hence, a mandate covering resumed arms inspections would also cover regime change. Finally, the United States maintained that the Council and its pronouncements were not really relevant. Authority to act already existed, either in the form of the right to preventative self-defence, or on the basis of the view that the United States could operate the revival doctrine unilaterally, without further involvement by the Council.

Ultimately, a compromise took shape in the form of Resolution 1441 (2002), which formally restored the revival argument to its good graces. It found that Iraq had been, and continued to be, in material breach and threatened serious consequences. This part of the Resolution, therefore, gave the United Kingdom what it would have needed to use force under the Desert Fox precedent. However, this concession had a price. The Council attached a process requirement, in effect suspending the implied authority to use force. Iraq would be given a final opportunity, in the form of a tougher arms inspection process. Should Iraq fail to comply, the UN arms inspectors would immediately report such violations to the Council for assessment. The Council would then consider the situation.

The United States claimed that the Resolution did not affect its already-existing right of action. Of course, one can only reserve that which one already has. In this case, US claims to pre-emption or the auto-administration of the revival argument were not based in international law, as understood by the rest of the world.

The United Kingdom was in a more difficult position. It had agreed to the two-step approach contained in Resolution 1441 (2002). There would be no authority to use force unless Iraq failed to make use of its final opportunity to comply. According to formal undertakings given by the United States and the United Kingdom upon adoption of the Resolution, there would be 'no hidden triggers' and 'no automaticity'. Hence, it would be up to the Council to determine if and when force would become available in view of Iraqi compliance.

The United Kingdom initially sought to preserve the right to act even outside a further pronouncement by the Council, in the event that subsequent action was blocked by a veto. It emphasized that the Council would need to meet its 'responsibility'. In truth, however, it remained up to the Council to decide whether or not to grant authorization.

It was later asserted that France, and others opposing a unilateral right of action, had had to accept the removal of the express right of the Council to 'decide' in Resolution 1441 (2002). By accepting that the Council would merely assess and consider, they had also accepted that mere discussion in the Council would clear the way for forcible action. However, this view was not in accordance with the understanding of the other delegations, or with assurances given by the United States and United Kingdom. Moreover, it represented a misunderstanding. The Security Council did not require affirmation of its power to decide upon action to enforce disarmament obligations. Clearly, it had the power to decide on the use of force in a wide range of circumstances. States, on the other hand, do not have such wide authority. Their right to use force is carefully circumscribed and limited to self-defence, arguably forcible humanitarian action, and implementation of a Council mandate. Neither self-defence nor humanitarian action applied in this instance. That left only the Council mandate. However, it had been the UK position throughout that revival of the mandate contained in Resolution 678 (1990) did require a Council decision. Hence, it could not claim this authority, unless it could demonstrate that the Council had taken such a decision in adopting Resolution 1441 (2002). That was impossible in view of the positions adopted by most members of the Council and the formal undertakings given by both the United States and United Kingdom. This was very clearly the understanding of most, including the UK's own Foreign Office Legal Advisers and the Attorney General.

For some time, the United Kingdom expected to remedy the situation through a second resolution, expressly authorizing force or at least rendering the revival argument operative. However, as Iraq appeared to be moving towards compliance, the majority of Council members favoured the continuation of the arms inspection process. Force, in their view, was to be used only as a last resort. Although the United Kingdom ultimately blamed France for unreasonably precluding a decision in the Council in favour of force, there was in fact no majority support for the US and UK position.

When force was used, it therefore did not have the backing of the Security Council. The United States might also have relied on its broad argument in favour of preventative self-defence. Such a doctrine would have profoundly destabilized the international system, permitting force according to the subjective determination by one state that another might, in the future, pose a threat. Instead, the overwhelming majority of states argued that the risks of terrorism and WMD could be accommodated by the existing right to self-defence in the face of an actual armed attack, or if such an attack appeared imminent.

The requirements of self-defence had already been expanded through the practice of the United States and United Kingdom. When maintaining the no-fly zones in northern and southern Iraq, coalition aircraft engaged Iraqi anti-air installations, whether or not they were at that time engaged in an actual or imminent attack against them. This was later expanded to include the support infrastructure, such as communication modes, including outside the no-fly zones. Self-defence was thus being claimed against more abstract threats than was previously the case. However, this finding operated at a tactical level. The US doctrine of pre-emption would have extended it far further, and applied it to the strategic question of whether or not a state would invade another in the absence of an actual or imminent threat of armed attack. Accepting this doctrine would have stripped the prohibition of the use of force of much, if not most, of its substance and returned the international system to the nineteenth century.

New threats had indeed emerged since the termination of the Cold War. But throughout the 30 years of the Iraq crisis, the UN made collective options available for engaging such threats. This included joint action to repress terrorism immediately after 9/11 and the whole series of measures adopted against Iraq in relation to its weapons programmes. Throughout, the United States accepted the benefits of collective action, but refused any of the constraints imposed by the UN. In relation to Kuwait, the legitimacy of the collective security label was adopted, without accepting UN involvement in the armed campaign. After the UN had established the cease-fire conditions, an informal consensus emerged supporting the use of force for limited humanitarian purposes and in relation to the arms inspection effort. When subsequently acting on this rationale in Kosovo, on a far more massive scale, many believed that the United States and NATO had abused this informal precedent. Similarly, increasingly unilateral action in relation to the auto-enforcement of the disarmament obligations was seen as violation of the trust that had underpinned the informal operation of the revival argument, on the strict understanding that it would operate only within the Council. The use of Resolution 1441 (2002) as principal justification for the very war that most states on the Council had sought to avoid by adopting it was seen as another, very severe, blow to the international system. The United States and, to a lesser extent, the United Kingdom, appeared to have arrogated to themselves the right to judge when force might be used on behalf of the organized international community, bypassing the institutional structure established for that purpose. War, it seemed, had again become a means of pursuing international policy, but administered by the United States, rather than the United Nations.

The case for war was undermined still further when it emerged subsequently that Iraq did not possess any of the WMD that had been alleged to exist. Moreover, the outbreak of severe internal conflict within Iraq confirmed the predictions made before the war was launched. However, in this instance the international system proved more resilient to the challenges posed by US and UK actions.

The episode is now widely seen as confirmation of the international rule of law, rather than its destruction. The UN membership and the collective security mechanism withstood tremendous pressure to render lawful a military action that could not be accommodated by accepted justifications for the unilateral use of force. The principle that war is not admissible as an extension of policy, save as a last resort and in the common international interest as determined by the Security Council, was maintained, despite its evident breach in this instance. Fundamental adherence to this principle has been confirmed by continued interest in this matter, even years after the operation. The Netherlands Inquiry into the war made an authoritative pronouncement on its illegality, and, at the time of writing, the United Kingdom was in the midst of a debate on how action could be taken in the face of clear advice that it had no justification in law. It can be expected that this interest will lead to a further strengthening of the institutional and legal safeguards which ensure that conformity with the rules of international law is seen as a necessary, if not sufficient, basis for the use of force.

Bibliography

Abiew, FK, (1999) *The Evolution of the Doctrine and Practice of Humanitarian Intervention*

Akehurst, M, (1984) 'Humanitarian Intervention' in H Bull (ed), *Intervention in World Politics* 95

Akermark, SS, 'Storms, Foxes and Nebulous Legal Arguments: Twelve Years of Force Against Iraq, 1991–2003' (2005) 54 ICLQ 221

Alexandrov, SA, (1996) *Self-Defence against the Use of Force in International Law*

Alston, P and Macdonald, E, (2008) *Human Rights, Intervention, and the Use of Force*

Amin, SH, 'The Iran-Iraq Conflict: Legal Implications' (1982) 31 ICLQ 167

Arend, AC, 'International Law and the Preemptive Use of Military Force' (2003) 26 *Washington Quarterly* 89

Auerswald, P, (2009) *Iraq, 1990–2006*

Bass, GJ, (2008) *Freedom's Battle: The Origins of Humanitarian Intervention*

Bedjaoi, M, (1994) *The Seurity Council and the Rule of Law*

Berdal, M and Economides, S, (2007) *United Nations Interventionism, 1991–2004*

Berger, L, 'State Practice Evidence of the Humanitarian Intervention Doctrine: The ECOWAS Intervention in Sierra Leone' (2001) 11 *Indiana International and Comparative Law Review* 605

Berman, F, 'The UN Charter and the Use of Force' (2006) 10 SYBIL 9

Bethlehem, D, (1991) *The Kuwait Crisis: Sanctions and their Economic Consequences*

Blix, H, (2004) *Disarming Iraq*

Blockmans, S, 'Moving into UN Chartered Waters: An Emerging Right to Unilateral Humanitarian Intervention' (1999) 12 *Leiden Journal of International Law* 759

Bothe, M, 'Terrorism and the Legality of Pre-emptive Force' (2003) 14(2) *European Journal of International Law* 227

Bowett, D, Collective Security and Collective Self-Defence' in M Rama-Montaldo (ed), (1994) *El derecho international en un mundo en transformacion* 425

—(1958) *Self-Defence in International Law*

Brenfors, M, 'The Legality of Unilateral Humanitarian Intervention: A Defence' (2000) 69 *Nordic Journal of International Law* 413

Brown, D, 'Use of Force Against Terrorism after September 11th: State Responsibility, Self-Defence, and Other Resources' (2003) 11 *Cardozo Journal of Comparative and International Law* 1

Brownlie, I, 'International Law and the Use of Force by States Revisited' (2001) 21 *Australian Yearbook of International Law* 21

—'Humanitarian Intervention' in JN Moore (ed), (1974) *Law and Civil War in the Modern World* 217

—(1963) *International Law and the Use of Force by States*

Brunnee, J and Toope, SJ, 'The Use of Force: International Law After Iraq' (2004) 53(4) ICLQ 785

Byers, M and Nolte, G, (2003) *United States Hegemony and the Foundations of International Law*

Byers, M, 'Terrorism, the Use of Force, and International Law after 11 September' (2002) 51(2) ICLQ 401

Cassese, A, 'Terrorism is Also Disrupting Some Crucial Legal Categories of International Law' (2001) 12 *European Journal of International Law* 993

—'A Follow-Up: Forcible Humanitarian Countermeasures and *Opinio Necessitatis* (1999) 10(4) *European Journal of International Law* 791

—'Ex Iniuria Ius Oritur: Are We Moving towards International Legitimation of Forcible Humanitarian Countermeasures in the World Community?' (1999) 10(1) *European Journal of International Law* 23

Carty, A, (2000) *Sir Gerald Fitzmaurice and the World Crisis: A Legal Adviser in the Foreign Office 1930–1945*

Chandler, D, 'Rhetoric without Responsibility: The Attraction of "Ethical" Foreign Policy' (2003) 5(3) *British Journal of Politics and International Relations* 295

Charney, JI, 'The Use of Force Against Terrorism and International Law' (2001) 95(4) AJIL 835

Chayes, A, 'The Use of Force in the Persian Gulf' in LF Damrosch and DJ Scheffer, (1991) *Law and Force in the New International Order* 3

Chesterman, S, (2001) *Just War or Just Peace? Humanitarian Intervention and International Law*

—*et al.*, (2008) *Law and Practice of the United Nations*

Clintworth, G, (1989) *Vietnam's Intervention in Cambodia in International Law*

Coates, D and Krieger, J, (2004) *Blair's War*

Cook, R, (2004) *The Point of Departure*

Cornell, ML, 'A Decade of Failure: The Legality and Efficacy of United Nations Actions in the Elimination of Iraqi Weapons of Mass Destruction' (2001) 16 *Connecticut Journal of International Law* 325

Cot, J-P and Pellet, A, (2nd edn, 1991) *La Charte des Nations Unies*

Craven, M *et al.*, 'We Are Teachers of International Law' (2004) 17 *Leiden Journal of International Law* 363

Crawford, J, (2002) *The International Law Commission's Articles on State Responsibility*

Currie, J, 'NATO's Humanitarian Intervention in Kosovo: Making or Breaking International Law' (1999) *Canadian Yearbook of International Law* 303

Daalder, IH, 'The Use of Force in a Changing World—US and European Perspectives' (2003) 16(1) *Leiden Journal of International Law* 171

D'Amato, A, 'Israel's Air Strike against the Osiraq Reactor: A Retrospective' (1996) 10 *Temple International and Comparative Law Journal* 259

Damrosch, LF, 'The Permanent Five as Enforcers of Controls on Weapons of Mass Destruction: Building on the Iraq "Precedent"' (2002) 13(1) *European Journal of International Law* 305

Daniel, D, 'The Kosovo Intervention: Legal Analysis and a More Persuasive Paradigm (2002) 13 *European Journal of International Law* 597

Danish Institute of International Affairs, (1999) *Humanitarian Intervention*

Danner, M, 'The Secret Way to War' (2005) 52(10) *The New York Review of Books* 70

David, AE, (1975) *The Strategy of Treaty Termination*

de Ceullar, J Perez, (1991) *Report of the Secretary-General on the Work of the Organization*

de Hoogh, A, (1996) *Obligations Erga Omnes and International Crimes*

Delbrück, J, 'The Fight Against Global Terrorism: Self-Defense or Collective Security as International Police Action? Some Comments on the International Legal Implications of the "War Against Terrorism"' (2001) 44 *German Yearbook of International Law* 9

Dettke, D, (2009) *Germany Says No*

Dinstein, Y, (1998) *War, Aggression and Self-Defence*

Doswald-Beck, L, 'The Legal Validity of Military Intervention by Invitation of the Government' (1985) 56 BYIL 189

Ehrenberg J. *et al.*, (2010) *The Iraq Papers*

Farer, TJ, 'An Enquiry into the Legitimacy of Humanitarian Intervention' in LF Fisler Damrosch and DJ Scheffer, (1991) *Law and Force in the New International Order* 159

Felix, KA, 'Weapons of Mass Destruction: The Changing Threat and the Evolving Solution' (2003) 34 *McGeorge Law Review* 391

Fielding, LE, 'Maritime Interceptions: Centrepiece of Economic Sanctions in the New World Order' (1993) 53 *Louisiana Law Review* 1191,

Fleck, D, 'Developments of the Law of Arms Control as a Result of the Iraq-Kuwait Conflict' (2002) 13(1) *European Journal of International Law* 105

Foreign and Commonwealth Office Paper, 'Iraq: Legal Basis for the Use of Force (2003)', reproduced in (2003) 52 ICLQ 812

Fowler, W, (2004) *Operation Barras*

Franck, T, 'The Use of Force in International Law' (2003) 11 *Tulane Journal of International and Comparative Law* 7

—'What Happens Now? The United Nations after Iraq' (2003) 97 AJIL 607

—'Inspections and Their Enforcement: A Modest Proposal' (2002) 96(4) AJIL 899

—(2002) *Recourse to Force: State Action against Threats and Armed Attacks*

—'Terrorism and the Right of Self-Defense' (2001) 95(4) AJIL 839

—and Rodley, N, 'After Bangladesh: The Law of Humanitarian Intervention by Military Force' (1973) 67 AJIL 275

Freedman, L and Boren, D, (1992) 'Safe Havens' for the Kurds in Post-war Iraq in N Rodley, *To Loose the Bands of Wickedness* 43

Freudenschuss, H, 'Between Unilateralism and Collective Security: Authorizations of the Use of Force by the UN Security Council', 5 *European Journal of International Law* (1994) 492

Gahlaut, S, 'The War on Terror and the Non-Proliferation Regime' (2004) 48(3) *Orbis* 489

Gardam, J, (2004) *Necessity, Proportionality and the Use of Force by States*

Gazzini, T, 'NATO Coercive Military Activities in the Yugoslav Crisis (1992–1999)' (2001) 12 *European Journal of International Law* 391

Glennon, M, 'Pre-empting Terrorism: The Case for Anticipatory Self-Defense' (2002) 7(19) *The Weekly Standard* 24

Goodrich, LM, Hambro, E, and Simons, LP, (1969) *Charter of the United Nations*

Gordon, M and Trainor, B, (2007) *Cobra II*

Gorst, A and Kelley, S (eds), (2000) *Whitehall and the Suez Crisis*

Gray, C, (3rd edn, 2008) *International Law and the Use of Force*

—'From Unity to Polarization: International Law and the Use of Force against Iraq' (2002) 13 *European Journal of International Law* 1

—'After the Cease-Fire: Iraq, the Security Council and the Use of Force' (1994) 65 BYIL 135

—'The British Position with Regard to the Gulf Conflict (Iran-Iraq): Part II' (1991) 40 ICLQ 464

Greenstock, J, (2009) *Development at the UN: Statement to the Iraq Enquiry*

Greenwood, C, 'International Law and the "War against Terrorism"' (2002) 78 *International Affairs* 301

—'Humanitarian Intervention: The Case of Kosovo' (1999) 10 *Finnish Yearbook of International Law* 141

—'Customary International Law and the First Geneva Protocol of 1977 in the Gulf Conflict' in P Rowe (ed), (1993) *The Gulf Conflict in International and English Law* 63

—'New World Order or Old? The Invasion of Kuwait and the Rule of Law' (1992) 55(2) MLR 153

—'International Law and the Pre-emptive use of force: Afghanistan, Al-Qaida and Iraq' (2003) 4 San Diego International Law Journal 7

Greig, D, 'Self-defence and the Security Council: What does Article 51 Require?' (1991) 40 ICLQ 366

Guillaume, G, 'Terrorism and International Law' (2004) 53 ICLQ 537

Haass, RN, (2009) *War of Necessity, War of Choice*

Hampson, FJ, 'Means and Methods of Warfare in the Conflict in the Gulf' in P Rowe (ed), (1993) *The Gulf Conflict in International and English Law* 89

Hannikainen, L, (1988) *Peremptory Norms in International Law*

Harris, DJ, (6th edn, 2004) *Cases and Materials in International Law*

Heinze, EA, 'Humanitarian Intervention: Morality and International Law on Intolerable Violations of Human Rights' (2004) 8(4) *International Journal of Human Rights* 471

Higgins, R, 'The Advisory Opinion on Namibia: Which UN Resolutions are Binding under Article 25 of the Charter?' (1992) 21 ICLQ 270

—(1963) *The Development of International Law through the Political Organs of the United Nations*

Hilpold, P, 'Humanitarian Intervention: Is there a Need for a Legal Reappraisal?' (2001) 12 *European Journal of International Law* 437

Hofmann, R, 'International Law and the Use of Military Force against Iraq' (2002) 45 *German Yearbook of International Law* 9

Holzgrefe, JL and Keohane, RO, (2003) *Humanitarian Intervention*

Howard, LM, (2008) *UN Peacekeeping in Civil Wars*

Independent International Commission on Kosovo, (2000) *Kosovo Report*

James, A, 'The Concept of Sovereignty Revisited' in A Schnabel and R Thakur, (2000) *Kosovo and the Challenge of Humanitarian Intervention* 334

Jennings, RY, 'The Caroline and MacLeod Cases' (1932) 32 AJIL 82

Johnman, L, 'Playing the Role of Cassandra: Sir Gerald Fitzmaurice, Senior Legal Advisor to the Foreign Office' (1999) 13(2) *Contemporary British History* 46

Joyner, CC, 'Sanctions, Compliance and International Law: Reflections on the United Nations' Experience Against Iraq' (1991) 31(1) *Virginia Journal of International Law* 1

Joyner, DH, 'The Kosovo Intervention: Legal Analysis and a More Persuasive Paradigm' (2002) 13 *European Journal of International Law* 597

Kaikobad, KH, 'Jus Ad Bellum: Legal Implications of the Iran-Iraq War' in IF Decker and HHG Post, (1992) *The Gulf War of 1980 to 1988* 51

—'The Gulf Wars 1980–88 and 1990–91' (1992) 63 BYIL 299

Kartashkin, V, 'Human Rights and Humanitarian Intervention' in LF Fisler Damrosch and DJ Scheffer, (1991) *Law and Force in the New International Order* 203

Kelle, A, (2002) 'Terrorism Using Biological and Nuclear Weapons: A Critical Analysis of Risks after 11 September 2001', PRIF Research Report, No 64

Kettell, S, (2006) *Dirty Politics?*

Kirsch, N, 'Review Essay: Legality, Morality, and the Dilemma of Humanitarian Intervention after Kosovo (2002) 13(1) *European Journal of International Law* 323

Kirsch, N, 'Unilateral Enforcement of the Collective Will: Kosovo, Iraq and the Security Council' (1999) 3 *Max Planck Yearbook of United Nations Law* 59

Knudsen, TB, 'The History of Humanitarian Intervention: The Rule or Exception?', Paper presented at the 50th ISA Annual Convention, New York, 15–18 February 2009

Koblentz, GD, 'Pathogens as Weapons: The International Security Implications of Biological Warfare' (2003) 28(3) *International Security* 84

Kress, C, 'Time for Decisions: Some Thoughts on the Immediate Future of the Crime of Aggression: Reply to Andreas Paulus', 20 *EJIL* (2009) 1129

—'Strafrecht und Angriffskrieg im Licht des "Falles Iraq"', (2003) 115 *Zeitschrift fuer die gesamte Strafrechtswissenschaft* 294

Kritsiotis, D, 'The Kosovo Crisis and NATO's Application of Armed Force against the Federal Republic of Yugoslavia' (2000) 49 ICLQ 330

—'1993 US Missile Strike on Iraq' (1995) 45 ICLQ 162

Lauterpacht, E *et al.*, (eds), (1991) *The Kuwait Crisis: Basic Documents*

Lavalle, R, 'The Law of the United Nations and the Use of Force, Under the Relevant Security Council Resolutions of 1990 and 1991, to Resolve the Persian Gulf Crisis' (1992) 23 NYBIL 3

Lietzau, WK, 'Old Laws, New Wars: Jus Ad Bellum in an Age of Terrorism' (2004) 8 *Max Planck Yearbook of United Nations Law* 383

Lillich, R, (1974) 'Humanitarian Intervention: A Reply to Ian Brownlie and a Plea for Constructive Alternatives' in JN Moore (ed), (1974) *Law and Civil War in the Modern World* 229

Litwak, RS, 'Non-Proliferation and the Dilemmas of Regime Change' (2003/4) 45(4) *Survival* 7

Lowe, V *et al.*, eds, (2008) *The United Nations Security Council and War*

—'Clear and Present Danger: Responses to Terrorism' (2005) 54 ICLQ 185

—'The Iraq Crisis: What Now?' (2003) 52 ICLQ 859

Major, J, (1999) *The Autobiography*

Malanczuck, P, (1993) *Humanitarian Intervention and the Legitimacy of the Use of Force*

Mallison, WT and Mallison, SV, 'The Israeli Aerial Attack of 7 June 1981' (1982) 17 *Vanderbilt Journal of Transnational Law* 417

Malone, DM, (2006) *The International Struggle over Iraq*

Marcus, IM, 'Humanitarian Intervention without Borders: Belligerent Occupation or Colonization?' (2002) 25 *Houston Journal of International Law* 99

Marston, G, 'Armed Intervention in the 1956 Suez Canal Crisis: The Legal Advice Tendered to the British Government' (1988) 37 ICLQ 773

Matheson, M, Legal Authority for Use of Force Against Iraq' (1998) 92 *American Society of International Law Proceedings* 136

Mayall, J (ed), (1996) *The New Interventionism, 1991–1994*

McCullough, HB, 'Intervention in Kosovo: Legal? Effective?' (2001) *7 ILSA Journal of International and Comparative Law* 299

McLain, P, 'Settling the Score with Saddam: Resolution 1441 and Parallel Justifications for the Use of Force against Iraq' (2003) 13(233) *Duke Journal of Comparative and International Law* 233

McLaughlin, R, 'United Nations Mandated Naval Interdiction Operations in the Territorial Sea' (2002) 51 ICLQ 249

Mendelson, M and Hulton, SC, 'The Iraq-Kuwait Boundary' (1993) 64 BYIL 135

—'Les décisions de la Commission des Nations Unies sur la démarcation de la frontière entre l'Iraq et le Koweit' (1993) *Annuaire français de droit international* 178

Merriam, J, 'Kosovo and the Law of Humanitarian Intervention' (2001) 33 *Case Western Reserve Journal of International Law* 111

Meyer, C, (2005) *DC Confidential*

Miller, JA, 'NATO's Use of Force in the Balkans' (2001) 45(1–2) *New York Law School Law Review* 91

Moir, L, (2010) *Reappraising the Resort to Force*

Moorman, W, 'Humanitarian Intervention and International Law in the Case of Kosovo' (2002) 36 *New England Law Review* 775

Morton, JS, 'The Legality of NATO's Intervention in Yugoslavia in 1999: Implications for the Progressive Development of International Law' (2002) 9 *ILSA Journal of International and Comparative Law* 75

Müllerson, R, 'Jus Ad Bellum and International Terrorism' (2002) 32 *Israel Yearbook on Human Rights* 1

—'Self-defence in the Contemporary World' in LF Damrosch and DJ Scheffer, (1991) *Law and Force in the New International Order* 3

Murphy, SD, 'Self-Defense and the Israeli *Wall* Advisory Opinion: An *Ipse Dixit* from the ICJ?' (2005) 99 AJIL 62

—'Assessing the Legality of Invading Iraq' (2003–4) 92 *Georgia Law Journal* 173

—'Contemporary Practice of the United States Relating to International Law' (2003) 97 AJIL 419

—'Efforts to Address Iraqi Compliance with UN Weapons Inspections' (2002) 96 AJIL 956

—(1996) *Humanitarian Intervention: The United Nations in an Evolving World Order*

Neuhold, N, 'Collective Security After "Operation Allied Force"' (2000) 4 *Max Planck Yearbook for United Nations Law* 73

Orakhelshvili, A, (2006) *Peremptory Norms in International Law*

Oudraat, CJ, 'UNSCOM: Between Iraq and a Hard Place' (2002) 13(1) *European Journal of International Law* 139

Parachini, J, 'Putting WMD Terrorism in Perspective' (2003) 26(4) *Washington Quarterly* 37

Paulus, A, 'Second Thoughts on the Crime of Aggression', 20 *EJIL* (2009) 1117, 1124

Paust, J, 'Use of Armed Force against Terrorists in Afghanistan, Iraq and Beyond' (2002) 35 *Cornell International Law Journal* 533

Pellet, A, 'Brief Remarks on the Unilateral Use of Force' (2000) 11(2) *European Journal of International Law* 385

Pogany, I, 'Humanitarian Intervention in International Law: The French intervention in Syria Re-Examined' (1986) 35 ICLQ 182

Poltak, C, 'Humanitarian Intervention: A Contemporary Interpretation of the Charter of the United Nations' (2002) 60(2) *University of Toronto Faculty of Law Review* 1

Powell, C, (1995) *My American Journey*

Quigley, J, 'The United States and the United Nations in the Persian Gulf War: New Order or Disorder', (1992) 25 *Cornell Int'l L. J* 1

Record, J, (2010) *Wanting War*

WM Reisman, 'Why Regime Change is (Almost Always) a Bad Idea' (2004) 98(3) AJIL 516

—'Assessing Claims to Revise the Laws of War' (2003) 97(1) AJIL 82

—'In Defense of World Public Order' (2001) 95(4) AJIL 833

—and Armstrong, A, 'The Past and Future of the Claim of Preemptive Self-Defence' (2006) 100 AJIL 525

Roberts, A, 'The So-Called "Right" of Humanitarian Intervention' (2000) 3 *Yearbook of International Humanitarian Law* 3

—and Guelff, R, (3rd edn, 2000) *Documents on the Laws of War*

Rodley, N, 'Collective Intervention to Protect Human Rights' in N Rodley, (1992) *To Loose the Bands of Wickedness* 14

—'Human Rights and Humanitarian Intervention: The Case Law of the World Court' (1989) 38 ICLQ 321

Romano, J-A, 'Combating Terrorism and Weapons of Mass Destruction: Reviving the Doctrine of State Necessity' (1999) 87 *Georgetown Law Journal* 1023

Ronziti, N, (1985) *Rescuing Nationals Abroad and Intervention on Grounds of Humanity*

Rosenne, S, (1985) *Breach of Treaty*

Rostow, EV, 'Until What? Enforcement Action or Collective Self-defence' (1991) 85 AJIL 506

Rytter, JE, 'Humanitarian Intervention without the Security Council, from San Francisco to Kosovo—and Beyond' (2001) 70 *Nordic Journal of International Law* 121

Sands, P, (2005) *Lawless World*

Santopadre, RC, 'Deterioration of Limits on the Use of Force and Its Perils: A Rejection of the Kosovo Precedent' (2003) 18 *Saint John's Journal of Legal Commentary* 36

Sapiro, M, 'Agora—Future Implications of the Iraq Conflict: Iraq: The Shifting Sands of Preemptive Self-Defense' (2003) 97(3) AJIL 599

Saraooshi, D, (2000) *The United Nations and the Development of Collective Security*

Schachter, O, 'United Nations Law in the Gulf Conflict' (1991) 85 AJIL 452

—'The Right of States to Use Armed Force' (1984) 82 *Michigan Law Review* 1620

Schaller, C, 'Massenvernichtungswaffen und Präventivkrieg—Möglichkeiten der Rechtfertigung einer militärischen Intervention im Irak aus völkerrechtlicher Sicht' (2002) 62 *Zeitschrift für öffentliches ausländisches Recht und Völkerrecht* 641

Scharf, MP and Williams, PR, (2010) *Shaping Foreign Policy in Times of Crisis, The Role of International Law and the State Department Legal Adviser*

Schrijver, N, 'Responding to International Terrorism: Moving the Frontiers of International Law for "Enduring Freedom" ' (2001) 48 *Netherlands International Law Review* 271

Shapiro, M, 'Iraq: The Shifting Sands of Preemptive Self-Defence' (2003) 97 AJIL 600

Short, C, (2004) *An Honourable Deception?*

Shotwell, JT, (1929) *War as an Instrument of National Policy*

Simma, B, 'NATO, the UN and the Use of Force: Legal Aspects' (1999) 10(1) *European Journal of International Law* 1

Simpson, G, 'The War in Iraq and International Law' (2005) 6 *Melbourne Journal of International Law* 1

—(2004) *Great Powers and Outlaw States*

Sofaer, AD, 'The Reagan and Bush Administrations' in MP Scharf and PR Williams, (2010) *Shaping Foreign Policy in Times of Crisis: The Role of International Law and the State Department Legal Adviser*, 65

—'On the Necessity of Pre-emption' (2003) 14(2) *European Journal of International Law* 209

Stahn, C, 'Enforcement of the Collective Will After Iraq' (2003) 97 AJIL 804

—'Terrorist Acts as "Armed Attacks": The Right to Self-Defense, Article 51 of the UN Charter, and International Terrorism' (2003) 27 *Fletcher Forum of World Affairs* 35

Stowell, EC, (1921) *Intervention in International Law*

Stuerchler, N, (2007) *The Threat of Force in International Law*

Sztucki, J, (1974) *Jus Cogens and the Vienna Convention on the Law of Treaties*

Taft IV, WH, 'The Bush (43rd) Administration' in MP Scharf and Paul R Williams (eds), (2010) *Shaping Foreign Policy in Times of Crisis: The Role of International Law and the State Department Legal Adviser* 127

—and TF Buchwald, 'Pre-Emption, Iraq and International Law' (2003) 97 AJIL 557

Teson, F, (3rd edn, 2005) *Humanitarian Intervention*

UK Foreign Policy Document No 148 (1986) 57 BYIL 614

Verwey, WD, 'Humanitarian Intervention' in A Cassese (ed), (1986) *The Current Legal Regulation of the Use of Force* 57

Vincent, R, (1974) *Non-Intervention and International Order*

Walker, GK, 'Principles for Collective Humanitarian Intervention to Succor Other Countries' Imperiled Indigenous Nationals' (2002) 18 *American University International Law Review* 35

Warbrick, C, 'The Invasion of Kuwait by Iraq (Parts I and II)' (1991) 40(3/4) ICLQ 482

Wedgwood, R, 'The ICJ Advisory Opinion on the Israeli Security Fence and the Limits of Self-Defense' (2005) 99(1) AJIL 52

—'The Fall of Saddam Hussein: Security Council Mandates and Preemptive Self-Defence' (2003) 97 AJIL 576

—'The Enforcement of Security Council Resolution 687: The Threat of Force against Iraq's Weapons of Mass Destruction' (1998) 92 AJIL 724

Weisburd, M, 'The War in Iraq and the Dilemma of Controlling the International Use of Force' (2004) 39 *Texas International Law Journal* 521

Weller, M, 'Access to Victims: Reconceiving the Right to Intervene' in WP Heere, (1999) *International Law and The Hague's 750th Anniversary* 353

—'The Threat or Use of Force in a Unipolar World: The Iraq Crisis of Winter 1997/98' (1998) 4(3–4) *International Peace-keeping* 63

—'Peace-keeping and Peace-enforcement in Bosnia and Herzegovina' (1996) 56 *Zeitschrift fuer Auslaendisches Offenliches Recht und Voelkerrecht* (Heidelberg Journal of International Law) 1

—'Sovereignty and Suffering: The Legal Framework' in J Harris (ed), (1995) *The Politics of Humanitarian Intervention* 35

—'The Afghanistan Peace Accords of 1988, 1991 and 1993' (1994/5) 5 *Finnish Yearbook of International Law* 505

—(1994) *Regional Peace-keeping and International Enforcement: The Liberian Crisis*

—(1993) *Iraq and Kuwait: The Hostilities and their Aftermath*

—'The United Nations and the Jus ad Bellum' in P Rowe (ed), (1993) *The Gulf War 1990–1 in International and English Law* 29

—'The Kuwait Crisis: A Survey of some Legal Issues' (1991) 3 *African Journal of International and Comparative Law* 1

—'The Use of Force and Collective Security' in IF Decker and HHG Post (eds), (1991) *The Gulf War of 1980–1988* 71

Welsh, J (ed), (2004) *Humanitarian Intervention and International Relations*

Weston, BH, 'Security Council Resolution 678 and Persian Gulf Decision-Making: Precarious Legitimacy' (1991) 85 AJIL 516

Wetzel, RG and Rauschnig, D, (1978) The Vienna Convention on the Law of Treaties: *Travaux Preparatoires*

Wheeler, NJ, 'Humanitarian Intervention after Kosovo' (2001) 77(1) *International Affairs* 113

—(2000) *Saving Strangers*

—and Dunne, T, 'Good International Citizenship: A Third Way for British Foreign Policy' (1998) 74(4) *International Affairs* 847

White, ND, 'The Will and Authority of the Security Council after Iraq', (2004) 17 Leiden Journal of International Law 645

—'From Korea to Kuwait: The Legal Basis of United Nations Military Action', (1998) 20 *International History Review* 597

—(1993) *Keeping the Peace*

Williamson, M, (2009) *Terrorism, War and International Law: The Legality of the Use of Force Against Afghanistan in 2001*

Wilmshurst, E, (2005) *Chatham House Principles of International Law on the Use of Force by States*

Wippman, D, 'Kosovo and the Limits of International Law' (2001) 25 *Fordham International Law Journal* 129

Wood, M, 'The Law on the Use of Force: Current Challenges' (2007) 11 *Singapore Yearbook of International Law* 1

Woodward, B, (2004) *Plan of Attack: The Road to War*

Yoo, J, 'International Law and the War in Iraq' (2003) 97 AJIL 563

Zacklin, R, (2010) *The United Nations Secretariat and the Use of Force in a Unipolar World*

—'Beyond Kosovo: the United Nations and Humanitarian Intervention' (2001) 41 *Virginia Journal of International Law* 923

'The Basis in International Law for the Military Intervention in Iraq', (2010) *Netherlands International Law Review* 81

'The Caroline (Exchange of diplomatic notes between Great Britain and the United States, 1842)' (1906) 2 *Digest of International Law* 409

Index